This book

Victorian Knight-Errant

Victorian Knight-Errant

A STUDY OF THE EARLY
LITERARY CAREER OF
JAMES RUSSELL LOWELL

By Leon Howard

UNIVERSITY OF CALIFORNIA PRESS
Berkeley and Los Angeles / 1952

UNIVERSITY OF CALIFORNIA PRESS
BERKELEY AND LOS ANGELES
CALIFORNIA

CAMBRIDGE UNIVERSITY PRESS
LONDON, ENGLAND

PRINTED IN THE UNITED STATES OF AMERICA
BY THE UNIVERSITY OF CALIFORNIA PRINTING DEPARTMENT
DESIGNED BY A. R. TOMMASINI

TO

HOYT HUDSON

(1893–1944)

FOREWORD

THE FATHER of James Russell Lowell once thought of christening his youngest son "Perceval," and, in later years, James regretted that it had not been done. "I think of altering my name to Perceval Lowell," he wrote his intimate friend George Bailey Loring on January 21, 1839; but, instead, he compromised by adopting "Hugh Perceval" as his pen name and beginning to sign letters with it in May. When he had a son of his own, his first notion was to give the child the ancestral name he had himself wanted—but, like his father, he changed his mind. The name, however, lingered in his consciousness as a vague symbol of nobility. One of the most devastating of his mature critical essays was directed against a poet who actually bore the name, failed to live up to its demands, and, in his failure, made Lowell feel the difference between his own mediocre achievements and the high aspirations of his youth.

This sensitive regard for a chivalric name does not, of course, provide a formula or even a clue for a psychological interpretation of Lowell's chaotic emotional and literary life. But it does suggest the most natural pattern by which Lowell's wayward questings may be arranged for presentation in a semblance of order. For it was a pattern of which he himself was not entirely unconscious. He thought of himself, during one period of his life, as Spenser's Knight of the Red Crosse—an aspirant to the House of Holiness, riding against error in the company of a lovely lady who was white in purity, as in name, yet marked with the sign of inward mourning. And when he doubted his own worthiness, he controlled his ignoble impulses by imagining his fate as a recreant Modred. In any case, whatever myth he lived during his early life was an errant one. Occasionally, like his own Sir Launfal, he dreamed of finding some sort of Holy Grail; but, usually, he merely alternated his desire to help the weak and the oppressed with his desire for temporary success or lasting fame. So long as he was driven by his inherent energy, rather than pulled by external circumstances, he was not able to settle upon any consistent purpose; and the effort to follow his life according to any kind of pattern, as the reader of the following pages will see, requires a considerable amount of zigzagging in time as well as direction.

My personal interest in Lowell, it will become evident enough, was not stimulated by an enthusiasm for his literary achievement so much as by a curiosity about the value of literature as a medium for human and historical research. The complexities of man, as a separate individual in the tide of history, are too great to be wholly discovered and laid out for display; but, to some minds, these complexities offer a challenge more exciting than the properties of matter or the intricacies of abstract thought. And, among men, the poet—perceptive and emotional, impractical and expressive, sometimes sublime and often silly—is the most revealing. He is often the highly sensitive person who has the power to catch and preserve in words the human complexities of his age, and, if we know enough to read his words with understanding, we can find in him the subtler forces of history which flow from the past to the present with an influence as pervasive as it is unsusceptible to generalization.

This book, which is based upon Lowell's early life and works, is neither a biographical nor a critical study in any conventional sense. Instead, it is an experiment in literary research. My purpose in undertaking it was to discover the extent to which a meticulous examination of an individual's entire literary output, within the human context of its origin, could improve one's understanding of the individual himself and of the age in which he lived. As a subject for such an experiment, Lowell proved at first satisfactory and eventually fascinating. From him, I learned something new about education at Harvard during his undergraduate years, something of unrecorded but primary significance in American intellectual history, something of the problems faced by the American writer of the early nineteenth century, and a great deal about the operation of literary influences from abroad and about the crosscurrents and internal conflicts which affected the great reform movements of the time. I also found the clue to several mysteries of Lowell's personal life and to his success as a critic, and I learned, from the consideration of his writings as personal documents, how sterile and unrevealing purely aesthetic criticism can be in its approach to certain kinds of literature. Such things as these were expected. But Lowell was more rewarding than I had guessed. He provided, I believe, some new insight into the peculiarities of the literary imagination, into the possible relationship between emotion or philosophy and the style of poetic expression, and into the general nature of human illusion. Whether I have been able to share these findings by recording them properly, of course, is a different matter.

The great problem was that of pursuing such a variety of interests through the life and works of a man who is not particularly fascinating to anybody's first glance. Often I was tempted to abandon Lowell in the pursuit of one of the tangential interests he aroused. But I was held to my original intent by a feeling of obligation to complete the experiment I was committed to attempt and by an increasing curiosity as to what the subject would next reveal. The work was finally brought to an end by the law of diminishing returns. When Lowell overcame his "failure to mature" (as one of his biographers put it) or (in words which I myself prefer) reached a state of arrested development, his occasional spurts of creative energy were too far apart for consideration in a manuscript already long enough to try the patience of the most sympathetic reader. At that point I did abandon him, with only enough attention to his later years to indicate that he had come to life in my mind while I was using him as an instrument of research.

The result is a book which may be specious in its coherence and lacking in any proper focus of interest. Although it tells the story of James Russell Lowell, it is more concerned with human nature and society; and it is difficult indeed to admire Lowell and be realistic about human nature or open-minded about the society in which he moved. At times, such art as I possessed failed to meet the demands made upon it—most lamentably, in chapter three, where I could not find the method for a suitable treatment of Lowell's youthful madness, and, perhaps, in the separate accounts of his simultaneous interests in chapter seven. The book's irremediable fault, however, is that it violates the proprieties of specialized interests while presenting the specialized evidence upon which its larger implications are based. That fault was implicit in the original purpose which caused me to make and others to support the experiment: the desire to escape the narrowness of conventional specialization without falling into the irresponsibility of uninformed generalizations. The only solution I could think of was that of standing firmly in my own field while looking beyond its borders. But after my own experience with the results of the attempt, I sincerely hope that somebody else will find a solution which is more generally acceptable.

The bit of novelty involved in this experiment has emphasized my miscellaneous shortcomings to such an extent that I have lost more productive energy through frustrations than I care to contemplate. For that reason, perhaps, I now feel unusually grateful to the many people who have contributed in one way or another to the work and have awaited, either with patience or with indifference, its outcome. The work was made possible by a fellowship from the John Simon Guggenheim Memorial Foundation and by a leave of absence from Northwestern University, and I wish to express my particular gratitude to those officers of the Foundation and of the University who enabled me to have that year of freedom for research and composition—especially to Henry Allen Moe, to Franklyn Bliss Snyder, and to William Frank Bryan. I am also indebted to my former Northwestern colleagues, Harrison Hayford and Ernest Samuels, who generously looked after my teaching duties in my absence, and to the members of the research committee of the Northwestern Graduate School who granted funds for certain incidental later research. The hospitality and coöperation of the Houghton and Huntington libraries, which so far exceeded any call of duty to a wandering scholar that I cannot adequately express my appreciation to the individuals responsible, made the work a pleasure; and, in addition, William A. Jackson of the Houghton Library took extra trouble to obtain permission for my use of additional manuscript material, and the late Dixon Wecter of the University of California placed at my disposal his microfilm copies of manuscripts that might otherwise have been unavailable to me. Staff members of the Widener, Boston Public, Swarthmore College, Congressional, Newberry, University of Chicago, Northwestern, and University of California at Los Angeles libraries were also coöperative in meeting the lesser demands I made upon them; and I am indebted, in various ways, to Virgil Heltzel, William Charvat, Carl Bode, George Clark, Glenn Gosling, John Stafford, Mrs. Anna McTeer, Mrs. Elsie Leach, Mrs. Harrison Hayford, Mrs. Philip Durham, and the late Mrs. Frederick Winslow—all of whom had something to do with providing me with information or correcting my errors. My final indebtedness is to the Board of Editors and the staff of the University of California Press who have made the following pages available to whom they may concern.

L. H.

Los Angeles
June, 1951

CONTENTS

Chapter I

THE YOUNG SQUIRE

I

WHEN THE Reverend Dr. Charles Lowell sailed for Europe in the spring of 1837, he was worried about the failure of his youngest son—then in the third term of his junior year at Harvard College—to live up to his intellectual abilities. As he sat in New York the day before going aboard ship, brooding over the things he had left undone, he finally decided that he might leave a good influence behind him in the form of a sliding scale of innocent bribery. "You know the necessity for economy," he wrote, informing his son of the fifty cents a week he was to receive as an allowance, "and you know that I shall never deny you, but from necessity, what will afford you pleasure." But, regardless of necessity, he promised that the allowance would be raised to seventy-five cents as soon as his son became a member of Phi Beta Kappa and to a dollar if he should be one of the first eight admitted. Scholarship would pay—and pay well—he made clear after another reference to the limited state of his finances when he added: "If you graduate one of the first five in your class, I shall give you $100 on your graduation. If one of the first ten, $75. If one of the first twelve, $50. If the first or second scholar, two hundred dollars. If you do not miss any exercises unexcused, you shall have Bryant's Mythology or any other book of equal value, unless it is one I may specially want." This should have been easy money for James Russell Lowell, for he already stood high enough in his class to receive a place on the program for the public exhibition that year, and, as his father observed, he could readily have become a fine scholar. But unfortunately, both for the father's pride and his son's later career, he did not collect a cent. It was to be nine years before he became a member of Phi Beta Kappa, and although he was graduated it was not until he had slipped down below the middle of his class.

Had the Lowells been able to think of themselves as members of the Brahmin caste of New England, they might have looked upon Jemmy as one who had carelessly defiled himself and consequently was obliged to endure a process of cleansing. There was, in fact, some trace of that attitude in the boy's family and in his own view of himself; but the descriptive phrase had not yet been invented, and if it had been, it would not have seemed superficially appropriate to the youngest Lowell who was neither pallid nor slender and who obviously had not taken to his books as a pointer or setter to his fieldwork. Yet there was a perceptible and enduring quality of the Brahmin in him in the sense that he was the product of a bookish and eminently respectable cultural environment and had his roots deep in the past and widespread through the New England present. The house in which he was born, although hardly more than a half-century old at the time, was rich in historical associations. When it was new, the citizens of Middlesex County, some four thousand in number, had gathered around it and defied the King by forcing Lieutenant Governor Thomas Oliver to resign his office as President of the Council. During the Revolution it had been used as a hospital for American soldiers and by the Committee of Correspondence. Later it had been a center of interest during the turbulent democratic era, for it had passed through the hands of the Federalist Cabots and into the possession of Elbridge Gerry who, in his turn, had received threats of violent treatment while serving as governor of the Commonwealth and giving his name to a new device of political ingenuity. There Gerry had taken the oath of office as vice-president of the United States. It had not been a popular house in those days, and the neighbors might have seen some signs of God's justice in the fact that the surviving family of a democrat had been unable to preserve the estate and had been forced to break it up and sell the house and ten surrounding acres to a Lowell. Tories and patriots, Federalists and democrats had slept in its rooms and passed through its doors, and there were people in the village of Cambridge who remembered them all. A boy born in such a home was born to the consciousness of a living past.

The past was alive in the village, too, and young Lowell knew that in the houses around the common there were still old women in old-fashioned dress peering at him through the windows from which they watched Lord Percy's men on their way to Lexington. Eyewitness accounts of the fighting around Boston were familiar to Lowell's boyhood, but the myth-making power of blending fact and fancy was already at work and people who remembered the retreat from Concord were also beginning to recall the picture of Washington reviewing his first command under what was to be called "the Washington Elm." The General's headquarters had been in the neighboring Craigie House where brief glimpses of the mysterious turbaned figure of Mrs. Craigie impressed a small boy on his way home from the village in the years before his Aunt Sally made her home there. Memorable battlefields were in walking distance, and, although the son of the long-time secretary of the Massachusetts Historical Society got through his sophomore year in college without having walked up Bunker Hill, he was fully aware of the local associations with Revolutionary and colonial events. But, to a youngster, history became most vividly and romantically alive in October when the annual "cornwallis" mustered the citizen soldiers of his own time for the purpose of playing at war in masquerade. It was the New England equivalent of Guy Fawkes Day, sharing the spirit of carnival with the college commencement and the spring election, which not only dramatized the surrender at Yorktown but released the inhibitions of the reserved Yankees and displayed something of the secret nature of the farmers who fired the shots heard round the world. Such an occasion was a remembrance of things past which translated the facts of history into pageantry while recapturing some of its life in a way that gave an impressionable boy the feeling of being connected with a tradition.

Outside Cambridge there were other evidences of a close connection with other times and other manners. The youngest Lowell had the privilege of traveling with his father when the latter preached outside Boston, and he was frequently impressed by the country people who stood by the side of the road and made their manners in the old way when the minister drove by. As New England edged its way into the nineteenth century, the up-country was far behind Boston, and Dr. Lowell's visits to rural meetinghouses moved through time as well as space. In some of them, old men "deaconed off the hymn" in the manner of the early Puritans, while others were modern enough to approve music provided by amateurs of the bass viol, the clarinet, and the fiddle. But all belonged to another era in comparison with the Boston churches whose organs so impressed local poets that all of them felt obliged to touch the diapason stop for their own verses at one time or another during the first half of the century. Dr. Lowell's own West Church was one in which the eighteenth century lingered and upon which the nineteenth century pressed. In the old building which Dr. Lowell had replaced in the first year of his pastorate, Jonathan Mayhew, in memory of the English Puritans, had preached the right of revolution and encouraged the contemporary application of his doctrine of the superiority of people to kings. Within the borders of its parish, a later minister could witness another revolution less agreeable to his desires, in which poverty was overcoming people and disease threatened the unalienable rights of life, liberty, and the pursuit of happiness. Dr. Lowell shared the feeling for tradition which helped bind his congregation together so closely that he was able to survive the Unitarian controversy without delivering his church exclusively to any sectarian group, but he ministered generously to the newly hungry and for their benefit established one of the first Sunday Schools in New England; and, although he was known as a conservative to the end of his life, he accepted as an assistant and—beginning in March, 1837—active associate and successor the Reverend Cyrus A. Bartol who was one of the members of the new Transcendental Club.

The Lowell family had achieved a respectable place in the past which had left so many impressions upon the physical surroundings of the future poet's boyhood. His ancestors had been in Massachusetts almost as long as Harvard College had, and although they were not among the aristocrats of the colony, they had acquired a social position that placed James's grandfather in the upper third of his college class. The grandfather had become a member of the general court, a delegate to the Continental Congress, a judge of the United States district court, and a chief justice of the circuit court, and for eighteen years was a member of the Harvard Corporation; but he was most frequently remembered in the household of his youngest son as the member of the state constitutional convention who had introduced into the Massachusetts Bill of Rights the clause abolishing slavery in the new state. There was a certain excess of family pride in giving Judge John Lowell personal credit for freeing the Negroes of the Commonwealth, but his son and his grandsons believed it appropriate that his portrait should face that of William Wilberforce in the house on Brattle Street, and it was the belief rather than the precise historical fact which affected his descendants. James's mother's family were relative newcomers from the Orkney Islands and the Highlands and had been loyalists during the Revolution. His grandmother, who was a member of the first generation born in America, regularly went into mourning on the Fourth of July; and his mother kept him aware of his Scottish heritage by singing ballads and by presenting him with the three volumes of Scott's *Tales of a Grandfather* when he was nine years old.

Like many other children of his generation, Lowell was brought up on Sir Walter Scott, whose influence was so pervasive that at the Harvard commencement a boy might mount a mechanical horse and tilt at a ring. The money he paid for the privilege, however, was a purely New England heritage, for the most common coins were those of the colonial period when it took six Massachusetts shillings to make a dollar and the smaller coinage reflected the odd proportion of exchange.

Lowell's cultural roots were as widespread in the present as they were deep in other generations. Judge John Lowell, who had started the family on its road to distinction, had married a Higginson and a Cabot as well as a Russell; and these families with the Lowells' more recent connections, the Jacksons and their friends, the Lees, formed a substantial portion of the Boston manufacturing aristocracy whose wealth and community interests made their names synonymous with the development of Boston as a cultural center during the nineteenth century. The Lowells in Cambridge were outside the sphere of prosperity in which their Boston relatives moved, for they never fully recovered from the attempt of the younger Charles to become a financier while managing the family property when his father was abroad during the depression of the late 'thirties. But they were not social outsiders, and there was an attitude of mutual respect between wealth and scholarship that made Nathan Appleton a welcome member of the Massachusetts Historical Society and the son of its secretary a welcome member of the society of Beacon Street. Young James Lowell was too ill at ease to dance at the first "grown-up ball" he attended at the home of his cousin, Mrs. I. C. Gray, and he never got over his awe of Mr. Appleton's stately and beautiful daughter; but he eventually became as thoroughly at home in Boston as in Cambridge.

The simpler and more informal manners of the village, however, were those to which he was born. While the Boston Lowells grew in dignity, Dr. Lowell began to put on a few gentle airs in Cambridge, and when he went abroad in 1837 he gave his home the name Elmwood—perhaps with some desire to have a home address that would not seem undignified or queer to his English friends. There was a good deal of decorous formality in the college community, of course, but Jemmy Lowell was aware that somehow literary and intellectual distinction left a man more pliable than did success on State Street. He never forgot how the elder Richard Henry Dana drew him and his Shetland pony through the front door of his home and, with the assistance of the college butler, tried in vain to coax the shaggy beast and its little rider upstairs. The incident was memorable because it was extraordinary, but it was a matter of everyday observation that playfulness and eccentricity were not avoided so severely by men of letters as they were by financiers and merchants. Young Lowell grew up to know the elder Dana as a man who was somewhat vaguely an author rather than as an author who was a shadowy figure of a man, and he had a similar knowledge of Judge Joseph Story, the famous authority on the Constitution. For the two Dana boys and William Story were his playmates and friends whose families he knew from a boy's point of view, and in later life he habitually looked for the man hidden behind the pages of a literary work and often judged the work according to the estimate he placed upon the author.

Some of the Cambridge men with whom he came in daily contact formed a personal connection, obscurely realized, between the growing boy and a world far beyond the borders of Cambridge and Boston. His father had studied in Edinburgh where he received personal attentions and particular kindnesses from Dugald Stewart, whose philosophical works were so highly thought of at Harvard College, and had visited Wordsworth and Southey and corresponded with the latter and with Sir Walter Scott. Anyone from Cambridge who took the new omnibus to Boston might, at Cambridgeport, have his toes stepped on and receive a courteous apology from one of Samuel Taylor Coleridge's—and Dr. Lowell's—most beloved friends, or he might ride into the city in the late afternoon with a member of the Harvard faculty who had talked with the notorious Byron and the great Goethe. A boy of good family in Cambridge regularly exchanged greetings with men who had received compliments from the most important literary men of the early nineteenth century, and if he was not especially impressed by the fact, it was because he knew no better than to take it for granted as the normal experience of a person who had a respectable place in the world firmly established by the cultural interests of his ancestors and his older contemporaries. The cultivated classes of Boston and Cambridge knew more about their ancestors and cherished a more unbiased interest in personalities across the Atlantic than they did concerning people in other sections of their own country, but young Lowell at least had the advantage of some firsthand acquaintance with the geography of the United States, for in addition to holiday visits and pastoral exchanges within a day's journey or so from Cambridge he had made a boyhood trip as far south as Maryland and Virginia and a youthful visit to the White Mountains, Niagara Falls, and Canada. Such tours, however, did little to enlarge the horizon of his imagination, and he seems never to have let his fancy dwell upon the Orient with which his seafaring connections in Boston were familiar. From childhood, books were a prime reality in his life, and vicarious contacts with other people had to be nourished upon literature before they could grow strong enough to make an impression upon him. Lowell was bred to a state of adaptability to European civilization, but in manhood he held to his childish notion that the Chinese were a fabulously topsy-turvy people who spoke a comic language and somehow violated the law of gravity, and a Virginian with whom he had no personal acquaintance was a citizen of a world almost as strange.

But Lowell's boyhood associations were by no means confined to the cultivated classes in his native town and the neighboring Boston. Cambridge was a village inhabited by a few dozen educated families, a couple of Scottish gardeners, a Dutch barber, a small number of Irishmen, several Continentals engaged in educational pursuits, and more than four thousand native Yankees. The dialect of the latter was not so pure as it was in the country, but their temper was unmodified. Such men as "Neighbor Pomeroy" (on whose wagon Jemmy frequently rode home from school) and the older of the two village constables knew exactly where each of his fellow townsmen belonged and gave each exactly his due of respect—and demanded his own precise measure in return. The spreading chestnut tree of the village blacksmith shaded a domain in which the smith was complete master of his bellows, and when the little son of Dr. Lowell was allowed to pump he was as proud of the privilege as he would have been of occupying a throne by permission of a king. The elderly Snow twins ruled their oyster cellar in the courthouse with a royal decree as immutable as the laws of the Medes and the Persians: "When oysters are good, they *air* good; and when they ain't, they *isn't.*" No fashionable superstition concerning the spelling of the month moved them in the least, and the eating habits of Cambridge people followed the Snows rather than the calendar. If Cambridge, apart from the weathered red brick of the college, was mostly a village of white and yellow, it was because the local Yankee painter preferred those colors; and while Smith Professors of Modern Languages, for example, had the right to prefer some other hue, they had the obligation to respect the right of Mr. Newman to paint or not to paint as he saw fit, and Elmwood and Craigie House stand today as fulvescent monuments to their owners' decent respect for the opinions of that portion of mankind which believed a man should be cock of his own roost regardless of the level on which he might be roosting. Such was the basic tenet of New England democracy to which a person had to subscribe or become a martyr, and New Englanders as a whole had gone through a process of natural selection that made them inclined to become martyrs for, rather than to, obstinate individualism. In Cambridge, as in all villages, there existed certain arbitrary notions of what was proper and seemly, but anyone who gave assent to the common standards of speech and conduct received a considerable amount of tolerance in return; and the more sophisticated citizens cultivated a sense of humor that relieved the friction between pressure of principles and the external necessity of toleration.

Such friction existed in the best regulated of small communities where petty violators of the Ten Commandments could not be avoided as easily as they might be in larger and more thickly populated places. It was a standing joke that sweet and sour apples were supplied from the same barrel in one of the village stores where it was a kind of second nature of the deacon who ran it to bend the Eighth Commandment rather than lose a sale. When, more dramatically, the spirit of violence took possession of some of the men of Cambridge and they helped burn the near-by Ursuline Convent in 1834, the mother of T. W. Higginson allowed her indignation to overflow upon the local butcher who was suspected of having taken part in the outrage. But her family continued to eat meat and acquired a good story from the butcher's defense. "Well, I dunno, Mis' Higginson," he is reported to have argued, "I guess them bishops are real desperate characters." There were occasions, of course, when humor was not appropriate. All the boys and probably most of the grown people of Cambridge knew that the barber prospered at the expense of his daughter's virtue, but it was not a part of the village philosophy even to ask the question: Since the barber is villainous shall the children's hair grow long? They closed their eyes to his villainy just as they ignored the perfume his young customers were compelled to endure, and young Lowell grew up to write publicly of the shop as a place of wondrous curios and evidences of wealth, the ill-gotten nature of which he was unwilling to recall although he had once discussed it in a youthful letter. Petty deceit, violence, and vice were known and discounted by village boys who hardly realized when they had learned the lesson of hoping for the best in humanity while putting up with the best at hand. When they later grew up to encourage the march of the intellect toward self-improvement, they may have allowed themselves an occasional excess of enthusiasm, but in their more relaxed moments they had few illusions about the length of the march.

As the child of fairly well-to-do parents, young Lowell had an intimate acquaintance with the plainest level of Yankee country folk which was not available to children reared with equal care in slightly less fortunate circumstances. Some of the family servants in his own home and in the homes of his close friends and relatives, though lacking the education or perhaps the early opportunity requisite to a completely independent existence, had become long-established members of the household and the trusted mentors of small boys who had to be initiated into the arts of the garden and the barnyard and of field and stream. Before the great immigration they were mostly natives; and although the Lowells' Job and Sam may not have had the perfect mastery of the incidental demands of life shown by the Nathan Hales's Fullum, their long service bore witness to the fact that they were good representatives of a class to which every boy in Lowell's position owed much in the way of early training. The man later attributed his Hosea Biglow side to the experiences of his childhood and particularly to his country visits with his father, but James's Hosea and his brother Robert's Elnathan Bangs had their origin in the common knowledge of the two boys which may have been acquired in part on their own ten acres. The two fictitious Yankees, of course, represented the concentrated essence of a wide observation of the type that was visible readily enough in the village and abroad, but if any faith may be put in impressions and testimony, Lowell had a more intimate acquaintance with the Biglows of New England than with the Birdofredom Sawins or even the Parson Wilburs.

II

A BOY BORN to Lowell's environment was destined to receive as substantial an education as his mind would admit. Jemmy followed the normal routine of being taught to read by his mother and entering Miss Dana's school where, as he recalled later, the birch often "told a tail of woe" among the children. He was soon transferred to another school taught by another Dana, Miss Sophia, who did not believe in thrashings but did believe that youngsters of six and seven should begin the study of Latin and French while they were too young to realize that languages were "hard." Jemmy Lowell and Ned Dana were the only two boys in the school, and although Jemmy was so sensitive to compulsory sissiness that he threw away the white hat with the gold tassel with which his mother had dressed him up for his little seminary, he acquired the rudiments of Latin and the ability to read children's stories in French. Miss Sophia gave up her school in order to marry the Reverend George Ripley when Lowell was only eight, but the boy kept up his French while continuing the formal study of Latin in a conventional grammar school and thus cultivated the interest in modern languages which was to flourish later. His grammar school, of course, was that kept by William Wells in the Fayerweather house near the Lowell home. There he went in 1827 with such enthusiasm of spirit at being among boys again and with so little training in strict discipline that he received a thrashing on his first day in attendance, but it taught him a lesson, for George Ticknor Curtis later recalled that Lowell's school days were singularly free from chastisement. He remained at the Wells school, usually as a day scholar but sometimes (probably while his family moved to Boston for the winter of 1828) as a boarder, for six years before he was sent to the Boston school kept by Daniel G. Ingraham for a year of variety and perhaps of maturing away from home before entering Harvard at the age of fifteen.

This customary grammar school education was designed to give a student a solid knowledge of Latin, an ability to read Greek, and enough training in mathematics to enable him to undertake the study of geometry and advanced algebra. It prepared him for college, where he learned to write and speak English, practiced Latin composition, and attempted to compose exercises in Greek, while he spent three additional years upon literature in each of the ancient languages and three years upon mathematics. Harvard students went through the motions of studying modern history for a couple of terms but spent more time upon serious recitations in logic and theology. The college's greatest emphasis, however, was placed upon the study of philosophy—moral, mental, and political "science"—and more credit was allowed toward graduation for a good exhibition in "moral and intellectual philosophy" than for any other exercise. A student was expected to learn at least one modern language before graduation, and if he had any serious interest in his academic record he usually learned several. The pattern of study was rigidly set and there were few variations in particulars. A young man with scientific inclinations could substitute chemistry for intellectual philosophy during two terms of his college course, and after all the students had gone through the three volumes of the *Cambridge Natural Philosophy,* they studied "the philosophy of Nature" and heard lectures on mineralogy and anatomy at the end of their senior year. The choice of modern languages, however, was entirely optional, and although French and German were the most popular, many of the boys studied Italian, some took Spanish, and a few showed an interest in Portuguese. The recitations in more than one modern language were "voluntary" and received only half credit in points toward graduation and academic honors, but the extra credit was an inducement to extra study and the "voluntary" system was so popular that the freshmen of Lowell's generation agitated for its extension and there was talk, three years after his graduation, of putting all classes on that basis.

The habit of Harvard was so thoroughly ingrained among New Englanders of the Brahmin caste that they looked upon the institution as a sort of distinguished but eccentric trustee of their sons' stability. The ideal student was one who conformed to the college regulations with amused tolerance and casually graduated near the top of his class. Richard Henry Dana, after the maturing experience of two years before the mast, could play the proper role; but a younger boy who had grown up in the village might assume, from too great a familiarity with academic peculiarities, that such casualness supplanted rather than concealed a serious respect for the advantages Harvard had to offer. The extent to which Lowell's scholastic troubles might be attributed to the immature contempt bred from long acquaintance with scholastic foibles is uncertain; but he was acutely aware of the "curiosities" who gathered to eat the annual alumni dinner, of the incongruity between President Kirkland's person and his position, of the absent-mindedness of his successor, and of the great horse laugh of one of the French instructors whom the boy's fancy always dressed in violet silk. "The world always judges a man (and rightly enough, too)," Lowell wrote many years later, "by his little faults ... rather than by his great virtues." As a boy, he had a quick and constant eye for little faults and incongruities and not much interest in virtues beneath the surface. The youngster who hid along the edges of the gravel pit while the more earnest students practiced their oratory and gestures in what they fondly believed was solitude was more impressed by the occasional absurdity than by the constant probity of the trustee to whose control he was destined. It was easy for a nimble-witted lad to feel superior to some of the solemn-minded students whose humorless mummery he had watched from concealment, and to be contemptuous in his judgment of faculty members by their little faults and eccentricities. But whatever his attitude might be toward it, he was given the intellectual training which Harvard thought proper for its students and in later life was to have little else to draw upon when he felt the need for mental sustenance and support.

Lowell had little trouble with most of the Harvard course of study. He was a good student of languages, Latin and Greek, German and Italian, and he had a natural facility in composition. Theology and rhetoric offered no difficulties to a young man with his background, and although he was a poor mathematician he was passable according to the standards that exist when the subject is required of all students. The ancient languages in which he was thoroughly grounded in school and the modern languages (including French) in which he perfected himself in later life became the prized tools of his literary trade and were, by all odds, the most valuable of his acquisitions from college. The time spent on theology was little more than his tribute to the Christian civilization of which he was a part. A boy reared in Lowell's environment hardly needed to follow William Paley through *A View of the Evidences of Christianity* in order to protect himself against the deists and skeptics of the late eighteenth century; nor did he particularly need Bishop Joseph Butler's defense of natural religion in the first part of his *Analogy of Religion,* which he was also required to recite. They were both respectable classics, and a student might incline toward either in his own private beliefs without giving offense to his fellows. Lowell was later to prefer natural to revealed religion, but there is no evidence that his opinions were materially influenced by his college course of theology, and if Butler had any direct effect upon him, it was probably by encouraging him in the common tendency to draw analogies between the natural and spiritual worlds. The formal rhetoric and logic of Richard Whately which he was required to study before he took up mental and moral "science" made even less impression upon him. He was struck by Whately's contention that "the highest degree of Energy . . . is produced by such Metaphors as attribute *life* and *action* to things inanimate"; but most of the good advice in the *Elements of Rhetoric* was ignored in Lowell's early writings, and only occasional allusions to "a syllogism in Barbara" in the autobiography for his classbook and in his letters show that he had ever studied the *Logic.* Natural science—particularly chemistry and astronomy—added to Lowell's vocabulary and occasionally contributed an image to his later verse and prose. But aside from such ornamental relics, the time spent on his scientific studies seems to have been of no more value to him than that consumed by his long struggle with mathematics—which, to all appearances, was a total loss.

The most difficult of all Lowell's Harvard studies to evaluate is philosophy. It was this that brought about his downfall as a student, kept him on an allowance of fifty cents a week, and made him a disappointment to his father and such a problem to his classmates that they held a formal meeting about it. Yet the patterns of thought which he followed throughout his entire early literary career were acquired before he graduated from college—whether he acquired them through direct study or through absorption from an intellectual environment which was epitomized and made formally visible in the Harvard curriculum. During his junior year the course in moral and intellectual philosophy was based upon Paley's *Principles of Moral Philosophy* and Dugald Stewart's *Elements of the Philosophy of the Human Mind,* and although the course continued throughout the year, students were permitted to drop it for the last two terms and hear lectures in chemistry and physics instead. Lowell elected to do so after only six recitations in the second term. His own reasons for the change may be suggested by the fact that seven of his ten excused absences from class during the first term were from this single course, but the reason why the Harvard authorities (who, at this time, certainly would not have accepted boredom as an excuse for a change in registration) permitted it is less clear. The most probable explanation is that the course was taught in such a way that the students went through both textbooks in as near one term as possible and those who failed to grasp this important subject were required to review it while those who succeeded were allowed to do something else. Lowell, despite his absences, was a good student. The average value of his recitations in this course was greater than in any other with the exception of German (his best subject); and his "exhibition" in moral and intellectual philosophy during the second term, though not brilliant, was distinctly above the average. During the vacation following his second term, he alluded to Stewart's *Elements* in a letter to a classmate as though it were a familiar book, and, however his course may have been taught, it is unlikely that he escaped recitations in the author who served as the very keystone of the philosophical arch through which all Harvard students from Emerson to Lowell were obliged to pass.

The immediate importance of Stewart's philosophy as a part of Lowell's intellectual background was that it provided him with a theory of knowledge which encouraged obedience to one's spontaneous impulses, even though they might run counter to the conventional rules calculated and set forth by such a utilitarian philosopher as Paley. For Stewart belonged to the Scottish "Common Sense" school of philosophers who insisted upon the existence of innate ideas (particularly of morality) which could be comprehended by some internal "sense" common to all men in all ages. Stewart himself avoided the controversial term "ideas" and called them the fundamental "laws" of belief, although he compared them, in the conventional manner, to the "intuitive truths prefixed to the Elements of Euclid." He was also inclined to refer to the faculty of perception as the "reason"—a term he considered practically synonymous with, though less restricted than, "intuition" and altogether preferable to the ambiguous "Common Sense." *"To appeal to the light of human reason from the reasonings of the schools,"* he wrote, "is surely an expression to which no good objection can be made on the score either of vagueness or of novelty." His distinction between the intuitive reason and discursive reasoning or (as he sometimes called it) the "understanding" was essentially the same distinction between the Reason and the Understanding that Lowell was later to find in Carlyle and Emerson, in Eckermann's *Conversations with Goethe,* and in Coleridge; and Stewart's *Elements* was, in effect, for Lowell a respectably dull introduction to a way of thinking that he was to find in some of the more spirited writers he read later.

In addition, Stewart provided the young man with a similar distinction between the creative "Imagination" and the "Fancy" which Lowell was to find less satisfactorily drawn by Coleridge; and he showed him the difference between Humor and Wit, pointed out the significance of Rousseau as an example of the "ill-regulated Imagination," and made other points which were to influence Lowell's mature literary criticism. But such matters as these touched lightly upon the consciousness of the Harvard undergraduate. For the moment, he was probably affected only by the high respect which the author of a college textbook showed for "the faculty of Imagination" as "the great spring of human activity and the principal source of human improvement." For the specific critical theories of the *Elements* had no immediate effect upon Lowell's mind. He was not yet ready for them. He was only beginning to think seriously about literature, and, in any case, he was at an age that required a more exciting mental stimulus than the Scottish philosopher could provide. His college course provided him with material to which he could return when he grew tired of the excitement offered by other, more stimulating thinkers. The philosophy of Dugald Stewart was the intellectual Elmwood into which Lowell was to relax, later in life, when he was through with youthful adventuring.

There were close associations, in fact, between the ideas of Stewart and Lowell's home environment, for Dr. Lowell had not only studied under him but had been taken into his home, and had kept up a correspondence with his leading disciple. The Harvard recitations should have been easy for his son. Nor should the younger Lowell have had any trouble meeting the philosophical requirements of the first half of his senior year which called for a study of John Locke's *Essay concerning the Human Understanding* with a formal provision, set forth in the college catalogue, to the effect that a written analysis was required of the student and a commentary from the instructor "exhibiting the opinions of other philosophers on controverted questions." The most controverted question in Locke's *Essay,* of course, was that concerning the existence of innate ideas, and Stewart was the philosopher in the Harvard curriculum who attempted to controvert Locke's denial of their actuality. Before he had entered the junior course which prepared him to approach the great Mr. Locke with the proper arguments, Lowell had absorbed the intuitive—if not quite transcendental—point of view which Harvard encouraged.

Yet it was as a senior philosopher that Lowell met his downfall. His recitations dropped to mediocrity and below, and they continued to get worse during the second term as the instruction shifted from Locke to Jean-Baptiste Say's *A Treatise on Political Economy.* In the third term, in which the class finished political economy and took up Judge Joseph Story's *Familiar Exposition of the Constitution of the United States,* Lowell's performance reached its nadir by falling considerably below his recitations in mathematics. Since this course constituted the most important part of his senior studies, the falling-off was serious; and in the three successive terms of his senior year the net total of credit points he earned toward graduation dropped from seven hundred and fifty-seven to five hundred and fifty-seven to eleven in contrast to the average of something more than one thousand per term for his first three years. He was so indifferent to classes that not even the new Professor Longfellow could attract him to a course of unrequired lectures on the languages and literatures that had already begun to arouse his informal interest. He was in love and writing for the Harvard literary magazine, and the college requirements allowed—and perhaps even encouraged—a student to relax to some extent in his senior year. But Lowell, in the opinion of Francis Bowen, was relaxing entirely too thoroughly, and this serious-minded young instructor in moral and intellectual philosophy began to refuse to accept his pupil's excuses for frequent absences. The result was that on June 25, 1838, a week before the end of his last term, the faculty of the college

Voted, That Lowell, Senior, on account of continued negligence in college duties be suspended till the Saturday before Commencement, to pursue his studies with the Revd. Mr. Frost of Concord, to recite to him twice a day, reviewing the whole of Locke's essay and studying also McIntosh's Review of Ethical Philosophy, to be examined in both on his return and not to visit Cambridge during the period of his suspension.

He was to be made a student in spite of himself. Furthermore, he was to be given a more comprehensive view of philosophy than any of his classmates received, for the faculty seem to have considered it unnecessary for him to review Stewart and, instead, assigned him the book by Sir James Mackintosh which was not to be made a part of the formal curriculum of Harvard until the following year.

To Lowell, the action was unexpected and unreasonable. Two years before, when he was no more than a sophomore, his seventeenth birthday had been marked by the reception of his term "circular" listing fourteen absences from prayers and fifty-six from recitations (a total of seventeen more than he had been guilty of this time) and nothing had happened. During the course of his college days he had "undergone with the patience of a martyr," by his own account, "privates and publics without number and three threats of dismissal." And now the dignity of his senior year was being upset by the rustication that might be meted out to any immature schoolboy. He had lost his summer vacation, and the prohibition against a return to Cambridge would prevent him from making his public appearance as class poet at the Class Day celebration scheduled for July 17. His classmates held a mass meeting in protest, but in the meantime, Lowell had taken a buggy for Concord, damning everything and vowing that he would neither smoke nor shave so long as he remained in the wilds.

III

The young Lowell who went so resentfully to Concord was also going through a crucial period of his life. He had passed his nineteenth birthday, reached his full height of five feet eight inches, stopped growing, and decided that he had become a man. For several years he had affected the maturity of cigars, smoking from eight to ten a day when he could afford them; and for almost a year he had been "hopelessly in love" but sufficiently a man of the world to take an interest in other attractive young ladies. Although he had been something of a timid wallflower at his first grown-up ball in Boston a few months before, no one about Cambridge would have suspected shyness in the young dandy in white pantaloons and the new black beaver hat he had purchased for the glorification of his last weeks in college. His lively eyes displayed a quick interest in everything around him, and he talked with a sparkling, witty incessance. In the dark of the moon he was not above cutting the top off a post in the college yard, and, soon after he left, some of the more sentimental of his classmates decapitated another in his memory, exclaiming "Damn that Bowen!" while they attacked the one and murmuring "Jimmy helped do that" when they contemplated its mutilated fellow. His absent father and his elder brother's wife Anna (who was keeping house at Elmwood) were aware of the quality of childishness that still lurked beneath his daylight air of assurance; but they, and many of his friends, also realized that his customarily frivolous manner concealed a profound earnestness which had not yet found expression except in occasional letters. He had shown both a private and public interest in religion and a concern for political liberalism and for a humanitarian policy toward the American Indians; and his college class, as a whole, was sufficiently touched by the new spirit of reform to be the first at Harvard to make a public gesture toward temperance at its graduation exercises. He had reached, perhaps rather late in comparison with some of his associates, that state of fluid unpredictability in which a young man's purpose in life can be so easily shaped by chance and circumstances.

Under happier conditions he might have found his mold in Concord. For he was ready for Emerson. Emotionally, as we shall see later, he needed an agent that would crystallize his vague desires to do good, to justify his moral being. Intellectually, he was prepared for transcendentalism. How readily the doctrines of Emerson soared out of the principles of Dugald Stewart may be illustrated by a paragraph from a lecture by the Concord philosopher which Lowell had attended during the preceding December:

> Long prior to the age of reflection is the thinking of the mind. Out of the infinite darkness it came insensibly into the marvelous light of today. Over it always reigned a firm law. In its period of infancy it has accepted and disposed of all its impressions from the surrounding creation after its own way. Whatever any mind doth or saith is after a law.... And this its own law remains over it after it has come to reflection or conscious thought. Our spontaneous action is always the best. Thus you cannot with your best deliberation and heed, command your attention upon any speculative or practical question with such success as shall follow the spontaneous glance you give to the matter as you rise from your bed

or walk abroad in the morning. Always our thinking is an observing. Into us flows the stream evermore of thought from we know not whence. We do not determine what we think; we only open our senses, clear away as we can all obstructions from the facts, and let God think for us. Then we carry away in the ineffaceable memory the result and all men and all ages affirm it. It is called Truth. But the moment we do not do so, but are wilful and ingenious in the matter, it is not Truth.

The first half-dozen sentences might have been composed as a poetic epitome of Stewart's theory of how the human mind gradually stored itself with impressions and associations ordered according to the "fundamental laws of belief." They were orthodox. But out of them arose the doctrines that Emerson was later to present as "Self-Reliance," the moral that he was to use for his poem "Days," and the theory that the highest knowledge comes not from experience but from the influx of the divine mind in the individual. The connection between the two parts of the paragraph might seem, to a cold scrutiny, specious; but to Emerson it was real, and to Lowell, who was never "wilful" (in Emerson's sense of "determined") or "ingenious" about intellectual matters, it could have been attractive.

There were also novitiates of Lowell's own age in Concord who might have assisted his initiation into the mysteries of transcendentalism. Thoreau could have helped, for, although they had hardly known each other in college the year before, the two young men had something in common; and they might have exchanged ideas if Lowell had been in a better mood and if Thoreau had been willing to tolerate a man who was as talkative as, and more elegant than, any of the women from whom he later escaped to Walden. More important, Emerson's other and more brilliant protégé, Charles Stearns Wheeler, whom Lowell so genuinely admired a few years later, was in the village, full of information about the very books that Lowell was to discover with such excitement for himself. But he would not have needed such intermediaries. Emerson's courtesy itself was a bridge to his high gospel, and the older man entertained the younger in his home, talked with him, lent him books to read, and was in every way kind to the involuntary exile. But Lowell would have little to do with the people who might have meant so much to him in the "horrible place" to which he had been sent. His friends teased him about dwelling among the transcendentalists, and he was so sensitive to their opinions that when he finally did see Thoreau, after more than two weeks of rustication, he wrote: "I saw Thoreau last night, and it is exquisitely amusing to see how he imitates Emerson's tone and manner. With my eyes shut I shouldn't know them apart." He was a superior young man, determined to disapprove.

Yet Lowell's mind was active during his stay in Concord, and if his temper led him to refuse the village philosophy, it did not allow him wholly to reject the system of Sir James Mackintosh which the Harvard faculty had prescribed for him. And if it was easy for a young man to move from Stewart to Emerson, it was just as simple to go from Stewart to Mackintosh whose chief contribution to mental and moral "science" was his insistence that *"Right, duty, virtue, moral obligation,* and the like" were not merely "thoughts" as Stewart had conceived them but "feelings" that had an active influence over the "will." For the great ethical discovery of the eighteenth century, which Stewart ignored, according to Mackintosh, had been the perception "that through whatever length of reasoning the mind may pass in its advances toward action, there is some principle wholly unlike mere reason,—some *emotion* or *sentiment* which must be touched, before the springs of will and action can be set in motion." These emotions or sentiments were, in other respects, remarkably like the "Common Sense" which the earlier Scottish philosophers had attributed to mankind in an effort to describe those intuitions which Stewart represented as knowledge through "reason." They were "dependent on emotion and sympathy, with respect to the objects of which, it is not only possible but natural for all mankind to agree." Or, as Sir James put it more concretely in the opening sentences of his "Preliminary Observations":

> There is no man who, in a case where he was a calm by-stander, would not look with more satisfaction on acts of kindness than on acts of cruelty. . . . There is no tribe so rude as to be without a faint perception of a difference between right and wrong. There is no subject on which men of all ages and nations coincide in so many points as in the general rules of conduct, and in the qualities of the human character which deserve esteem.

This was his answer to Locke on one of the "controverted questions" with which the "Common Sense" philosophers also dwelt: Mackintosh merely translated their common perceptions of right and wrong from the head to the heart and so placed them more positively among what Stewart called the "active powers" of man.

Before he left Concord, Lowell was to indicate in his *Class Poem* a preference for the emotionalism of Mackintosh over the inspiration of Emerson, and in the course of the next few years he was to base a temporary philosophy of poetry upon the theory that all action-provoking thought was derived from the common sentiments of mankind. But his diligent recitations of Mackintosh were not accompanied by any enthusiasm, and the only philosophical work from which he received any positive stimulus during his rustication was the first volume of Carlyle's *Miscellanies* which Emerson and Stearns Wheeler had recently seen through the American press. He had hardly finished reading proof on the denunciation of Carlyle in his *Class Poem* when he picked up the new book and discovered "fine passages in all" its essays and felt the particular attraction of "the one on German Playwrights." But the article on Burns, he wrote to his classmate George B. Loring on August 9, "is worth all the rest to me." His enforced study of Mackintosh against the background of Dugald Stewart bore unexpected fruit in his enthusiasm for an author who, although Lowell of course did not know it, was no admirer of the one and actually professed to have been "hurt" by reading the other.

For Carlyle's essay on Burns, interpreted within the limits of Lowell's intellectual experience, served as a synthesis of the Harvard course of study and made it applicable to the problems of a would-be poet. The essay, as Lowell read it, took the admirable emotion of sympathy which Mackintosh had made the foundation of morality and turned it into the foundation of poetic greatness. As he contemplated Burns as "a true Poet" and "the most precious gift that can be bestowed on a generation," Carlyle exclaimed over the "inborn riches" of his soul:

> How his heart flows out in sympathy over universal Nature; and in her bleakest provinces discerns a beauty and a meaning! . . . But observe him chiefly as he mingles with his brother men. What warm, all-comprehending fellow-feeling; what trustful, boundless love; what generous exaggeration of the object loved! His rustic friend, his nut-brown maiden, are no longer mean and homely, but a hero and a queen, whom he prizes as the paragons of Earth, . . . Poverty is indeed his companion, but Love also, and Courage; the simple feelings, the worth, the nobleness, that dwell under the straw roof, are dear and venerable to his heart: and thus over the lowest provinces of man's existence he pours the glory of his own soul; and they rise, in shadow and sunshine, softened and brightened into a beauty which other eyes discern not in the highest.

This quality of sympathy for nature and man, which Carlyle called "the essential gift of poetic feeling," played the same part in the aesthetics of his appreciation of Burns that the "imagination" played in the more formal aesthetics of Dugald Stewart. This sympathy likewise bore the same relationship to the "fancy," which Carlyle called "clearness of sight" and considered, as Stewart considered the fancy, "the foundation of all talent" and the attribute of a "lively" mind, although it gave "no sure indication of the higher endowments that may exist along with it." Carlyle implied that these higher endowments might be "fire," "force," or "strength"; but, on the whole, he was clear about what he prized most in Burns as the higher supplement to his power of sight: Burns "saw, and not with the eye only," for his descriptions were "of the heart as well as of the eye!"

Thus, Carlyle's essay brought together Lowell's other two Scottish philosophers by doing—inadvertently, perhaps—for aesthetics what Mackintosh had done for ethics: it substituted emotional for intellectual activity as the highest requirement of the poet who possessed the necessary faculty of perception but would rise above the prosaic level of Richardson and Defoe. In effect, Carlyle identified sympathy with imagination. Like Mackintosh, he thought of this emotion as an active power quite different from the "weak-eyed maudlin sensibility" he attributed to Keats and as something which went with, rather than against, those vigorous "strictly intellectual perceptions" that Stewart had found in Burns. Such perceptions were, he thought, "at all times the very essence of a truly poetical endowment"; but he was inclined to emphasize the poet's *"light"* less than his *"warmth":* "a Poet without Love were a physical and metaphysical impossibility." Yet Carlyle believed no more than did Mackintosh that a poet should make a naïve display of his sympathies. The fact that "Indignation makes verses" was not a contradiction of his principle, for, he explained: "The Indignation which makes verses is, properly speaking, an inverted Love; the love of some right, some worth, some goodness, belonging to ourselves or others, which has been injured, and which this tempestuous feeling issues forth to defend and avenge." The young poet who first read such lines in Concord was not at the moment so particularly interested in the inverted principle as he was in its more positive application, but in the course of years he was to find some need for a double-edged theory of poetry which was as sharp on one side as it was soft on the other—although by the time he needed such a justification for his indignation he had almost forgotten Carlyle and was more concerned with those "moral feelings" which Mackintosh held could be cultivated by "indignation against the wrong-doer."

The stimulus that Lowell found in Carlyle's essay, although he could hardly have experienced it without the background of his college studies, was entirely extra-curricular. It did not affect his attitude toward Concord and toward most of the people he found within its bounds. He maintained as low an opinion of the Reverend Barzillai Frost, his host and preceptor, as he did of Thoreau. He found his rhetoric ridiculous when he listened to his sermons, and he even developed a perverse interest in the empirical philosophy of John Locke when he discovered that Frost was a confirmed admirer of the English philosopher and could be easily distressed by a student who claimed to find the great man incontrovertible upon such questions as whether inherent moral sentiments could make an impression upon the *tabula rasa* of the human mind. Mrs. Frost, however, won the schoolboy's admiration by kindness and good cooking; and, in spite of himself, he found a few people to like. He soon broke his vow not to shave and became so attracted to Miss Caroline Brooks that he wrote a poem about her and seems to have regretted that her serious affections were already engaged. But he was free to admire, and he made a lifelong friend of her fiancé, E. R. Hoar. There was an occasional other "good fellow" to be found in Concord, but the rest of the people, although he found them inclined to lionize him, were unendurable. "The chief characteristic of our ladies," he wrote Loring in the letter of August 9, "is that they don't clean their nails, and of the gentlemen that they don't ditto their teeth." He was glad to get away from a place of so many unpleasant suggestions; and although he returned a year later when Concord provided the only platform that would support him as a lecturer, the four-dollar fee he received for his performance did nothing to restore the town to his good graces. To the young man whose habit was to look upon himself as a guileless member of a chosen group, Concord was Nazareth, and his later admiration for Emerson was always tempered by a skeptical wonder that any good thing could come out of such a place.

Cambridge was his home. More than thirty years later, when he wrote "On a Certain Condescension in Foreigners," he referred to a person he knew who was "singular enough to think Cambridge the very best spot on the habitable globe"—and the same person had probably begun to suspect as much during a schoolboy exile in Concord. The roots that he had put down in Cambridge found the sort of nourishment that enabled him to flower in the civilization which the English-speaking peoples of the nineteenth century were to produce. He had a respectable background in the past which made it unnecessary for him to endure the condescension of any one, and sufficiently broad connections in the present to be assured of a decent welcome into almost any society he chose to enter. Despite his academic troubles, he also had the foundations of what passed as a good education in his own day, for he possessed a reasonable competence in the two dead languages which still haunted the European mind and some acquaintance with the three most highly approved living foreign tongues. He could enter a Boston drawing room, an English country house, or a German university without feeling completely lost; and he could return from any one of them to Elmwood with a feeling of relaxation which was in no sense a let-down. And he always returned. Circumstances were to call him away from Elmwood on numerous occasions, and three times his emotions—anger, misery, and heartache—were to drive him to seek a different residence. But his voluntary departures were never for long. The house in which he was born provided the young squire and the older man with a feeling of stability which he could never possess anywhere else, and of the five Lowell children who grew to maturity, he was the proper one to inherit Elmwood and die there.

That a person who was so persistently attracted, physically and emotionally, back to the environment in which Lowell was bred should have become a radical poet and impassioned reformer was almost a violation of nature. That his radicalism and his reforms should have had a less solid and substantial base than his good-natured conservatism was, perhaps, inevitable. His extremes were tolerated, with some distress, at Elmwood; but Lowell could hardly have endured the distress they caused unless he had been able to rationalize them and look upon them as something more than erratic deviations from the social pattern to which he had been bred. He got much of the material for that rationalization from the writing of the three Scots with whom he became acquainted before he was allowed to return to Cambridge and take his bachelor's degree. The confidence in a knowledge that transcended Locke's "Understanding," a belief that the moving spirit of morality existed in emotions common to every man, and a conviction that the imagination was either identical with or closely related to sympathy—these, however decorated with other notions, were fundamental to Lowell's later attempts to justify his literary and radical activities. He was to support them from other sources—from the New Testament, from Emerson, and from the writings of Coleridge, Wordsworth, and Shelley—but such support from known sources was merely a verification of the "Truth" in which his youthful mind was shaped. In his later prose works, Lowell was to speak disparagingly of Carlyle's tendency to confuse moral and aesthetic values, and he was never to mention the philosophy of Mackintosh or to refer to Dugald Stewart at all. But from his early reading of them, there was to flow into his consciousness a stream of thought from he knew not whence, and, intuitive thinker that he was, he seems to have placed more confidence in that stream than in any of the thoughts he found for the first time in other writers.

From this social and intellectual environment of Cambridge and Concord, Lowell derived most of the contradictions and restlessness that marked his early literary career—his feeling of insecurity when he was away from Elmwood in body or in spirit and his uneasy conscience when he stayed comfortably at home and failed to follow his wayward impulses. When he had attended Emerson's lecture on the evening of December 20, 1837, he had been greatly impressed by a figure of speech which is applicable to his own condition: "The walls of the mind's chamber are covered with scribblings," Emerson had said, as Lowell recalled it in a letter to Loring, "which need but the bringing of a candle to make them legible." The early scribblings in his own mind were often on opposing walls, and for nearly twenty years after he graduated from college his various candles wavered from side to side without illuminating, consistently, either the comforts of security or the message of his radical emotions. To say that Lowell was temperamentally unstable would be true enough as an indifferent observation upon his character. But such an observation would do little to explain his peculiar literary failings and achievements, for the stability of a phlegmatic temperament is rarely to be found among poets, who normally succeed, as poets, by imagining what they want to be and do and by utilizing even the vagaries of temperament to that end. Lowell tried more seriously than any of his contemporaries, except possibly Whitman, to set a definite aim for himself as a poet; and at one stage, at least, his aim was remarkably like Whitman's. His failure to hold consistently to it was in part a result of the conflicts and contradictions inherent in his early environment and exhibited in his later life. But he also suffered from a certain peculiarity of the imagination which may be revealed most clearly, perhaps, by an account of his early travels through what Keats called "the realms of gold."

Chapter II

REALMS OF GOLD

PROBABLY NO young American of Lowell's generation ranged more widely than he did through the regions of imaginative literature. From earliest childhood he had been brought up in a house full of books by a family with literary inclinations and varied tastes who exposed the youngest member to their own enthusiasms and encouraged him to read and make his own collection of books at an age when most children were still spelling through their primers. Long before he was able to spell, his sister Mary used to reconcile him to his daily naps by reading to him from *The Faerie Queene* to such an effect that his active fancy led him to see visions in medieval costume during childhood, and Spenser became "the first poet" he "ever read as a boy." His mother sang him Scottish ballads, and it was probably with her encouragement that he was reading *Waverly* at the age of eight before she gave him the three volumes of Scott's *Tales of a Grandfather*. Dr. Lowell stood at the opposite pole from his womenfolk; he had "kissed the great toe of Pope" in his own youth, according to his son, and tried—with altogether contrary results—to bring Jemmy up "in the old superstition that he was the greatest poet that ever lived." His brother Robert's taste for Byron was more attractive to him, although it was not necessarily influential at a time when almost every young man interested in poetry had to go through his Byronic period, and three years' seniority merely meant that the older brother was the first to reach that inevitable stage.

Surrounded by such a variety of literary tastes, with access to a home library of over four thousand volumes and with the power of borrowing abroad, Lowell was remarkably free to explore the many goodly states and kingdoms of the imagination. The actual record of his explorations is no more than sufficient to show that they were precocious and unrestrained. He had "got quite a library" of his own at the age of nine, he reported in one of his earliest letters, and he later recalled specifically having read Cowper during the administration of John Quincy Adams, which came to an end a few days after his tenth birthday. But there is little information about the order of his interest in the many poets and several prose writers who cropped up and received the tribute of allusion in his undergraduate letters, essays, and verses. He recalled in later life that Marlowe was "the first man of genius" he "had ever really known" and that having made his acquaintance "during the most impressible and receptive period" of his youth he was "naturally bewitched" by him. But his writings, including his letters and commonplace books, are singularly free from allusions to Marlowe in comparison with other of the "Old English Dramatists" and he evidently was bewitched without being captivated into the constant re-reading that he gave to Spenser. Shakespeare made a more lasting impression upon him in his youth, although his reading had not been systematic, for he expressed his astonishment, in a letter of November 6, 1835, that he had read all the plays except two or three including *Hamlet* which he resolved to get at "instanter."

There can be little doubt but that the fifteen-year-old book collector who entered Harvard in 1834 had already formed an acquaintance with the major English poets. The boy who wrote in 1836 that Samuel Butler's *Hudibras* "always was and always will be a great favorite" of his as an "inexhaustible source of mirth from beginning to end" certainly knew Butler's great opposite whose life he was reading at the time, whose works he was acquiring in a new and "beautiful" edition for his own library, and who was exciting his ambition to "read all the Greek and Latin classics which he did." Lowell never, at this time or later, alluded to Milton as a new planet swimming within his ken, but always as a writer so familiar that his first acquaintance with him might be dated back to his childhood. Wordsworth was another with whom he apparently grew up, without enthusiasm but with the familiarity of long acquaintance. During his last year in college, Lowell parodied Wordsworth, criticized him, and once or twice alluded to him in his letters; but he recorded no quotations from him in his commonplace book and refused to admit the fascination which the author of *Lyrical Ballads* quite evidently exercised over his mind. Wordsworth was to require more space in the index to his complete prose works than any other English poet including Shakespeare, and Lowell's refusal from the beginning of his career to face the fact that he was more bewitched by Wordsworth than by Marlowe was one of his most unfortunate reactions to his early reading, for it meant that he kept his editorial eye turned away from the influence which made so much of his own early poetry seem slightly secondhand.

The modern poets for whom he did admit an enthusiasm were the pirated three—Coleridge, Shelley, and Keats—whose works he obtained in an American reprint of the Galignani edition in 1834. To find "such infinite riches in a little room" was a "delight" to him, as he remembered it after more than half a century, and in the case of Coleridge the delight was not exaggerated in the recollection. He would settle down, in the summer of 1835, to consume the better part of the day with Coleridge's poetical works before him; and he was delighted when his father gave him the three-volume "Aldine Edition" as a New Year's present. He obtained the two volumes of *Remains* the following December and reread the Aldine volumes in 1838 and the "Ancient Mariner" (for years his favorite single poem) over and over again. Keats aroused less excitement at first, for Lowell had not yet begun to read for technical instruction in the art of poetry, and he had to pass through several stages of his apprenticeship to it before he recognized in Keats a quality of mind so akin to his own that he could fully appreciate him. Shelley, although read thoroughly, apparently made the least impression of the three. As late as the spring of 1838, Lowell was unwilling to agree with his friend Loring that "the fire of poetry abounds" in the author of *Queen Mab,* and when he did agree, after being attracted by Shelley's theory of poetry and the Platonic imagery of *Adonais* some years later, he called the fire "ineffectual." The Galignani collection gave him an immediate and lasting enjoyment of Coleridge's poetry but merely laid the foundation for his gradual appreciation of Keats and for a more fluctuating interest in Shelley.

When Dr. Lowell gave his son the edition of Coleridge on New Year's Day, 1836, he was making his contribution to the library of modern—or relatively modern—poets which the boy was beginning to build up. He spent some of his own New Year's "cash" on an edition of Beattie, observing that *The Minstrel* was in the stanza of his beloved Spenser, although it was fifteen months before he really got around to reading the poem "carefully." He also received a fine edition of Akenside as a college "detur" on February 1, without giving any evidence that he was as impressed by the contents of the volume as he was by its binding. It was apparently during this year that he received his first light touch of Byronism, for by Christmas he had discovered that there were at least two points of personal resemblance between himself and the English poet—a discovery which caused Loring to write earnestly on December 28: "I hope your resemblances to Byron are in his good qualities and if so that you may hold on to them." Lowell had no reason, at the moment, to try to multiply the points of similitude, but he did read Byron's poetry and during the next few months showed himself able to quote it readily and speak casually of the "tears" that "some parts" of it brought to his eyes. But Thomas Campbell also had the same effect of sometimes bringing tears to his eyes and sometimes sending a cold but not unpleasant chill along his spine. Campbell on the whole seems to have pleased him more than Byron did during the winter term of his junior year in college, and his classmate Loring was so impressed by his enthusiasm that he offered to present him with the expensive, six-dollar-and-a-half edition (probably the new one announced by Moxon, with illustrations by Turner) he coveted. At this particular time, the content of Campbell's works appealed to Lowell more than did that of Byron's. His portrait of the noble Oneyda in *Gertrude of Wyoming* interested a young man who had already expressed his sympathy with the fate of the Indians then being moved to reservations, and his representation of Kosciusko and the struggle for liberty in Poland appealed to Lowell's awakening interest in European politics. *The Pleasures of Hope,* too, expressed emotions that Lowell shared and found again in a companion poem, Samuel Rogers' *The Pleasures of Memory,* which he read during the same spring. He was laying his hands "on a very pretty edition of Cowper" in two volumes which he "intended to keep" for his own library at the same time, reading the poems of Southey and the same author's prose compendium of miscellaneous information, *The Doctor,* and, by August, quoting James Montgomery. Southey's poetry, however, seems to have made no great impression upon him until the following February, when he made extensive extracts from *Thalaba* for his commonplace book.

Lowell had begun keeping a commonplace book in 1836, and from that time until 1838 his miscellaneous reading may be fairly well traced despite the fact that he apparently let memorable quotations accumulate until they impelled him to periods of industrious copying between long intervals of laziness. Except for *Thalaba,* the personification of war in *Childe Harold,* a bit from Scott's *Lord of the Isles,* Thomson's *The Seasons* (which he read in 1836), and Cowper's *The Task* (which may have been one of the few entries made after 1838), his interest in non-dramatic poetry during this period was almost entirely in what he liked to call the "old poets" of the seventeenth century or earlier. He found something worth copying from Chaucer's "Knight's Tale," Shakespeare's Sonnets, Sir John Davies' *Nosce Teipsum,* and shorter poems by James I, Richard Crashaw, Thomas Carew, Richard Lovelace, Robert Herrick, James Shirley, Samuel Daniel, George Wither, and William Drummond of Hawthornden—in addition to Spenser whom he was rereading. He was also quoting George Herbert and Dryden in his letters and reading Sylvester's translation of DuBartas.

The determination he had made in November of 1835 to read *Hamlet* "instanter" was—as so many of Lowell's determinations were to be—more easily made than carried out, but Shakespeare remained on his mind, and when Hillard and Gray announced the publication of a new and "beautifully printed" edition for February, 1836, Lowell announced his own intention of buying it if he could raise the necessary fourteen dollars. In March he was neatly copying choice passages from *Hamlet* into his new commonplace book and following them, apparently (for these quotations are undated), with occasional selections from *Much Ado About Nothing,* and the first part of *Henry VI.* He was also reading *The Merry Wives of Windsor* and, though hardly for the first time, *Twelfth Night* a day or so after twelfth night in January, 1837. None of these extracts indicates more than an interest in a good quotation: Lowell could not have said at this time that he "really knew" Shakespeare as "a man of genius" in the sense that he claimed to have known Marlowe. They mark merely the beginning of a new acquaintance that grew in intimacy throughout his college days until the habit of quotation, allusion, and echo became an unconscious part of his literary style.

Lowell was also quoting Milton's *Comus* in his commonplace book under the date of April 26, 1836, but the only other poetical drama, in English, that appears to have interested him before his senior year in college was the contemporary *Ion; A Tragedy* by Sir Thomas Noon Talfourd. This sweetly sorrowful account of a young man with immortal impulses and an appropriately Platonic name charmed him with its noble sentiments and "exquisite" imagery, in March, 1837, and he copied out passage after passage from it. During these middle undergraduate years he was also working his way through verse dramas in other languages: selections from the plays of Metastasio, whom he translated in part and straighway forgot; Goethe's *Faust;* Sophocles' *Oedipus Tyrannus, Oedipus Coloneus,* and *Antigone;*

Euripides' *Alcestis;* and apparently several dramas by Aeschylus. But they represented languages rather than literature and probably contributed little, if anything, to his developing interest in the poetic drama. Although he occasionally copied out a line from Aeschylus, the only comment he made upon any of them concerned *Faust:* "Hard, isn't it?" he wrote an older friend early in 1836. He purchased a German edition of Schiller before January 6 of that year, but English offered him, in every way, an easier fare. Henry Taylor's *Philip Van Artevelde* so pleased him, in January, 1838, with its representation of a high ideal drawn from an age ruder than the decadent present that he reread it in October of the same year; and in February he turned again to his beloved Coleridge, reading through the entire collection of dramas, though recording only a few quotations from *Remorse* and the translation of Schiller's *Wallenstein*. All of these had "idealistic" implications: Van Artevelde felt that he was knit to the bondsmen of the world by their affections as firmly as they were bound to their feudal lords; Coleridge's theme was the power of conscience over the darkest heart; and Duke Wallenstein bore witness to the inability of the firmest mind to devote itself exclusively to practical matters without recourse to some source of confidence that lay beyond the common power of understanding. They reflected the normal interests of a very young man with transcendental leanings, a feeling that poetry was something apart from the practical world, and a disposition at the moment to identify poetry with rather superficial sentiments.

He was still in the mood to use somewhat superficial sentiments as the touchstone of poetry when he began to read widely in the older dramatists. He first made the acquaintance of the contemporaries of Marlowe and Shakespeare in the arched alcoves of the college library during the last two terms of his senior year. He wrote fifty years later:

> There, with my book lying at ease and in the expansion of intimacy on the broad window-shelf, shifting my cell from north to south with the season, I made friendships, that have lasted me for life, with Dodsley's "Old Plays," with Cotton's "Montaigne," with Hakluyt's "Voyages," among others that were not in my father's library. It was the merest browsing, no doubt, as Dr. Johnson called it, but how delightful it was! All the more, I fear, because it added the stolen sweetness of truancy to that of study, for I should have been buckling to my allotted task of the day.

The twelve volumes of Dodsley's *Select Collection of Old Plays* and the six volumes of Dilke's *Old English Plays* that supplemented them provided an extensive acquaintance with Elizabethan and Jacobean dramatists whom Lowell cultivated according to his mood. At first he was attracted by the romantic prettiness of Beaumont and Fletcher, and on March 14, 1838, he withdrew some of their *Works* from the college library in order to transcribe passages from *The Maid in the Mill, Love's Pilgrimage,* and *Love's Cure, or The Martial Maid* into his commonplace book. Eleven days later, on the day he was rusticated to Concord, he withdrew some "Old Plays" which he probably took with him—evidently one or more volumes of Dilke's supplement to Dodsley, which was commonly abbreviated in that way. When he returned to Cambridge, he also returned to the Jacobean dramatists, taking home the two-volume edition of Ford's *Dramatic Works* from Harvard Hall on September 12 and reading such plays as *The Broken Heart, Honor Triumphant, The Ladies Trial, The Lover's Melancholy,* and *'Tis Pity She's a Whore* with more emotion than he had yet spent on the old playwrights.

During the course of his reading from the dramatic poets, Lowell's own attitude toward literature had changed. Most of his early traveling through the realms of gold had been that of an idle but impressionable tourist to whom the pure serene of different imaginative worlds had little personal meaning, although the breathing of it was pleasant enough and he loved to collect souvenirs of his trip. Parts of his collection were preserved in his commonplace book and not placed on exhibition until several years later, if at all. Others were presented to the public view almost at once in the pages of *Harvardiana,* the undergraduate literary magazine which he helped to edit and for which he wrote during his senior year. In it, for example, his allusions to English poetry included quotations from Shakespeare's *Hamlet, Othello, Julius Caesar, Henry IV, Part I, As You Like It, Twelfth Night,* and *The Tempest,* from *Paradise Lost,* from Gray's *Elegy,* Burns's "Jolly Beggars," Tom Moore's "Oft in the Stilly Night," Byron's *Childe Harold* and *Don Juan,* and Shelley's "Letter to Maria Gisborne"; parodies of passages from *Hamlet, King Lear, Twelfth Night, The Tempest,* and of Pope's Homer, the English "Pindaric" ode, Wordsworth's sonnets, Burns, and Rogers; and references, direct or indirect, to *Much Ado about Nothing,* Pope's "Song by a Person of Quality," and Goldsmith's *The Deserted Village,* in addition to a considerable number of passing references to authors or titles that he had quoted or parodied. He referred, somewhat satirically, in one contribution to the use of a comprehensive index of Shakespeare "for glibness of quotation," but his own glibness did not come from any book of reference or from his own commonplace book: he was demonstrating, in college, that retentive memory for a good phrase which filled his later critical writings and, somewhat inadvertently, his verses with literary allusions and echoes of other writers.

The first unmistakable signs of his new attitude toward literature appeared in the spring of 1837 when he left his room near the college at the beginning of the holidays and returned to the lonely house which was soon to be designated Elmwood. His father, mother, and sister Rebecca had sailed for Europe less than a week before; Mary, of course, had long since married and moved away; and his brother Robert had a room in Boston. The house itself was lively enough with the children of his oldest brother Charles, who was looking after the family home in his father's absence; but Charles himself was occupied by business, and his wife, Anna Cabot Lowell, although the kindest of older sisters-in-law, was probably too busy with her own brood and a new routine of housekeeping to have much care for the feelings of a young man who had merely taken a twenty-minute walk up the street in order to return home for his college vacation. His only real welcome was from the family dog whom Dr. Lowell had named Argus, and it made Lowell feel like Odysseus. He retired to his room and under the influence of his father's farewell letter read twenty pages of Cicero and eight chapters of Herodotus, but by three o'clock in the afternoon he was so overcome by loneliness that he took his pen in hand and addressed himself to George Loring who had also gone home that morning: "Well, I suppose you are at home, 'sweet, sweet home!' So am I, and it does my heart good. As I run about over the same familiar spots which I trod in joyous, careless infancy, my heart leaps up again, and the innocent days of my childhood come over me like a dream." But there was a mixture of sadness in the joy of revisiting the "home of one's childhood," he confessed, and amid his melancholy reflections on the mixture he resolved to read his Bible every night and publicly satirize "those *fools* that are ambitious of appearing to despise religion, etc., etc."

In an effort to express his pleasurable sensations at returning home, Lowell not only borrowed phrases from William Wordsworth and John Howard Payne but drew upon *The Pleasures of Hope* and *The Pleasures of Memory* for several quotations which he excused on the ground that they were "so much, so infinitely, superior to anything *I* could say." Yet a week later he had his own say in a little poem "Our Old Horse-Chestnut Tree" which recalled his "careless infancy" and that of his brother Bob. He undoubtedly thought of it as an intensely personal expression when he sent it to Loring—

as, in a sense, it was. But the "family mansion" mentioned in the part of the letter which introduced it, the "casements" that first "brought the light" to him in the poem, the childish laughter, the bird's nest, and the hoary evidences of age were all directly—and in most cases verbally—out of Samuel Rogers' *The Pleasures of Memory* into which he had earlier looked for a "superior" expression of his feelings. The boy was childishly lonesome for his parents and suffering from the melancholia of a bad conscience aroused by his father's letter, but he had discovered, without fully realizing it, that a person's emotions often look better when reflected by the pleasant distortion of the mirror of literature. He was to find other mirrors than that of *The Pleasures of Memory* and prepare a few of his own, but he was to continue for many years to see himself through some sort of literary reflection; and when he protested, as he so often did, his desire to be true to himself, it is practically impossible to know exactly what he meant without looking first for the mirror in which he saw that momentary self represented.

II

LOWELL'S TENDENCY to find his own image in the realms of gold was stimulated—and perhaps made a settled habit of his youthful mind—by a chain of circumstances which began during the July vacation of 1837 when he went up to Waltham to visit the family of his sister-in-law. Anna's brother, Patrick Tracy Jackson, Jr., was James's classmate in college, and the two young men were later to occupy neighboring stools in the Boston counting-house where Robert Lowell was already working. But James seems to have known none of the other children of the family until he paid them a visit and was completely bowled over by an auburn-haired younger sister named Hannah. After his return home, he wrote Loring enthusiastically about the meeting, and a day later confided to an older friend, W. H. Shackford, that he was in love and had "been so for some time, hopelessly in love." But there was little he could do about it at the time. He had been obliged to return to Cambridge and represent the Hasty Pudding Club with a poem at the time of the undergraduate public exercises, and both young people had apparently scheduled holiday visits immediately afterward. Lowell made an "excursion into the country," where, he wrote Shackford rather superciliously, he busied himself in "shooting and fishing and going through the usual routine of country amusements." He was glad to get home where he had better opportunities to write Loring to keep an eye on his "forlorn and desolate Hannah," who was visiting in his friend's home town of North Andover and who, he obviously feared, might be prevented by a certain "Captain" from becoming as forlorn and desolate as he hoped.

She returned safely, however, and bowled him over again when he first met her on August 22; and Lowell, who had been shy about expressing his feelings in English prose to anybody who knew her, let himself go the next evening in a verse letter to Loring in the Scots of Bobby Burns. While he was in ecstasies over her eyes, curls, smiles, voice, and blushes, she had come down to Cambridge and had dropped in to stay for dinner. "Wasna *that* queer?" he asked in astonishment, after she had gone and he had returned to his poem. Loring had found it difficult to understand his friend's distrust of his own attractions, but Lowell continued to be genuinely timid and was equally surprised when he discovered that Miss Jackson was expecting to be in Cambridge again for Emerson's Phi Beta Kappa address on August 31. Lowell, of course, attended, but he did not find his inspiration on the platform as he implied when he recalled the occasion some thirty years later: His references to it in *Harvardiana* for the following March were mildly humorous and perhaps more nearly satiric than appreciative. But his lady, it developed, was an admirer of Emerson, and he was thinking of her on December 22 when he wrote to Loring of the lecture by Emerson which had so impressed him with the figure of the candles lighting the mind's chamber and which had inspired him to keep a journal. She may have been more interested, in fact, in the "Human Culture" advocated by Emerson than in balls, for Lowell was disappointed when she did not show up at the one given by his cousin on the day after Christmas, and his disappointment may have been partly responsible for his own social failure on that occasion.

So far, there was nothing unusual in the first love affair of a young man who was rather shy at heart but not in manner, and who was more attractive to the opposite sex than he was willing to believe. When he drew the works of Beaumont and Fletcher out of the Harvard library in March, it was only normal for him to copy into his commonplace book the pretty passages relating to his emotion; and while he was in Concord, a teasing verse letter from his brother Robert referring to a visit from the young lady did not discourage him from looking with enthusiasm into the charming black eyes of Miss Caroline Brooks. After he returned home, however, he fell into a mood darker than that of his irritating but not unrelieved rustication. September was a bad month in every way. He had been planning to study law, but as the time approached he was not eager to begin his studies and wondered whether he should not enter the Divinity School instead, although he felt no particular calling to the ministry. "If I did not think that I should some day make a great fool of myself and marry (not that I would call *all* men fools who marry)," he wrote Loring on September 22, "I would enter the School tomorrow." His trouble was not with any belief in a celibate priesthood but entirely financial: having been for some time so completely without funds that he could not pay postage on a copy of Emerson's Dartmouth College oration he had wanted to send his friend, he was suffering the dejection of a poverty which was infuriating in its pettiness. The only solution he could see for the problems of normal life was an independent income. He also had too much time in which to brood, for although he insisted to Loring that he was "in good health and spirits" he wrote that his eyes were so weak that he was prevented from reading in the evening.

It was while he was in this state of disconsolate emotional impotence that he brought home the works of John Ford. A few years later he was to discover that Ford was "sentimental," but at the time the "great deal of tragic *excitability and enthusiasm*" which he found in his works—especially in *'Tis Pity She's a Whore*—was an incitement to his own mood. He seems to have recognized a kindred soul in the hero of the play, that "miracle of wit" Giovanni, who had been so applauded by the university until he lost himself in his own emotions. Lowell himself had been a promising student who had thrown away the academic success that could so easily have been grasped and was now restless in his inability to settle upon a profession. He was "hopelessly in love," doubtful of his attractions, and so awkwardly backward about confessing his state of mind to the young lady concerned that nearly a year later he was still addressing her in letters as "Miss Jackson." But in his own mind his feelings were intense, and he copied from the play numerous passages that seemed appropriate to his own situation. "Let pouring bookworms dream of other worlds," he transcribed under the general heading "Love"; "My world, and all of happiness is here." Under the heading of love that fears to speak he copied:

> For every sigh that thou hast spent for me,
> I have sighed ten; for every tear shed twenty;
> And not so much for that I loved, as that
> I durst not say I love, nor scarcely think it.

The barrier between James and his beautiful Hannah was not at all like that which separated Giovanni and Annabella, of course, but Lowell was in the position of suffering so acutely from minor difficulties that he had to magnify and dramatize them in order to justify the misery in which he was luxuriating.

Driven by this need for self-dramatization, Lowell apparently allowed his unoccupied imagination—for, although thinking of a dramatic poem on a seventeenth-century theme, he was not actually writing poetry at the time—to dwell upon the parallel between himself and Giovanni until it was exaggerated beyond all reason. How much he may have brooded over the fact that his "hopeless" love was for his brother's sister-in-law is, of course undeterminable, because such thoughts bordered upon matters about which no well brought up young man would speak. But it was probably at this time that he turned to *Manfred* and *The Cenci,* the two other plays he listed among the books read in 1838; and it seems to have been soon after this that he began to speak darkly of his own emotions with a "wildness" that disturbed his friends, although, incidentally, no trace of it may be found in the few surviving verses or notes he addressed to the young lady herself. Two or three years later he was to look back at his youthful love affair and see it through a "lurid and sulphurous glow," and it was to be a decade before he could remember it as anything other than something terrible. But the terrible glow seems to have come from an excited imagination kindled by the poetic drama of the Jacobean and Romantic periods.

There is no clear indication of when Lowell read the numerous other "old plays" from which he made extracts for his commonplace book, but since they do not appear among the books read in 1838 or those drawn from the library at Harvard in 1837 or 1838, they probably represent a continuation into the following year of the interest so greatly stimulated by Ford. Tourneur's *The Revenger's Tragedy,* of course, made use of the theme that had attracted him during the fall; but Lowell's attention to certain other plays was directly related to his unenthusiastic attitude toward the law, which, after some thought of medicine and business, he was unhappily studying in 1839. Webster's *The White Devil, The Devil's Law-Case,* and *Appius and Virginia* and Ben Jonson's *Volpone* all contain satirical portraits of lawyers; and there is a legal tone at least, as the titles suggest, in Nash's *Summer's Last Will and Testament* and Shirley's *The Contention of Ajax and Ulysses.* It is hardly a coincidence that these formed a majority of the miscellaneous plays quoted in the commonplace book, although the quotations themselves were as likely to deal with love and women as with the law, and Lowell found more to interest him in *The Duchess of Malfi* than in any of Webster's other plays. Three additional works from which he quoted briefly and casually are Massinger's *A Very Woman* and *The Bondman* and Dekker's *Old Fortunatus.*

The old English dramatist who, after Ford, aroused Lowell's sympathetic imagination was George Chapman. The volume of Dilke's collection which included *Old Fortunatus* also contained *Bussy D'Ambois* and *Monsieur D'Olive* by the relatively unknown playwright whose translations were familiar enough but whose plays had not yet been collected into a complete edition. Chapman's passionate, defiant heroes were apparently the sort of men whom the wishy-washy young law student envied in 1839 when he dated his reading from the former play. The Earl of St. Anne, in the latter, spoke to the point of Lowell's own situation when he provided the following exclamation for his commonplace book:

> Yet in this case of love, who is my brother?
> Who is my father? Who is any kin?
> I will pursue my passion; I will have her.

For his affair ended with a dramatic, but somewhat less than Jacobean, catastrophe in early September, 1839, when Lowell quarreled violently with his brother, moved out of Elmwood, and took a room in the village. More than a year later, on November 24, 1840, he confessed to Loring: "I now feel that my love for Hannah Jackson was no *true* love else I had never felt toward my brother as I did." But he gave no other details. Charles Lowell was at the time in the process of losing, by unfortunate management, the greater part of his father's personal fortune and some seven thousand dollars for his maiden Aunt Sally (who was consequently forced to give up her breakfasts with Mr. Longfellow in Craigie House and move into a small cottage) and was in no state of mind to tolerate the emotional imperatives of an erratic younger brother. Loring had been urging marriage upon his friend, and the quarrel probably grew out of nothing more than Charles's natural reaction, under the circumstances, to an awkward assertion by James that such was his intention. Having found it impossible to make a Phi Beta Kappa out of his charge and extremely difficult to turn him into a lawyer, Charles could do no less in the midst of his other difficulties than attempt to keep him single until their parents' return.

The younger brother's emotions were more tumultuous, and he confessed later that he went so far as to put a cocked pistol to his head without having the courage to blow out his brains. There is no reason to doubt his recollection of the gesture, although it may be that his memory substituted courage for intention in the recollection of his reasons for not acting out more completely the plot of *The Sorrows of Young Werther* or of a Jacobean drama. For Lowell seems to have remembered this exciting period of his youth often in later life and considered it as the material for an incident in a novel and for the plot of a narrative poem. One of his notes for a novel which was to be based upon life as he had lived it (as he explained his intention later) was the suggestive fragment: "After first disappointment in Love could not lose appetite could not go crazy." More seriously, in another unpublished fragment designed for a narrative poem to be included in "The Nooning," he seems to have tried to get at the truth of the affair:

Was I in love, or was it love's pretence
The shallow cheat of idleness and sense?
Did she love me, or filled I but the void
Of will unsated, passion unemployed?
I knew not, know not, do not care to know,
Enough for me that village life was slow
And that she gave my blood a joyous feel
Of virtue masculine from head to heel.

It is improbable that he plucked such lines out of a void in which his own early experience had no place, and whether or not he was speaking here in his own person or in that of his intended hero, these words are about the best that could be said in retrospect about his violent passion.

But at the time there was no question in his own mind concerning the reality of his emotion. His imaginative citizenship in the world of George Chapman was fervently acquired, and he found his own emotions reflected with satisfying distortions in the completely uninhibited Bussy D'Ambois from whom he found more lines to quote than from any other dramatic hero. Bussy's opening speech was fascinating: his belief that "Fortune, not reason, rules the state of things" in which "Reward goes backwards" and great men are but empty strutters in colossal roles represented a moody cynicism which coincided with Lowell's temper, and so did the consoling thought that although "Man is a torch borne in the wind" he has a private "virtue" which will determine his fate at the last. D'Ambois, the "complete man" who as a law unto himself needed no other law, struck Lowell's imagination; and although the play illustrated Tamyra's observation,

> Our bodies are but thick clouds to our souls,
> Through which they cannot shine when they desire,

Lowell found it a true tragedy in which the hero fell because he solidly resisted the winds of chance that blew through empty men and let them stand. He found another such hero in *Byron's Conspiracy*—a "Great Spirit" (as he indexed it in his commonplace book) who, "on life's rough sea" loved to have "his sails filled with a lusty wind" that drove him fiercely and made him also a law unto himself. Lowell may have discovered Byron in Lamb's *Specimens of English Dramatic Poets,* but the plays by Chapman that were readily available to him roused him, as did the works of few other poets, to go out and discover more. From some source he obtained a copy of the rare *Gentleman Usher* and in it found further allusions to heroic self-reliance and, in particular, at least one passage which linked the self-reliance exemplified by Chapman's heroes with the transcendentalism which was again beginning to attract Lowell after a temporary renunciation of it in Concord.

During the next few years Lowell was to work up Ford, Chapman, and Massinger more thoroughly for critical purposes and to discover, as the material for an essay, the plays of Thomas Middleton. But no other dramatists were going to interest him in the way Ford and Chapman had. They absorbed him and recreated him in their own image, and the violence of Chapman was to prove a secret means of emotional release during another period of frustration and to have a more direct influence upon his own poetry and upon his course of action. As a critic, Lowell was to acquire a greater admiration for Shakespeare than for either of his two contemporaries who had meant so much to him personally; but the quality he was to admire in Shakespeare was his ability to identify himself with the original creations of his own imagination as Lowell had once identified himself with the creations of Chapman's. This was the quality of "sympathetic imagination" which the critic Lowell, combining the teaching of Dugald Stewart and Sir James Mackintosh, was to place first among the powers of a great poet. But the youthful Lowell, who practiced the art of sympathetic identification for his own emotional satisfaction rather than as a means of creation, was not yet ready to stand aside from it and contemplate it critically. He had, by special action of the Harvard faculty, been taught to trust his emotions rather than his rational powers; and this teaching, fertilizing a temperamental bias he had revealed earlier, was already bringing forth its fruit in the form of a sincere self-deception which became characteristic of all his early thought and action.

Lowell did not live entirely in his Chapman mood, and after his outburst at home, having had an unsatisfactory experience in a countinghouse the preceding spring, he settled down to the study of law. He was trying to accept his universe and wrote his friend Charles W. Scates soon after he left home:

I begin to like the law; but I shall let my fate be governed by circumstance and influence. There are those who would have a man *act out himself;* it is very much a dispute about words. For is not this acting out ourselves, a man giving its due weight to every influence? A man should not only regard what is *in* him, but also what is *without* acting on that within.

He had a great deal to say "that would stare at you cold and meaningless from paper"—and he kept his confidences for an atmosphere of cigar smoke. But he apparently renounced his love affair with none of the dramatics that occurred in most of his references to it, for there seems to have been nothing, at any time, sufficiently "lurid" in the relationship between the two young people to embarrass their later acquaintance. A year or so afterward, when Hannah was engaged to someone else, Emelyn Eldredge reported having been "glad to see" Lowell walking with her and her friend Elizabeth Lee one evening and that Hannah "looked laughingly happy." She may never have suspected the morbidness of the seething emotions she roused in the bosom of the young man whose imagination haunted the brazen realms of Jacobean drama while his wit amused her in Waltham, Cambridge, and Boston.

While Lowell was reading the "old dramatists" with such intensity, he was also introducing into his commonplace book notes from a variety of other sources. But his habit of finding his own emotions reflected in books and trying to live up to the reflection was transferred, early in 1840, from the drama to the novel and was preserved almost exclusively by that form of literature. He seems to have been a constant reader of fiction from childhood, when he read Scott and *Robinson Crusoe;* and his comments upon Cooper's *The Pathfinder* when it appeared in 1840, indicate that he had kept up to date with the leading American novelist of his generation. His commonplace book, letters, and contributions to the Harvard undergraduate magazine reveal a variety of interests ranging from well-established classics in fiction to the twenty-five cent paper-backed novels of his own day. His commonplace book shows that he was reading Bulwer's *Rienzi* and Susan Ferrier's *Marriage* in 1836, and a letter of the same year contains an allusion to Dickens's Sam Weller; and among the books he withdrew from the

Harvard library was Sannazzaro's *Arcadia*. Undated quotations in his commonplace book include passages from D'Israeli's *The Young Duke* and *Vivian Gray, Tristram Shandy, Joseph Andrews,* an English translation of *The Hunchback of Notre Dame,* and Rabelais; and his contributions to *Harvardiana* include casual allusions to *Don Quixote,* "one of Richardson's novels," Bulwer's *Paul Clifford, Pelham,* and *Ernest Maltravers,* and another passing reference to *The Pickwick Papers*. His letters indicate that he was also reading *Eugene Aram,* that Chamisso's *Peter Schlemihl* exercised a certain fascination over him, and that he had some acquaintance with Jean Paul Richter.

Much of this reading was idle and time-killing, indicating little more than that Lowell had the habit of consuming fiction regularly whether or not it made any great impression upon him. Often it did not, for a parody in *Harvardiana* shows that he had looked into Carlyle's *Sartor Resartus* in 1837, and its inclusion in his list of books read in 1838 suggests that he had picked it up a second time without being particularly impressed by anything but its superficial peculiarities. He could read and reread one of the most exciting books available to a young man of his background without being stirred until he turned to it again after he had been emotionally prepared to receive and respond to its impression. A young man whose imagination dwelt in the passionate, demanding world of John Ford and George Chapman would not be likely to find himself attracted to an infinite shoeblack who discovered happiness by demanding nothing. He would need first to humble his pride in "virtue masculine from head to heel."

III

Lowell's pride had been humbled to some extent by his quarrel with his brother in September, 1839, and his emotions were brought back to a quieter life on the first day of December when he went home with another classmate, William A. White, and met another younger sister. He was not overcome by the meeting, but he was impressed, and wrote Loring the next day that Maria White "is a very pleasant and pleasing young lady, and knows more poetry than any one I am acquainted with. I mean, she is able to repeat more. She is more familiar, however, with modern poets than with the pure wellsprings of English poesy." He was ready to be pleased by a pleasant young lady who knew a lot of poetry. Maria was possessed by the same mixture of earnestness and lively fancy that characterized Lowell, but she was much quieter in spirit and had a more firm confidence in the power of high-mindedness. Lowell himself was trying, despite the distractions of too many parties and the persistent memories of his disappointment, to cultivate a more high-minded attitude of his own. "I have been reading nothing but novels lately," he wrote Loring on March 26, 1840, "a way of keeping all *thought* out of one's head which I find very good." But one of them had made him think, for he exclaimed over Goethe's *Wilhelm Meister:*

> *that* too I have read or rather from it I have drunken. The more I see of that wonderful man, the less I wonder at Carlyle's great reverence of him. So full of thought and earnestness, and something which seems like music to interpret for us thoughts which were ours indeed, but locked up in some (as it seemed) unknown tongue.

Wilhelm Meister came close to being the candle which Emerson had declared every man needed in order to make legible the scribblings on the wall of the mind, and under its influence Lowell planned to change his life and—during the next winter—indulge in fewer parties. "I will amaze the fools," he promised Loring, "sympathize with the loving and softhearted, and measure swords with the thinking."

Wilhelm Meister was to have a more direct influence upon Lowell's theory of what the poet should be, however, than upon his social behavior. Yet it did serve to reawaken his sympathetic imagination and get him out of the realm of the Jacobean drama. Lowell could discover a great deal of himself reflected in a hero who had known the peace and torment that members of the opposite sex could bring to a young man's soul without destroying his artistic impulses. Wilhelm, of course, had learned from experience what Lowell had learned at secondhand from Carlyle's essay on Burns: that a man of the world with habits of dissipation could not feel the complete devotion to art which was necessary to its perfection. But Lowell, as the account of his poetic theories will show, had taken the lesson to heart, and he was ready to sympathize with another young man who felt the attractions of literature while his family urged upon him a life of practical usefulness. The desire to be a public character of some influence, to indulge a love for poetry and everything connected with it, and to cultivate his mind to the point of esteeming nothing but the good and the beautiful—this was as good an expression of Lowell's current ambition as it was of Wilhelm Meister's during the years of his apprenticeship.

Maria White encouraged such ambitions and gave him an opportunity to "sympathize with"—and receive sympathy from—"the loving and soft-hearted." She *"is* beautiful—so pure and spiritlike" he wrote Loring on May 17 after another visit to Watertown. She was inspiring him to verse by June 3, and a little more than a week later he found himself in a situation that revived his old memories of Hannah and brought them into sharp contrast with his growing new feeling for Maria. As he described it in a letter to Loring on June 13, he had been to Watertown for a party given by Sarah Hale and was spending the night with the Whites. Walking home in the moonlight with Maria on his arm, he reported:

> not only did my body go back, but my spirit also over the footsteps of other years. Were not the nights *then* as lovely and was not she hanging on my arm and did not earth's most glorious eyes look up to me and fill me with sweet hope that on life's road that arm would be within my own and those eyes would look up to me for a strength and a stay? Alas the evil days are many! How often has my soul lifted up its voice and cried with an exceeding bitter cry—Entreat me not to leave thee, nor to return from following after thee, for whither thou goest there would I go! Could she have looked into my soul last night as we walked together she would have [seen] far darker shadows lurid and sulphurous sweeping up over my soul than those that floating over the moon gave such beauty to the night. And then the river that we gazed down into—think you those water-parties are so soon forgotten?

But as they sat on the steps and talked, "the full waves of her tumultuous thought" (which became "full-hearted talk" when he thought it over before publishing the lines as part of his poem "Ianthe") flowed over him, and he was convinced that she was "truly a glorious girl with her spirit eyes." "They tell me I shall be in love with her," he added somewhat unnecessarily. "But there is but one *Love*. I love her because she is a woman, and so was another being I loved."

It was on the day before making this visit to Watertown that Lowell obtained a copy of *Sartor Resartus* for his own library and wrote the date, June 11, 1840, on the title page. He probably began reading it, for the second or third time, soon after his return home, and marking those passages which particularly impressed him by their wit or vividness. It is apparent from his markings that at first he was primarily struck by Carlyle's humor and by his tendency to question the validity of appearances—a tendency which Lowell himself was developing at the time, possibly with the encouragement of Maria who was considered "transcendental" by her friends. At any rate, as his markings became frequent they included such transcendental passages as "Rightly viewed, no meanest object is insignificant; all objects are as windows, through which the philosophic eye looks into infinitude itself" and the sentence which Captain Ahab was to parody in the diagnosis of what Melville called his "monomania": "All visible things are emblems; what thou seest is not there on its own account; strictly taken, it is not there at all; matter exists only spiritually, and to represent some idea, and *body* it forth." But as he reached the second, autobiographical book he began to realize that the autobiography was curiously like his own. He found his own experience reflected in the passages he marked on the happiness of childhood and in one beginning "My active power (*Thatkraft*) was unfavorably hemmed in"—although when Carlyle observed that "obedience is our universal duty and destiny" his young reader wrote an emphatic "No!" in the margin and then, as a second thought in a period of emotional change, crossed the denial out. There were few examples, however, of such doubtful reactions. References to attending church as a sort of "parade duty" and to "the dead letter of religion" aroused Lowell's approval, and the two paragraphs beginning " 'My teachers,' says he, 'were hide-bound pedants' " reflected an experience to which Lowell was willing to lay claim without reservations. By the time he reached the fourth chapter, "Getting Underway," in the second book he had identified himself thoroughly with Carlyle's hero and was marking the book heavily with signs of their common experiences.

Up to this point Lowell was finding in *Sartor Resartus* a reflection of what he liked to consider his own past, but little that affected his immediate situation by encouraging him to that ambiguous combination of identification and emulation that had been aroused earlier by Ford and Chapman. But in the chapter on "Romance," Carlyle began to speak to the problems that beset Lowell's mind as he read. He marked the assertion that "a certain orthodox Anthropomorphism connects my *Me* with all *Thees* in bonds of love; but it is in this approximation of the like and unlike, that such heavenly attraction, as between negative and positive, first burns out into a flame": he had only recently partly expressed and partly suggested the same notion in his letter to Loring, and something of the sort had been in his head as he walked home with Maria in the moonlight and remembered other walks with Hannah. As he sat on the steps and listened to Maria's voice, however, he had experienced happier thoughts, and he found occasion for emphatic double marks when Carlyle wrote: "and the poor claims of *Me* and *Thee,* no longer parted by rigid fences, now flowed softly into one another; and life lay all-harmonious, many-tinted like some fair royal champaign, the sovereign and owner of which were Love only." The flowing together of his and Maria's lives was to become a favorite figure of speech with him and one which always seemed to express a happy contrast to the "flame" of his feeling for Hannah. He also placed double marks in the margin of the chapter on "The Everlasting No" opposite a reference to "the folly of that impossible precept, *Know thyself;* till it be translated into the partially possible one, *Know what thou canst work at*"; and he underlined the related exclamation: "Alas! the fearful unbelief is unbelief in yourself." That he was acquiring wisdom drawn from the bitter experience of a kindred soul he was sure when he found and double-marked the reference to restraint from suicide by "a certain after-shine of Christianity" and "a certain indolence of character" which was, Carlyle added in a sardonic explanation that Lowell underlined, "a remedy I had at any time within reach."

Lowell was also evidently affected by Carlyle's description of the state of "continual, indefinite, pining fear" in which his hero lived until he reached the "Centre of Indifference"—a chapter which struck the young American less forcefully than did that on "The Everlasting Yea" which followed. The marginal markings for the latter were made more from hope than from imaginative identification with the hero, for Lowell could not yet say truthfully that "With other eyes, too, could I now look upon my fellow-man; with an infinite love, an infinite pity." But he could appreciate and be encouraged by the discussion of the value of sorrow and be inspired by the belief that man's happiness came from his greatness; and the last three paragraphs on the Ideal were worth the attention he indicated—especially the doubly impressive peroration: "O thou, that pinest in the imprisonment of the Actual, and criest bitterly to the gods for a kingdom wherein to rule and create, know this of a truth: the thing thou seekest is already with thee, 'here or nowhere,' couldst thou only see!" In none of his other reading had Lowell ever found his past life, his present emotions, and his hopes for the future reflected so convincingly as he found them in *Sartor Resartus.* Of all the goodly states and kingdoms in the realms of gold, it was there that he found himself, perhaps to his own surprise, most completely at home.

A few weeks later, in July, Lowell followed Maria to Nantasket beach and there he looked at her with the eyes of a Diogenes Teufelsdröckh who, with a happier chronology than Carlyle permitted his hero, had passed through his Centre of Indifference and was ready for The Everlasting Yea when he found his Blumine. He spent an entire evening alone with her on the rocks where she sang ballads to him and he thought he heard the songs the sirens sang. Love, "silent as one who treads on new-fallen snow," had crept upon him ere he was aware, and it differed from his old love for Hannah—as he put it a half-dozen times in verses and in letters—as the peaceful rising of the evening star differed from the burst of a rocket or (as Maria suggested) the lurid flash of a meteor. His mind was not entirely at rest afterward, for he had fits of melancholy and kept brooding, as he disclosed in letters to Loring on August 25 and 31, over how different his life would have been had he met Maria three years before. But he had learned his lesson from the inhabitant of the lonely tower of Weisnichtwo and knew the value of sorrow. "I would not give up the bitter knowledge I gained last summer for much—very much," he wrote—and quoted Carlyle's translation of the verses on finding the "Heavenly powers" through sorrow, which Wilhelm Meister had heard the blind harper sing. Lowell began to think of writing his own *Sorrows of Young Werther* (as Longfellow had recently done in *Hyperion,* using his own translation of the same verses as a motto) for serial publication in the *Southern Literary Messenger* or of composing a "psycho-historical" tragedy. He even reported that he had the plot for the latter "nearly filled out," but neither plan came to any result. Instead, he tried to discover the reflection of "the greatest woman I ever saw" in the writings of other authors where he so habitually looked for his own.

He thought he had almost found her in Bettina Brentano after he had succeeded, by August 25, in obtaining Goethe's correspondence with her, from which Maria had once read him some "beautiful extracts." Maria's soul was "nearer" to Bettina's cloud of glory than any he had ever seen, and it made him "mournful" to think that all the love of such a divine child had been given to so cold and hard a person as the German poet appeared to be by contrast. But the literary version of Maria which he seems to have settled upon as the most perfect resemblance was the heroine of that "sweet" novel *Philothea,* by Lydia Child, which Maria had given him to read. She had evidently talked about the book on the June evening when they sat on the steps in Watertown and Lowell was made to see "the calm majestic forms and godlike eyes of early Greece" all around him, for *Philothea* was "A Grecian Romance" of a Platonic, transcendental sort, with a contemporary American application in the contrast it offered between the industrious though corrupt and fickle democracy of Athens and the more wholly depraved slave-supported Sparta. The unresentful disposition of the novel's heroine was such that she had caused even Plato to exclaim over the "most lovely union when the Muses and the Charities inhabit the same temple"; and the strength of her gentleness, the wisdom of her purity, and the power of her loveliness made her the dominating character of the book. She knew through the revelation of a vision that her romance with Paralus would end in death, and immediately after reading the book Lowell had a dream that his romance might also—and told the dream and recommended the book to Loring in almost the same breath. Maria, too, wrote three months later that when she told James she loved him, she almost felt as if she had said "and I will espouse sorrow for thy sake." Her willingness represented the wisdom of experience to her, and it was the "common sense" of "genius" to James; but it also represented the voluntary self-abnegation that caused Philothea to follow her dying father into exile and marry the son of Pericles when he was incurably ill of the plague.

The resemblance between the heroine of Lowell's life and that of Mrs. Child's book was not entirely accidental, for Maria was a favorite among Mrs. Child's younger friends; and after the burning of the Ursuline Convent which Maria attended before 1834, the girl received much of her education from the older woman's "book filled study" in Watertown which was still occupied by Mrs. Child's brother, Convers Francis, who directed his young neighbor's poetic taste and may have taught her to translate German poetry. At any rate, when Lowell sat down that year to describe his feelings toward Maria in a blank verse poem entitled "Love," he described the sort of sentiment that Philothea aroused:

> A love that in its object findeth not
> All grace and beauty, and enough to sate
> Its thirst of blessing, but, in all of good
> Found there, it sees but Heaven-granted types
> Of good and beauty in the soul of man.

Both young people were rather afraid of sexual attraction, and they seem to have agreed that James's earlier experience should be a lesson for them both. Yet on the hazy afternoon of November 4, as they sat on the hill overlooking Watertown, tossing flowers into a pool they called "the Fairy Well" while Maria recited Wordsworth, they became formally engaged and James became "a new man." He described his new self and its superiority to the old one in a letter to Loring on November 24, but his friend, who had followed him through so many ups and downs, reserved judgment until he had a chance to observe the change with his own eyes. He made his inspection on the day after Christmas and reported the next day: "—you have become a new man most thoroughly. You used to frighten me with your wildness—and distress me with a strange ogre-like levity—but yesterday—what I have a thousand times wished for—a certain 'stilling of the waters' as near as I can express it satisfied my most fond wishes. 'Richard's himself again.' "

During the long while that Lowell was finding himself (and eventually Maria) reflected in the books he read, he was showing curiously little interest for a would-be poet in the experiments and technical achievements of other poets. As a schoolboy he imitated, as schoolboys will, but the only English poets among his predecessors to whom he went seriously to school were Burns, Byron, and, apparently, Samuel Daniel. The account of his relationship with them, however, is a part of the story of his initiation into the art of versemaking. His conscious efforts at imitation were only momentary, in any case, and his desire for originality usually enabled him to avoid any lasting similarity between his own style and that of other poets who had once been his models. When Lowell failed to achieve his desire, as he so often did in his early verse, his fault lay not in a willingness to imitate but in the very blindness of his determination to look in his heart and write "naturally" as his heart dictated. For Lowell's habit of seeing his own emotions reflected in somebody else's book made the "heart" he trusted a somewhat protean organ. When he so regularly found consolation for his melancholy in recollections of his boyhood and days of "careless infancy," he was indulging a not unusual human impulse to which he gave an unusual value because it had been magnified in his mind by Campbell and Rogers and Coleridge and because he breathed so easily the air of that particular kingdom of the imagination ruled by William Wordsworth. His own heart leaped up at the recollection, in part, because the heart of an Englishman had leaped up when he saw a rainbow in the sky and had caused him to write of primal sympathies and second births. Yet it was his own heart performing antics which could most naturally be described in the Wordsworthian terms that inspired them. The more naturally and sincerely he wrote, the more he wrote like a man whom he found more annoying than almost any of the other English poets.

That a spontaneous expression of heartfelt emotion might result in nothing more than literary imitation was a fact which Lowell's mind refused to accept or to consider. A recognition of it would strike at the roots of his intellectual being which were in shallow and friable soil but perhaps in as solid ground as his temperament could endure. The Wordsworth who recollected his childhood in octosyllabic or irregular verse—and to a lesser extent Coleridge—became his literary blind spot. As an unfortunate answer to Poe's later charge of plagiarism was to show, Lowell could never place one of Wordsworth's poems by his own and compare them objectively. His sympathetic imagination was too literary to create a world entirely its own without a greater discipline than he was permitted, by temperament and by teaching, to exercise upon it. Yet the world it did create was so real to him personally that he could not realize the extent to which he inhabited it in partnership with other poets.

IV

ALTHOUGH LESS disciplined than his equally well or better known contemporaries, Lowell was not especially remarkable in his possession of an imagination strongly moved by particular combinations of words or by words that seemed to have a peculiar aptitude for expressing ideas or attitudes current in his own time. That property is common enough among poets. Lowell's own verses remind the reader of poems by Elizabeth Barrett, Thomas Hood, George Meredith, and occasionally Robert Browning which were written after his, almost as often as of those written before, and the historian of the American interest in Tennyson has discovered as evident an "influence" upon Lowell of poems he probably had not read at the time as of those he certainly had. It is this sensitiveness to one's literary environment which gives poets of one generation the sort of common coloring that enables the literary historian to speak of "periods" and "ages" despite the extraordinary individual differences existing among the writers thrown together by time. Lowell possessed this sensitiveness to a rare degree. As his moods changed and as he moved from one field of literary subject matter to another he took on the appropriate color. More than any other writer in English he was to become the chameleon of nineteenth-century literature. It was his primary virtue as a critic and perhaps his primary fault as a poet: but his early habit of throwing himself into the books he read and living so much of his life as a citizen of the world of someone else's imagination made it impossible for him even to recognize that he possessed the characteristic. For a young man who was so earnestly to preach and so honestly to practice the gospel of sincerity while expressing such a variety of opinions under so many different circumstances, however, the ability to turn from brown to green without hypocrisy was necessary. Without it, he might have been a better poet, but more probably, as the opportunities of his particular life opened up to him, he would have been no poet at all.

Difficult as it is to estimate the effects of any particular contemporary upon the writings of such a person as Lowell, it is impossible to avoid the question of his relationship to Tennyson, whose poems, like some of those by Wordsworth and Coleridge, aroused his sympathetic imagination and opened up a new world in which he made himself at home. Emerson lent him a copy of the 1833 *Poems* when he was in Concord, but while the mood of his rustication was upon him he seems to have found little to admire in the new poet. At any rate, the only sign of his immediate reaction was the introduction into the notes of his *Class Poem* of a stanza from "O Darling Room" as a specimen of the "floods of verses with *all* the childishness and none of the redeeming points of Wordsworth's earlier style." But he took the book back to Cambridge with him, and it was probably this, rather than the 1830 volume, that Edward Everett Hale remembered as being "passed reverently from hand to hand" and recognized by "everybody who had any sense" as the work of a great poet. For Lowell listed only one volume of Tennyson among the books he read in 1838, and neither his commonplace book nor his correspondence reveals a familiarity with the 1830 *Poems, Chiefly Lyrical* at this time. The *Poems* itself was scarce, and it was probably Emerson's copy again that Lowell had in his hands on May 2, 1839, when he copied a half dozen extracts in his commonplace book, one of which, from "The Lotus Eaters," he quoted in a letter eight days later. He also set out to make a longhand copy of the entire volume of one hundred and sixty-three pages for his sister, and he sent Loring, on August 4, a copy of the verses composed upon finishing it. "Thus hath Toil ended that which Love began," he wrote in an incomplete "sonnet" which represented his task as the emblem of a manly skill in living that could bridge by industry the gulfs of chance and "Go on from loving Will to perfect Deed." After such exercise, he could have no other poet more firmly fixed in his memory.

The actual evidence of Lowell's tendency, on occasions, to write like Tennyson is a part of a story other than that of his visits to the kingdom of another man's imagination. His failure to curb the tendency, however, was a result of that complex mixture of literature and physiology that formed his emotional life during the years that followed his graduation from college. A page in his commonplace book records the progress of his private emotions through his two love affairs by quotations from Beaumont and

Fletcher, John Ford, and Spenser's "Hymn in Honour of Love"; and he was willing enough to parade the first and last varieties of emotion reflected in the three quotations. But the public admission of a Jacobean or Byronic passion, however darkly he might hint of it to a classmate, was a different matter. He found a more respectably poetic passion in the author of "Margaret," "Eleänore," and "The Miller's Daughter"; and in the last poem, especially, he found the same combination of love, melancholy, and recollections of the past that he himself so often indulged in. Beginning with some verses which he sent to Hannah in August, 1839, soon after he had copied out the 1833 *Poems,* Lowell often wrote like Tennyson when he had a lady on his mind. He did so less regularly, however, after he had become engaged to Maria and decided that he had not known her well enough to do her justice in his earlier poems. Then he developed something of the feeling that caused him to write, after her death: "All that was written of Lady Digby, all that Taylor said of the Countess of Carbery and Donne of Elizabeth Drury—belongs as well to her, she was so beautiful and good." But it was probably Spenser's "Hymn," or Daniel's epistle to the Countess of Cumberland, and the lines on the concord of well-tuned minds (which he copied into his commonplace book apparently some time after making the entries from Tennyson) that first caused him to seek for Maria in the Platonic atmosphere of the Renaissance imagination. At any rate, after identifying her there, he seems to have fallen into the Tennysonian style only when writing of fictitious ladies and his own less serious emotions.

"It is not the star but the comet that gathers a tail," Lowell was to write later with reference to the tendency of imitators to copy the flashy rather than the substantial qualities of their models; and Tennyson was a comet rather than a new planet in his literary skies. The evidence of "Passion" that he copied from "Eleänore" into his commonplace book was a showy but reputable substitute for the feelings that really occupied his imagination. When he made himself at home in the world of Tennyson's youthful fancy (for the effect of the 1842 *Poems* upon him was quite different), he was more concerned with the costume and the incidental customs of the country than with its spirit, which, on the whole, was an effete one that perhaps expressed itself best in superficialities. Although Lowell himself was notoriously incapable of successfully carrying a tune, he had an enthusiastic fondness for music, and one of his unfailing delights was to relax while Hannah or Maria (who were both musical) sang to him. It was while in a mood of this sort that he entered most thoroughly into the world of the poet who was so fascinated by the phrase "languid Love" and by the notion of music lying gently on the spirit, and the ladies in the most Tennysonian of his personal poems were almost always engaged in singing. He was also attracted by the feminine music of Tennyson's melodies and, after leaving college, imitated them more deliberately than he did the work of any other poet. When he wrote like Wordsworth, Lowell was usually unconsciously and blindly identifying himself with the other poet; when like Tennyson, he was more nearly, though not entirely, the tail of a comet.

The writers who interested Lowell as versemakers and those who attracted his sympathetic imagination represented by no means all or even the greater part of his youthful reading. They were selected from a large body of reading by a young man whose varied interest included a fondness for literary gossip which gave him at least an introduction to almost every writer of any importance in English and to many in other languages. His commonplace book shows that while reading the older dramatists he was also reading John Payne Collier's *Poetical Decameron,* and he undoubtedly read Lamb's *Specimens of English Dramatic Poets.* He could have made a fairly thorough survey of early English verse through Joseph Haslewood's two volumes of *Ancient Critical Essays upon English Poets and Poësy* from which he made remarkably large numbers of extracts in June, 1839. He also made notes from Horace's *Ars Poetica* which he was studying during his sophomore year in college and from the works of Dr. Johnson in which he seems to have been browsing extensively at about the same time. He quoted from Pope's letters in the seventh volume of his *Works,* from the letters of Thomas Gray, and from those by Charles Lamb which had recently been edited by the author of *Ion.* Among the modern miscellanies, in addition to Southey's *The Doctor* and to Carlyle's which he read as rapidly as the successive volumes appeared, he read William Hazlitt's *The Plain Speaker* and Coleridge's *Table Talk*—although it was apparently "much later" before he bothered to look up the latter's *Biographia Literaria* and *The Friend.* He was also reading in the *Library of Useful Knowledge* and rather extensively in magazines and reviews. From his correspondence with William H. Shackford and Loring, it appears that he took a certain amount of pride in keeping up-to-date in literary matters, and he seems to have followed the successive prose miscellanies of N. P. Willis with more attention than enthusiasm. Among the more curious books from which he made quotations were the *Merrie Conceited Jests of George Peele,* John Bulwer's *Anthropometamorphosis,* Sir Charles Blount's *Philostratus,* John

Gaule's *Select Cases of Conscience,* and the Abbé de Villars's "diverting history of the Rosicrucian Doctrine of Spirits," *Count de Gabalis*—and he probably included Rabelais in the same category.

Lowell's total reading among the older prose writers was almost as extensive as that from the poets and dramatists. His account of having discovered Cotton's translation of Montaigne and Hakluyt's *Voyages* at the time he ran across Dodsley's collection of old plays has already been quoted. His commonplace book shows that he was also reading Sir Thomas More, Thomas Fuller, Isaac Walton, Sir Walter Raleigh, Sir Thomas Browne, and Francis Quarles, and an unidentified Baxter who may have been Richard. His reading in history included Gibbon's *The Decline and Fall of the Roman Empire,* Carlyle's *French Revolution,* Thomas Maurice's *The History of Hindostan,* and, apparently, the eleven-volume edition of John Jortin's works whose "Remarks" on various subjects he quoted regularly. In biography he was reading Cellini's *Autobiography,* Maria Graham's *Memoirs of the Life of Nicholas Poussin,* the life of Kepler in the *Library of Useful Knowledge,* a life of Cardinal Wolsey and one of Sir Dudley North. He quoted Dante in Italian and Petrarch in English, Homer and Aeschylus in Greek, and Horace and Cicero in Latin; and his extracts from Landor's *Imaginary Conversations* all dealt with Italian and classical subjects. He appears to have used Rabelais in Duchat's edition, but the only literature he made any attempt to survey with a peculiar regard for its national origins was German. In addition to the works by Schiller and Goethe that have already been mentioned, he quoted Richter's *Flegeljähre* (in the "Boston translation"), Ludwig Börne's *Fragments and Aphorisms,* Luther's *Colloquies* (in the London, 1652, edition), and Eckermann's *Conversations with Goethe.* He made numerous other notes concerning German authors, but they all seem to have come from Heinrich Heine's *Letters Auxiliary to the History of Modern Polite Literature in Germany* which had been translated from the French and published in Boston in 1836 and which Lowell used as his guide through a realm in which he obviously felt not nearly so much at home as he thought he should be.

The literary allusions in the essays Lowell published in the *Boston Miscellany* soon after he quit keeping his commonplace book show that he remembered more than he ever wrote down and so left no record of his first acquaintance with a number of familiar writers—particularly eighteenth-century poets—whom he apparently neglected. Nor does the record reveal his interest in such fellow-Americans as Longfellow, Whittier, and Emerson which is hinted at in his letters or, in the case of Emerson, rather fully revealed in the history of his own literary career. The miscellaneous mass of stuff which attracted his fancy long enough for him to sit down and copy out bits of it, however, does show that while going through the last two years of college and through the two years of casual legal study which followed, he had not neglected his books. Some he had read with idle curiosity and others with an absorbing passion. He had not only traveled much in the realms of gold but had become a naturalized citizen of the land of the imagination.

Lowell's passionate interest in literature, however, was not the best possible omen of his own success in practicing the art—especially the art of poetry. For, although learning is a surer path to originality than is ignorance, an original poet must learn from others without so losing himself in them that he cannot tell their feelings and words from his own. It was altogether proper, as Lowell (with Coleridge's help) was to realize, for a poet to lose himself in his subject or to absorb his subject into himself. That was the essence of the poetic imagination. But the sympathy that led a man to identify himself primarily with literature rather than with life was the imagination of a subjective critic rather than that of the poet. It was not, as his later writings were to show, a necessary or inherent characteristic of Lowell's mind; but his youthful indulgence of it affected almost all of his early poetry, and he was never to write with the appearance of naturalness and originality until he got over the notion that every poem ought to be a sincere expression of his whole mind and heart.

Chapter III

INITIATION

THE UNMINDFUL behavior of the Harvard faculty which rusticated Lowell to Concord upset most of his classmates as much as it did the young man himself. While some of them were decapitating another post in his memory and damning Bowen all over the yard, his more mature associates tried to do something practical about the matter. For literature was the fashion in those days, and Lowell, as class poet, was expected to make the exercises on July 17 memorable. His admirers attempted to persuade the class to hold its meeting in Boston, from which Lowell was not explicitly prohibited, but James Ivers Trecothic Coolidge (who was as unquestionably the orator as Lowell was the poet) refused to perform off the traditional grounds, and the class as a whole was unwilling to defy the college authorities. The meeting had to be held without him, and although he sent in a little "Supper Song" which was printed as a broadside and distributed on the occasion, the ambitious class poem was not completed until nearly commencement time and consequently turned out to be somewhat different from what it otherwise might have been. The circumstances which caused the poem to be printed rather than read and which induced Lowell to postpone finishing it until after the original date set for its completion probably affected his entire early literary career, for they shook him out of the groove he normally would have followed and set him publicly at odds with his environment.

As a child Lowell did not lisp in numbers, and there is no evidence that the schoolmates who expected so much of his talents discovered them before the middle of his sophomore year in college. At that time, like many another undergraduate, he had a notion that if he had to translate Horace he might as well try his hand at putting him into English verse. "Apropos of poetry," he wrote his older friend, Shackford, on January 6, 1836, "I myself (you need not turn up your nose and grin)—yes, I myself have cultivated the Muses, and have translated one or two odes from Horace." After studying Italian for some three months, he also attempted a bit from one of Metastasio's plays, preserving the result in his commonplace book under the date May 3, 1836. His earliest surviving original verse is neatly copied out in the same volume—a neo-classic "Impromptu" quatrain addressed to a young lady in Boston and dated in September of that year. He seems gradually to have discovered that he had a knack for rhyme and during the Christmas vacation wrote to Loring, somewhat self-consciously, that he was surrounded by the works of various poets and some of his "own compositions." He was still "engaged in several poetical effusions" by the end of January, 1837, when he wrote to his mother that he was dedicating one to her as "the patron and encourager of my youthful muse."

The most ambitious of these effusions was a long poem in Spenserian stanzas from which he sent extracts to Shackford on February 26. As a proper young American, Lowell opened his poem with an appeal to the muse who had long "roam'd Europa's shore" but "Perchance with Liberty" had sought the western world, and the stanzas which have been preserved show that he was going to deal with such purely American subjects as the Hudson River scenery, the white man's cruelty to the Indians, and the red man's revenge. Otherwise, the few stanzas he selected as those most worth showing have little in them that is not a composite reflection of the English imitators of Spenser in whom he had been interested for the past year and, though to a surprisingly small degree except in the use of archaisms, Spenser himself. The description of Sleepy Hollow is somewhat suggestive of the gloomy dell in which Orgoglio captured the Red Crosse Knight but not so much so as of the vale of Indolence in what Lowell was later to call "the most delightful" of Thomson's poems. The stanzas contain a touch of the digressive melancholy of Beattie's *The Minstrel,* which had attracted him by its stanza-form a year before but which he had not yet read with sufficient care to become disappointed in it; and the sentiments of a travel poem which broods on the impermanence of man's work in contrast to the everlasting mountains, upon the historical associations of the stopping places, and upon the "Spirit of Freedom" are those of *Childe Harold.* As much of the rhetorical concern for freedom, however, was derived from Campbell as from Byron, for Lowell's representation of her spirit weeping over

Kosciusko came directly from *The Pleasures of Hope;* and perhaps the original idea of dealing with Indian materials in Spenserian stanzas was conceived in imitation of *Gertrude of Wyoming.*

Lowell also sent some Spenserian verses to Loring on April 10, accompanying them with a short and cynical epigram on marriage. But such efforts represented only an elementary trial of his abilities about which he was extremely self-conscious. "How do you like the rhyme?" he had asked Shackford, adding: "poetry I won't call it." And he had spoken more elaborately than necessary about his failure to "correct" any of the examples he had sent. The little poem on his "careless infancy" with the title "Our Old Horse-Chestnut Tree" which he had sent Loring on April 12 was a more finished performance despite its dependence upon *The Pleasures of Memory* for its substance. But a certain easy fluency is the only thing to be found in any of these early experiments that was at all indicative of Lowell's poetic future.

Nevertheless, his schoolmates were impressed with his talents, and he was at some time elected to Alpha Delta Phi, the *sub rosa* secret society which controlled the undergraduate magazine and attempted to bring into association the future men of letters who were starting their careers at Harvard. He was also made a member of the Hasty Pudding Club in February, 1837, and its secretary for the remainder of the year, with the obligation to continue the club's tradition of keeping the minutes in rhyme. When his "rhyming powers" were "brought into notice" (apparently by his first minutes) he was given the further task, by a vote of twenty to four, of representing the organization publicly with an "anniversary poem" to be delivered at the undergraduate exercises in July. He took his assignment seriously and worked upon it diligently, finding a "pretty good" subject, and one which kept "enlarging" as he progressed, in his intention to satirize "those *fools* that are ambitious of appearing to despise religion." His delivery was a success, for President Quincy told a member of his class that the performances in general were "highly creditable," and this performance seems to have been the source of his classmates' expectation of further successes from him along similar lines. The surviving fragment of the poem which appeared in the undergraduate magazine nearly a year later, however, hardly justifies any particular expectation of wit or satire, for its heroic couplets were imitative of *The Deserted Village* or perhaps of Campbell or Rogers with occasional cadences from Gray's *Elegy* and only rare touches of irony. The couplets of his club minutes are, somewhat naturally, even more flimsy and unfinished. Lowell did not have the sort of mind that could adjust itself easily to what Holmes called the "square-toed measure." He was already showing that his talent was for fluency rather than for craftsmanship, and good satiric couplets required—at least during the cultivation of the style—the sort of craftsmanship that sometimes meant working backwards in order to make cunning preparation for an inspired second line. Lowell did not have the temperament to mix inspiration nad cunning, and in his earliest work revealed something of his lifelong tendency to compose by rushing ahead in spasmodic bursts of energy.

By the time Lowell had finished his Hasty Pudding poem he had been selected as one of the editors of *Harvardiana* for his senior year, and during the summer vacation he worried over his responsibilities and his seeming inability to produce anything for the September number. He finally managed three contributions in verse but in order to do so fell back entirely upon parody and imitation. The first was a burlesque review of a "New Poem of Homer" (supposedly translated and *herausgegeben* by Diog: Teufelsdröckh at Weisnichtwo) in which sample passages parodied the sublime style of Pope's Homer and other eighteenth-century epics and made it ridiculous by introducing undergraduate vulgarisms and applying it, with all its supernatural machinery, to a freshman-sophomore football game. The "Imitation of Burns" was a fragment of the poem on Hannah Jackson he had sent Loring on August 22; and the "Dramatic Sketch" was a composite parody of passages from five or six of Shakespeare's plays, with quotations from some of them and from *Paradise Lost* and *Childe Harold,* all forming a high-sounding account of an imaginary meeting of the board of editors. For the second number, he answered the question "What is it?" with a description of "Love's Young Dream" and wrote a comic "Serenade." For the third, he again attempted both serious and humorous verse. "Saratoga Lake" was one of the many youthful products of the theory, so popular at the time, that the way to make American scenery poetic was to give it the sort of historical and legendary associations that the Old World possessed in such abundance. In it Lowell took an Indian superstition quoted from N. P. Willis's *American Scenery* as his justification for creating a legend of a "pale face and his bride" who violated the silence of the lake and were swallowed by its waters. Whether he intended it as an imitation or not is doubtful, but the subject matter is like that of Bryant's "Monument Mountain," and the melancholy restraint of the blank verse in which it is presented is so reminiscent of the same poem with overtones from "Thanatopsis" that it certainly should be classed as belonging to the school of Bryant. Lowell's brief attachment to the school, however, was not intellectual, for the associationist theories that lay back of the poem were not a part of his own equipment at this time. The humorous poem, telling how care killed a cat, was a "Sonnet in Imitation of Wordsworth" supposedly contributed to Lowell's miscellaneous column of "Skillygoliana" or literary soup; but, like most of the other alleged contributions, it and the accompanying fragment of a sonnet on Niagara probably came from the author himself. Called a satire on modern bathos, it was really a burlesque in sonnet form of Wordsworth's use of the pathetic style in his ballads.

Harvardiana did not appear during December, and during this vacation period Lowell seems to have taken stock of himself and decided to depend less upon other poets for his compositions. Although the "Scenes from an unpublished Drama" in the issue for January, 1838, suggests that he may possibly (for the lines are not certainly his) have been looking into the heroic drama of the Restoration and finding amusement in its improvements on Shakespeare, a little poem of sixteen lines that he "contributed" to his column of "Skillygoliana" shows that he was striking out on his own in an effort to achieve—through the use of numerous feminine rhymes—a lightness of musical effect which had not yet appeared in his verses. In a letter to Loring on the day after Christmas he had referred to Milton as "the great archpriest of the English temple of the muses," and he may have found in Milton's youthful poems the inspiration, though not the model, for his own experiment. He was to try another poem in alternating masculine and feminine rhymes and novel line lengths in "A Dead Letter" for the May number of his magazine, but except for the unusual stanza forms of two of his three translations from Uhland (in April and June) that was the extent of his experimentation as an undergraduate in Cambridge. Most of his other contributions in verse have little significance. The "Pindarick" in Irish dialect for the January "Skillygoliana" shows merely that he had certainly not yet developed the admiration for Gray which he was to cherish later; the "Skillygoliana" for February is in the sort of heroic couplets that were familar to most New Englanders in annual New Year's verses; the April "Fragment of an epistle to a sister in Europe" is like his imitations of Burns of the year before, and "A Cape Cod Ballad" in the same issue is a burlesque of ballad imitators in general. Lowell was breaking away from dependence upon particular English poets, but he was not yet showing any real signs of cultivating an individual style of his own.

THIS WAS THE sort of "poet" from whom some members of the Harvard class of 1838 expected so much that they were willing to risk the anger of the faculty and hold their exercises off the college grounds. He was erudite and apparently more clever than posterity might gather from the record—a fit versifier for a small circle—but in no way remarkable for originality. He had written some four hundred lines or almost half his poem according to his classmates' expectations before the faculty sent him to the country, and it is evident from this preliminary part that he was expecting to achieve an undergraduate brilliance by looking to Byron as his literary model with an occasional glance at Campbell and perhaps Keats. It was also to be a repetition of his success of the year before in satirizing those "fools" who did not adopt the opinions and attitudes agreed upon by the right-thinking people who attended undergraduate public exercises at Harvard.

The objects of his satire were to be the persons who were ambitious of appearing to admire the German philosophers "From heaven-high Fichte up to viewless Kant" (about whom Lowell knew nothing except that the latter was obscure and had a name on which he could easily pun); Thomas Carlyle and transcendentalists in general who were the most noted admirers of the Germans; and those other "canting fanatics," the abolitionists—especially the English workers in the cause who ignored "Erin's mournful cry," the "hybrid race" of women abolitionists who had forsaken the gentleness of their sex, college students who neglected their studies and violated the college laws in order to hold anti-slavery meetings, and Americans in general who exaggerated the woes of the slave while doing nothing about the poor Cherokees who were suffering from the Jacksonian policy of removing Indians to reservations across the Mississippi. His poem opened with a series of light Byronic stanzas, suggestive both of *Don Juan* and of *The Vision of Judgment,* in which he expressed a thoroughly Byronic attitude toward philosophy in an ironic expression of his own desire to soar above "each *common* thing" such as "common metre, words, and common sense"; and it continued in couplets, not quite so suggestive of *English Bards and Scotch Reviewers,* which expressed a similar attitude toward those leaders of "cant" who had no time to learn from the past but, with more enthusiasm than judgment,

rush to bring Millennium by force,
And in the holy warfare growing warm,
Would take the New Jerusalem by storm!

There was a suggestion of Campbell in his Cherokee lament in what was to be the nineteenth section of the finished poem and possibly a recollection of Pope's "Lo, the poor Indian" in his account of the woes of the exiled tribe. But there was much in the first part of the work to show that he had deliberately adopted Byron as his literary mentor and little to indicate that he consciously thought of any other.

When he left for Concord he left the manuscript of his unfinished poem with his sister-in-law Anna for reading and criticism, and when the week's supply of clean shirts he had taken with him ran out, she responded to his first letter home with a detailed commentary on the poem which showed that she had read it with the "great interest" she professed and that although some of the things that the author and his classmates might think best had escaped her, little else did. She was "most pleased" with his introduction, his address to Cant, and his remarks on the abolitionists; but she thought he had gone too far in his attack upon Carlyle, and in a note upon one of the lines she urged a change of attitude:

> Can Carlyle's genius truly be said to be buried in lethargic sleep—are you not more severe on him than your heart faithfully listened to, would counsel—I know that plenty of satire is needed to season such discourses—but if at the same time you could greatly acknowledge his genius would you not feel better satisfied—every one can see his faults and abuse him—cannot you show the public that you appreciate his powers—I believe that now and hereafter Carlyle will be in your judgment a great and wonderful man in spite of his faults—yet in this poem you appear only to be sensible of his blemishes.

She was eager for him to finish it in order that it might be read for him at the class meeting, for her younger brother Patrick had walked out to Elmwood on the evening of July 3 to report that such was one of the schemes his class had in mind. The other plan was to print it, and Charles, who seemed to have less confidence than his wife had in his younger brother, asked her to advise him "strongly against" doing so. He argued, sensibly enough, that James would "gain more reputation by having it read than by putting it in the hands of critics" but spoiled his argument, to a person of his brother's temper, by adding that no one had ever printed at his age without regretting it.

But Lowell was in no mood to take good advice. Anna had also referred to their Aunt Sally's response to Charles Scates's insistence that James had "but one fault in the world": "indolence and the Spense negligence" was her sharp and characteristic diagnosis. Anna did not agree:

> My opinion of the case is that it proceeds more from negligence than indolence and more from a blind confidence in your own powers and your own destiny than either. Those who possess the more showy and striking gifts of nature may be deficient in her most important and noble endowments without discovering their own deficiencies—each moment is to the self-conscious man a mirror of the powers he possesses—but on that mirror the faculties he exerts not, be they ever so comprehensive ever so elevated, appear not.

She also observed that "While we bow zealously before those who possess creative power before all the more active manifestations of the soul," a wise observer might find in the passive state of insight and humility "a higher merit and a closer communion with its Source." Her message was as bitterly received as it was kindly sent. In a long letter to Loring, written from Concord on July 8, Lowell summarized his family's criticism without any effort to distinguish between his Aunt Sally's and his sister Anna's—although he did acknowledge the justice of some of it after he had reworded it in more flattering terms that laid claim to the somewhat transcendental attitude she had urged upon him:

> Everybody almost is calling me "indolent," "blind dependent on my own powers" and "on fate." Damn everybody, since everybody damns me. Everybody seems to see but one side of my character, and that the worst. As for my dependence on my own powers, 'tis all fudge. As for fate, I believe that in every man's breast are the stars of his fortune, which, if he choose, he may rule as easily as does the child the mimic constellations in the orrery he plays with. I acknowledge too that I have been something of a dreamer and have sacrificed perchance too assiduously on that altar to the "unknown God," which the Divinity has builded not with hands in the bosom of every decent man, sometimes blazing out clear, with flame (like Abel's sacrifice) heavenseeking sometimes smothered with greenwood and earthward like that of Cain. Lazy quotha! I haven't dug, 'tis true, but I have done as well, and "since my free soul was mistress of her choice, and could of *books* distinguish her election" I have chosen what reading I pleased and what friends I pleased, sometimes scholars and sometimes not.

Truth, he continued, might be sought but it was rarely found in academic groves; and for his own part he was "almost a mind to turn idealist and believe with Emerson that 'this world is all a fleeting show, for man's delusion given.' "

The remark about turning to Emerson was not entirely a joke. As his paraphrase of his sister's diagnosis of his trouble shows, Lowell was inclined to place his willfulness on higher grounds than his Aunt Sally or even Anna would admit; and although he might not have ascended seriously into the clouds of idealism, he could easily have been brought to worship the unknown god whose altar was in his own bosom. His philosophical training at Harvard had been such that it was only necessary for some one to kindle the light of "Reason" in order to set the altar ablaze, and he had been sufficiently affected by Emerson's words in the past to have become possible tinder to the older man's spark. He was later to express his gratitude for "the mental and moral *nudge* which he received from the writings of his high-minded and brave-spirited countryman"; and if his later recollections of the Phi Beta Kappa address as "our Yankee version of a lecture by Abelard, our Harvard parallel to the last public appearance of Schelling," attributed to it an "inspiration" that was not evident in his reactions at the time, nevertheless he listed Emerson's "works" among the books he had read in 1838, began to keep a journal upon Emerson's recommendation, and read Landor simply because he had heard of the "great store" Emerson set by him. Had he been less inclined when he went to Concord to take out his own bitterness upon his surroundings and had he been free from the pressure of others' opinions, he might have sought Emerson out and found a refuge in his kindness and a consolation in his philosophy. Damned as he felt himself to be by his Cambridge friends and relatives, Lowell would have needed little persuasion to give himself to the Over-Soul if by doing so he could achieve justification.

But no one called him publicly before the altar of the unknown god. On the contrary, his friends, though sympathetic with his situation, were disposed to tease him about his enforced associations. "I hear from the Transcendentalists who harbored with you yesterday, that you are tolerably comfortably settled in your new abode," wrote his classmate Nathan Hale, Jr., on July 5:

> What do you make of the Concord lion—the original of the day—the author of the review of one John Milton—R. Waldo Emerson—the Carlyle of the West? Have you *hived* with him at all? I believe he is a good conversation man when he can get a good listener, such as, I judge, *are not* you—although I never saw you in contact with one of these wholesale talk-venders.

Lowell's reply is not available, but when he wrote Loring on July 12 of his meeting with Thoreau at Emerson's dinner party, he indicated, without making any direct comment on Emerson, a certain awareness that if he appeared to take the "lion" too seriously, his smart young friends would find him as amusing as he professed to find Thoreau. Yet there is no suggestion in his correspondence that he felt any antagonism toward Emerson or anything other than an inclination toward his doctrines until "the original of the day" committed his Divinity School *faux pas* two days before the class exercises for which Lowell's poem had originally been expected.

Lowell, of course, was not present for the address in which Emerson applied his doctrines of self-reliance to religion, but he soon began to get reports of the disturbance it had caused. He apparently sent Hale an inquiry concerning the "talk" and received a reply from Boston on July 24:

> I didn't hear Emerson's lecture and was very glad that I didn't, when I was told what it was. Dr. Palfrey appeared very much hurt about it—It seems there were two divisions; the first asserting that *no* ministers of the present day (he made *no exceptions*) did their duty or did anything; doing away with all the good the poor Divinity teachers hoped they had been doing for three years—the second was an express denial of *all* the divine claims of our Savior—proclaiming we might all be his equals, he only having "acted out," farther than any other *person* (so he insisted on saying, couldn't say *being*) ever had, the inward idea of man—The elect were enraptured—Miss Eliz. Peabody &c—but the moderate I think are a little frightened—As for the Divinities I want to kick every one I see—I think it was actually insulting in them to choose Emerson, knowing what must come, for such an occasion, and doubly so to have it printed when they have heard the work. I think it will ruin him however, he has gone too far.
>
> As you say he is not worth so much talk but as you said you had not heard an opinion on the subject I thought I would give you a bit of my mind....

Other reports that came to him are not extant, but their nature may be guessed from a retrospective letter of September 19 from Loring:

> I learnt in Salem that Jones Very has become insane—and imagines he is another Christ divinely commissioned—Now I can easily conceive of all this; but then that he should be thus blown up by Emerson, as on dit, is too strange—Perhaps between them they have put the standard of perfection found in Christ so low that one if not both think they have reached it—or *think he has reached it*—The latter is preferable—My Salem cousin ... sat down to Emerson's address a devoted admirer of the man, and rose up filled with gall and wormwood—I don't know whether to believe the man or not—and yet it is time that my mind should be settled—One must read both sides—for I would as soon espouse one doctrine as another—if the choice were to be made without examination.

Lowell, by this time, was willing to talk calmly about Emerson's doctrines; but his earlier response to comments on the Divinity School Address was completely intolerant. When William A. White (his classmate and future brother-in-law) asked him to put his name on a subscription paper for three or four copies of the address, Lowell wrote Loring: "I told him that if I saw such a document I would certainly comply with his request, though at the same time I was sorry to write the name of any of my friends where I should consider it writing him down an ass." In a melancholy letter of August 9, he spoke of an inclination to go down to see Emerson as the desire of one "fool" to seek the sympathy of another. Yet he added: "He is a good-natured man, in spite of his doctrines." Plainly he thought that these doctrines, as Emerson had so recently applied them, were intolerable to any right-thinking person. It was in this state of mind that Lowell turned to the commencement poem about which both he and his classmates had become worried. For at the meeting on July 3 which Patrick Jackson had reported at Elmwood, the class had really decided that the anticipated masterpiece should be published, and about half the members had subscribed for more than a hundred and seventy copies. The prospective author, however, had been having trouble. He had not been able to get it ready for the proper occasion, and, in fact, saw no prospect during the early part of July of writing "half a line" so long as he remained in Concord. He had decided by July 25 that he would follow the direction of the class and let the poem be printed, which meant that it would have to be ready by commencement time, yet on August 2 he wrote Loring: "I have not begun to finish my poem yet confound me! but I intend to soon." Such reports on his lack of progress, however, cannot be taken entirely at their face value, for the young man who wrote on August 9 that he was again in doubt about whether to have his poem printed and added "I haven't written a line since I have been in this horrible place," had boasted to the same friend of the "hit" made by his broadside "Supper Song" and had sent him his stanzas "To Mt. Washington on a Second Visit" with a suggestion that they were good enough for publication in the Boston *Courier* or Nathan Hale's "Respectable Daily." But he did begin printing the part he brought with him to Concord before he had completed the entire poem, and his additions were made under such pressure that his friend Scates, who was seeing it through the press, removed one indiscretion from it without having time to ask permission and took upon himself the responsibility of approving some of the proof.

The greater part of the poem which Lowell wrote in Concord was a continuation of the manuscript he had brought with him, and he actually seems to have begun work on it a day or so after his letter to Loring, for he took it up with a further treatment of the Cherokees and the military campaign against them as it was reported in Nathan Hale's "Respectable Daily" for August 2. He paid tribute to Emerson for his public letter of April 23 telling of "Our country's baseness and the Indian's wrong" and tried to "rouse" his own audience in the interest of "right" and "justice"

> ere the bloody vintage yet be trod
> To fill the wine-cup of the wrath of God!

But most of the continuation was a satire on "canting fanatics" he had not got around to attacking in the first part. He was rather bitter about the "ultra-temperance men" who showed that

> The worst intoxication a man can feel
> Is that which drains the burning cup of zeal;

and he ridiculed the "Graham nerves" of those who could not bear the thought of the nightmares that beset the sleep of normal people who knew no better than to eat what they wanted. His own preference was for "that golden age" at Harvard before the popularity of reforms, when students had beer for breakfast and freshmen knew their places, and all were so little bothered by transcendental philosophy that

> They little thought that in their beef or roll,
> They swallowed parts of "Universal *Soul.*"

He wound his poem up in a burst of sentiment, lamenting the death of a classmate who had been drowned at the end of his freshman year and bidding first his friends and then his muse a properly mournful farewell.

Had this been all of the poem, it would have had little significance except for the ironic fact that the boy who wrote it was soon to become the enthusiastic advocate of almost all the "cant" he denounced. But the most important part of the entire work, in its effect upon Lowell's later career, was an interpolated division of three numbered sections dealing with Emerson and modern literature. They were necessarily written before the poem (which was sent to the printers sheet by sheet) was completed and were probably composed while Lowell was receiving the first wave of gossip aroused by the Divinity School Address and protesting that he could not write. His reference to the address was explicit. "Woe for Religion," he began:

> When men just girding for the holy strife,
> Their hands just cleansed to break the bread of life,
> Whose souls, made whole, should never count it loss

With their own blood to witness for the cross,
Invite a man their Christian zeal to crown
By preaching earnestly the gospel—down,
Applaud him when he calls of earthy make
That *One* who spake as never yet man spake,
And tamely hear the anointed Son of God
Made like themselves an animated clod!

Emerson's greatest offense, to the mind of the confused young man whose father's pulpit was being occupied by a Unitarian, was in denying the peculiar divinity of Christ; and his second greatest, perhaps, was in having followers, for with reference to the strangeness and newness of such doctrines Lowell sneered: "But then they're *his,* you know, and must be true." Not having heard the address and not having had the opportunity to read it, he of course misrepresented it—most grossly in a passage which gave the false appearance, by the use of quotation marks, of being a direct echo of Emerson's own words:

For miracles and "such things" 'tis too late,
To trust in them is now quite out of date,
They're all explainable by nature's laws.

Nothing could be more opposite to Emerson's main doctrine than that attributed to him in the first two lines, nothing could have been further from his attitude than the suggestion of contempt in the quoted "such things," and nothing could be more alien to Emerson's customary line of thought than the eighteenth-century rationalism implied in the third line. It was this heedless propensity to give the wrong interpretation to an original misunderstanding that enabled Lowell, like some of Emerson's other critics, to find infidelity in the Divinity School Address and accuse it of presenting "the views of Gibbon and Voltaire."

Lowell placed too much faith in the accounts of the Divinity School Address given by his friends, but his criticism of Emerson was not based entirely on hearsay. He had read and remembered *Nature* well enough to allude to one of its most grotesque figures of speech in the couplet:

But all mankind are not transparent eyes,
They only see things of their usual size;

and *The American Scholar* was fairly clear in his mind as he wrote. There was a sharp play of verbal allusiveness to the Phi Beta Kappa Speech in his ironic introduction to the general subject of modern philosophy:

Hail progress days! Farewell! thou good old age,
When talking nonsense did not make a sage,
Bacon and Locke, your day of empire's o'er,
To dust and book-worms sink for evermore!

And in his discussion of modern poetry which immediately followed the attack on Emerson, Lowell deliberately selected for ridicule the most favorable "sign of the times" that had been held up before the young Harvard scholars the year before. "The literature of the poor, the feelings of the child, the philosophy of the street, the meaning of household life, are the topics of the times," Emerson had said, declaring that they marked "a great stride" forward in literature. By way of reply, his former hearer chose the "nursery" poetry of Wordsworth and others as an object of particular attack, implying that if it were a stride forward it was a regretable one:

Oh let us cherish still
The hallowed sprites of fountain, dell, and hill!
Cling fondly to the lovely dreams of eld,
Nor fling away the faith our fathers held
For all that now for deepest pathos passes,
For fifty Peter Bells and half-starved asses!

Such differences of opinion were considered. Lowell was careful to distinguish between Emerson as a person and his "cant," and he probably thought that he was expressing a carefully considered, commonsense judgment on the man and his doctrines when he concluded his sketch with the patronizing lines:

Alas! that one whose life and gentle ways,
E'en hate could find it in its heart to praise,
Whose intellect is equalled but by few,
Should strive for what he'd weep to find were true!

During a spell of petulance, the future zealot had made his choice. He would not become one of the Emersonian "elect."

In ignorantly making the mistake against which his sister-in-law had warned him—that of writing something to please his classmates which he would later regret—Lowell had turned away from the one American who might have helped him most. The transcendental movement was peculiarly suited to his temperament, and, as the next few years were to show, he could not avoid being affected by it. Yet during this time his relations with Emerson were marked by a self-consciousness and awkwardness that grew out of this attack from Concord. Furthermore, in making the attack he had incidentally made an intellectual commitment from which he was to find it hard to escape. In his final address to the muse, he had defined, in terms of his Concord studies, the "reality" which he had held up as his guide:

> Reality! more fair than any seeming
> E'er blest the fancy of an angel's dreaming,—
> Be thou my muse, in whose blue eye I see
> The heaven of my heart's eternity!

One might sympathize with Lowell's lament for philosophy turned over to "misty rhapsodists" who

> having made a "universal soul,"
> Forget their own in thinking of the whole;

but such sympathy does not obscure the fact that a young man of his general temperament would have been better lost in the currents of universal being than in a reality which frankly mirrored his own emotions.

Lowell had some second thoughts about his poem before it was finally printed in time for distribution on the Commencement Day of August 29. Although he sent the first part to press without doing anything about Anna's criticisms except improving one transition and perhaps revising an occasional line, he went over her letter with care before he finished sending in his copy, and in his notes cited literary precedent for some of the imagery she had queried and added a comment on Carlyle which seems to have been inspired as much by her letter as by his own recent reading of the essay on Burns: "No one admires Mr. Carlyle's genius more than I do; but his style is execrable, though, for a change, entertaining. His tying himself down to such a diction, &c. reminds one of a punishment still practiced in China, chaining a living criminal to a dead body. Of course the ridicule is meant for his imitators—the 'servum pecus,' as Horace calls them." He also qualified his condemnation of the abolitionists by supposing that "there is not a man in New England who is not an abolitionist at heart" (although he still had nothing good to say of the fanatics and the females of the species); and he tried to modify his more recently composed satire by qualifying his condemnation of Wordsworth and emphasizing his praise of Emerson's Cherokee letter. As an over-all apology he added a "Preface" in which he disavowed all responsibility for publication and stressed the fact that much of the poem represented merely a rough draft which circumstances, by cooling his interest in the performance, had prevented him from revising.

His friend and editorial supervisor, Charles Scates, exercised even better judgment in Lowell's behalf, for the author's interest in his performance had evidently been sufficiently hot for him to plan another satiric attack even less justifiable than that upon Emerson. He had heard in Concord that Francis Bowen, who had been responsible for sending him there, was to be made Professor of Moral Philosophy at Harvard, and he had written Loring on August 2: "I am sorry for it—we have too many half-bearded professors there already. As for Bowen I don't believe he'll ever have any more beard, the soil isn't rich enough." Exactly what he expected to do about the matter in his poem is not altogether clear, but he seems to have planned to introduce into his notes a supposedly "suppressed dedication" to his instructor. Scates gave the only indication of its contents when he wrote on August 20 that he would not send the proof of the notes and also explained: "I have taken the liberty to *suppress* the *suppressed* Dedication, because I think you will thank me for it in good time. Your personal feelings ought to find no place there. If Bowen is no gentleman, as I grant you, dignified contempt is the best treatment."

Unfortunately, it seems to have occurred to no one that Lowell might thank him "in good time" for curbing the attack on Emerson. Yet as soon as the author read his printed lines after he had received his degree and the commencement excitement was over, he realized that he had made a mistake. Three days after the exercises, on September 1, he took his pen in hand to make the apologies which were due.

> In my class poem are a few lines about your "address." My friends have expressed surprise that after I had enjoyed your hospitality and spoken so highly of you in private, I should have been so "ungrateful" as ever to have written anything of the kind. Could I have ever dreamed that a man's private character should interfere with his public relations, I had never blotted paper so illy. But I really thought I was doing rightly, for I consider it as virtual a lie to hold one's tongue, as to speak an untruth. I should have written the same of my own brother. Now sir I trouble you with this letter because I think you a man who would think no wise the worse of me for holding up my head and speaking the truth at any sacrifice. That I could wilfully malign a man whose salt I had eaten and whose little child I had danced on my knee—he must be a small man who would believe so small a thing of his fellow.

The letter reveals all the gaucherie of a very young man with a very bad conscience and the desire to make the best of an impossible situation even at the expense of complete honesty. He hoped that Emerson would accept a copy of the poem and "read it *through*" in order to find—although he did not say so—the lines of praise that came near the end and so find reason to "acquit" him "of all uncharitableness." Emerson answered in a charitable and, for his correspondent, a face-saving letter, sending in return for the poem a copy of his Dartmouth College oration which he hoped Lowell would like better and expressing the hope that Lowell would visit and walk with him in Concord. The younger man had made his peace with the older if not with himself.

Peace with himself was less easy to make. Lowell wanted to be a poet, but his first serious effort, written primarily to please his classmates, had led only to a bad conscience and to confusion. He knew that his brother and his sister-in-law questioned the wisdom of his performance. He probably felt like a naughty child when he thought of the charitable Emerson whose bread he had broken. The most admiring of his classmates had edited the poem "for his own good" with the patronizing expectation of thanks "in good time." And the poem itself, he must have realized, was a factitious rather than a genuine expression of his sentiments and talents. Without putting his necessity into words, he knew that he needed a positive ideal—a vision or a philosophy of what poetry should be—before he could go further.

III

LOWELL HAD insisted when he went to Concord that he would write no more for *Harvardiana,* but the July issue, like his own *Class Poem,* was late in appearing and apparently was published for the commencement at the end of August rather than for the undergraduate exercises held six weeks before. By the time it was ready to go to press he was in better spirits, and under the inspiration of the charming Caroline Brooks (who, he confessed, "runs in my head and heart more than she has any right to") he sent Loring on August 17 a poem beginning "A pair of black eyes" which he promised to copy out as a "'A Song" for the periodical. The lines "To Mt. Washington" which he had sent earlier also appeared in *Harvardiana* rather than in the *Courier* or in the *Advertiser;* and although Scates's intention to reprint the "Supper Song" among the notes to the *Class Poem* was not carried out, the young man who did not expect to compose "half a line" in Concord actually graduated in a blaze of literary if not of academic glory. He had managed, at the last moment, not to disappoint his classmates, and he had every reason to be confident of his literary powers. His poetry may have shown little more original talent than many other young men could have matched had they put their minds to it, but he demonstrated by his trial efforts that he possessed a store of energy which could burst the bonds of laziness and negligence and find expression in verse. He had passed one stage in his initiation into the practice of poetry. The next was to be more solemn—a test of his purpose rather than of his valor.

Precisely how he should go about discovering his purpose Lowell did not know. Shortly after the college commencement, while still meditating his treatment of Emerson, he wrote his friend Loring:

> About Emerson's doctrines—I hardly know what to say. As far as his were practical opinions (of man's independence &c) I always have said the same myself. As to religion—I don't know whether we poor little worms . . . ought not to *condescend* to allow that there may be something *above* his reason. We must sometimes receive light like the aurora without knowing where it comes from. And then on the other hand we may be allowed to doubt whether our wise creator would have given us a dispensation, by which to govern our everyday life, any part of which was repugnant to our reason. It is a question which every man must settle for himself; indeed he were mad to let any settle it for him.

He was not prepared to follow the gleam of transcendental intuition, but he was ripe for enthusiasm of some sort. His interest in the poetic drama had turned his thoughts to "writing a sort of dramatic poem on the subject of Cromwell," and he explained his motives in the same letter to Loring:

> It always struck me that there was more true poetry in those old fieryeyed, buff-belted warriors, with their deep, holy enthusiasm for democracy political and religious, with their glorious trust in the arm of the Lord in battle, than in the dashing, ranting Cavaliers who wished to restore their king that they might give vent to their passions and go to sleep again in the laps of their mistresses deaf to the cries of the poor and the oppressed.

He was turning away from Byronism and reacting against his own opposition to reformers in the *Class Poem,* but he did not know how or where to turn.

His method and his direction were both suggested by the essay on Burns which he had read soon after writing the lines on Carlyle in his *Class Poem;* and it was in a mood of self-criticism and good intentions, encouraged by this essay, that he recalled how Henry Taylor had "capitally exposed" the "Satanic School" of Byron and Shelley. He reread *Philip Van Artevelde* for its critical preface and perhaps with the thought that it might serve as a model for his own drama. Of the "popular poets" of the early nineteenth century, in general, Taylor had written:

> These poets were characterized by great sensibility and fervour, by a profusion of imagery, by force and beauty of language, and by a versification peculiarly easy and adroit, and abounding in that sort of melody, which by its very obvious cadences, makes itself most pleasing to an unpracticed ear. They exhibited, therefore, many of the most attractive graces and charms of poetry—its vital warmth not less than its external embellishments; and had not the admiration they excited, tended to produce an indifference to higher, graver, and more various endowments, no one would have said that it was, in any evil sense, excessive. But from this unbounded indulgence in the mere luxuries of poetry, has there not ensued a want of appreciation for its intellectual and immortal part?

Taylor was emphatically of the opinion that most of the poetry of the nineteenth century lacked "subject matter" and that contemporary poetry consisted "of little more than a poetical diction." Lowell evidently agreed, for although his dramatic poem did not materialize, he immediately set about composing verse designed to exhibit the "intellectual and immortal part" of poetry in its subject matter without sacrificing its "most attractive graces and charms."

He was, in fact, hardly capable of dramatic composition, for he was too wrapped up in the emotions of his prolonged love affair and the unhappy necessity of preparing to earn a living. The restless young man felt as Coleridge did when he compared himself with a "Solitary Date Tree," blossoming but unmated and unfruitful. He quoted Coleridge's "lament" at least twice in his letters of this time, and the only poem he "shaped" during his first six weeks after leaving college was a sonnet, "Oh! do not weep that thy estate is lowly," in which he, like Coleridge, counted the blessings that might console a person who could not have what he wanted. It was completely opposed to anything that might be called Byronism, and it contained a certain amount of vicarious personal consolation in its praise of charity that endureth much and of love that does not seek yet always finds. He had other pieces on his "mental anvil," but he was not to finish any of them for nearly three months, and the only one on which he worked very steadily was an ambitious "ballad" which he did not complete at all. The single specimen that he gave of it in a letter to Loring on November 15 was in the form of two stanzas that sound as though they might have been part of an Ancient Mariner's account of Wordsworth's Martha Ray; and the "Song" which he copied from it and included in another letter of January

7 indicates that Lowell had deliberately turned back to the simplicity of *Lyrical Ballads* in an effort to avoid an "unbounded indulgence in the mere luxuries of poetry."

The letter which contained the "Song" from the ballad also included a reference to a fragmentary essay on poetry Lowell had recently read at an Alpha Delta Phi meeting, and Loring's response to it indicates that his friend had by this time developed a formal if incomplete "theory of poetry" for his own guidance. The fragment, in its original form, appears to be lost; and the surviving revision of it which Edward Everett Hale remembered as having been incorporated in Lowell's essays on the old dramatists, so far as it can be identified with any plausibility, deals entirely with the ideal poet rather than with the art of verse-making. Yet Lowell's earliest notions concerning the art—or, perhaps more properly, the artlessness—of making original verses was so closely connected with his notion of the poet that the two cannot be separated. He had learned from Carlyle's essay on Burns that a true poet should be characterized by a breadth of love, depth of sincerity, and a life as elevated as his genius; and his earliest attitude toward the art of poetry seems to have been, in the words of one of his songs written a few months later, that what his spirit spoke to him he would as simply tell.

But the fact is that neither the speech of his spirit nor the method of his own telling was entirely simple. To say that the true poet possessed "love" is one thing; to define the word is another. When Carlyle exclaimed over the "warm, all-comprehending, fellow-feeling" of Robert Burns, Lowell himself recognized in the exclamation, as we have seen, a tribute to Mackintosh's "sympathy" which was somehow related or parallel to what he had learned from Stewart to call the "imagination." In his own reading, he had already begun to exercise it as what he was later to call the "sympathetic imagination" which enabled him to have a comprehending, fellow-feeling for other authors or their creations. In his early and over-ambitious theorizing, however, he refused to limit the "love" which a poet had to possess in order to avoid being "a physical and metaphysical impossibility" to anything so unpretentious as the imagination. He identified it, further, with the most firmly rooted of his religious beliefs, for had not Carlyle said that "Poetry, as Burns could have followed it, is but another form of Wisdom, of Religion; is itself Wisdom and Religion"? Growing up in a household whose head always avoided sectarianism and insisted that "Christian" was label enough for his church, Lowell had been trained from childhood in the Christian doctrine of brotherly love. His home was the sort, if circumstantial evidence can be trusted at all, in which a child would normally have been brought up to believe that the first and great commandment was not one of the Ten but to love God with all his heart, soul, and mind, and that the second was to love his neighbor as himself. He would have been thoroughly and earnestly familiar with St. Paul's assurance that the "more excellent" way of life—and, incidentally, the way to prophecy—was the way of love or charity; and he would have been equally familiar with the Olivet discourse in which the Lord was represented as rewarding charity with the words: "Inasmuch as ye have done it unto one of the least of these my brethren, ye have done it unto me." Nor were such doctrines mere intellectual conceptions to the young man whose earliest published sonnet expressed a "yearning of the soul for brotherhood" and who confided to a friend: "I go sometimes with my heart so full of yearning toward my fellows that the indifferent look with which even entire strangers pass me brings tears to my eyes."

The ambiguity of the word "love" was such that Lowell found it relatively easy in theory to unite his yearnings toward a particular object with those toward all humanity and to identify his feelings with the more intellectualized doctrines of Pauline charity. Yet in practice even he was sometimes confused. The loss of personal feelings in the spirit of universal love was not, as he implied in a poem with that title, "Something Natural." Writing to Hannah Jackson in 1839, he told how his "heart yearned" to her "instantly" and expressed his dilemma in his concluding stanza:

> We should love beauty even as flowers—
> For all, 'tis said, they bud and blow,
> They are the world's as well as ours—
> But thou—alas! God made thee grow
> So fair, I cannot love thee so!

Yet he struggled manfully with his natural inclinations. In "Love's Altar," written in June of that year, he told of the sacrificial flames that would not rise to *one* alone. But after love had been broadened by knowledge, he boasted:

> The love, that in those early days
> Girt round my spirit like a wall,
> Hath faded like a morning haze,
> And flames, unpent by self's mean thrall,
> Rise clearly to the perfect *all*.

In another mood and in a private poem sent to Hannah on August 9, however, he was recalling his early days as those in which the impulses of his heart went upward "Like Abel's offering to the mercy seat." He could not solve his problem of definition; but in December he dedicated a poem called "Bellerophon" to his college friend, John Francis Heath, and announced that he was "a Maker and a Poet" and that "Love, wide Love, is the *one* light" whose attraction made him soar.

The reconciliation of his particular emotions with his general humanitarianism seems to have been necessary to Lowell's theory of poetry, for he appears to have been determined to avoid the "error of Burns" which Carlyle had mourned over. Burns's "error" had been "the want of unity in his purpose, of consistency in his aims; the hapless attempt to mingle in friendly union the common spirit of the world with the spirit of poetry, which is of a far different and wholly unreconcilable nature." To avoid it, Lowell followed Carlyle's advice to adopt "a true, religious principle of morals; and a single, not a double aim in" his "activity." In the passage from the essay which referred to poetry as religion Carlyle had been explicit in his insistence that the "single aim" should be to follow the "spirit of poetry" rather than the "common spirit of the world":

> He loved Poetry warmly, and in his heart; could he but have loved it purely, and with his whole undivided heart, it had been well. For Poetry, as Burns could have followed it, is but another form of Wisdom, of Religion; is itself Wisdom and Religion. But this also was denied him. His poetry is a stray vagrant gleam which will not be extinguished within him, yet rises not to be the true light of his path, but is often a wildfire that misleads him. It was not necessary for Burns to be rich, to be, or to seem 'independent'; but it *was* necessary for him to be at one with his own heart; to place what was highest in his nature highest also in his life; 'to seek within himself for that consistence and sequence, which external events would ever refuse him.' He was born a poet; poetry was the celestial element of his being, and should have been the soul of his own endeavours.

As Milton had said, "He who would write heroic poems must make his whole life a heroic poem"; and Carlyle felt that the words were never truer than in the present age: "If he cannot first so make his life, then let him hasten from this arena; for neither its lofty glories, nor its fearful perils, are fit for him."

In his growing desire to make a man of himself, Lowell brooded over such words. It was at this time that he thought of altering his name to "Perceval" (or to "R. Graves L.") and adopted "Hugh Perceval" as his pen name. By July 22 he was writing:

> I live now artistically. Everything comes to me artistically. This line which I found quoted in old Sam Daniel's Apologie for rime, seems to me to contain all

the rules of poetic art, "Carmen amat quisquis carmine digna gerit." Milton seems to have borrowed from this his noble thought that the life [of] a poet should be an heroic poem.

Loring, having found the same sentiment in a dissertation on Ossian, encouraged him: "I doubt not the longer you live... you will feel that whoever loves to tune the lyre must live things worthy to be sung"; and Lowell on the same day, July 26, was announcing that the *"real"* and *"poetical* men" had become synonymous terms since he had begun to write about only his "real feelings." But there was little opportunity for a youth of twenty to be heroic in Cambridge in 1839. He could only be "manful." Heroism might be possible at some time in the future, but at the moment he could do no more than versify his good intentions in what Loring called a "noble stanza":

The present is becoming past;
Live then each moment manfully
If you would wish your deeds to last,
For none can tell what destiny
Fills the next moment of To Be.

The manfulness that he was discovering at the time in the swaggering heroes of George Chapman was not entirely inconsistent with the semi-transcendental humanitarianism involved in his decision to make "love" the inspiration of his verse, for he copied into his commonplace book a Platonic explanation of the doctrine of universal sympathy from *The Gentleman Usher:*

the eternal acts of our pure soules
Knit us with God, the Soule of all the world.

But he was less interested in explanations than in the fact itself. "I am now content to understand a mystery without a rigid definition in an Easy and Platonic description," he quoted from Sir Thomas Browne in December, 1839, and he also copied out another sentence from the *Religio Medici:* "I love to lose myself in a mystery, to pursue my reason to an 'O altitudo!' " If he elevated himself above the "common spirit of the world" and refused to compromise with it, he believed, he would become a "true poet" and eventually be recognized as such; and to support that conviction he transcribed another passage from *Bussy D'Ambois:*

There is a deep nick in Time's restless wheel
For each man's good, when which nick comes it strikes.

As a result of this confidence in his own destiny—to which he held much more consciously in the middle of 1839 than he had at the time Anna Lowell attributed his rustication to that mistake—Lowell's verses were filled with arguments against ambition. In one of his "Thoughts" for June 4 he wrote:

> Strive not for fame, but wait beneath the tree,
> And goodly fruitage will drop down to thee.
> Who shakes the bough to get in on the hour,
> Gets unripe fruit that turns his stomach sour.

He had been "Choked by ambition's siroc blast," he told Hannah Jackson in August; and although he changed "ambition" to "convention" when he used that line in a published poem, "The Departed," he printed intact the sonnet which referred to the noble life and continued in the strain of his other verses:

> If we live thus, of vigor all compact,
> Doing our duty to our fellow-men,
> Than our poor selves, with earnest hand or pen
> We shall erect our names a dwelling-place
> Which not all ages shall cast down agen.

Such, he concluded, was the secret of the old poets who were still guiding posterity heavenward.

His distrust of verses written in ambition was in keeping with the contempt for fashionable modern poets which he had expressed in a long letter to Loring on June 28, 1839, and with his enthusiasm for the "fat little" volume of classical poets he had recently discovered. It was also in keeping with the "capital" criticism of contemporary poetry by Henry Taylor and with the condemnation in Carlyle's essay of "tawdry, hollow, wine-bred madrigals" and other music "from the throat outwards, or at best from some region far enough short of the *Soul*." And it was all part and parcel of Carlyle's doctrine of sincerity: "Be true, if you would be believed. Let a man but speak forth with genuine earnestness the thought, the emotion, the actual condition of his own heart; and other men, so strangely are we all knit together by the tie of sympathy, must and will give heed to him." Here again the essay on Burns had picked up an attitude which Lowell had been trained to accept as virtuous and made it a means to literary greatness.

The young man's attribution to the "old poets" of the virtue which he did not find in the moderns probably was the result of his enthusiasm for Joseph Haslewood's edition of *Ancient Critical Essays Upon English Poets and Poësy* which he had discovered in the spring of 1839 and from which he was making numerous extracts in June. In it Lowell had been struck by George Puttenham's attempt, in two chapters of *The Arte of English Poesie,* to dignify the profession of verse-making by showing how poets had been the first priests, prophets, legislators, politicians, philosophers, astronomers, historiographers, orators, and musicians of the world; and he probably found some personal satisfaction in another chapter explaining how poets, through no fault of their own, had fallen from their earlier high reputation into the contempt which still existed to such an extent that a young American had to study law instead of letters. Puttenham also had introduced into English the term "Maker" for the poet, according to Sir John Harrington, from whom Lowell copied the observation into his commonplace book; and Lowell adopted it in its "high and supernatural" sense, also noting that Harrington had himself called poetry "the verie first nurse and ancient grandmother of all learning." But it was in Samuel Daniel, who was more inclined to take the dignity and the importance of the art for granted, that Lowell found the attitude which appealed to him most strongly at the time: "There is but one learning, which *omnes gentes habent scriptum in cordibus suis,* one and the self-same spirit that worketh in all. We have but one body of Iustice, one body of Wisdome throughout the whole world, which is but apparalled according to the fashion of every nation." It was Daniel whom he quoted in the letter to Loring in support of the heroic life which, as an attribute of the poet, Carlyle had approved in Milton. And it was Daniel who in another passage—which Lowell copied into his commonplace book a few weeks before he began to express the same opinion in his own verse—specifically warned that "the greatest hinderer to our proceeding, and the reformation of our errours, is this Selfe-love, whereunto we Versifiers are ever noted to be especially subject."

Such meditations as these were preliminary to Lowell's vision of the ideal "Maker." He was reasoning himself out of the self-love—the desire to show off—which had led him astray in his *Class Poem.* Whether he could transform these negations into a more positive ideal, which he could follow to some advantage, was another question.

IV

CERTAINLY THE negative influence of Lowell's readings and meditations on the subject of poetry was most evident at the time. In his vague and humorless efforts to be high-minded, he ignored the naturally acute perceptions of his senses and curbed the impulses of his active wit. Furthermore, his notions induced him to disregard the discipline of poetic form before he had even begun to master it. His correspondence with Loring, early in 1839, indicates the practical effect of his aspiration. On January 7 he sent his friend a collection of verses, including one poem "written down straight as it came from my heart" and another entitled "From the 'Freedom of the Heart.'" Two weeks later he sent a couple of epigrams on "Youth" and "Age" which were both addressed to the "Heart" and another addressed "To a Spring of Moss in Winter"—and Loring, commenting on January 30 upon the "heartfelt" quality of some lines in the last poem, remarked significantly: "You seem to practice your Theory of Poetry."

So far as Lowell's "Theory" dealt with the actual art or craft of verse-making at all, it seems to have gone no further than to maintain that conformity to metrical laws should not interfere with the freedom of the heart to overflow in spontaneous expression. He wrote to Loring on May 9 of his brother Robert's comments upon the irregular meter of one of his poems, describing them as being made "unphilosophically and without much perception of the *true* rules of poetry." The one rule which appears to have satisfied him followed: "In my opinion no verse ought to be longer than the writer can sensibly make it." To its "senseless" violation, he attributed the "abundance of useless epithets" borne like Robinson Crusoe's "cats" upon the shoulders of English Poesy, who had to go "cramming her fingers into her ears to shut out their prolonged caterwaul." The rule was a cardinal one to him for some time, and in early June of the following year he was still insisting upon it in a letter urging Loring to put a dream he had recorded in his journal into irregular verse, because, he added, "In my judgment all lyric poetry should be so written."

It is possible that Lowell may have found some authority for his theory in a too literal interpretation of Wordsworth's definition of poetry as a "spontaneous overflow of powerful feeling"; but there is no real evidence that he had been at all impressed at this time by the Preface to *Lyrical Ballads,* and he certainly had given no thought to its words concerning the occasion of the overflow. Nor did his theory grow out of any belief in poetic inspiration. As a youth of sixteen or seventeen he had played with that notion, but he renounced it at least twice after graduating from college, and in a letter of August 4, 1839, made a distinction between "*inspiration* or *perception* of *real* truth, and *enthusiasm* or *longing after ideal truth.*"

Poetry was the product of enthusiasm, and his own theory of its practice was nothing more than a belief that the enthusiasm should be sincere and that sincerity was incompatible with syllable-counting. It was a beginner's naïve notion that there was an inevitable conflict between form and subject matter in which sincerity required that form should give way.

The license of his easy-going "theory of poesy" allowed Lowell to fill his letters to Loring, during the first half of 1839, with verses. In addition to his address to the sprig of moss and the several poems formally appealing to the heart, he wrote allegorically on "The Death of the Old Year," laid bare his heart in "Spring," declared his allegiance to nature in "The Poet," became humorous over his "breeks" and over the effect of an attack of erysipelas upon his nose, became melancholy over "Time," translated one of Allston's pictures into a sonnet on "Miriam," put one of the Psalms into verse, and versified a miscellaneous collection of "Thoughts" on various subjects. "I don't know how it is," he wrote on April 29, "but I sometimes actually *need* to write somewhat in verse." He wrote as the spirit moved him, and the spirit moved him so often that he had no time to make copies of all he wrote. On July 16 he sent Loring a new poem entitled "Isabel" and an itemized list of others that his friend had not seen: "Threnodia on an Infant," 123 lines (which had appeared in print); "Astrology," a sonnet; "Moonlight," 84 lines; "Love's Death," 48 lines; "The Longing," 22 lines; "Old Age," 136 lines; and "The Maniac," 110 lines, plus "many scraps." He had "several others" in his head but he had "resolutely determined that all those likely to be at all good" should be finished before he began more. Most of these were eventually lost, and although some may have been deliberately destroyed, others were simply mislaid—in a few cases, to the author's distress, by editors to whom the only copies were sent. Nathan Hale's *Daily Advertiser* lost the sonnet "Miriam" and the *Knickerbocker* apparently either lost or mutilated another poem of which he had "no full copy."

Although Lowell's theory enabled him to be productive to the point of wastefulness, its effect upon the quality of his verse was unfortunate. The young man who so often discovered his own emotions reflected in other poets expressed them too often in spontaneous echoes of the language in which they had been stated before. Even the "heartfelt" lines which Loring praised from "To a Sprig of Moss in Winter" were reminiscent of a part of Burns's "Winter Night" which Carlyle had cited as evidence of the Scottish poet's ability to see with the "heart" as well as with the eye. It was only natural, of course, that a beginning poet should find difficulty in putting other writers out of his mind; and when Lowell published the first of his poems to seek and find an audience beyond the purlieus of Harvard (a call for war against England if the Maine boundary dispute could not be settled) in the Boston *Morning Post,* his appeal to "Ye Yankees of the Bay-State" suggested Campbell although the poem as a whole was not an imitation of "Ye mariners of England." Few poets can strike an entirely original note in their first published work. But few poets have ever been more completely misled than Lowell was by his efforts to be original.

"Ye Yankees of the Bay-State" was a ballad in which Lowell was not attempting to practice his theory of poetry. His second publication in a periodical, the "Threnodia on an Infant" which appeared in the *Knickerbocker* for May, 1839, was an ambitious illustration of "natural" expression in irregular verse. It followed his theory that "no verse ought to be longer than the writer can sensibly make it" by mixing five- and three- and occasionally even two-foot lines into its octosyllabic measure, using feminine endings and broken rhymes, and shifting at times from iambic to trochaic rhythm without regard to regularity. Although it was printed in the magazine with the lines displayed like those of an irregular ode, Lowell himself seems to have thought of it not as an ode but as a poem in verse paragraphs which represented his spontaneous expression rather than the calculated adoption of any particular form. There are no signs that the author was consciously trying to imitate Wordsworth's Immortality Ode in structure or in art. Yet it was a poem which touched upon the emotional theme of the Ode—an emotion which Lowell had discovered when he returned with a bad conscience to his lonely home just after his parents and Rebecca had gone abroad in the spring of 1837 and which was regularly aroused in him by periods of unhappiness. He had learned from Wordsworth (and to some extent from Coleridge) rather than from Samuel Rogers to glorify the child as father to the man and the days of careless infancy as the happy period of invulnerability to trouble. And when he philosophically contemplated the eyes of a child

Wherein the fortune of the man
Lay slumbering in prophetic light,

or when he exclaimed over

the infant soul
(How mighty in the weakness
Of its untutored meekness!)

he inevitably slipped into the diction and the cadences of the English poet whose emotions were so inextricably mixed with his own. He could no more avoid it than a child can avoid an equally unconscious imitation of the gestures of a parent. Nor was he capable of recognizing such lines as expressing anything more than his own individual feelings.

Such feelings were strong in him for two years after he graduated from Harvard. The habitual desire to escape from immediate unhappiness into memories of his childhood became almost an obsession with him after he moved back to Elmwood, and it followed him as he changed his residence, during the course of 1839, to Boston and back to Elmwood and then to a room in Cambridge. Missing the stabilizing influence of his parents, uncertain about his career, and discouraged over his prospects, he let his mind turn often to the contrast between his present restless and worried state and the carefree days before he left home for college. The line from Coleridge's "The Blossoming of a Solitary Date Tree" which kept recurring in his mind was that which found consolation in "The buoyant child surviving in the man," and he seems to have let his thoughts dwell on the Ode to Dejection as well; for it was that poem, rather than Wordsworth's Ode, which most strongly marked the lines beginning "Oh for my childhood back agen" which he sent to Hannah Jackson in July with the comment: "Rather the expression of a feeling than of a steady thought but shows the spring of the thoughts that were discussed." Whether the young man decided to follow Wordsworth's advice to find strength in the philosophic mind or whether the discussion led to a suggestion from the young lady that he might occupy himself with other matters, he later reversed himself on the same theme and in August sent her a series of three sonnets beginning "I would not have my childhood back agen" and developing the notion that if a person paid attention to the present, worked earnestly from a full soul, and strove to exalt the race rather than himself, he would neither fear age and death nor grow weary of life. He reiterated the same attitude in the "noble" stanzas he sent Loring during the same month, but he also retained the emotion of the Coleridgean lines and printed some of them later as parts of "The Departed" and "A Feeling."

Lowell found support for his theory of poetry in another poet who had salvaged enough from the shipwreck of his ill-adventured youth to write noble verses. There were many things in Daniel's *Defense of Rhyme,* such as his warning against trying to answer a feminine number with a masculine rhyme, to which Lowell paid no heed. But the old poet's less technical advice appealed to him. He shared Daniel's impatience with "unnecessary intrications" in the profession of poetry and agreed with his attitude toward ancient writers: "We are the children of nature as well as they." Daniel also encouraged him to accept the ear as the supreme arbiter of metrical differences although it might mean that the decision could vary with different individuals: "I must confess," he wrote, for example, "that to mine own ear, those continuall cadences of couplets used in long and continued Poems, are very tyresome, and unpleasing." Yet he would not condemn such writing out of his own "daintiness," although he added his opinion in a statement that Lowell copied out into his commonplace book as a justification of "irregular verse": "Methinks sometimes... No bound to stay us in the line where the violence of the matter will breake through, is rather graceful than otherwise." Daniel confessed his own difficulty in managing to "disuse" his ear enough to write according to his theory, but Lowell would have anticipated no such trouble in adopting the older poet's advice to follow "Nature that is above all art." He was too innocent, however, to realize that an ear used to the irregularities of Wordsworth and Coleridge was not the same as one disused from the sound of such well-filed lines as Daniel's.

So, while Daniel encouraged the young poet to listen to the music that sang in his own head, Lowell did not realize that in listening to the songs of old and happy far-off things he was hearing a music which was not his own. Most of the verses he wrote during the year following his reading *A Defense of Rhyme* were written in accord with the belief he expressed to Loring at the end of that period when he said of all lyric poems: "It takes from their lyric charm to think that the poet *had* to put certain words in certain places." "Music" and "Bellerophon" of December, 1839; "The Serenade," "The Departed," and "Flowers" of the following January; "The Bobolink" of May; and "A Feeling" of June—all are in the irregular verse Lowell had first used for his "Threnodia." Every one of them also contains an expression of the notion that his life had turned to dust and ashes in which a memory of his childhood was the only vital spark, and in most of them the metrical variations are more suggestive of Wordsworth and Coleridge than of the violence of the matter gracefully breaking through the form. The irregularity and something of the mood and manner of this period survived in "Ianthe" (which was partially composed in June, 1840), but as soon as Lowell came to a full realization that he and Maria White were thoroughly and equally in love with each other, he quit longing for childhood and quietly abandoned his theory of irregular poetry. The return of his parents from abroad and his successful completion of his law course may also have had something to do with his new feeling of security, but, whatever the cause, his emotions, his plans, and his meters and rhymes all became less erratic after the late summer of 1840, and the influence of Wordsworth and Coleridge dropped beneath the surface of his literary style and reappeared only rarely thereafter.

Lowell's emotional life was too closely intertwined with literature, however, for him to shake off Wordsworth and Coleridge without replacing them with another poet in whom he could see himself. There may have been a recollection of his earliest reading of Tennyson's "The Lady of Shalott" in two lines from his "Threnodia," but Tennysonian echoes did not begin to appear regularly in his verse until he had copied out the 1833 *Poems* for his sister and had begun to feel the emotions Tennyson expressed. Some of them were associated with Hannah Jackson. One of the poems he sent her in July, 1839, as "a chapter of heart-history," was a sweet and melancholy dream of an impulsive young woman who had passed away. "Isabel" was not retained in the collected editions of Lowell's poems—probably because the marks of its origin were so clear in such lines as:

A sunbeam struggling through thick leaves,
A reaper's song mid yellow sheaves,
Less gladsome were;—my spirit grieves
To think of thee, mild Isabel!

The mood and the music, however, were to be preserved in later poems which were free from any signs of direct indebtedness to Tennyson. For example, when Lowell published "Isabel" in *A Year's Life* he was tactful enough to change the epithet describing her eyes from "mild" (which Tennyson, incidentally, had used for Aphrodite, and Lowell, while copying out Tennyson, applied regularly to Hannah) to Maria's "blue," and it was this same dear but slightly revised dead lady who reappeared a year and a half later in the same metrical dress in the poem "Rosaline."

Lowell was later to remove the Tennysonian class consciousness from "Rosaline," and he was probably aware at the time that many of his imitations of the English poet were entirely artificial. For example, he originally composed a little "Song" beginning "Lift up the curtains of your eyes" on July 23, 1839, under the inspiration of Hannah's singing, and then expanded it into the elaborate poem "Donnazetti" which he sent her on August 9. The new version clarified the "spell" which music cast over the poet by explaining how it bore him back to the joyous days of early childhood; but it also contained too much of Tennyson's affected "Dandyism," as its author noted at the time, and the version he chose to print in *A Year's Life* was the original. Yet two years later, after Maria had begun to sing to him, he used the idea of the reversionary effect of music in another poem, "To Perdita, Singing," and the Tennysonian association remained. The later poem was free from "Dandyism" but contained combinations of trochaic rhythms and feminine iambic lines which gave a new cadence to Lowell's octosyllabic verses—one found in neither Wordsworth nor Coleridge but clearly audible in "The Lady of Shalott." Tennyson was having a more subtle effect upon him than can be explained in terms of literary imitation.

Tennyson remained in Lowell's mind, as a conscious literary influence, for a while after he met Maria White. Some of the melody and a good deal of the visual imagery found in "Ianthe," which was inspired by his evening walk with Maria in early June, 1840, were borrowed or adapted from "The Lady of Shalott" and "Mariana in the South." And the most obviously Tennysonian of all his published poems is "The Sirens," which he wrote at Nantasket in July and always printed with the date and place as a sort of souvenir of his discovery of Maria's love. Although it contains some verbal recollections of "The Ancient Mariner," it makes no attempt to disguise its resemblance to "The Lotus Eaters" and "The Hesperides" and was probably intended to be read not as an imitative but as a companion piece to these poems, with Lowell trying to show that the songs the sirens sang were very much like those sung by the eaters of the lotus and the guardians of the golden apples.

There are suggestions of Tennyson's music and of his early affectations in other of Lowell's early verses, but after the middle of 1840 the young American's willingness to fall into archaic language and sensuous music may be indicative of his interest in Spenser as much as of his liking for the Spenserian qualities of a contemporary. Lowell dedicated *A Year's Life* to Maria in a little poem of Spenserian allusions and included in it a tributary sonnet "On Reading Spenser Again," in which he credited the author of *The Faerie Queene* with feeding his fancy with "sweet visions" and inspiring him to behave like the Red Crosse Knight. He had deliberately allowed "some small savor" of "the old poets," as he was to put it in a sonnet of 1842, to creep into his rhymes; and he probably justified, in his own mind, his use of archaisms by recalling that Spenser had been quaint before him. Coleridge and Keats had both sung of knights and paladins in aged accents and untimely words, Tennyson was beginning to sing with them, and

Lowell joined in—partly because of their example and partly because he shared their fondness for the old poets. His impulses were so inextricably mixed that it is possible only to say that he would not have written like Tennyson for so long had Tennyson not made it seem up-to-date for him to admire Spenser. For it was the Elizabethan rather than the modern poet who suggested to Lowell a working relationship between art and ideals.

This relationship was summed up, somewhat speciously perhaps, in the idea of harmony—the harmony of poetry growing out of a life in tune with the universe. Lowell found the idea developed at some length in the second book of *Wilhelm Meister* when the poet was described as "a teacher, a prophet, a friend of gods and men." In "the old enraptured world," according to Goethe, the poet "found a home in every habitation" and inspired the great and the lowly; and it was the business of the modern poet to live so harmoniously that he could capture some of the ancient dignity of his kind. More recent German literature, Lowell learned from reading Heine's *Letters Auxiliary to the History of Modern Polite Literature in Germany,* had turned against this high and universal ideal in its effort to achieve a narrow nationalism. But Heine warned against the new movement, and Lowell copied into his commonplace book the exiled poet's observation that "Herder regarded the human race as a mighty harp in the hand of a mighty master; every people appeared to him a string of this great harp, tuned to a peculiar measure, and he comprehended the universal harmony of its divine sounds." Such were the sentiments that Carlyle and Henry Taylor, and the Elizabethan critics, had prepared him to accept.

The inexperienced young man was being absurdly literal-minded, of course, when he tried to harmonize his numbers with his emotions; and he could only do so because his poetic rhythms and his emotions were unconsciously but closely related to his reading. Had he been more impressed by the Platonism than by the melancholy of Wordsworth's Intimations Ode, he would not have been able to follow a "theory" of poetry which rationalized so perfectly his reluctance to discipline his feelings or his art.

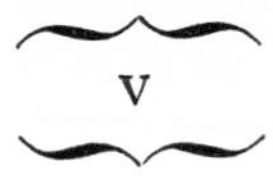

V

LOWELL ACHIEVED a discipline of his emotions, at least, by means of the Platonism he found in the Elizabethans and, later, in Mrs. Child's *Philothea* and in *Sartor Resartus*. But he was not seriously impressed by it until he had fallen in love with and become engaged to the transcendental Miss White and had succeeded, with her encouragement, in making his love for a young woman so nearly Platonic that it made him long for "all" rather than merely for "her." The universal love which had been an intellectual aspiration to him when he wrote "Bellerophon" in December, 1839, was expressed as a genuine emotion a year later when he realized the difference between the feelings aroused in him by two different people. The contrast which he drew so often in his letters was made occasionally in such poems as the sonnet "Much have I mused of Love" that he sent to Loring on January 2, 1841, with the explanation that it had been written "the other day" with reference to his own experience. Other sonnets that he produced soon after his engagement in order to round out the volume he had decided to publish emphasized the universal quality of the emotion he had for Maria, and one of the two from this group which he chose to preserve in his collected poems, "I would not have this perfect love of ours," was explicit in saying:

> That love for one, from which there doth not spring
> Wide love for all, is but a worthless thing,

and in insisting that

> our pure love doth ever elevate
> Into a holy bond of brotherhood
> All earthly things, making them pure and good.

Such an attitude was quite different from the one he had expressed in a little poem entitled "Impartiality" which he had written in June, 1839, and in which, with Hannah on his mind, he had expressed his delight in certain scenes because of the "dear memory" of having gazed upon them with her. It was also different from that found in the sonnet, "Verse cannot say how beautiful thou art," which, though undoubtedly written to Maria, was composed and published before he had either reread *Sartor Resartus* or admitted his love for her and received her ideas on the subject. Gradually, but within two months of the time of his engagement, he discovered in his feelings toward an individual the "universal Love" which he had demanded a short time before, in a poem by that title, of "The Church."

This feeling of "universal Love" pervaded the little volume of verse which he decided, in November, 1840, to publish because "Maria wishes me to do it, and that is enough." It appeared during the latter part of the following January with punctuation "in the latest style" by courtesy of Mr.

Folsom, whose suggestions, the author wrote Loring while his book was going through the press, were "given *through* his nose, but I believe *from* his heart." He called it *A Year's Life* with reference to the time between his introduction to the "gentle Una" to whom it was dedicated and his preparation of the manuscript for the printer, and he took as its motto a line from Schiller's *Wallenstein: Ich habe gelebt und geliebet.* Had he been entirely accurate in these hints concerning its background and contents, he might have confessed to the two years of living reflected in it and might have attached *zweimal* to the second verb of his motto. But it was a worshiper's privilege to take such offerings as he had and place them upon the altar of his choice. Anyway, the poems to Hannah which he selected for inclusion could, with a few changes, be made just as "universal" as those written to Maria.

If the new poems included in the volume were more universal and calmer in their emotional content, they were also more regular in meter. This curious correspondence between Lowell's mind and metrics may be particularly observed in "Irenè," which he had written to celebrate his engagement to Maria in November. The second and to his mind the most accurate of his attempts to describe his future wife (for he wrote Loring that he "did not know her" when he had first tried in "Ianthe"), the poem was so different from his other work that when it was published anonymously in the *Daily Advertiser* it was not recognized as his. He was pleased by the "good opinions" it had gathered, but he was a bit annoyed to realize, as he wrote Loring on November 24, that "Some wise and good people have discovered something in 'the author of Irenè' which they could not see in your good friend J. R. Lowell." The discovery should not have been surprising, for the difference was a clearly audible one. The author's unawareness of it, in fact, is perhaps the only evidence we have that "Irenè" does not mark the beginning of a deliberate effort to smooth his verses with Samuel Daniel's file instead of following his critical advice. The balanced pentameter lines begin and usually come to a conclusive end as equally distant from the caesura as those of Daniel's "The Complaint of Rosamond" and "Musophilus"; and although Lowell did not share the misguided passion for diaeresis which slowed the older poet's lines, the rhymes are no more irregular than those of the latter's address "To the Reader" and the poem is one of the few published in *A Year's Life* which would have pleased the ear of the "well-languaged" author of *A Defense of Rhyme.*

The other poems Lowell wrote during the latter part of 1840 were almost all smoother and more regular in form than those he had composed earlier. In particular, he began to cultivate the sonnet and wrote more than half of the thirty he included in *A Year's Life* shortly before the volume was published. He also experimented with a number of new stanza forms, including the rare *abba* quatrains of his "Fourth of July Ode." He was obviously changing his theory concerning the proper form of lyric verse, for his greater regularity seems to have been less the result of practice and experience than of emotional relaxation and the desire to follow new models. The sonnets, in particular, were not the work of a practiced master of the form. Lowell wrote later that he had tried with unusual care to make his sonnets original, but it is difficult to see that he was making any great effort in that direction at this time: the large majority of them follow the Wordsworthian pattern of the modified Italian octave, and most of the others have the sort of irregularity which is more characteristic of Coleridge and Tennyson than of the experimental extremes to which Keats went in his calculated efforts to attain originality. Sometimes he slipped back into his older practices. Of the two irregular lyrics that he wrote during this period, one ("To E. W. G.," written in September) was introduced by a quotation from the sestet of Wordsworth's "It is a beauteous evening," and the other (a "Serenade" beginning "From the close-shut windows") is rather clearly an imitation of the four-beat measure of Coleridge's "Christabel." But, on the whole, he had settled down both emotionally and metrically before he received his vision.

The vision, however, was not to come until he had gone through a further process of transcendentalization which led him toward Emerson under circumstances more favorable than those which affected his stay in Concord. He had been interested enough in transcendental notions in July, 1839, to write a poem called "The Beggar" in which he had made the poet beg steadfastness of the oak, "unyielding might" of the granite, mournfulness of the pine, contented merriment of the brook, and modesty—as an afterthought—of the violet. The point of view was that of Emerson who, finding "Discipline" in the language of nature, asked: "Who can guess how much firmness the seabeaten rock has taught the fisherman?" How seriously Lowell adopted it at the time he was writing his satiric *Class Poem* is uncertain. But he and Maria had fallen in love with each other practically in Emerson's presence at Nantasket Beach, where they saw a great deal of the man whom Maria, at least, so greatly admired.

Maria probably succeeded in breaking down much of the self-consciousness the author of the *Class Poem* felt toward the author of the Harvard

Divinity School address, and Lowell was both serious and willing to admit the Emersonian quality of his attitude toward nature before November 19, 1841. For when he sent Emerson a peace-making letter containing a second apology for his undergraduate impertinence, he enclosed a sonnet written during the previous April which touched upon the same theme: "When in a book" he found "a pleasant thought" which had been spoken to him by nature, he wrote, he would not feel distressed that he had lost the chance to put it into verse, for the discovery only proved that nature would always speak to those who could understand and in time would speak still "sweeter" truths to him. "Mr. Emerson," Maria had exclaimed as soon as she heard it, "would like that"; and Lowell was sending it on the chance that Mr. Emerson would—which he did to the extent of printing it in *The Dial* for the following January. Another sonnet, "I love those poets of whatever creed," written on April 20, 1841, also dealt with the discovery in books of such high thoughts as nature had put into his own mind and into the minds of the old poets who had expressed them before.

The process of transcendentalization that Lowell went through during the first year or so of his love for Maria White was by no means complete. It drove him toward Emerson—especially in his consideration of the relationship between human beings and external nature—but it did not drive him all the way. Like Emerson, Lowell was more interested in the "presence" that Wordsworth felt dwelling in the light of setting suns and in the mind of man than he was concerned with any theory of the harmonious blending of the affections by their reciprocal action upon each other. Yet he was not willing to follow the Concord philosopher in his identification of the "presence" which the author of "Tintern Abbey" had left something of a mystery. To Emerson, the spirit shining through the universe (though not, of course, dwelling in it) was the Over-Soul; but Lowell, even while writing Emerson that the transcendentalist's Waterville address revealed "what we are groping after," was still not prepared to accept the theological implications of the Concord philosophy. He had expressed his own "philosophy" six weeks earlier, on October 11, 1841, in "The Lesson—To Irenè." The generosity of a flower had taught him that although he could feel the earth, his home was not there; and a star had encouraged him to exclaim hopefully that he was not made "To glimmer on a gross and bodily sense." He was negatively anti-sensuous rather than positively transcendental, misty rather than visionary.

Emerson was probably beyond either Lowell's or Maria's comprehension.

In one of his most revealing sonnets, "My Father, since I love," written on November 29, 1841, James displayed clearly the intellectual limits of his transcendental theorizing. Since he had discovered the meaning of love, he declared, the presence of God cried forth to him from every object of nature, he had himself become identified with God, and therefore "all things fugitive" had drifted from him until he was left alone with the "Eternal One." In his highminded enthusiasm, he was permitting himself the poetic license of pantheism and mysticism, but in his mind he was addressing his poem to an anthropomorphic "Father" and writing "Eternal One" with an orthodox accent on "Eternal" rather than with a Platonic stress on "One." It was his ability to go into a sort of intellectual trance in the middle of so brief a poem as a sonnet that enabled him to make a solemn assertion to the effect that by identifying himself with a divinity that existed in nature he thereby estranged himself from everything physical. By deserting thought for thoughtful-sounding words, he was unconsciously attempting to reconcile Wordsworth's incipient pantheism with Emerson's dualism and both with the divinity of the old-time religion in which he had been reared.

Yet despite the inconsistencies, incoherences, and general obscurity of his religious conceptions, the religious impulse was the basic measure—as Carlyle said it should be—of the harmonious life which he held up as his poet's ideal, while he continued to think about the perfect Maker and his art after he had published his first volume and entered upon his professional career. In a sonnet to "Reformers" probably written in November, 1841, and published in the abolitionist *Liberty Bell* for the following year, he was specific: "If ye have not the one great lesson learned . . . That only full obedience [to that which makes the leaves grow, the tides move, and the stars shine] is free," he asked them,

> how, in Truth's name, have ye earned
> The holy right to fight for Liberty?

Be "free" in that sense, the "Red Crosse Knight" warned the practical men who were trying to save the abolitionist movement from total collapse, and God would give them a sword bright enough for Orion's belt and their "lightest word" would have the power to put down evil. His own mind was not greatly concerned with abolition of slavery but with the higher problem of the poet and how he could be restored to his old position as the friend of—and perhaps intermediary between—God and man.

Lowell was, in fact, even then engaged in summarizing his two years of theorizing about the poet in an "Ode" which he completed in December and published in the *Boston Miscellany* two months later. It had taken its origin from Carlyle's essay on Burns recollected amidst the thoughts of Goethe, Emerson, the authors of the *Ancient Critical Essays on English Poësy,* and Maria White. In it Lowell drew the contrast pointed out by the Elizabethans, by Wilhelm Meister, and by Carlyle and Henry Taylor between the "empty rhymers" of modern times and poets "In the old days of awe and keen-eyed wonder" when, as Puttenham and Sir John Harrington had noted, they received the title "Maker" which might well be preserved among the moderns. The ideal poet for whom Lowell was seeking in his own day was one who had learned wisdom from nature after the fashion he had described in the sonnet Maria expected Mr. Emerson to like, and who had not pampered his soul by wasting his body in the manner Carlyle had attributed to Burns and Byron. Furthermore, he was one who followed "the One Will obediently" instead of making Burns's mistake of dividing his purpose, who looked at the best and not the "worthless clay" of life, and who practiced universal love while heeding "not how the lower gusts are working" as he himself had determined to do after his engagement to Maria.

It was not until some years later, after Lowell had thought more precisely upon the advent of his ideal poet, that he supplemented Carlyle with Mackintosh and specifically made "Love the heart's-blood of his song" and gave full expression to the doctrine of universal brotherhood. While writing the first version of his "Ode" he was still a little confused and seemed somehow to believe that a love capable of discovering "reverence and love" beneath the "foulest faces"—that the sort of poet he was seeking (and later, in Whitman, refused to recognize)—could be found only "Among the toil-worn poor." But he was sure that such a poet, striking his harp "with a toil-embrownèd hand," would make a music like that of the wind and ocean and make mankind as aware of his soul's sublime superiority as he himself had been made, according to his recent sonnet on that subject, by his second love affair. This was the sort of music he wanted in contrast to that of the "scrannel-pipes" of contemporary verse-makers. Nor did he seem to think that it would be impossible to achieve. "Oh, prophesy no more, but *be* the Poet!" he exclaimed to his imaginary fledgling Maker whose "hero-spirit" was supposed to strike the harp "And tell the age what all its signs have meant."

For a man of talent to write "such pieces of rhetoric, setting forth the dignity of poets, and their innate independence of external circumstances, could be no very hard task," as Carlyle said of Goethe after quoting Wilhelm Meister on the poet in the first volume of *Miscellanies* which Lowell read in Concord. "But to adopt these sentiments into his sober practical persuasion . . . heartily and in earnest to meditate all this, was no common proceeding; to bring it into practice, especially in such a life as his has been was among the highest and hardest enterprises which any man whatever could engage in."

Lowell, who had gradually acquired similar high sentiments and had found the rhetoric in which to express them, had no notion of the difficulties required to bring his theory into practice within the limits of his professional field of endeavor. He did not know how greatly his vision was influenced by his vigil over literature rather than by an awareness of the realities of life. He could not have been aware that all the natural tendencies of his mind—his wit and his waywardness, his inbred conservatism and his innate perceptiveness—were opposed to the achievement of his ideal. He probably did not quite know himself what some of his rhetoric meant. There is an indication in the middle section of his "Ode" that boldly "to speak out for the Truth" meant the same to him as to

> Lay on her altar all the gushings tender,
> The hope, the fire, the loving faith of youth!

He had found a purpose, and his initiation into the art of poetry was complete. But all it did for him was to leave him in a sort of fluent haze.

VI

The fluent haziness which characterized Lowell's vision of the ideal poet was not a superficial manifestation of youthful simplicity. It represented a genuine—though not a transcendental—experience which detached him from normal physical reality. For the refined residuum of passion which he praised as pure gold so often in his poems to Maria could not have been achieved without a considerable sublimation of the feeling evident in his earlier attitude toward Hannah Jackson. As it appears in the sonnets of *A Year's Life,* it might be taken as little more than a "savor" of such "old poets" as Spenser and Daniel which he had deliberately allowed to "creep" into his rhymes. But it was really neither a personal pose nor a literary affectation. There was a strange fear of intensely personal feeling on the part of both James and Maria at the time they became engaged. In a poem called "The Two," written a few weeks after that November afternoon and never included in one of the collected volumes, Lowell portrayed a young couple who were frightened by the discovery of their love for each other and determined to keep it as that of a "sister and her brother" even while realizing that henceforth their "life-streams" must join and thus "flow on forever." It may not have been an autobiographical poem of the sort that can be taken as a precise account of personal experience. Yet one or two of his letters, written after his marriage, would have required only a normal amount of the simplification and exaggeration that goes with expression in verse in order to become the attitude expressed in the poem. After one experience with the "lurid" emotions of John Ford, Lowell was willing, in reality as well as on the printed page, to discipline himself in the opposite extreme represented by Thomas Carlyle—although he of course thought of the extreme as an ideal rather than as an abnormality.

There was, in short, a genuine repression of physical feeling in Lowell's verse at the time he was forming his concept of the ideal poet. It is most obvious in the Platonic substance of his poems to Maria, though repression and literary tradition are so inextricably mixed in Platonic poetry that they cannot be separated. It is to be found, more subtly but just as ambiguously reflected, in his rhythmical forms—whether they are a direct reflection of controlled feeling or a reflection of the "old poets" in whom he found his emotions expressed. In considering an imagination so equally compact of literature and life as was Lowell's, it is impossible to distinguish between discreet literary imitation and the spontaneous overflow of feeling into earlier channels of expression. Evidence of the important underlying literary effect of his repression is to be found, most clearly, in his poetic imagery.

For *A Year's Life* reveals one curious thing about Lowell's initiation into the art of verse-making: so far as a reader might judge from this public record of his service, he had devoted only a single sense to the requirements of his novitiate. He had trusted his ear—which was not particularly good—but he had not opened his poetic eyes. Or, if they were opened, they were willing to look upon objects in public only through a haze of moonshine. In most of the poems in *A Year's Life* the "wildly scattered hair" of "midnight clouds" disappeared in the "mellow sky" of a daylight that made snow and flowers both "bright" while ladies with "dreamy" eyes and "moonbeam" hair might either talk with "fluttering" lips or silently weave a "coronal of amaranth" about the "duly-sobered head" of a little child. The poems that dealt with objects of immediate sight in more clearly descriptive terms were usually those in which the visual imagery reflected that of Tennyson—which was itself not remarkable for its clarity of outline. There is little evidence in the book that its author had ever been taught from Dugald Stewart that an active poetic fancy presupposed "an extensive observation of natural objects" or had noted that Carlyle had praised Burns highly for his ability to see with his eyes as well as with his "heart." Yet there is unmistakable evidence, in the poem entitled "Summer Storm" which was written in 1839 although not published until 1847, that Lowell possessed "a mind susceptible of strong impressions" from natural objects which Stewart observed "almost always" characterized "poetical genius." Even in *A Year's Life* such a poem as "The Bobolink" attributes a full consciousness of the language of the sense to the poet in boyhood. The evidences of its existence in maturity appear to have been deliberately avoided, except for the sense of hearing, in the little book dedicated to "The snowy maiden pure and mild" who had so changed the author's life.

The nineteen-year-old girl—who was to be so distressed, two years later, when Frank Heath confessed to a sensuous enjoyment of the moonlight and the music in Berlin—probably should bear a large part of the responsibility for the attitude which dictated the selection and to some extent the composition of the poems that went into the volume. She had been taught to fear "sensuousness" more, perhaps, than the fires of hell. A few months before she met Lowell, she had copied out a poem she liked and sent it to her spiritual mentor, the Reverend Convers Francis, who commented: "There seemed to me too much of the actual, sensuous world in it, for the exquisite idea which it symbolizes; but I know I am wrong, and shall find it more truthful to its ideal significance." It was this sort of attitude that Maria, in turn, was to express in a long letter to Heath; and she had probably passed it on to Lowell much earlier and had encouraged him to find it in the books he read, for in a little poem describing "The Song of the Poet" (which he wrote in 1840 and never published) he insisted that "Earth should not thicken its element." However he might have defined "Earth" in that particular line, he gave it little chance, in any definition, to "thicken" the songs he sang in the small volume of which the Reverend Mr. Francis could hardly have disapproved.

This sort of objection to sensuousness in verse did not forbid the use of visual images in poetry: it was aroused only by the sort of use which so thickened the lines that they arrested the mind's eye and forced the reader to a conscious effort to penetrate through them to the ideal meaning that lay beneath the surface. It was part of the transcendentalism which looked upon physical objects as windows through which one might view infinitude or as emblems of the spirit they bodied forth. Lowell had marked Carlyle's use of both these metaphors in *Sartor Resartus;* and although he probably realized that they both expressed the same thought, he let the former guide his own poetic composition—possibly from the fear of being misunderstood if he dealt too much in emblems. He enjoyed the sensation of looking closely at the world about him, but he was unwilling to portray it in his published verse lest he be suspected of greater enjoyment of material objects than awareness of their spiritual significance. He was determined to make his own poetry conform to what he thought "the song of the poet" should be: free, sweet, mild, bright, modest, and pure. In doing so he also made it pale.

There were some emblems in Lowell's early poetry, of course, and some of them, in the form of ideal ladies clothed in tresses and clouds, later inspired a pictorial-minded artist to illustrations which would have surprised the young poet who undoubtedly did not visualize what he described. For the vagaries of interest will cause one person to look through an image which will arrest the mind of another, or they will cause the same mind to act in contradictory ways. Convers Francis' sister, Lydia Maria Child, for example, was extraordinarily sensitive to images of human suffering, and the faintest picture of unhappiness was never emblematic but always real to her. Yet she asked for an extraordinary emblem of her philosophy, which she apparently expected to penetrate even as she looked upon it in concrete form. Writing to James of the pleasure she had received from his volume of verse, she added:

> I have a request to make of Maria. For some reason or other, my brain has a strange tendency to make *images* of every idea. The faculty is so active, and presents such vivid pictures, that at times it is almost like seeing visions. For instance, I never hear the word transcendentalism without straightway seeming to see a giraffe, feeding from the top of a palm tree, by moonlight, amid the glittering sands of the desert. This has not its birth in my favorite theory of *correspondences;* for I do not know whether there is any affinity between the spiritual idea and the natural image. All I know is that they always present themselves to my mind together. If it *comes* to Maria to do it, I want her to send me this in one of her paper-cut transparences.

Maria White shared much of her older friend's sensitiveness to images of everyday life and probably, despite her humor, something of Mrs. Child's blindness to the most grotesque representation of abstractions. Lowell was cultivating the same ability to see clearly or through a veil, and Maria encouraged him to transform his natural earth into a veil of symbolism. Although he later was to come around to Milton's belief that poetry should be simple, sensuous, and passionate, he was to continue to deal—especially in his anti-slavery writings—in images that were not sensuously interpreted in his own mind, and he was to experience no difficulty at all in placing side by side the realistic portrait of a country parson and the emblematic Birdofredum Sawin.

Some poets, who lack the power of creating spontaneous visual imagery, might have found their release from earthly bondage in a philosophy which placed the ideal above the real—as Shelley possibly did after struggling with "Alastor." But Lowell had the inherent mental temper of such a poet as Keats. When he rose above sensuous experience, he lost completely his artistic moorings. He was inevitably to find them again in the course of time, for the natural disposition of the mind cannot be wholly denied; but for a while he was lost in his haze, and his work was never to be secure from the sort of imagery he was not equipped to handle with genuine sensitivity.

The young squire turned visionary was as unfortunate in his initiation into the art of verse-making as he had been in his introduction to philosophy. But if his natural powers were weakened, his assurance was strengthened. He had a gleam to follow as he entered upon the fields of literary endeavor which his contemporary world spread before him.

Chapter IV

THE FIELD OF ENDEAVOR

I

IF LOWELL published *A Year's Life* only because Maria wished it, he nevertheless used the volume to launch his career as a professional man of letters. The undertaking was an ambitious one, for neither Bryant nor Longfellow, the two most highly paid American poets of the early nineteenth century, had yet been able to support himself by writing verses; and Lowell had no reasonable expectation of doing better. Yet the hope of doing so had been in his mind since before June 28, 1839, when he wrote Loring: "If I could get any bookseller to do it for me, I would publish a volume of poems. Of late a fancy has seized me for so doing. If it met with any commendation I could get paid for contributions for periodicals." He was still dwelling on this hope three and a half weeks later when he wrote of his "blind presentment of becoming independent in some other way" than through the practice of law, although he professed to realize that "to be able to sit down and do something literary" for the rest of his natural life meant a life of celibate poverty. In the meantime, he continued his law studies, going into the office of Charles Greely Loring in Boston after graduating from the Dane Law School and remaining there for the two years before being admitted to the bar in 1842. He also gained experience, as an amateur, in the periodical world with his poems in the Boston *Morning Post* and the *Daily Advertiser* and with one or possibly two contributions to the *Knickerbocker* magazine. The Democratic *Post* soon discovered that the young man from Cambridge did not think according to its fashion—except on the issue of the Maine boundary line—and soon became one of his most persistent critics. The *Advertiser* remained friendly for a longer time, but both it and the *Knickerbocker* were careless of the copy he volunteered, and there is no evidence that the editor of either encouraged his contributions.

The newspapers did not, in any case, offer a satisfactory field of operation for a young man who wanted to become a professional poet. They might print his contributions, but they would neither pay for them nor spread an author's reputation very far abroad. On the other hand, the magazines generally paid for the material which they printed and circulated throughout the country for critical attention. They offered the only practical medium through which an ambitious young man could make a trial venture of his professional talents.

But the American magazine, just before the middle of the nineteenth century, was not a well-established institution. Most of the literary periodicals were short lived, and all of them were speculations—some by ambitious printers or business men who knew little about literature, and others by enthusiastic young writers who were anxious for a medium of expression but were ignorant of business. The more business-like operators followed standard business practices by trying to acquire a monopoly over the talent reflected in their pages: they might pay relatively well, but they usually did so only on condition that their contributors should have no dealing with rival publications. The more enthusiastic amateurs might pay little or nothing, and the substance of their publications was made up of items composed by personal friends or mutual admirers. The result was that the entire magazine world was made up of coteries held together by financial inducements or by a community of literary tastes or intellectual interests. Hopeful new recruits and disappointed former enthusiasts drifted in and out of these groups without greatly disturbing their rivalries, and a man's original work was often judged by his critic's opinions of his associates. It was not a world which offered the best possible training for a young poet, but it was the only one in which Lowell was able to venture.

His first real success was with J. W. White of the *Southern Literary Messenger,* who published a "Song" and two of his sonnets in March, 1840, and printed ten more of his poems in the next four numbers. Lowell was disappointed, however, for he wanted more than generous recognition and complained to Loring that the editor had responded to his first contributions with "Hammydiddle in plenty but no pay." It had been his misfortune to catch the *Messenger* and its editor at about the nadir of their financial careers. White had confessed the preceding November that he was so "confoundedly hard run" and "confoundedly in debt" that he had to reject all contributions that were not gratuitous; and even when influential pressure was put upon him, in June, he would promise only a dollar and a half a Bourgeoise page with the understanding that he should be allowed to take his own time about paying that pittance. That may have been one reason why his columns were so wide open to the unknown "Hugh Perceval" from Cambridge. But the "Hammydiddle" was inspired in part by White's hope that he had caught a Harvard professor who would add dignity and prestige to the *Messenger* at a time when professors were expected to—and did—write better than the ordinary run of journalists. Lowell had been amused to receive a letter with the title hopefully attached to his pen name, and, whether or not he disillusioned his correspondent, the compliments continued while he himself continued to send in verses. Yet he was in financial difficulties of his own, and although he was just beginning to realize the extent of his father's recent losses, he knew that his Aunt Sally had been forced to move from Craigie House and that he ought to have some personal source of income. When White asked him in August to translate a long poem of Victor Hugo's, he made up his mind to reply that "reading and writing come by nature, but to be a translator is the gift of Fortune." " 'Tis a bad habit to get into for a poor man, this writing for nothing," he told Loring on August 18; "Perhaps if I hang off he may offer me somewhat." A week later he was thinking of writing a continued prose narrative for the *Messenger,* if White would pay him. But White could not, and Lowell made a permanent literary withdrawal across the Mason and Dixon line.

In the meantime, he had been attracted by the hundred-dollar prize contest offered by Burton's *Gentleman's Magazine* and in March had copied out one of the longest, and poorest, of his poems as his entry. In June, however, while he was still sending contributions to the *Messenger* in preference of fame to fortune, he was "correcting" the same poem with the notion of sending it to Miss Fuller and the *Dial.* "Callirhöe" needed correction, for the verse was crude and the imagery strange. If the poem ever went to Miss Fuller, it did not go beyond her; and Lowell's next attempt to find his way into the *Dial* was through Emerson, to whom he sent a group of poems in the autumn with the request, apparently, that they should be forwarded to the editor as anonymous contributions. She selected a sonnet, "To a Voice heard in Mount Auburn, July, 1839," reminiscent of Wordsworth's "To a Highland Reaper," for inclusion in the January issue above the signature "M.L.O." The others went, as the unenthusiastic Emerson put it in a whimsical effort at tact, "in the vast editorial Drawer to take their chance for future insertion with other sylphs and gnomes now imprisoned or hereafter to be imprisoned in that limbo." Lowell evidently insisted that his sonnets should be printed together and quickly if at all, but Margaret Fuller was not the sort of editor who would take dictation from a contributor, and only one appeared. The others may have accompanied it in *A Year's Life* instead of disappearing permanently into the editorial drawer, for Lowell's only other verse in the *Dial* for that year was a July sonnet signed "Hugh Peters" which began "Where are the terrors that escort King Death" and could hardly have come under Emerson's description of the "gay verses" considered in December.

"Callirhöe" had a better, if not entirely happy, fate. The first manuscript which had been sent off for Burton's prize contest remained among the miscellaneous mass of material which, upon the sale of the magazine, passed into the hands of George R. Graham and under the eyes of his assistant editor, Charles J. Peterson. It was the kind of verse that Peterson liked, for he had no objection to the metrical irregularity which characterized this in common with so many of Lowell's other early poems, nor did he have the sort of mind easily arrested by visual imagery. Accordingly he was not bothered by the statement that a lady named Callirhöe had a spirit "like a squirrel caught at play" or by the fact that her hair was golden in one line and auburn in another. Furthermore, his acquaintance with English poetry and his habits of reading were so superficial that he would hardly have recognized the sudden emergence of Coleridge's "sacred river" in Lowell's assertion that his heroine's

inner soul flows calm forever;
Dark and calm without a sound,
Like that strange and tractless river
That rolls its waters underground.

The editor of what was to become the most prosperous of American magazines wrote "Hugh Perceval" for permission to use the manuscript and, without waiting for a reply, had it set up and printed as the featured poem of the February number of *Graham's*.

The publication of his longest poem to date without permission and without pay was a death blow to "Hugh Perceval," because even though the incident was explained as a regrettable "misunderstanding" Lowell knew that editors would not take such liberties with the author of *A Year's Life* whose name was fairly well known through favorable reviews in a half dozen or more respectable periodicals. For his book had been a quick success. By February 18 he had learned that he was to be reviewed in the *North American* and the *Christian Examiner* and heard that "the Dial Clique seems sufficiently well pleased" and would probably mention him in the next number. Less than a month later he was pleasantly aware that all his notices so far had been "very favorable" except for one in the Democratic Boston *Post* and was especially delighted by the fact that the *Arcturus* in New York had given him "a *very* pleasant notice" without the stimulus of any acquaintance with him except through the book. There were few reviews outside New England—although *Graham's Magazine,* in the course of time, was to give him an extraordinarily elaborate criticism—but numerous friends and some strangers wrote to him of their pleasure in the volume. Not many copies were sold, it is true, but Lowell had not expected to sell many; and if he followed his original intention of printing only four hundred or less, the sale of three hundred which he reported to Loring on March 15 represented either a satisfactory public response or an optimistic estimate of it. The important point was that he was being talked about in a way that gave a commercial value to his name. He was not yet aware that the highest market value of American magazine poetry represented a small honorarium for the verses and a larger bribe to the author for keeping his name out of rival periodicals, but he knew from experience that verses printed over an unknown name were usually paid for in mere words of praise. It was with a highly commercialized and not unenvious ear that N. P. Willis listened to the talk and described Lowell as "the best-launched poet of his time."

One of the first responses Lowell got from his launching was an invitation, in February, to contribute to an annual which was supposed to be edited *sub rosa* by Longfellow, Felton, Hillard, and "that set" and published in Boston as *The Token and Atlantic Souvenir.* He was flattered by the prospect of appearing in such "good company" as Hawthorne, Emerson, and Longfellow and possibly Bryant and Halleck; and when the publisher, D. H. Williams, made the invitation formal with an offer of five dollars a page, he copied off a four-page poem as one of what he seems to have vainly hoped would be several contributions. In the months following his engagement to Maria, his poetic fancy was playing often with youthful love affairs that ended in death rather than in marriage, and "The Ballad of the Stranger" (which he confessed to Loring was "beautiful") told the story of a girl who had been beset by strange fancies of her dead mother while waiting for her lover and who, when he at last appeared, followed him "right gladly" into the "pleasant land" of death to which he had been taken by the "stranger" while on his way to her side. His success in selling it apparently encouraged him to further efforts along the same line, for he composed another "Ballad," which, during the course of his correspondence with Peterson concerning the "misunderstanding" over "Callirhöe," he offered to *Graham's*. Peterson was so impressed that in August he described it as "highly imaginative," sent the author a draft for ten dollars, and requested regular contributions. The ballad in *Graham's* was not published until October, and the annual, of course, did not appear until December, but with the acceptance of the two poems and with the unusual advance payment from the magazine, Lowell's career as a professional poet began.

It also began under somewhat unfortunate auspices of which Lowell was not aware. For before purchasing the "highly imaginative" ballad and making his request, Peterson had acquired an editorial associate and adviser who coöperated with him in encouraging some of the worst faults in his new contributor. Edgar Allan Poe had a preference, stronger and more positive than Peterson's, for the theatrical over the real in visual imagery, and he showed an equal inability to observe gaucheries with his mind's eyes. The October "Ballad" which Poe described as "a very beautiful little poem" in his article on "Autography" in November, for example, combined some of the most obvious characteristics of Coleridge with those of the Monk Lewis school of ballad makers and several of the worst faults of the early Tennyson. It set the atmosphere with the opening line, "Gloomily the river floweth," and told the story of a frightened lady whose murdered ancestor haunted the family hall while the wind wailed through withered poplar leaves, a waning red moon shone through clouds like dead faces, and an owl screeched and a dog howled. The climactic last stanza was like a bad imitation of Tennyson's original description of the death of Iphigenia:

A gleam across the chamber floor—
  A white thing in the river—
One long, shrill, shivering scream, no more,
  And all is still forever!

Neither editor thought to ask—as he could have asked more legitimately than Lockhart did of Tennyson's heroine—"what more she would have"; nor did either visualize the scene in which the ghost, if he were supposed to exist outside her imagination, jumped around in the most extraordinary manner before frightening the girl to death. Instead, Poe praised Lowell for the "vigor of his *imagination*" and despite the fact that he found "his ear for rhythm" to be "imperfect" gave him "at least the second or third place among the poets of America"—largely, it seems, on the basis of this "Ballad."

For Poe had not read *A Year's Life,* gave no indication that he recalled the contributions of "Hugh Perceval" to the *Messenger,* and expressed the opinion that "Merry England" in the November *Graham's* was "not quite so fine" as the "Ballad." The former poem, indeed, was hardly the sort that the editors of the "Lady's and Gentleman's Magazine" would have accepted from a contributor they were not trying to cultivate. Inspired, perhaps, by the author's and Thomas Carlyle's appreciation of Ebenezer Elliott and by the Lowell family's more recent report on conditions in England, it used an ironic title to express a concern for the "slaves of the forge and loom" and the "factory children thin" in a lyric manner that was soon to be made widely known by the publication of Hood's "Song of a Shirt" and Elizabeth Barrett's "The Cry of the Children." It foreshadowed Lowell's later social consciousness; and, in its reference to the repression of the people in order

> That one weak Guelphic girl may wear
> Her plaything of a crown,

it showed his reckless habit of firing away at random whenever he began to attack an evil. But he was not encouraged to pursue such subjects in *Graham's.* Peterson, apologizing for Poe's criticism of Lowell's "ear for rhythm," wrote that he did not share his coadjutor's "fancy for numbers 'In linked sweetness long drawn out.' " But the poetry he did like was not the sort represented by "Merry England." "Give me," he exclaimed, "a bold, free, imaginative style, in preference to a dulcet, wishy-washy one—give me a cataract shut in by mountains, rather than the gentlest stream that ever stole through a meadow." Yet even Peterson wished that Lowell's poems had a little less ruggedness in them and a little more perfection in their rhymes, and he and Poe seemed to have agreed on the specific poems that they preferred.

Among the new ones sent in, they passed over "To Perdita, Singing" (although Peterson quoted it in a burst of January enthusiasm), published "A Song" beginning "Violet! sweet violet" in January, 1842, and settled upon "Rosaline" for the February number and for their favorite of all Lowell's poems. "Some of its verses," wrote Peterson on January 10, "display a loftiness of imagination which you have never yet surpassed. One shudders in reading 'Rosaline'—that is not all, one may analyze and yet admire it." Poe had evidently both analyzed and admired, for on February

8 Peterson wrote again: "Rosaline *is* a fine poem. Poe, Griswold, all of us say so. In the March number, in a review of Longfellow, Poe, after doing justice to you, says of Rosaline *'that no American poem equals it in the higher elements of song.'* Griswold has taken it for his 'American Poets'—a splendid work soon to be published and in which he assures me he will do you justice." The review duly appeared with the words that Peterson had promised, but Griswold dealt the poet something less than the "justice" Peterson expected in his book, and Lowell was to appear only once in *Graham's* after Griswold took over Poe's job as literary editor. The loss of Poe's supervision over his verses was no misfortune. Poe had praised him as "a young American who, with ideality not richer than that of Longfellow, and with less artistical knowledge, has yet composed far truer poems, merely through the greater propriety of his themes." The theme of "Rosaline" was the theme of the "Ballad": the death of a beautiful woman under gruesome circumstances. It was one which was supposed to excite the phrenological bump of "ideality," according to a psychology to which Peterson and Poe both subscribed; and although Lowell showed no signs of taking seriously this shady compromise between materialism and transcendentalism, it did him no harm to escape from the influence of editors who paid in both cash and public praise for the rhythmical creation of vague creeps.

The editors of *Graham's* were evidently prepared to offer Lowell a steady income of at least ten dollars per issue, and perhaps more if they paid extra for the sonnet on the "old poets" which they published in addition to "Rosaline" in February. For March they used "Fancies about a Rosebud Pressed in an Old Copy of Spenser," and only Lowell's failure to get his contribution in on time prevented him from appearing in the April and May numbers. He appeared in review, however, in April when a five-page notice entitled "Lowell's Poems: A New School of Poetry at Hand" quoted liberally from *A Year's Life* and later magazine verse, showered him with praise, and reached the largest group of readers in America. "The genius of Lowell is surpassed by no contemporary," the anonymous critic told forty thousand subscribers who had never heard of the poet six months before; but he should be saved from his faults: "He can display the taste of Coleridge without his absurdities, he can be as intellectual as Shelley without his mysticism, he can emulate the ideality of Tennyson and Keats without the affectation of the one, or the redundancy of the other. He has high genius, susceptible of improvement, but capable of perversion." The reviewer's specific, pretentious attempts to save his genius from perversion, however, were not of a sort that might make Lowell a more careful poet. He discovered an unfortunate influence of "Spencer" in Lowell's "tendency to push his metaphors to the verge of allegory" and in his "quaintness," although he implied that he looked upon the use of such words as "poisèd" and "inspirèd" as an echo of "the barbarous jargon of Carlyle"; and he attributed Lowell's fondness for compound epithets, especially in his earlier poems, to his reading of "Spencer and others of the quaint old writers." But Lowell knew, as little interested as he was in the dark conceits of *The Faerie Queene,* that Spenser's allegory was not just a carelessly extended metaphor; and he could not have avoided observing that the one little allegory he had adapted from Spenser, the lines on chastity which he wrote for "Callirhöe" and was to transfer to "Ianthe," had been singled out for quotation and particular praise as one of his more exquisite pictures. Furthermore, he had himself recognized the fault of false accentuation nearly three years before and damned it with Carlyle's own term "Dandyism." To find that his critic associated such violations of "the purity of our tongue" with Carlyle's influence must have surprised him as much as to discover that compound epithets were "mongrel expressions" more common among "the quaint old writers" than in the pages of Pope. The most elaborate criticism that Lowell had yet received was, in short, superficial in its treatment of his poetic failings and uninformed to the point of stupidity in its use of English literature for purposes of comparison. Yet it was of such stuff that Peterson had written: "I could not have had an article on you more to my mind if I had written it myself." When Peterson later wrote that Poe, although he did not write the article, expressed himself as being in agreement with it, Lowell must have closed his mind to critical comments as indicating anything more than the current state of a particular market.

He had already learned that what was gristle for one editor might be meat for another; and although he refused, as a matter of principle, to fit his singing to editorial prides and fancies, he was not averse to selecting from his accumulating store of manuscripts the poems most likely to please the men to whom they were sent. The critic in *Graham's* had revealed his intellectual kinship to Peterson and Poe by declaring of Lowell: "In one faculty he is certainly equal to any contemporary, and that faculty is the highest one a poet can possess—we mean *ideality.* The imagination of Lowell is of the loftiest character." And he cited the "Ballad" and "Rosaline" as indisputable evidence of the truth of his assertion. Other such poems went to *Graham's.* "Farewell," which appeared in June, was a melancholy, Tennysonian poem with echoes of Wordsworth and hints of Coleridge addressed to a missing and presumably dead fair one named Marian. "A Dirge," in the July number, varied the formula by making the corpse that of a poet—a sort of composite Shelley and Keats—who had been both literally and allegorically drowned. By this time, Graham was willing to pay Lowell twenty dollars a poem if he would become a contributor to his magazine exclusively, but Poe had left his advisory position on the editorial staff and Peterson's wish that the dirge were a little more condensed may have reflected the opinion of his successor who had disappointed all Lowell's friends by the notice in his *Poets of America.* In any case, Lowell hoped for other markets and could find no profit in making an exclusive agreement with Graham even if the new editor had encouraged it—which he apparently did not, for the only poem by Lowell that was accepted by *Graham's* while Griswold served as editor was a little one called "The Moon" which he seems to have assigned, through Peterson, to Poe in payment for one of the latter's contributions to Lowell's own magazine and published as a partial discharge of Poe's indebtedness to Graham.

Not even Lowell, perhaps, could have told whether his disappearance from the pages of *Graham's* was primarily the result of his unwillingness to limit his financial prospects, his failure to please the new editor, or his inability to devote his talents entirely to the particular kind of verse so stupidly praised by his Philadelphia critics. Try as hard as he might to avoid sensuous imagery and to keep his eye on "the ideal," he could not prevent the visible world from making its appearance in his verses; and he knew that some readers liked his more sensuous poetry much better than he would admit liking it himself. He may have felt the need of an outlet for the sort of verse he wrote in spite of his ideal, and he probably longed for an editor more sympathetic than Rufus W. Griswold. He certainly wanted a better market than he had yet found if he was to endeavor to make a living at literature.

II

A BETTER market than *Graham's,* Lowell thought, might be the *Boston Miscellany* which was begun in January, 1842, by his friend, Nathan Hale, Jr., who was willing to publish several contributions in each issue without expressing Peterson's fear that he was writing "too much." Whether or not Lowell was paid for his first contributions, he expected eventually to be offered fifteen dollars per poem and in September had reason to anticipate that amount in the future—with no objections to his writing for others. Hale had been the editorial genius of *Harvardiana* and depended upon Lowell's assistance in his new enterprise, asking five months in advance of the first number for "some bright, joyous prose" and indicating that it would not be amiss for Lowell to be "funny." The prose was not immediately forthcoming, but Lowell sent poems in abundance—some of them from manuscripts that had been available for *A Year's Life* but had been rejected and brought to light again, apparently because, as Lowell wrote Emerson in November, Hale did not generally like the same pieces he himself did. As his undergraduate letters had made clear to his friend, Hale found transcendental mistiness ridiculous and admired the poetry of Keats; and, appropriately enough, the first poem in the *Miscellany* was a "Sonnet—To Keats" in which Lowell paid the tribute of imitative allusion to the sensuous images of "The Eve of St. Agnes" and "An Ode on a Grecian Urn" and praised Keats for the warm and "right good English blood" that ran through his heart even in its "most Grecian mood." Hale also printed "To Perdita, Singing" in his first number, and an unsigned poem "Agatha." The signature may have been omitted from "Agatha" because the editor wanted to avoid giving the impression of depending too heavily upon one poet, or it may have been that Lowell chose to have the poem anonymous because it was, in fact, a rewritten version of "Irenè," composed after he had been engaged for nearly a year and had become capable of a more precise analysis of virtues he had observed in Maria from the beginning.

The growing appreciation of Keats, which Lowell was expressing in his correspondence with Charles Peterson but not revealing in the poems sent to *Graham's,* is clearly evident in the sonnet "Like some black mountain glooming huge aloof" that appeared in the February *Miscellany.* Written during the preceding September, two months before the "Ode" on the poet which appeared in the same number, its theme was the inner demand for some "afterwork" which would be superior to anything he had ever written or anything that the world or custom required of him. Yet instead of idealizing—or, perhaps more properly, de-materializing—a physical object as had been so often his custom, he compared his imperative feeling with the glooming mountain in such a way that the dominant effect of the sonnet was that of the sensuous image; and the literary influence which helped release his visual imagination is revealed in the reference of the last line to "A cricket's chirp among the easeful grass." In his light prose sketch in the

March number entitled "Getting Up," Lowell exhibited further evidence that his interest in Keats was so alive that he had probably been recently rereading him. "Lamia" was certainly in his mind as he wrote of his dream-gathering of authors and literary characters, and he permitted Chaucer and Milton to express the hope that a newcomer to their circle might be either Dante or Keats; and, near the close of his dream, he found himself springing at the ghost of Gifford with "carving-knife in my hand and the thought of poor Keats in my heart." There was a good deal of sentimentality in this, just as there was in the sonnet "To the Spirit of Keats" which he published in *Arcturus* in January and chose to preserve in his collected works, but there is also an indication that at the time he found a sympathetic publisher for his own more sensuous poetry he was finding in the life and works of John Keats the distinction between sensuousness and sensuality which Maria had failed to draw.

Lowell's increasing use of visual imagery for its own sake and his more intense appeal to other senses are apparent in other poems that show no signs of Keats's influence. Although the whole picture of the poet's grave in "A Dirge" in the July *Graham's* is inconsistent and at times contradictory, the poem contains lines of visual imagery that ten years later would have been called Pre-Raphaelite; and there are numerous signs that Lowell, who had never shut out the visual world from the privacy of his study, had acquired a new conception of his art that made him willing to open his poetic eyes in public. He quite evidently wanted readers of "The Forlorn," in the March *Miscellany,* to see the sleet stiffening on the pavement and hear it rattling on the street-lamps that flared through the white gusts and revealed the bleakness of the flat brick walls separating the outcast from shelter; and the memories of "clear blue summer days" were visual memories in which meadows shimmered through the rising heat and changed hue under a rippling western breeze. He was not yet sure in the exercise of this element in his imagination, for his mind's eye certainly blinked when he let the girl's bare feet freeze to the sidewalk without bringing her to a stop. But his description of the environment in which one more unfortunate went to her death makes an appeal to his reader's knowledge of the visible world—not to any phrenological faculty of "ideality" or to any other theory that developed under what Lowell called, in his "Disquisition on Foreheads" in the same issue, "the influence of Lavater and his execrable book."

By the end of March, 1842, Lowell had finished his legal apprenticeship in the office of Charles G. Loring and had set up an office of his own a few doors away on Court Street. For more than a year he had been boarding in Boston at his father's expense, and the new establishment increased his indebtedness to his family. He had already "had a client," he wrote his friend Heath on the last day of the month, but he was conscious that it would be "a long while" before he would be "able to support a wife." The privacy of a rarely visited office, however, gave him the opportunity for more sustained literary activity than he had been able to engage in before; and the first products of his independence seem to have been two of the three essays on "The Old English Dramatists" which he published in the *Miscellany* that year. The criticism of George Chapman and John Webster appeared in the April number as an anonymous contribution but was easily identifiable as coming from the same pen which had produced *A Year's Life,* "Callirhöe," the "Ode" on the poet, and "The Forlorn." Lowell's insistence that "Love never contracts its circles" was a repetition of the theme of the sonnets in his published volume; and the angel of poetry, sitting silently "at the soul's gate" in the essay, was the image of Spenserian Chastity which he had transferred from "Callirhöe" to the revised version of "Ianthe." He drew upon his "Ode" to justify the appearance of his essay in a "Miscellany of Literature and Fashion": "For, under this thin crust of fashion and frivolity throb the undying fires of the great soul of man, which is the fountain and centre of all poesy, and which will one day burst forth, and wither like grassblades all the temples and palaces which form and convention have heaped over it." It was "the high and glorious vocation of poesy to make our daily life and toil more beautiful and holy by the divine ministerings of love," he added in the same strain; for "She is the true preacher of the word." From "The Forlorn" he recalled "the poor wanderer whose bare feet know by heart all the freezing stones of the pavement"—a wanderer whom, he declared, poetry loved better "than the rich maiden for whose tender soles Brussels and Turkey are over-careful." His professional leisure had given him time to gather together many of the thoughts and impressions he had recently used separately, and his friendly editor allowed him to develop his own stream of consciousness at the expense of the two dramatists with whom he was supposed to deal.

The second of his essays, which dealt with John Ford and appeared in May, was equally discursive. In the first section he turned again to a discussion of the poet, dealing with him in sentences of Emersonian sententiousness that were transcendental in their point of view and sometimes specifically reminiscent of the Phi Beta Kappa Address. It may have been this part of the essay which grew out of the paper on his theory of poetry which he had read, with illustrations from the old dramatists, at the January, 1839, meeting of Alpha Delta Phi and which Edward Everett Hale remembered as the basis of the essays in the *Miscellany*. While reconsidering the attitude toward Emerson expressed in his *Class Poem,* Lowell may have told the Harvard undergraduates that the poet, "Unsupported by any of the earth's customs or conventions, . . . leans wholly on the Infinite"; and he may also have told them that the Elizabethans were indifferent to anachronisms and to the facts of geography because "They laid their scene in the unchangeable heart of man, and so 'Made one little room an everywhere.' " But some of his general observations, like those of the first essay, were the products of his more recent meditations. Lowell could hardly, in 1839, have criticised Lamb's comments on the death scene in *The Broken Heart* by saying that the English critic matched "a selfish with a universal love" and by adding, as his own opinion: "Love's nobility is shown in this,—that it strengthens us to make sacrifices for others, and not for the object of our love alone. Our love for one is only so made preëminent, that it may show us the beauty and holiness of that love whose arms are wide enough for all." Such words were those of the man who had written the sonnets to Maria and the "Ode" on the poet—and of the incipient radical who, in the same essay, claimed that if creeds should be credited with doing good by concentrating the will and energy of a strong mind on a single point, "the credit should be given rather to concentration and resolution than to creeds."

Most of the effort that Lowell spent on these papers apparently went into his long and somewhat irrelevant introductions, for, although some of his remarks upon particular passages reveal the penetration and acuteness which made him a good critic in spite of his faults, his quotations show that he did little more than cull his commonplace book and review two or three plays by each of his subject dramatists. Even in the midst of his series of illustrative quotations, he frequently digressed into attacks upon such miscellaneous notions as the "thought that a certain rudeness and ungraciousness of bearing was most befitting a radical," the belief that propriety required ladies to expose their bosoms on formal occasions and keep them covered in the privacy of the home, and the assumption that a "slavish and emasculate" polite language was preferable to directness in speech. Yet these irrelevances were perhaps responsible for the popular success of his first two essays, and there is some irony in the fact that their widely acknowledged success made him work so diligently upon the third that he devoted it exclusively to the subject of Massinger and made its few digressions (such as those on the faults of Byron and the virtues of Keats) almost entirely literary. In preparation for it, he wrote Loring, he marked over a thousand passages from Massinger's plays; and he delayed its publication from June to July and eventually to August. It is not certain whether the author was wearied by such industry or whether his readers were wearied by its results, but the paper on Massinger was the last of his critical essays to be published in the *Miscellany*.

Lowell composed two other prose sketches for Hale's periodical, however, "The First Client" in the May issue and "Married Men" in September. Both were published anonymously, as were all his lighter prose sketches, and neither was particularly successful. The former was the most original of all his attempts at narrative essays and reflected enough idle observation from his own experiences in an empty law office to be more amusing than his customary artificial humor. But Lowell did not have the sense of timing necessary for a writer of good narratives. When he could see his audience face to face, he was an excellent storyteller; but on paper he was too self-conscious to put himself in his reader's place and seems never to have known precisely when he had made his point. By the time he had composed his sketch on "Married Men," he had begun to feel that he could not write well in his "cramped-up lawyer's office" and had also begun to plan a more "lucrative employment" in the form of his own magazine. He thought for a while of writing a pamphlet on slavery, but he actually composed only a few bits of rhyme which were dashed off as the spirit moved him; and his publications, during the latter part of 1842, were almost all poems taken from his portfolio.

These garnerings for the *Miscellany* are made readily identifiable by the fact that the human relationships among the little "Band" of friends with whom Lowell was formally allied were not as perfect as his biographers have implied. In particular, Lowell felt obliged to protect himself against the rivalry of his classmate, William Story. Imitation was a tribute that he appreciated until it became too close in time as well as manner, and Story had been treading so closely on his heels that his irritation mounted until, on April 11, he had written Loring:

I was very much annoyed at first, the more so because he had read many of my unprinted poems and I feared to see the duplicates before I could publish the originals. It is provoking to have a train of thought taken directly out of one's mouth. My sonnets were original, as far as my reading goes. I never saw any in the same strain in English or any other language. But W. S. imitates them *very* closely, and as he is not always very particular about dates, many people would never know which were originals.

Hale, who also belonged to the "Band," evidently avoided a quarrel by having both young men date their contributions to the *Miscellany* by the year, month, and usually day of composition whenever any question of priority might possibly arise; and by the time Lowell expressed himself upon the matter he had "got over the vexation," though he still wished that Story "would get over the habit as well." Of the ready-written poems he contributed after having begun his critical essays, the most interesting is "The Two" in the May issue, in which he gave the clue to the relationship between his own emotional experience and the development of his conception of the poet as he had expressed it three months before. Others suggest the literary influences under which he was working at various times. A sonnet, "Whene'er I read in mournful history," although strictly Italian in form and in the customary "strain" that Lowell considered original, was in its general mood a clear reflection of the "divine fury" he was reported to have had for Shakespeare's sonnets at the time he composed it in the autumn of 1841. The vague and incoherent imagery of the original version of "A Fantasy," published in July but dated January 12, 1842, shows the effect of the generous praise of his "ideality" which he was receiving at the time, and the poem should, in justice, have gone to *Graham's* whose editors were largely responsible for it.

The only other poem signed by Lowell to appear in the *Miscellany* was "The Shepherd of King Admetus" in September, which was dated June 25 of that year. This, like certain other poems of the same period, however, is a part of the story of "Prometheus" and the changes in Lowell's conception of the ideal poet between the publication of the "Ode" and the 1844 *Poems*. The number of his occasional unsigned contributions is doubtful. The lines of free verse entitled "The True Radical" printed in August have been assigned to Lowell by his bibliographer, and his later use of the idea that the business of such a person was to water the roots of the tree of progress rather than lop off its dead branches probably justifies the attribution. The undated, unsigned six lines of verse headed "Poetry:—A Simile" in the June *Miscellany,* although never attributed to him, are equally characteristic and equally in keeping with his habit of composing brief poetic thoughts that were occasionally used to fill out an incomplete magazine page. A longer poem attributed to him by his bibliographer, "To an

Aeolian Harp at Night" in the December issue, is much less characteristic; and it seems hardly probable that the *Miscellany,* after promising him fifteen dollars a poem, would accept a solitary contribution from one of its best-known writers and then publish it without the author's name.

There is no evidence that Lowell profited very much financially from his connection with the Boston *Miscellany.* He may have been paid for some of his contributions—most probably for the essays on the old dramatists, and possibly for "The Shepherd of King Admetus"—but his greatest rewards came in increased reputation and an encouragement toward literary criticism and a more sensuous richness of poetic style. The press notices printed in the October number of the magazine included one from the *Traveller* which listed Lowell's among the half-dozen "eminent" names mentioned as contributors to the July issue while it grouped vaguely as "others" Mary E. Hewitt, William A. Jones, Cornelius Mathews, and Evert A. Duyckinck; and the December cover boasted of him as one of the "Male Writers" in the "Unrivalled List of Eminent Contributors!" who would appear in the magazine for the coming year. He had received considerable acclaim for his critical efforts, from his friends and from strangers, and there had been some favorable recognition of his anonymous essays at light prose. He was no longer merely a poet but a promising young man of letters. But he was primarily a poet, and he had become a better poet for having Nat Hale as an editorial counterinfluence to Peterson and Poe. Hale demanded far less in the way of metrical perfection than did Poe, and he overlooked echoes of Keats and Shakespeare as readily as the editors of *Graham's* overlooked those of Wordsworth and Coleridge; but he preferred the imagery of this world to that of transcendental idealism or of the misty mid-region of phrenological ideality, and Lowell needed any influence that would help bring him part way down to earth.

III

WHILE LOWELL was busy supplying the two major journals upon which he placed his professional hopes, he was also engaged in disposing of a surplus of the sonnets that apparently formed a considerable part of his literary output from the time he rounded out "a year's life" with this form until the end of 1841. Some of them found their way around Margaret Fuller and into the *Dial.* His new approach to Emerson, after the several weeks with him at Nantasket during the summer of 1841, was largely a matter of spontaneous impulse on Lowell's part, yet if he had searched his soul he probably would have discovered a feeling that it would do a professional literary man no harm to have some connection with what he called "the Dial clique," even though the *Dial* itself stood at some distance from the world of commercial literature. The inclusion of the sonnet "When in a book I find a pleasant thought" in his letter of November 19 may not have been accompanied by any thought of publication; but when Emerson asked permission to print it, Lowell's response with two other sonnets, by return mail, revealed a genuine eagerness to appear over his own signature among the transcendentalists. "Only as thou herein canst not see me" and "To Irenè on her birthday" were selected—if the first was not written especially for Emerson—with reference to the recipient's philosophy and sent with an allusion to the quaintness of his poetic taste, and permission to use them was accompanied by delicate pressure in the form of a hint that if Emerson did not want them the author's friend Hale would probably be glad to get them for his magazine. The *Dial* published all three in January, 1842, and Lowell received a complimentary copy of the issue for his generosity. But he made no attempt to crowd the *Dial* with his poems, although Emerson would doubtless have accepted others. His next gift of sonnets was to another little clique.

Arcturus, A Journal of Books and Opinion had been established in December, 1840, by Evert Duyckinck and Cornelius Mathews, and Lowell had been a subscriber from its beginning, sending it a copy of *A Year's Life* for review and receiving a complimentary and fairly long notice by Duyckinck in the fourth number. He delayed expressing his appreciation, however, until an article on "The Sonnets of Keats" in the last issue for 1841 inspired him with the wish to see two of his own sonnets "enshrined in the same volume"—just as three others were in the process of being enshrined in the *Dial*. Accordingly, on December 5, he made Duyckinck a gift of "To the Spirit of Keats" and "Sunset and Moonshine" and explained suggestively, if not quite accurately, that "other engagements" alone had prevented him from making earlier contributions to the magazine with which he felt so sympathetic. First Mathews and then Duyckinck accepted his sonnets with appreciation, the latter writing on December 17 that "the moon-led pulse of ocean" was one of "those amulet phrases which a man may carry about in his head and have popping out over the fire or along the walk to cheer and inspire him—the 'open sesame' to a whole region of thoughts and fancies going beyond." The poems were printed in the January number, but neither editor requested further contributions for which he might be obliged to pay. Lowell, however, gave freely out of his abundance, supplementing the sonnet to Keats with another beginning "Poet! thou art most wealthy, being poor," which was its logical sequel although more closely connected emotionally with the first of the two sonnets sent to Emerson two days after composing this. The obscure last line of the "Only as thou herein canst not see me" sonnet in the *Dial* appears, as it is printed, to be an early expression of that willingness to glory in imperfection which is to be found in his papers on the "Old Dramatists" and which later helped him to appreciate so quickly the poems of Robert Browning. But Lowell attempted to explain it to Emerson as an expression of the theme found in the *Arcturus* sonnet on the poet: although his ears are earthly, he can hear celestial harmonies with them and respond by achieving nobility on earth. The *Dial* sonnet was evidently in his mind when he wrote the one on the poet, for he used the same imagery of the music of the spheres to describe the transcendental source from which the poet drew his inspiration. When his "Ode" on the poet appeared in the *Boston Miscellany* of February, 1842, Lowell received a prompt and enthusiastic letter of praise from Mathews and, in a notice of the Boston magazine in the April number of *Arcturus,* a flattering number of public compliments. In appreciation, he reached into his portfolio and contributed to the May issue three further sonnets.

Two of these, "My Father, since I love" and "I love those poets, of whatever creed," had played a part in the evolution of the "Ode." The third, "The hope of truth grows stronger day by day," which was dated December 10 and therefore probably written while the "Ode" was in the process of composition, is indicative of a new field of interest into which Lowell had been led by his professional meandering. The boldest and most imaginative (in a Miltonic sense as opposed to the sort of imagination found in him by Poe) of all his poems up to date, it foresaw the soul of Man breaking its fetters like a frozen sea and grinding continents together like icebergs as it threw heavenward the sunlit spray of its free spirit. For, the sonnet continued, the memory of former glory lingers in every heart as the sound of the sea remains in a shell—a murmur of "inward strife for truth and liberty" which swelled hour by hour until it inspired the poet to his prophetic vision. The generalized abolitionism of this poem did not appear in the first version of the "Ode"—although it was introduced into the second—because Lowell had not yet succeeded in establishing, to his own satisfaction, the proper relationship of a poet to a specific reform movement. A few weeks before, he had touched upon the problem in a sonnet published in *The Liberty Bell* for 1842 as a tribute to John Pierpont, whose poetic resources were being devoted to the anti-slavery cause, but at the time he could do little better than maintain that poets suffer more for truth than do more active martyrs. Later reprinted as "The Fiery Trial," the Pierpont sonnet made the somewhat curious claim that harder than "The hungry flame" to bear were certain unrecognized martyrdoms for Truth: scorned hope, seemingly wasted faith, the knowledge of baseness wrongfully elevated, and delayed fame. To endure such torments, it continued, God had sent poets, who had been content to suffer humbleness and poverty in order to "sow one grain of Love's eternal seed." The poem reveals the same sort of self-pity that is found in the *Arcturus* sonnet "To the Spirit of Keats" and shows that the feeling was cultivated under the influence of Shakespeare's sonnets, but it does not indicate that Lowell had given any serious attention to the possibility that he might become personally involved in the abolition movement.

This and the two other sonnets, "Great Truths are portions of the soul of man" and "If ye have not the one great lesson learned," that Lowell contributed to *The Liberty Bell* for 1842 are probably no more indicative of the author's interest in the anti-slavery cause than of his desire for literary reputation in as many circles as possible. He was soon to become a staunch abolitionist at some expense to his professional reputation, but in the autumn of 1841 the abolitionists were little more to Lowell than a group of worthy people with whom Maria was associated and from whom he was receiving flattering attentions. Mrs. Child was one of the editors of the *National Anti-Slavery Standard;* and after she had assured him—despite his fears to the contrary—that there was "reform" implicit in the humanitarianism of his poems, he allowed her to print "The Loved One" in the *Standard* for December 16, 1841, and reprint two of the sonnets from *The Liberty Bell* on January 27. He also permitted her to use for February 3 a "Sonnet written in a copy of the Liberty Bell, presented to a beloved friend at Christmas," which encouraged the lady to whom it was addressed to continue her interest and activity in "the blessed cause of truth" but showed no awareness whatsoever of the sort of activity that some of the female abolitionists engaged in. As for Lowell himself, his only other contribution to the *Standard* for that year, a sonnet beginning "Poet, if men from wisdom turn away," in the issue of September 1, was apparently a monologue in which he advised himself to "Sing to the hearing of the Eternal ear," thus keeping things light within regardless of how dark they might appear outside. In his "Elegy on the Death of Dr. Channing," which was written in November, 1842, as his only contribution to the 1843 *Liberty Bell,* he took his own advice and, asserting that "Truth needs no champions," praised Channing as a man of peace whose great soul gleamed from another world to "clothe the Right with lustre more divine."

Lowell's own intention at the time was to do no more than let his light so shine that it would clothe the right with greater lustre, and when he did take up his poetic arms on the side of a specific reform it was to cross sonnets with another poet in an indubitable attempt to further his own professional career. In March, 1842, the *United States Magazine and Democratic Review* (which was supposed to pay its contributors fairly well) published an article on "Wordsworth's Sonnets on the Punishment of Death," reprinting the sonnets from the *London Quarterly,* attacking Wordsworth's defense of capital punishment, and promising further commentary in an early number. Lowell quickly volunteered the additional commentary in the form of six sonnets expressing his own antagonistic response to Wordsworth's series and sent them to the editor, John L. O'Sullivan, in time for publication in May. They were evidently a gift, but after a decent interval the giver entered into direct negotiations with the editor concerning the possibility of becoming a regular contributor and received, on September 9, an offer of five dollars per poem which he somehow, by the twentieth, had changed into an arrangement that would "probably" give him ten or fifteen. The only poem that he sold that year under this arrangement was "An Incident in a Rail-Road Car" which he had written in May—possibly with the *Democratic Review* in mind—and which was published in October. The sonnets and the poem are closely related, and both reflect the change in attitude toward poetry through which he went between the publication of his "Ode" and the appearance of his 1844 *Poems.* For once, however, his generosity with his sonnets had brought results—his samples had persuaded a customer. But his experience had proved that the profession of letters required more of the fine art of salesmanship than a high and somewhat fuzzy-minded young poet possessed.

Lowell's first two years of professional authorship had not been financially profitable. He had earned twenty dollars by his first contribution to an annual and probably eighty and certainly no more than one hundred dollars by his contributions to *Graham's.* The *Boston Miscellany* had printed seven prose sketches from him and seven or eight poems longer than sonnets, but there is no record of how much, if anything, he was paid for them. "I am to have," he wrote Loring on September 20, 1842, "fifteen dollars a poem from the 'Miscellany' "; but that magazine, which had printed from one to three contributions from him in every previous issue, did not publish anything by Lowell after that date unless the anonymous, and doubtful, "To an Aeolian Harp" in the December issue was his. That could hardly have been the fault of the young man who, in the same letter, looked upon the *Miscellany* as the mainstay of his optimistic hope to earn four hundred dollars a year by his pen and get out of "debt" by the following June. Probably Lowell had appeared in its pages so frequently because most of his contributions were gratuitous, and his earnings from that source are unlikely to have been as great as those from *Graham's.* The *Democratic Review* evidently paid him five dollars for "An Incident in a Rail-Road Car" after accepting the sonnets on Wordsworth as a gift. His contributions to the *Dial, Arcturus,* the *Anti-Slavery Standard,* and the *Liberty Bell* were usually voluntary and mostly—if not always—unpaid for. At the most generous possible estimate, free-lancing in literature for two years brought in less than one-quarter of the dollar a day at which he estimated his living costs.

In return for this possible twenty-five cents a day (which is, in all probability, almost double his actual earnings) and for the fame brought by his free-will offerings, Lowell nearly exhausted his portfolio of manuscripts and displayed a remarkable versatility in pleasing such an incongruous assortment of editors as Peterson, Poe, Nathan Hale, Jr., Emerson, Cornelius Mathews, Evert Duyckinck, John L. O'Sullivan, Maria Chapman, and Lydia Child and her associates on the *Anti-Slavery Standard.* A majority of them had only one quality in common: a sensitiveness to the interests of their female following, for although the *Democratic Review* and perhaps *Arcturus* were masculine periodicals, Emerson was commonly reputed to be an intellectual squire of dames and the editors of *Graham's* and the *Miscellany* made no secret of their dependence upon subscribers who looked first at the fashion plates and then at the poetry. There was an unmistakable feminine cast in the editorial eyes that admired Lowell's verses. A graduate of Harvard college and of the law school who prized his academic connection enough to take his Master of Arts degree might have been expected to achieve success with such a variety of editors representing such a large number of superficial readers only at the expense of his intellectual integrity; but Lowell at the time had little intellectual integrity to compromise. He needed discipline of exactly the sort that his initial *succès d'estime* made impossible. He needed acute readers who would point out his inconsistencies rather than sympathtic ones who would praise his beauties. He needed fewer literary friends and friends who would not admire so many different things. He needed, above all, a single associate with a strong, aggressive intellect that would either dominate and shape his opinions or force him to develop a tough mind of his own. Instead, he had Maria and the authors of books which he could shelve at will.

Nearly every one of his editors knew better than to encourage him in the course which they were not free to obstruct. As early as January 10, 1842, Peterson had written: "I confess I often think you write, or at least publish too much. A too general communion with the public will make you common—you understand in what sense I use the word—and men of less merit will win greater repute." Yet he kept begging contributions for *Graham's*. O'Sullivan, of the *Democratic Review,* in a letter of September 9 agreed to make an exception to his general rule of not paying for verse but added "a hint of advice":

—not to write too much, of the fugitive verse with which we are so surfeited. I make the suggestion because strongly inclined to believe that you can produce fine fruit which all men will recognize as ambrosial, if you do not allow the vine of your genius to "run too much to wood," as it is termed. Magazine verse writing is very apt to lead to very bad habits in this way. You would the more readily excuse this liberty if you knew the sincere friendliness of feeling from which it proceeds.

Mathews, whose conception of a hint was somewhat less Irish than O'Sullivan's, had been content to urge the cultivation of a more "compact and energetic style of expression"; and Poe, later, merely urged him to abstain from narratives. Except for Hale (whose opinions would have been expressed orally instead of by correspondence) and the ladies of the abolitionist press, Lowell seems to have had no editor who was entirely easy in his mind about what Mathews called his "extraordinary fluency." Others shared their uneasiness and volunteered similar advice. George Lunt, who had been stirred by the "Ode" on the poet to an enthusiastic communication in February, 1842, yielded to his conscience on March 4 and, holding too much fluency responsible for the low reputation of poetry in America, begged: "permit me to entreat you not to write too much." Lowell was ready to admit, at almost any time, that his verses were below his abilities and unworthy of his true self; but he was aware of the dilemma set forth in O'Sullivan's letter accepting him as a paid contributor to the *Democratic*

Review. As a friend, O'Sullivan had been realistic and frank in his warning against the danger of too much magazine writing. As an editor, he was equally realistic and frank almost to the point of brutality when he wrote: "Poetry is a kind of *merchandise,* like old pictures, for which Editors pay rather for the reputation of the name in the corner than for that essential virtue of color and design which no more admits of estimate in dollars and dimes than *light,* of measurement by the peck." O'Sullivan stated clearly the problem which seems to have been more or less perceptible to other editors: a talented American author of the 1840's had to make a deliberate choice between quantity and quality, to strive either for a profitable notoriety or for permanent fame. Lowell was never sure afterwards that the choice had ever really been his. He had to take the cash—even if there was very little of it—and let the credit go; and when his early attempt to achieve notoriety did not prove profitable enough he was impelled to try the more promising field of publishing.

IV

MAGAZINE publishing was perhaps the most mortal of all fields of literary endeavor during this period of American history, but Lowell was too young and too naïve to realize it. He was "very happy," he wrote Loring on September 20, 1842, because, among other things, he had "quite a reasonable prospect of getting into a lucrative literary employment next year" about which he was willing to talk but could not bring himself to write. Superstitious though he may have been about putting his plans on paper, he was sure that he had found a good opening for a literary periodical of his own. The *Boston Miscellany* had absorbed *Arcturus* in June, and the high aims of the latter magazine, with which Lowell had expressed himself as being particularly sympathetic, had been lowered to the level of the factory girls who bought the former for its fashion plates. His friend Hale was leaving the editorial chair of the *Miscellany* at the end of the year, and Lowell, although he certainly did not contemplate dissociating himself from it as a contributor, probably expected a lessening of its literary and artistic character in its effort to get further into the graces of what he described to Heath as "the worst judges—namely, the majority." It was a curious attitude for a young man looking for "lucrative literary employment" to adopt, but Lowell evidently felt that the situation left an opening for an editor like himself who would not feel "obliged to sacrifice the best interests of literature to those of his publishers." He would be his own publisher and his own editor and thereby strike a balance.

Robert Carter, a young man with literary ambitions who had come to Boston from Albany two years before and had recently tried to publish a magazine devoted to mesmerism, became interested in the project; and the firm of Emerson Leland and Willard J. Whiting, booksellers and magazine distributors, assured them that it would be possible to dispose of five thousand copies of a monthly, three-sheet magazine of the sort Lowell had in mind. On November 1, 1842, they signed a formal contract for six months (which was renewable up to eighteen) from the first of the following January. Lowell and Carter agreed to furnish five thousand copies of a magazine of forty-eight royal octavo pages, containing one or more engravings, on the twentieth of the month preceding the date of publication; and Leland and Whiting agreed to pay for them at the rate of twelve and one-half cents per copy in the form of three notes for each issue payable two, three, and four months from the date of delivery. Lowell and Carter also agreed to forfeit the sum of five hundred dollars if they failed to make their delivery on time and to buy back, at ten cents each, all copies unsold at the end of six months provided these copies had never left the hands of their publishers. In return, Leland and Whiting contracted to make every proper effort to distribute the periodical widely and to "publish" no other magazine. The new journal was to be called the *Pioneer* and was to be sold at the retail price of twenty-five cents a copy or three dollars a year.

Such a contract was an extraordinary one because it provided, in effect, that Lowell and Carter should do all the work, take all the risk, and still publish their periodical without any likelihood of profit. They probably did not bother to get adequate estimates of their expenses before signing their contract, but during the next two months the chilling facts became evident. The first issue, Lowell found, would require thirty-four reams of printing paper at five dollars a ream, three and a quarter reams of colored paper for binding at five dollars and a half, and three reams of "plate" paper for engravings at fifteen dollars—a total of $232.87 for paper alone. The stitching and binding in paper covers, according to the extant bills, cost thirty dollars more, and the charge for printing five thousand illustrations from each of the engraved plates came to seventy-five dollars. Other charges cannot be accurately fixed by surviving documents, but later receipts show that as late as 1846 Lowell owed J. G. Chandler a "balance" of twenty-five dollars presumably for the two pages of wood engravings illustrating Lowell's "The Rose" in the first number, and that he paid J. Andrews one hundred and twenty-five dollars for a single engraving he never used. Since the two engravings by Andrews in the first issue could hardly have been made for less than fifty dollars each, and Chandler's bill could not have been for less than its "balance," the cost of preparing illustrations was at least one hundred and twenty-five dollars, and the expense of publishing the first number of the magazine amounted to $462.87 exclusive of typesetting, printing, and payments to contributors. If Boston printing costs were comparable to the depression rates prevailing in Philadelphia at the time, the composition would have cost thirty-seven and one-half cents per thousand "m's" or about $71.25 per issue, and the thirty thousand impressions required for printing on half sheets with six signatures to a number could have been made at a charge of forty-eight dollars for presswork. The covers, at the same rate, would have cost about fourteen dollars. Thus the most conservative possible estimate of the expense would amount to $596.12; and although the editors had between fifteen and twenty dollars worth of paper left over and may have saved a few dollars on typesetting by large margins for poetry, they could not have paid office rent and spent much on contributors without exceeding the six hundred and twenty-five dollars anticipated from Leland and Whiting.

The Prospectus for the *Pioneer* had been issued to "the intelligent and reflecting portions of the Reading Public" on October 15, 1842, and promised relief from "thrice-diluted trash" in the form of "a healthy and manly Periodical Literature, whose perusal will not necessarily involve a loss of time and a deterioration of every moral and intellectual faculty." As this promise was amplified in the Introduction to the first number, it assured readers of "a *natural*" rather than "a *National* literature," based upon an impulse from within instead of influences from without. But the inner impulse Lowell affirmed on this occasion was not the immutable feeling he usually asserted in his poetry: it changed from youth to age, from radicalism to conservatism, and "both gasses must be mixt ere the cooling rain" of Truth could fall on the human "seed field." He sounded like the older and wiser Emerson who was later to write the essay on "Experience," but he was actually asking for tolerance of his proposed radicalism which he promised would not be offensive. "Radicalism has only gone too far when it has *hated* conservatism," he explained, and his "humble hope" for the *Pioneer* was that it should "be one exponent of a young spirit which shall aim at power through gentleness, the only mean for its secure attainment, and in which freedom shall be attempered to love by a reverence for all beauty wherever it may exist."

Such unusually apologetic wisdom represented Lowell's effort to arrive at a basis of understanding with the unknown public upon whom so much depended and of whose ways he understood so little. But when he considered literature in the abstract he was less practical. Poetry, whether composed in youth or in age, was no longer bits of colored glass in which the white radiance of eternity was broken down, for better understanding, into its constituent rays. It was the white light itself; and Lowell, in fact, began his essay on "The Plays of Thomas Middleton" for the first number of the *Pioneer* with a quotation from Shelley's *Defense of Poetry,* comparing a great poem with an inexhaustible fountain "forever overflowing with the waters of wisdom and delight," for successive persons in successive ages a "source of an unforseen and unconceived delights." Written hurriedly in late November and early December, the essay is, in its discursive parts, a prose recollection of the sonnets on Wordsworth's defense of capital punishment. It also included a passing reference to his avowed "radicalism" which was more closely parallel to the verses on "The True Radical" in the August *Miscellany* than to his defense of his point of view in the Introduction to the *Pioneer.* The three clarifying stanzas that he was to introduce into the second version of "An Incident in a Rail-Road Car" had evidently not yet been written, for in the haste of composing his essay Lowell did not pause to consider whether the "Love" which inspired a poet represented the intellectual perception of Plato or the emotional motive power of Mackintosh. On the whole, he seems to have leaned toward Plato at this particular moment, for he spoke of poetry as the "distant utterances of those far-heard voices which, in the too fleeting moments of a higher and clearer being, come to us from the infinite deep with a feeling of something heard in childhood, but long ago drowned in the din of life." Yet such a statement may represent nothing more than the fact that Lowell's mind, dwelling on Wordsworth while he wrote, was automatically expressing a preference for the author of an Ode on "Intimations of Immortality" over the defender of capital punishment. Lowell was spending less conscious thought upon his own contributions to his magazine than upon the problem of getting the magazine ready to receive them.

Lowell was very busy during the month of November collecting what Graham liked to call a "card" of writers for the *Pioneer,* arranging for engravings, getting printers' estimates, and buying paper for the first number. "I have been harassed more than you can well think," he wrote Loring on November 30, "by the *business* of my magazine"; and by business he apparently meant the physical details of publication, for he was rather negligent of his writers. John Neal was really the only professional "magazinist" he obtained for his first number, and John S. Dwight, the music critic from Brook Farm, and Jones Very were the only other contributors from outside his immediate circle of associates. As a result of a fortunate accident that the new editor of the *Boston Miscellany* had been a victim of Poe's critical remarks, Lowell was able to obtain the rejected manuscript of "The Tell-Tale Heart" in time to compensate for his failure to write Poe promptly for contributions; but he was not able to print work from Hawthorne and Whittier (two other good names that he wanted) until his second issue.

Yet with the help of his friends he succeeded in making the first number of the *Pioneer* a remarkably well-balanced magazine of criticism and literature. The fine arts were covered by Dwight's paper on "Beethoven's Symphonies," the editor's own essay on "The Plays of Thomas Middleton," and W. W. Story's review of the exhibition of paintings at the Boston Athenaeum. Story, who shared the editor's fondness for punning, signed his review—and other contributions in later issues—I. B. Wright and increased the apparent number of writers for the first number by a poem over his own proper signature. W. H. Burleigh, who had recently discovered, in an exchange of correspondence and sonnets, that his "orthodoxy" and Lowell's "transcendentalism" (defined by the latter as "freedom and love") were essentially the same, allowed three of his sonnets to be printed under the title "Acceptable Worship"; and Thomas W. Parsons, a young local contributor to the *Miscellany,* provided a long poem, "Hudson River." The issue also contained the first installment of an anonymous tale, by Carter, of contemporary Bagdad entitled "The Armenian's Daughter," a sonnet "Our love is not a fading earthly flower" signed by Lowell, a long poem "The Rose," two other unsigned bits of verse by him, and a poem on "The Poet and Apollo" over the signature "H. P." which probably represented the ghost of Hugh Perceval and another attempt to add to the number of contributors listed in the table of contents. Five pages of "Literary notices" (including reviews by Lowell of Hawthorne's *Historical Tales for Youth* and Dickens' *American Notes, for General Circulation*) and two pages of "Foreign Literary Intelligence" completed the number, although Lowell was hoping, if it did not conflict with the interests of the *Dial,* to expand the latter section into a thorough coverage of German literary matters and of American literature in Germany.

It was a beginning of which Lowell could be proud, and the press notices (which Carter collected for the cover of the February number) were all highly favorable with the exception of one by N. P. Willis of the *Brother Jonathan,* who took the attitude that it was much too good for the common people who might be expected to support it. "Half a dozen articles" in the first number, he prophesied, "will fall still-born under the notice of the nineteen in twenty of the readers *who pay* for what they read." But Lowell, who knew enough simple arithmetic to realize that after Willis had excepted Poe's story from his general condemnation there were not a half-dozen prose articles left to damn, failed to recognize the good professional judgment that lay beneath Willis' extravagance and probably would have been encouraged by his attitude, had he been given a chance, to seek for further articles of a "very refined and elevated character."

His second number, however, showed that he was moving toward greater refinement and elevation without any encouragement. For it, he had further contributions by Neal, Dwight, Poe, Parsons, and Story (as I. B. Wright), and another critical article, "Song-Writing," by himself; and he added a new visit to "The Hall of Fantasy" by Hawthorne, a long poem by Whittier, some sonnets by G. S. Burleigh, and a "Song" by Henry Peters, the rechristened "Hugh Peters," perhaps, who had contributed to the *Dial* and was better known as James Russell Lowell. The refinement was the result of substituting Hawthorne's sketch for Poe's tale of terror in the January number, and of Story's change from humorously sarcastic art criticism to leaves from a fanciful journal headed "Dream Love." Neal, too, lost some of his vigor in turning from historical portraiture to a more general discourse on "Newspapers." The foreign intelligence from Germany did not materialize, and Lowell's only contribution of poetry under his own name consisted of a sonnet addressed to Mary O. Story, which he had composed during the early summer. The plates were also refined by the substitution of two of Flaxman's "outlines" illustrative of Dante for the fuller engraving of Circe and by the use of an original illustration of Coleridge's "Genevieve" by Story instead of the more detailed historical engraving in the issue before. The editor's older sister Mary Putnam felt that there was a falling-off in quality and began to worry about her brother's judgment.

Lowell came down nearer to earth, pictorially, in preparing for the March number of his magazine by ordering a cheap etching based upon Dickens'

American Notes, but he used Flaxman again for his second plate and arranged for Story to do an article, under his own name, about the artist with whom his readers had become so well acquainted. But before he was able to prepare the issue for the press, his eyes failed him, and he was forced to go to New York for a series of operations by a specialist. He left Boston before he had been able to learn much about the success of Leland and Whiting as promoters, and although he was impressed by the advertising handbills that faced him "everywhere" on the streets he was on tenterhooks of anxiety over "money matters" and the actual sales. Within less than a week, however, he was growing more panic-stricken concerning the contents for the March number. He had not been writing ahead of his deadline in prose, and his portfolio of verse had grown thin from his desire to make a reputation in other periodicals. "*Something* I will send you for the next number," he vowed to Carter on January 15, "besides what I may possibly glean from others." Four days later he had picked up a poem against capital punishment by a new friend, Charles F. Briggs, who wrote under the name of Harry Franco, but he had no "scent" of any prose. Carter would have to collect the copy, and Lowell had little faith in his judgment. "Do not ask any conservatives to write," he begged. Actually, Carter was inviting contributions from a Miss Gray and from Elizabeth Peabody—who frightened Lowell more than a conservative would have, and despite his inability to use his eyes for more than a few minutes a day he demanded to see their articles before they went to press. He sent one of four poems he had just received from Elizabeth Barrett and spoke of reading proof on that and his own "pieces," although he had not yet written them and proofreading put a greater strain on his eyes than composition did. On January 24 he was sure he could write something good about Keats, and he continued promising copy until early February.

The report that Carter planned to make the leading article a "Vision" by Elizabeth Peabody stirred Mary Putnam into writing a frantic letter to her younger brother: she distrusted Miss Peabody's ability to do a leading article for anything and was certain that the prejudice against her name would be an almost insuperable barrier to the success of the *Pioneer.* She wanted Lowell to come to Boston for a few days to take over the editorial responsibility and let Carter finish one of his articles on Japan, Afghanistan, or Animal Magnetism in order to give substance to the number, for she thought that it was a crucial one which should better be late than thin. Lowell sent an excited précis of most of her advice to Carter, promising copy from himself within four days, suggesting the possibility of coming to Boston, and recommending a delay until the middle of March. Mary evidently did not know, and neither young man in his excitement remembered, that the distributors' contract carried a five-hundred-dollar penalty clause for such a delay.

Lowell did not get to Boston and his "copy" consisted of only a single sonnet, "The Street," and a brief poetic "Love Thought." But the issue appeared in full size, with Miss Peabody's "Vision" signed only by her initials and without the article by Miss Gray. William Story had risen splendidly to the crisis, extending his "Dream Love" to almost double the length of its first installment, writing nine pages on John Flaxman, and producing a two-page poem. He contributed, in all, almost a third of the issue. Poe's "Notes upon English Verse" (which was probably intended for three ten-dollar articles of the customary length) ran to ten pages and Hawthorne's "The Birth-Mark" to seven. Parsons had slightly more than a page of verse, and there were two sonnets by Maria White signed "V" and a long letter from Charles Stearns Wheeler in Germany which, unfortunately, duplicated material printed earlier in the *Dial.* It was not necessary to use the offering by Briggs, although Miss Barrett's poem, "The Maiden's Death," of course did appear; and it was possible to cut down the length of the installment of "The Armenian's Daughter" about which nobody seemed to be very enthusiastic. Miss Peabody's vision was classical and related to the plate by Flaxman. The issue, though somewhat ragged, was nothing to be ashamed of. Furthermore, it was ready for the distributors as early as either of the others had been.

By the time the sheets were ready to be "done up" into individual magazines, on or shortly before March 1, Lowell was back in Boston and in difficulties. The first number of the magazine had not been delivered to Leland and Whiting until after Christmas, and their first note for $208.33 did not become due until February 26. When it was presented, they let their period of grace come to an end and then formally refused to pay. Their position was not a good one, for they had already accepted 1,050 copies of the March *Pioneer* and had not only taken the January number after a delay of a week or ten days, but had accepted the second issue as late as February 10. Nevertheless, they did have the clause in their contract penalizing Lowell and Carter five hundred dollars for late delivery and nearly four-fifths of the March copies were still in the hands of the binders. Accordingly, they took the aggressive by getting a writ of attachment against Lowell and Carter for goods to the value of one thousand dollars "or their bodies" and filed an absurd suit for a total of twenty-five hundred dollars (including five hundred dollars for "interest" on "money lent" the young editors). On the next day, March 3, Lowell and Carter got a writ of replevin which ordered the sheriff to seize the subscription books of the *Pioneer* then in the hands of Leland and Whiting, gave a bond signed by Charles Sumner and George S. Hillard to appear in court on the first Tuesday in April, attached the property of Leland and Whiting, and filed suit against them for nonpayment of their note. In retaliation, the publishers purchased a new writ against the editors for the value of three hundred dollars and filed a new suit for two hundred and fifty dollars borrowed by Lowell and Carter on December 26. The *Pioneer* died of the shock, for, although each plaintiff was primarily interested in getting rid of his copies of the magazine to the other, the most valuable property attached by each proved to be the *Pioneer*—forty-one hundred unsold copies of all three issues in the hands of Leland and Whiting, and nineteen hundred and fifty bound and two thousand unbound copies of the March issue in the possession of Lowell and Carter. The most important result of their action was to prevent any sale of the magazine before March 15, when Lowell got his property released from the keeping of a deputy sheriff.

There can be no doubt that Leland and Whiting, in their anxiety to escape from a bad bargain, were willing to kill a magazine which had been puny from the beginning and was growing steadily weaker. The number of unsold copies listed in the inventory of their attached property indicates that with their discounts to agents (amounting to from thirty-three and a third to more than forty per cent of the retail price) they were losing money on their contract, and, although they were supposedly protected against any great eventual loss, they would have been without protection if Lowell and Carter's creditors had become worried and forced the young editors into bankruptcy before the end of six months. They seem to have had genuine financial difficulties at the time, they had every reason to be cautious after the failure of the Boston *Miscellany* only a few weeks before, and they certainly must have realized that the uncertain state of Lowell's eyesight was an added risk to the enterprise. As businessmen, they had every practical reason for getting out of their bargain as ruthlessly as they did.

They may never, in fact, have realized how near the *Pioneer* was to failure at the time they took their drastic action. For Lowell and Carter were more improvident in their editorial business than they were careless about their financial obligations, and it seems hardly possible that they could have got out an April number on schedule even had they been entirely free from trouble with their publishers. Three poems by Elizabeth Barrett, a poem against capital punishment by Charles F. Briggs, a thin and well-picked-over portfolio of Lowell's own verses, and perhaps the continuation of an unsuccessful serial formed the known sum of their literary resources at the time; and there was little that could be added on the spur of the moment to form the substance of a dummy for the next issue. They could undoubtedly depend upon the good nature and energy of William Story, who in any case was planning to continue his "Dream Love" indefinitely; and they had the good will of other contributors, but with the exception of Parsons these were all at a distance, and they had already discounted the coöperation of Poe. Carter had not finished any of the essays he talked so much about, and Lowell's own essays were usually printed near the end of the magazine not because of modesty but because he wrote them while the first sheet was being set up and printed. "Indolence and the Spense negligence" would have been Aunt Sally's explanation of her nephew's failure, as it had been of his troubles in college, although she might have found an excuse for him in the condition of his eyes. But from the most charitable point of view not even Poe appears to have been a more irresponsible editor than the youthful Lowell.

For months afterward he was busy paying the penalty for his misguided ambition. During the April term of the Suffolk County Court he was involved in five different legal actions, but the three suits by Leland and Whiting were postponed in order to give them time to file additional evidence after Lowell and Carter had succeeded in getting their own actions placed first on the calendar and had brought them to a successful conclusion. For Leland and Whiting defaulted on the suit involving the subscription books, and the young editors were awarded the books and one cent damages. In the second suit, over the unpaid note, Lowell and Carter were awarded damages of $338.30 plus costs of $51.39, and the judgment was ordered executed on June 19. The suits against them dragged on through June and were finally brought to trial during the July term of the Court. The first, involving the forfeiture clause in the contract and other penalties claimed by the publishers, was judged a nonsuit and Lowell and Carter were awarded $22.59 for their costs as defendants. The second was entered "neither party" on July 31 on the grounds that Lowell had not signed the two notes by which he and Carter had obtained a loan from their publishers at the beginning of their venture; and the third, against Carter alone, was settled by a technical award of $72.67—the amount of a somewhat inflated-looking bill claimed by Carter as due from the plaintiffs—and $24.93 in costs. Lowell sued again during the same term, but a settlement was probably made out of court, for no judgment is recorded on the index of actions. A settlement of $478.43 would, in fact, have cleared Leland and Whiting of all their legal responsibility; for against Lowell and Carter's claim for $1379.13 due them for 11,033 copies of the *Pioneer* accepted, the two editors had received the judgment for $338.30, a profit of $152.40 from having settled a $250 debt for $97.60, and an obligation of the distributors to pay $410 for the copies of the magazine they had attached. Whether the editors collected anything in an out-of-court settlement is uncertain.

How much Lowell and Carter's actual losses would have amounted to in a final accounting of course depends upon whether or not they reached a settlement with Leland and Whiting and upon how much they realized from the sale of copies of the *Pioneer* which remained in their possession. When Lowell wrote Poe on March 24—nine days after he had recovered his office from the deputy sheriff and before his damage suit had been brought to trial—that he had "incurred a debt of $1800 or more," he was putting the worst possible face on the matter and dramatizing his inability to meet a distressingly small business obligation to a friend in need. His real loss was certainly less. Although he effected certain economies after the first issue by making a more careful estimate of his paper requirements, by using "outlines" less expensive than full engravings for February, and by turning to engravers cheaper than J. Andrews for March, he had an extra printing charge for the second number and ordered one new plate from Andrews which was never used; so that the conservative estimate of $596.12, plus payments to contributors, may stand as the average approximate cost of each issue—that is, a total outlay of something more than $1300 above the amount recovered by court actions. Some copies of the March *Pioneer* were certainly distributed, for copies are extant bearing the imprints of Bradbury and Solden (the former publishers of the *Boston Miscellany*) in Boston and New York, and of Drew and Scammell in Philadelphia. The proceeds from these posthumous sales would have gone to the editors (who had the copies remaining in sheets bound on March 10) and may have reduced their loss by several hundred dollars. The most plausible guess is that the young editors had to divide a deficit of about a thousand dollars between them.

In addition to this they were responsible for payments to contributors but, by all appearances, these did not amount to very much in actual cash. Few magazines in America at this time paid for everything they printed. Young or relatively unknown authors, as Lowell had learned from several years of experiences, were expected to write for public credit rather than for cash until their professional reputations were established; and, among the contributors to the *Pioneer,* W. W. Story, T. W. Parsons, Jones Very, the two Burleighs, and apparently Elizabeth Peabody belonged to this category. The editors and Maria White certainly wrote without pay, and Elizabeth Barrett's contribution may have been a gesture of good will. On the other hand, Hawthorne, Whittier, John Neal, and perhaps J. S. Dwight were professionals to whom Lowell's offer of ten dollars per "article" would have been a minimum rate—although a letter from Neal on November 20, 1842, casually acknowledging that "the quid came safe," indicates that he may have been sent only a single "quid" or five dollars. All told, it is doubtful whether the editors paid out more than seventy-five dollars to their authors while their magazine was alive.

The case of Poe was a particularly unhappy one. Hard up as always, he eagerly volunteered regular contributions as soon as he heard that the magazine was to be established; and Lowell accepted his offer with enthusiasm, giving him "carte blanche for prose or verse" within reasonable limits and promising to make himself "personally responsible" to his contributors if the magazine should fail. Instead of paying Poe for "The Tell-Tale Heart" which he had taken from the files of the *Boston Miscellany*, however, Lowell instructed Peterson to collect ten dollars from Graham and pay it to Poe upon the publication of his own poem "The Moon." Poe acknowledged having "duly received" that amount on February 4, but from a memorandum of his account with Graham it appears that he received credit on an accumulated indebtedness rather than actual cash. In any case, he begged that future remittances be made directly to him. When "Lenore" appeared in the February *Pioneer,* however, Lowell was in New York, and no remittance was made until after Poe was forced to write a reluctant dunning letter in September. Carter immediately responded with five dollars, and after a few weeks delay Lowell sent five dollars more. But there is no evidence that he was ever paid for his "Notes upon English Verse" (which he had originally sold to *Graham's* for thirty-two dollars and then withdrawn for publication in the *Pioneer*) and in later years Lowell could not remember, although he argued somewhat ungraciously, in 1884, that if Poe had not been paid in full Mrs. Clemm would certainly have reminded him of it.

By that time, though, Poe had been dead for nearly thirty-five years; and his biographer, while realizing that Poe was "very considerate" of Lowell's embarrassment during a summer when he was "very poor," did "not think the circumstances need to be made known—few as are the good things that *are* to be said of him."

Whether or not Lowell and Carter divided their indebtedness to other creditors as equally as they divided their obligation to Poe, Lowell took the responsibility for settling the debts of the *Pioneer* and the young men were probably saved from financial disgrace only because one of them bore a creditable name. Some debts were settled promptly on March 3 when Leland and Whiting's suit became public knowledge, others came due and were paid at intervals during the summer, and some were renewed and extended for as long as three years. Dr. Lowell evidently came to the conclusion that it was less expensive to maintain a poet at home than a lawyer and publisher abroad, and in April, 1843, the young man who was—as N. P. Willis put it—"merely a man of genius" closed up his law office, returned to the house in which he was born, and began raising chickens. Carter, apparently, came out to Cambridge with him.

The whole experience was a sobering one for Lowell. He trimmed the long hair and shaved off the Messianic beard which William Page had painted in New York and which was to characterize the familiar image that most of his readers had of him. He stayed out-of-doors with his chickens and in his father's garden as much as possible in order to restore his eyes. And it was a full month before he could lose himself in his own poetry and announce to his friends that he was again "very happy."

Chapter V

FIRST ENGAGEMENTS

"About a fortnight since he began to scribble vigorously and has within that period written about a thousand lines," wrote Robert Carter to Poe on June 19, 1843, in a report on their mutual friend Lowell. One of the new poems, he continued,

> contains nearly four hundred lines I think, and was written in seven or eight hours. At least I left him one day at 11 A.M. and he had concluded to begin it immediately and when I saw him again at 8½ P.M. the same day he read to me upwards of two hundred and fifty lines he had written besides [,] before he began [,] some stanzas of a long poem in ottava rima which has occupied him chiefly for the last two weeks.

In addition, Lowell was to have a new poem in *Graham's* and another in the next *New Mirror*. The long poem scribbled with such extraordinary vigor was "Prometheus" which appeared in the *Democratic Review* for August; the work in ottava rima was "A Legend of Brittany" which served as the mainstay of the 1844 *Poems;* the poem in *Graham's* for August was "In Sadness"; and the contribution to the *New Mirror* for July 1 consisted of three stanzas beginning "There is a haven of sure rest" which were reprinted in the *Anti-Slavery Standard* for September 7 under the title "Forgetfulness." All were different reflections of the melancholy mood which beset Lowell frequently and harassed him more than usual during the weeks following the failure of his magazine.

"In Sadness" was the most conventional of his reflections, for its brooding words on the slowness of fame and the poverty of the poet were reminiscent of his sonnets on Keats and Pierpont, his "Dirge" over the poet, and various earlier expressions of similar self-pity—although in this case there was a new note of consolation in his belief that "High natures must be thunder-scarred With many a searing wrong" in order that the soul might be exercised and greater poetry be drawn from sorrow. In contrast to this, the poem in the *New Mirror* played with the theme of escape into forgetfulness in order to be rid of duty and care, sorrow, and the noise of life. The two longer poems were dramatized expressions of the feelings revealed in the lyrics, the impulse toward martyrdom and the desire for a quiet refuge from the active world. These two emotions seem to have been fairly well balanced in Lowell during the spring of 1843, but the latter was merely temporary. The more lasting impulse toward martyrdom—at least in Lowell's own mind, if not in actuality—was the result of a self-dramatization closely connected with his thoughts about the poet after he had published his "Ode" on that subject. Prometheus, as Lowell conceived him, was a new version of his ideal poet; and his poem was composed with such speed because it represented the culmination of a line of thought revealed in earlier poems and an outburst of emotion that Lowell had for months been keeping under restraint.

Lowell had begun to reconsider his notions about the poet and his place in the world within a month after the publication of his "Ode" in February, 1842, when the *Democratic Review* printed Wordsworth's series of sonnets in defense of capital punishment. The sonnets indirectly raised the question whether it was proper, after all, for the ideal poet to sit "enthronèd" on a mountain top, far above life's "thunder," while "An old man faithless in Humanity" betrayed his divine power over the human heart by showing himself an "atheist" to truth and love. Lowell immediately began to consider it in his own series of six sonnets in reply. Into the true believer, he decided as the basis of his argument, "Life" flows from the "universal Heart" and enables him, "by instinct of God's nature," to achieve "some conquest of the eternal Wo" which mankind suffers. The poet, living above all creeds and sects, is inspired by "A fuller pulse of this all-powerful Beauty" to serve "Truth" because he feels God flowing perpetually "through his breast." Natural poets, however, are rare. One of them appears hardly once in a cycle, and if he sells his birthright "true Culture" will be kept from the "longing soul of man" for another age. For culture, Lowell implied, depended upon poets who moved the hearts rather than minds of men: "By inward sympathy" the world would be won "to the law of meekness, faith, and truth." Yet the worst a poet could do would be to delay the progress of mankind. He could not reverse its direction, because the poet dies when a man begins to strive against freedom: dealing in lies and hate rather than truth and love, he becomes an atheist, whereas the true knower of God perceives an inevitable progress toward perfect goodness. Each "great Soul" looks into the future and foresees the flower of perfection, and each of his successors will see it open further, for no human being will ever witness the infinite blossom which exists "in the forethought of the Eternal One." Yet it is the business of a poet to keep his eyes forever fixed upon the "Endless Promise," accepting as a matter of faith the belief that "Good" lies hidden in the "sin and crime" of the ordinary world.

> His nobleness should be so Godlike high,
> That his least deed is perfect as a star,
> His common look majestic as the sky,
> And all o'erflooded with a light from far,
> Undimmed by clouds of weak mortality.

Although Lowell was not yet ready to admit that a poet should take an active part in a specific reform movement—and it is noticeable that he himself was writing with reference to Wordsworth rather than the capital punishment the English poet defended—he did take a step downward from his mountain top by deciding that the literary value of a poet's sentiments might be determined by their practical effect upon such a specific movement.

His "Ode" had been founded upon principles originally clarified in Carlyle's essay on Burns. His sonnets, based upon essentially the same principles, had acquired a new quality of high-minded social consciousness from his rediscovery of Shelley. Whether he had yet read the recently published *Defense of Poetry* (from which, within the year, he was to take the motto for one of his essays in the *Pioneer*) is uncertain, for the common ideas in his sonnets and Shelley's essay are not sufficiently individual to be conclusive; but the poems, which he had been defending to Peterson within the past few weeks, left unmistakable marks on his sonnets. The imagery and some echo of the philosophy of *Adonais* are both clear. The variety of synonyms which he used to describe the being—or whatever it was, for Lowell himself obviously had not thought precisely upon the matter—that flowed into the poet was borrowed from *Adonais,* and so were the "clouds" of "mortality" and some of the cadences and rhymes of the concluding sonnet. But Lowell, although more willing than he had been to adopt an "easy and Platonic description" for a mystery, had not absorbed intellectually the Platonism of Shelley's poem any more than he had accepted the transcendental theories of being he had found in Carlyle and Emerson. The first of his sonnets against Wordsworth based his argument upon a Platonic theory of knowledge—or at least upon a reasonable facsimile thereof. But the third shifted grounds to the system of Sir James Mackintosh, which taught that the intellect had no motive power in affecting human behavior and that the foundation of ethics was an emotional "sympathy"; and this sympathy was tacitly represented in the succeeding sonnets as widening out to a knowledge of the "Best." The shift was an unconscious result of Lowell's admiration for Platonic language and indifference to its meaning. To Shelley, and usually to Emerson, such words as "Truth," "Beauty," "Light," "Love," and "the Eternal One" were synonyms used to express a single idea. Lowell borrowed their synonymous use for its flashy effect; but when he repeated the individual words with reference to some meaning that lay beneath the surface, they took on conventional meanings quite different from their significance in the vocabulary of Platonism. Beauty became prettiness, the Eternal One became a personal God, and Love became the feeling that made him want to live the rest of his life with Maria. He was to improve somewhat in logic but was always to be a sort of intellectual Della Cruscan.

The silent transition from Plato to Mackintosh in these sonnets resulted only in an indication rather than in a clear revelation of Lowell's settling back into the system of moral philosophy which the Harvard faculty had forced upon him in his boyhood. He was more explicit in another poem, "An Incident in a Rail-Road Car," which he wrote in the same month and published in the same magazine for October. In this effort to give a concrete illustration of the way a poet influenced humanity, Lowell attempted to explain the inspiring effect which a casual reading of Burns had upon the "rude and rough" men in a railroad car. He was clear in his statement that inspiration came from the men's discovery of their own germinal hopes flowering in the words of the poet. These "germs" originally came from God, but in the mass of men they existed merely as a "feeling deep" until they became "Thought" in the breast of the poet. Thus:

> All thoughts that mould the age begin
> Deep down within the primitive soul,
> And, from the Many, slowly upward win
> To One who grasps the whole.

As if this were not clear enough, Lowell added three stanzas, when he prepared the poem for republication in a volume about a year later, in which he attempted to reconcile his own elaboration upon Mackintosh's psychology with a transcendental theory of knowledge and Pope's definition of true wit:

All thought begins in feeling—wide
In the great mass its base is hid,
And, narrowing up to thought, stands glorified,
A moveless pyramid.

Nor is he far astray who deems
That every hope which rises and grows broad
In the World's heart, by ordered impulse streams
From the great heart of God.

God wills, man hopes; in common souls
Hope is but vague and undefined,
Till from the poet's tongue the message rolls
A blessing to his kind.

Such a plausible combination of emotionalism, religiosity, and popularization—if properly supplemented by the current gospel of activity—could have given the "liberal" movement of the nineteenth century the representative poet that it never acquired in early nineteenth-century America. But Lowell, having been helped into his poetic role by the belief that literature was an activity in itself, was not ready to adopt the more common notion of an active life which might have compelled him to look upon himself as a mere inspirer and recorder of other people's activity. When Carlyle, following Dugald Stewart rather than Mackintosh, set thought and action in opposition to each other in *Sartor Resartus,* Lowell had indignantly written in the margin: "Thought *is* action." He was still in this state of mind and while in it proceeded to draw a moral for people who thought otherwise.

It seems probable that by the end of June, Lowell had read *A Defense of Poetry* and that Shelley had suggested to him the possible falsity of the contrast his "Ode" had drawn between the past and the present—that in the "old days of awe and keen-eyed wonder" men had been no quicker than the moderns to exclaim "Behold the Seer!" as soon as they saw a poet. "In the infancy of the world, neither poets themselves nor their auditors are fully aware of the excellence of poetry," Shelley had written, "for it acts in a divine and unapprehended manner, beyond and above consciousness; and it is reserved for future generations to contemplate and measure the mighty cause and effect in all the strength and splendour of their union." This, in any case, was the theme of "The Shepherd of King Admetus," which was dated June 25, 1842, and published in the *Boston Miscellany* for September.

The shepherd was represented as a surpassing wise but generally misunderstood young man, patronized by the king and called "a shiftless youth" and "good-for-naught" by his fellows who "unwittingly" made "his careless word their law." After his death the world became more sweet and full of love because of him, and when he had become a myth, he was recognized as a god. Although the first of the "old poets," he was—except for his slim waist line—very much like a young Boston lawyer who was running in debt for office rent while hoping that he could put into his own songs some thing that would compensate for his present ineffectuality. Even the hope was a little forlorn to Lowell, however, for he felt that from an ideal point of view the pretense of practicing law was a waste of time; and six weeks after he wrote the poem, he confided in Frank Heath that he was in his office "feeling all the while that I am giving the lie to my destiny and wasting time that might be gaining me the love of thousands."

Gradually he became so convinced of the visionary powers of the poet, whatever his contemporaries might think of him, that he allowed himself to be dazzled by the very nebulosity of his bright ideas. "I have got a clue to the whole system of spiritual philosophy," he announced to Loring on September 20:

> I had a revelation last Friday evening. I was at Mary's, and happening to say something of the presence of spirits (of whom, I said, I was often dimly aware) Mr. Putnam entered into an argument with me on spiritual matters. As I was speaking the whole system rose up before me like a vague Destiny looming from the abyss. I never before so clearly felt the spirit of God in me and around me. The whole room seemed to me full of God. The air seemed to waver to and fro with the presence of Something I knew not what. I spoke with the calmness and clearness of a prophet.

Whether Mr. Putnam found him so calm and clear is not recorded. But Lowell himself recalled his words if not as an unheard melody at least as one piped to the spirit in a tone not yet heard with sufficient clarity to be recorded on paper: "I cannot yet tell you what this revelation was. I have not yet studied it enough. But I shall perfect it one day, and then you shall hear and acknowledge its grandeur. It embraces all other systems." When he attributed a somewhat similar experience to Prometheus nine months later, he allowed his titan to explain that whereas the awful shadows or forms that rose around him were "clear-felt at heart," when he "turned to front them" they disappeared as a sort of shudder through the dense stillness of the midnight. Lowell apparently had the same experience when he examined the system that had loomed before him like a vague Destiny from the abyss, for it was never perfected, although the emotional value of the experience remained with him and enlarged his imagination.

He put together the results of his new meditations on the poet—the unrationalized vision, the theory of inspiration implicit in the sonnets on Wordsworth, and his consoling second thought that all poets were without honor in their own times—in the opening sentences of the essay on "The Plays of Thomas Middleton" which he was writing at the end of November:

> Poets are the forerunners and prophets of changes in the moral world. Driven, by their fine nature, to search into and reverently contemplate the universal laws of the soul, they find some fragment of the broken tables of God's laws, and interpret it, half conscious of its mighty import. While philosophers are wrangling, and politicians playing at snapdragon with the destinies of millions, the poet, in the silent deeps of his soul listens to those mysterious pulses which, from one central heart, send life and beauty through the finest veins of the universe, and utters truth to be sneered at, perchance, by contemporaries, but which become religion to posterity.

There was a good deal of Shelley's *Defense* in the essay; and, despite the decision of the editors of the *Pioneer* that their journal would follow Bacon's advice to reform without giving offense to the past, Lowell's representation of his own "radicalism" was very much like that to which Shelley had come after his early period of practical reform. "Progress is Janus-faced," wrote Lowell, borrowing a comparison which Shelley had used for religion and adapting it to the Baconian motto of his magazine, "looking to the bygone as well as to the coming; and Radicalism should not so much busy itself with lopping off the dead or seeming dead limbs, as with clearing away the poisonous rottenness around the roots, from which the tree has drawn the principle of death into its sap." He would have agreed with Shelley (for both young men had studied Mackintosh) that "Ethical science arranges the elements which poetry has created"; and it is quite clear from his essay that he believed with Shelley that the manner in which poetry acted "to produce the moral improvement of man" was by lifting "the veil from the hidden beauty of the world" and making its representations "stand thenceforward in the minds of those who have once contemplated them, as memorials of that gentle and exalted content which extends itself over all thoughts and actions with which it coexists." As Lowell put it:

> A love of the beautiful and harmonious, which must be the guide and forerunner to every onward movement of humanity, is created and cherished more surely by

pointing out what beauty dwells in anything, even the most deformed, (for there is something in that, also, else it could not even *be,*) than by searching out and railing at all the foulness in nature.

He had known, of course, long before he read it in Shelley's *Defense,* that "the great secret of morals is love"; but although he had studied Dugald Stewart's exposition of the connection, he was not ready in his essay to follow Shelley's explanation that the link between beauty and goodness was the imagination—that the sympathy of which he made so much had to be accompanied by an intense imagination (which poetry could stimulate) if it were to comprehend all humanity. For his essay, he preferred the brilliance of Shelley's Platonism and that of Wordsworth's Intimations Ode to the plain light of "common sense" reflected in this section of the *Defense.*

How little this Platonism meant to Lowell emotionally in comparison with its meaning to Shelley may be seen in his attempt to use it for elegiac purposes in his "Elegy on the Death of Dr. Channing" which was written in November, 1842, for the next year's *Liberty Bell.* The poem contains many of the ideas and none of the elevation of *Adonais.* The undying strength of Truth was transfused through the veins of nature in a way that kept it steadfast despite change and death and the temporary triumph of evil until "sovereign Beauty wins the soul at last." No power that ever wrought for Truth could die: it remained fresh after the individual who called it forth had become no more than a name, and what the world called death was not sleeping but a release of Love to soar higher than ever before. But Lowell could not take wings from such philosophy, for it had no substance to him. Channing's spirit was a source of prophecy and inspiration, but, when it beaconed from the abode where the eternal are, it appeared in the form of an orthodox "angel" existing in a "calm divine."

From this unsustained elegy Lowell turned, in December, to the essay on "Song-Writing" for the second number of the *Pioneer* and touched again upon the relationship between the poet and radicalism or reform. "In the inspired heart, not in the philosophic intellect," he wrote, "all true reforms originate, and it is over this that the songwriter has unbridled sway." Thus the song writer—who, like Burns, was a true poet though not necessarily a great one like Milton—was inevitably a reformer because he found a "ready welcome in those homespun, untutored artistic perceptions which are the birthright of every human soul, and which are the sure pledges of the coming greatness and ennoblement of the race." It was this birthright to which he had accused Wordsworth of being false in the sonnets in the

Democratic Review, for the test of a true song was that it touched "no feeling or prejudice or education, but only the simple, original elements of our common nature." Yet by this time Lowell was ready to go a step further: "All poetry must rest on love for a foundation, or it will only last so long as the bad passions it appeals to, and which it is the end of true poesy to root out." The rooting was evidently to be done in a very general way, but the poet was beginning to contemplate moving further down from his mountain top and taking his place in the world.

It was at this point that Lowell's eyes failed him and he practically gave up writing until he commenced the rapid "scribbling" that Carter described to Poe. Nevertheless, he seems to have been able during this period to compose, for the February, 1843, number of the *Democratic Review,* "A Parable" which represented "the Prophet" as acquiring vision at the foot of his mountain. Standing at the foot of the "holy hill," he asked God for a sign and waited for the thunder. Instead, a violet blossomed out of the rock beneath his eyes, and he drew the moral that he had been "hard of heart and blind" to look to the mountain for "the gift of prophecy":

> Had I trusted in my nature,
> And had faith in lowly things,
> Thou thyself would'st then have sought me,
> And set free my spirit's wings.
>
> But I looked for signs and wonders
> That o'er men should give me sway;
> Thirsting to be more than mortal,
> I was even less than clay.

The lesson of his parable was directed against ambition and toward the encouragement of more humility than had hitherto characterized him.

But there were parallel signs that however attracted, intellectually, Lowell may have been to the ideal of self-abasement, he experienced numerous contrary impulses. For he had started another commonplace book or "Private Journal" in which the entries, although undated, reveal something of his general state of mind between the time he began it in 1840 and the middle of 1843 when he incorporated some of its contents in completed poems. He had obviously become interested in blank verse, probably under the influence of the Elizabethan and Jacobean dramatists to whom he devoted so much critical attention during that period, and some of the fragments scattered through this "Private Journal" reveal clearly that he did not always think of himself as a suffering Teufelsdröckh or a neglected Apollo:

there were times when again he strutted around in his own mind like Bussy D'Ambois or Chapman's other heroes of impatient merit who took their spurns so defiantly. As boldly as Chapman, if not aloud, he spoke out in one entry:

> There is life enough
> In this wild heart to fill a thousand such
> As we meet every day.

On another occasion he exclaimed:

> Oh God! God!
> I could blaspheme as if this poor weak tongue
> Could in its insect bitterness outvoice
> Thy loudest thunder and as if this hand
> So fiercely doth my spirit stir my breast
> Could pluck black fate and stay the eternal wheels
> Of all things and shake heaven.

Such outbursts were not necessarily the expressions of James Russell Lowell in his own proper person: he worked other lines from his journal, expressing similar sentiments, into his poems on Prometheus, Cromwell, and Columbus. Yet it was the mood of Lowell as expressed in these lines that led to the creation of these characters and, through them, the gradual transference of the attribute of prophecy from the poet to the man of action.

II

THE TRANSFER was preliminary to Lowell's first major literary engagement upon the field of reform. The engagement began in his own mind when he mailed "Prometheus" to the *Democratic Review* on June 15, 1843, and described it to Loring on the same day as a poem representing "the Greek archetype of St. Simeon Stylites, the first reformer and locofoco of the Greek Mythology." He had high hopes for it, both from a professional point of view and from his new desire to be influential in a particular way: "It is the longest and best poem I have ever written, and over-running with true radicalism and antislavery. I think that it will open the eyes of some folk and make them *think* that I am a poet, whatever they may say." By creating Prometheus he had achieved a catharsis of his own feeling of impotence, and, after a reference to his poem in *ottava rima,* he added:

> I feel much more assured every day that I shall yet do something that will keep my name (and perhaps my body) alive. My wings were never so light and strong

as now. So hurrah for a niche and a laurel! I have set about making myself ambitious. It is the only way to climb well. Men yield more readily to an ambitious man—provided he can bear it out by deeds. Just as much as we claim the world gives us, and posterity has enough to do in nailing the base coin to the counter. But I only mean to use my ambition as a staff to my love of freedom and man. I *will* have power and there's the end of it. I have a right to it, too, and you see I have put the crown on already.

"I was never so happy as now," he began the next paragraph.

Lowell thought that he had at last succeeded in throwing off the curse of belonging to some literary "school" and had achieved something that was not only original but prophetic of a new poetry for the future. Although Goethe, Byron, and Shelley had handled the subject of Prometheus in modern times, he wrote Briggs on August 9, he had "looked at it from a somewhat new point of view":

I have made it *Radical,* and I believe that no poet in this age can write much that is good unless he give himself up to this tendency. For Radicalism has now for the first time taken a distinctive and acknowledged shape of its own. So much of its spirit as poets in former ages have attained (and from their purer organization they could not fail of some) was by instinct rather than by reason. It has never till now been seen to be one of the two great wings that upbear the universe.

Lowell's recent rereading of Shelley's poetry had obviously been from his Galignani edition which did not contain Mary Shelley's notes on the allegory of *Prometheus Unbound,* and he had failed to note the word "solely" in the sentence from the author's own preface which said: "But it is a mistake to suppose that I dedicate my poetical compositions solely to the direct enforcement of reform, or that I consider them in any degree as containing a reasoned system on the theory of human life." The lack of curiosity that enabled Lowell to read through Spenser at least twice with apparently a complete indifference to the hidden meanings in *The Faerie Queene* would easily have permitted him to read *Prometheus Unbound* without finding much more radicalism in it than was observable in Aeschylus' drama, for the Greek representation of the prophet kicking against the pricks was more in keeping with his current mood than was Shelley's patient hero. In fact, the Prometheus of Aeschylus, who had drawn knowledge from his mother earth, who was tortured for having had too great a reverence for humanity, and who was able to endure his restraint from activity only by keeping his eyes fixed upon the promise of the future, was almost an ideal prototype for Lowell's new conception of the poet.

Lowell kept the pattern of the Aeschylean myth although he was no longer inclined to stress the notion of drawing wisdom from nature, either by a recognition of "correspondences" or by any other means. His "radical" Prometheus was entirely the product of his thinking after his sonnets for the *Dial* and after his "Ode." It epitomized—against the background of the defiant emotion revealed in his "Private Journal"—the ideas expressed in the various poems written during the preceding year. As Prometheus characterized himself in his dramatic monologue, he revealed the uncompromising character that Lowell, in his sonnets, criticized Wordsworth for not possessing. He believed, with the author of "An Incident in a Rail-Road Car," that knowledge had its source in the heart, for it was his "wise heart" that enabled him to "foreknow" the "end and doom of all." With the wisdom of the poem "In Sadness," however, the titan realized that wisdom did not come to the inexperienced: it was his "immortal woe" that had made his "heart" a "seer." Like the author of the "Elegy on the Death of Dr. Channing," he knew that peace was stronger than war, for in one of his figures of speech he pointed out that the "invincible tenderness of Peace" was more powerful than the mightiest thunderbolts of Jove, and he looked upon the simple joys of everyday life as the "bloodless daggers" with which men destroyed tyrants who had already fallen victims to the discovery that the bonds of tyranny were ropes of sand which could be broken by "the thought of some great spirit" taking hold of the "hearts of men." Prometheus also understood the meaning of "A Parable" that taught trust in one's own nature and in lowly simple things, and he realized that the "master-spirits" who passed such doctrines on would, like "The Shepherd of King Admetus," have their words eventually become "part of the necessary air men breathe." Swelled up to titanic proportions, Prometheus was the sum of all Lowell's imaginary poets.

This new impersonation of the poet on the mountain top was bound to his peak by force, but Lowell, who had been almost ready to say that a "Maker" did not belong so high above the world, did not develop the radical elements implicit in this part of his myth. His Prometheus was not being restrained from threatened activity but, as in the original, was being punished for past actions; and there is no suggestion in the poem that the world would be better off if this type of poet, whose nature was wise from "finding in itself the types of all" men, were released and permitted to take part again in human affairs. Lowell was still holding, however loosely, to the attitude expressed in his marginal annotation in *Sartor Resartus:* "Thought *is* action." The only other proper activity he attributed to the poet was spiritual martyrdom of the sort he had described as "The Fiery Trial" in his sonnet to Pierpont and had reflected in the self-pitying sentiment of his sonnet "To the Spirit of Keats." Lowell had grown more self-conscious about this somewhat maudlin side of his own disposition, for he made Prometheus disavow "that hunger after fame" which besets "souls of a half-greatness" and boast that in resisting the desire for fame he had braved something more powerful than his tormentor. Yet he taunted Jove with the loneliness of oblivion in contrast to his own assurance of a posthumous fame that would make him "a power and a memory" and a "name to fright all tyrants," and he defied the god to destroy him and thus set free his "essence" to become part of that spirit which forever dwelt in "man's deep heart" and scattered hopes that would grow to be "A roof for freedom in all coming time." This gloating anticipation of future influence and the self-pity of the titan's references to the ages of immolation yet in store for him are more thoroughly elaborated and more impressive than the disavowal of a desire for fame: Lowell, although ready to admit in this poem that the world was so constituted that "Evil its errand hath, as well as Good," was still inclined to think it especially deplorable that poets should be forced to suffer the slings and arrows of outrageous fortune.

Prometheus, as a type of "radical" poet, was active in mind and, by necessity of the myth which Lowell voluntarily adopted, passive in behavior; and even his kicking against the pricks was the result of resentment rather than a desire for action. Yet his monologue is colored by some suggestion of that vision of the active life that moved Tennyson's Ulysses. For despite the definite link in Lowell's "Private Journal" between his blank verse poems of 1843 and the Elizabethan drama, there can be little doubt but that publication of Tennyson's 1842 *Poems* had a stimulating influence upon his actual composition of "Prometheus." Although the poem contains several figures of speech that recall *Adonais* and "An Ode to the West Wind," some imagery reminiscent of "The Eve of St. Agnes" and "An Ode on a Grecian Urn," and the sort of suggestion of Coleridge that had become commonplace in Lowell's verse, the prevailing literary influence noticeable in it is that of the author of "Ulysses," the "Morte d'Arthur," and, in one place, "Sir Galahad." The opening and two concluding verse paragraphs of Lowell's poem give the same suggestion, in their visual imagery, of a misty-eyed Keats that is to be found in the "Morte d'Arthur" and have something of the same tone of resigned and philosophical optimism. And the doctrine of

Keats's Oceanus (which Lowell, incidentally, had noted in his early commonplace book as having been derived by Sir Charles Blount from Aristotle) that the "first in beauty should be first in might" gave way to a Tennysonian "higher purity is greater strength" as a justification for a prophecy of the eventual overthrow of Jove. But the new poem by Tennyson which evidently fascinated Lowell and from which he could not escape was "Ulysses." Prometheus had undoubtedly learned from Ulysses

> that the memory of noble deeds
> Cries shame upon the idle and the vile,
> And keeps the heart of Man forever up
> To the heroic level of old time;

and Ulysses probably suggested to him that his wrongs represented experiences from which his revenge, he said,

> builds a triumphal arch,
> Through which I see a sceptre and a throne.

He reversed the experience of Tennyson's hero by having already communed with "eternal silence" and expecting to become a "name" in the future; but these and other verbal echoes of the earlier work—and the sonorous blank verse which was new to Lowell's pen—indicate that the bound Prometheus had more in common with the roaming Ulysses than his creator probably realized.

Lowell had hardly finished "Prometheus" before he began for the next number of the *Democratic Review* another poem in the same verse and in a similar spirit which he described as being "still more radical than Prometheus, and in some respects better, though, from its subject, incapable of so high a strain as that." The subject was Cromwell, about whom he had thought of writing "a sort of dramatic poem" as early as September 22, 1838. "A Glance behind the Curtain," however, was not dramatic but a continuation of the manner of "Prometheus," so close to it in certain qualities that some of the scattered passages in the "Private Journal" which were used for one poem might easily have been designed for the other. Lowell concluded his poem by calling Cromwell "One of the few that have a right to rank With the true Makers," but the closeness of the connection he made between his representation of this hero and his conception of the poet is most evident in a mutilated section of the journal in which parts of the poem were originally composed. The first version of the twenty-one lines beginning "And, for success, I ask no more than this," for example, develops the theme of bearing "unflinching witness to the truth" and concludes with words almost identical with those published:

Get but the truth once spoken, and 'tis like
A star newborn, that drops into its place,
And which, once circling in its placid round,
Not all the tumult of the world can shake.

The continuing paragraph in the manuscript evidently expresses Lowell's first notion of the way to get the truth spoken:

So do nought else but garner every hour
My golden harvest of sweet memories
And count my boundless revenues of smiles
And happy looks and words so kind and gentle
That each doth seem to give thy love anew
Content to let my waveless soul flow on
Reflecting but the blossoms on its marge
And thy clear spirit bending like a sky
O'er me . . .

These are the words of the poet who had fallen back into the mood which, in 1841, had caused him to write a sonnet to Maria describing how he had found in "The Haven" she provided a quiet "love that makes things common rare" and thereby enabled him to see more clearly the "calm, vast presence of Eternity." The same mood was upon him when he wrote "A Reverie" for the October number of *Graham's:* his longings after freedom, his love of human kind, and the vague yearnings of his undirected mind, all "find safe fulfilment" in the love of the sweetheart of whom he thinks as he loiters through the moonlight. But he removed these lines from "A Glance Behind the Curtain," and when he used them, in a slightly revised form, for "L'Envoi" in the 1844 *Poems,* he introduced them as description of "barren" joy rather than as an illustration of the way to achieve success. The earlier lines on success and outspoken truth which he retained in his narrative poem were placed in a different context entirely. Cromwell uttered them as the foundation of his decision not to emigrate to New England. The way to get truth uttered was not to garner sweet memories for poetic purposes but to seize "the great chance of setting England free." Affected like Prometheus by the new spirit of Tennyson, Cromwell revolted against inaction with a decision that "an hour" of activity in England was to be preferred to "a cycle of New England sloth." The passive poet of the "Private Journal" had become the man of action in the pages of the *Review.*

The man of action retained a good many characteristics of the ideal poet, however, for Lowell's Cromwell was as far removed from the historical character as Daniel Neal's legend on which the poem was based was removed from historical fact. His hero was as unconventional a Puritan as Mrs. Anne Hutchinson. His action was determined by the whispers to his "inner ear" from his soul in "that inward voice which never yet Spake falsely," and he expressed an entirely un-Calvinistic trust in what was "called for by the instinct of mankind." He had the consoling belief which Lowell's poet had so frequently expressed that "The future works out great men's destinies" whereas "common souls" were the clay "wherein the footprints of their age" were left "petrified forever." He had no doubt that God's increasing purpose ran through the ages, and knowing

that God brings round
His purposes in ways undreamed by us,
And makes the wicked but His instruments
To hasten their own swift and sadden fall,

he determined to act upon the principle that "New times demand new measures and new men" and upon the realization that truth is not absolute but something which grows as the world "advances." As for his own philosophy of behavior, it was a combination of Tennyson and Carlyle:

We cannot hale Utopia on by force;
But better, almost, be at work in sin,
Than in a brute inaction browse and sleep.
No man is born into the world whose work
Is not born with him; there is always work,
And tools to work withal, for those who will;
And blessed are the horny hands of toil!

And if he had to choose between the tendency toward compromise found in the former and the radicalism of the latter, he made his choice in a passage which expressed the sentiments of *Sartor Resartus* in a parody of the language of Tennyson's Arthur:

there is more force in names
Than most men dream of; and a lie may keep
Its throne a whole age longer, if it skulk
Behind the shield of some fair-seeming name.

"Men in earnest have no time to waste," exclaimed the outspoken hero, "in patching fig-leaves for the naked truth." Of the sufferings that Lowell had portrayed in his sonnet to Pierpont and to which he had referred again in his "Elegy" on Channing and in "Prometheus," Cromwell was impatient: they were "mean and buzzing grievances" and "petty martyrdoms." Yet he understood how people could endure them because they—the poets—had within them the "same prophecy" or "inward feeling of the glorious end" that inspired him to stay in England and become one who ranked with "the true Makers" and the friend of John Milton—

> A man not second among those who lived
> To show us that the poet's lyre demands
> An arm of tougher sinew than the sword.

In the character of Cromwell, Lowell united his poet with the man of action, and the radicalism of the man who translated the poet's dreams into military campaigns apparently encouraged him to try his own sinews by striking his lyre to some practical purpose.

He began with an occasional poem with a Wordsworthian title: "Stanzas Sung at the Anti-Slavery Picnic in Dedham, on the Anniversary of West-India Emancipation, August 1, 1843." Is it true Freedom, he asked, to be free from one's own bonds while others are in chains? The question was entirely rhetorical: the men and women of New England were not truly free so long as they kept silent and were unwilling to suffer hatred, scoffing, and abuse in order to be "In the right with two or three." In his poems for the general public, however, Lowell was less outspoken in his abolitionism—for most of his poems that had served the anti-slavery cause up to this time owed their significance more to the context in which they appeared than to Lowell's own words, which were considerably less forthright than those of Longfellow in the poems that Lowell criticized as lacking in "force." His abolitionist sentiments were rather diffuse, for example, in "The Fatherland" published in the *Democratic Review* for October. The poem was an imitation in metrical form and in some of its lines almost a translation of Ernst Moritz Arndt's "Des Deutschen Vaterland," but it was also a criticism of Arndt from the point of view that Heinrich Heine had taken in his *Letters* toward German nationalism and some of the German patriotic poets. Lowell's poem was not merely anti-provincial but anti-national. A "true man's fatherland" should be broader than his native country and more wide-spread than all the land of freedom: it should include all places inhabited by the human spirit, whether in joy or sorrow, and especially any spot of earth wherever a "slave doth pine." In the spirit of Tom Paine, Lowell was adopting the slaveholding South as his province of active reform.

He did not, however, move directly in. His next poem to take up directly the anti-slavery cause was "A Chippewa Legend," contributed to the *Liberty Bell* for 1844 and probably written about the time "The Fatherland" was published. The legend itself was a moral narrative of two Indians who had decided that they were not their brother's keeper, but Lowell was specific in pointing out that his story had "an inward sense" relative to the "poor, the outcast, and the trodden-down" who were bequeathed to the love and care of their more fortunate brethren by "our dear Father, in his Testament"—particularly, of course, by the implication of Christ's words in the Olivet discourse. Tactfully he made the application first to England, threatening her, in the spirit of his earlier poem "Merry England" with a volcano-like eruption of the "pent-up wrath" from her "starving millions" who were not only being deprived of their "body's bread" but of the "bread of life" while a great land was playing off its "empty farce Of Queenship to outface a grinning world." When he turned to his own country, whose charge it was to be "Freedom's apostle to a trampled world," he was less violent: although he could "hear the loathsome serpent hiss" over the ruins of the Capitol and see "those outcast millions turned to wolves" unless something were done about the "ugly sin" of three million slaves, he spoke more in sorrow than in anger. He was sure that the wrong could be conquered:

Serener thoughts
Befit the heart which can, unswerved, believe
That Wrong already feels itself o'ercome,
If but one soul hath strength to see the right,
Or one free tongue dare speak it.

Wrapping himself in the new-styled mantle of his ideal poet until he became oblivious of Pierpont and Whittier and Longfellow, Lowell was, in effect, announcing that he was about to become the Milton of the abolitionist cause.

It was in this spirit that he revised his "Ode" on the poet for publication in his new collection of verses, adding eight extra lines to each of its three sections. One addition followed the first two quatrains of the original version and expressed a "faith in holy sorrow" as Lowell had learned to value it before writing "In Sadness" and "Prometheus." Another, which preceded the last two quatrains of the second part, reflected the spirit of the Dedham "Stanzas" and "The Fatherland" by an expression of need for "martyrs and apostles" wherever there was a shadow of wrong and introduced the idea of progressive evolution toward the right that had appeared in the sonnets on Wordsworth and in the concept of radicalism dominating the *Pioneer*. The last addition provided an entirely new conclusion to the description of the ideal poet "for whom the world is waiting" by representing him as one

> Who feels that God's and Heaven's great deeps are nearer
> Him to whose heart his fellow-man is nigh,
> Who doth not hold his soul's own freedom dearer
> Than that of all his brethren, low or high;
> Who to the right can feel himself the truer
> For being gently patient with the wrong,
> Who sees a brother in the evildoer,
> And finds in Love the heart's-blood of his song.

In this final version of the "Ode" Lowell's poet, while not completely abandoning his mountain top, bent down considerably closer to his fellow man. The "Love" that kept him from being a "metaphysical impossibility" as a poet had become more actively humanitarian than it had been two years before. Such aggressive campaigners in behalf of humanity as Pierpont and Whittier might not have recognized in the author of these poems a new recruit to their cause, but Lowell was imaginatively involved with them. He had adopted the role of a poet who was sufficiently a part of the world to be heroic as well as high-minded in the interest of mankind.

III

ALTHOUGH LOWELL had committed himself to becoming a man of poetic action, he knew that he would have to conquer the public before he could be of any use in any role. Accordingly, he waited anxiously for the popular reaction to his new "radical" poetry. "My Prometheus has not received a single public notice yet," he wrote Briggs, "though I think it the best thing I have done, and though I have been puffed to repletion for poems without a tithe of its merit." But except for appreciative letters from Briggs, William Page, and Charles J. Peterson, "Prometheus" received little notice of any sort and "A Glance Behind the Curtain" none at all. He had sent only two poems to *Graham's* during that period, and only three to the *Democratic Review*. These, with the single poem printed in both the *New Mirror* and in the *Anti-Slavery Standard*, were not enough to keep him in the public eye. Nor did he receive his customary diet of editorial flattery. Griswold was not one of his particular admirers and Graham was careless about his correspondence, and O'Sullivan, while paying him twenty dollars for "Prometheus," had no regard for tender feelings. "Among other things it is not the least provoking to write for a man who neither appreciates me nor the tendency of my poetry, nor the true worth of any real poetry," Lowell confided in Briggs, shortly after O'Sullivan had accepted the poem on Cromwell—perhaps without paying any more for it than he had paid for "Prometheus." The editor of the *New Mirror* had been complimentary enough, but with an almost insulting air of giving an unknown amateur a pat on the back. Lowell needed attention in order to get back in the professional groove, and since Poe's intention to puff him in his *Stylus* had fallen through and Graham was showing no activity in printing the article on Lowell that he was supposed to be planning, there was nothing to do except publish a new volume of poems.

Lowell had the material for a substantial new volume in the large quantity of magazine verse he had published since *A Year's Life* and in the narrative poem in *ottava rima* which was too good to waste, although his new interest in reform and radicalism had dominated the escapist mood that produced it and left its author without much enthusiasm for his brain child. He had no resources for financing a book, for debts from the *Pioneer* were hanging over his head and his father (who had never recovered from the losses suffered through Charles) was using his own credit to save his son from bankruptcy. John Owen seemed eager to publish the collection there in Cambridge, however, and while doubtful about the "speculation" involved entered into a "treaty" with Lowell to do so. Throughout the autumn of 1843, Lowell was living at Elmwood and working on his new volume, which was published just in time, apparently, for the local New Year's trade. It seems to have occurred to neither publisher nor author that it might be good business to attempt the Christmas market outside New England; and they printed only about five hundred copies, although Owen had enough hope for the book to have it stereotyped.

The new volume contained thirty-five poems and thirty-seven sonnets. Fifteen of the poems and twenty-seven of the sonnets, forming more than half the substance of the book, had not been printed before; and, as a group, these new compositions show that, while appearing in magazines in a progressively active role, Lowell was dominated by his escapist inclinations during a considerable part of the time spent in his study. The longest of the poems, "A Legend of Brittany" in one hundred and eighteen *ottava rima* stanzas, was not only a medieval narrative but so far as it had a moral it was a sermon against ambition—against the love of power to which Lowell had confessed in his letter of June 15 to Loring, although it distinguished between the desire for power for its own sake and the ambition to do good which Lowell professed. It told the story of a maiden named Margaret who was dominated in will, seduced, and finally murdered by Modred, a Knight Templar, who first fell under the influence of her innocent beauty, then yielded to his desire to be master of all he surveyed, and was forced by his own ruling passion to destroy her because her condition endangered his chances of becoming head of his celibate order. Having hidden her body beneath the altar in the church, Modred fell victim to an inner compulsion which made him remain near the corpse and form a part of the congregation which witnessed the miracle of Margaret's singing until her unborn child was baptised. When the spectators turned toward the villain, they discovered that his "loathing spirit had spurned off the clay" and left it "stark and cold," overcome by its remorse.

"A Legend of Brittany," as a retelling of on old story with Coleridgean overtones, was the most careful piece of narrative fiction that Lowell had yet attempted. The story was entirely removed from his own time and environment. Modred was a villain who belonged in a Jacobean drama, and his characterization was reminiscent of Coleridge's *Remorse*. The verse form was that used by Boccaccio for a somewhat similar romance and was almost entirely free from any signs of the Byronic quality that appeared in the same stanza as Lowell used it for contemporary allusions in his *Class Poem*. The verse itself was closer to Spenser and to the Spenserian verse of Keats, in cadence and in imagery, than anything that the author had yet done even in the occasional poems that might have been imitations of Spenser. There would be considerable justice in describing it as "pure romance," produced in a mood of escape from the material interests and practical concerns that beset Lowell before he began it and continued to occupy his mind from time to time as he wrote.

But if Lowell was writing fiction, he was drawing upon his own past and immediate experience to give it life; and in some respects "A Legend of Brittany" was a more intimate, personal poem than "Prometheus," "A Glance Behind the Curtain," and other magazine verses that were positively concerned with the personal question of the poet's relationship to the world of action. A man who is placing himself before the public is likely to strike a pose. One who is posing a dummy may give it more of his own attributes than he realizes. It does not destroy the fiction to say that Lowell and Maria might have discussed Modred and Margaret and said "There, but for the grace of God, go we." Lowell had believed himself blasted by excessive ambition in his early youth, and, having "set about" making himself ambitious in a deliberate effort to gain "power," he was naturally inclined to dwell upon the pitfalls that might lie before him. Some of his comments upon his friend Story a year before had revealed how solemnly he took a poet's obligation to live up to his noble utterances and how sensitive he was to an attitude of cynicism in private, and high-mindedness before the world. His more recent acquaintance with N. P. Willis also had probably given him something to brood about. If a willingness to give the public what it wanted was the secret of success, Lowell was living at Elmwood, unable to afford the moderate expense of a visit to New York, because he had been too virtuous to succeed. Yet he was a nimble-witted young man whose personal relationships flourished, and he could have had few doubts but that if he limited his ambition to a sufficiently narrow end he could achieve it with ease. That was his tempation and Modred's tragic flaw. In the interest of his "self-blinded" willingness to take "Ambition's meanest footstool for a throne" Modred had entered upon a career of "steady fraud to keep his soul at bay" until all his noble "instincts" gave way to his love for power for its own sake. Lowell moralized about it with unmistakable reference to his own situation as he had described it in the letter to Loring:

> A healthy love of power thaws the ice
> Wherewith sloth fetters oft the gushing will;
> But when the soul lusts after it, no vice
> Is half so deadly.

This was the lust of Modred for Margaret, first for her heart and then for control over her body—as Lowell made clear,

> not for the glut of sense,
> But to enjoy his mastery to the core,
> And probe the depth of his bad influence;
> Such hunger gnawed him and such fierce unrest,
> As one who hath a serpent in his breast.

After Modred had gained his end, the story of murder and remorse was that which Lowell had already told in "Rosaline" until the scene in the church when Margaret's voice sings of the superiority of the spirit to the body and of hope for Modred after he learns from ages in purgatory that "faith is but ambition purified." While Lowell was convincing himself that it was the poet's business to take a more active part in life, he became so subtly preoccupied with his problem that even his purest "romance" evolved into an exhibition of one of the dangers that threatened the course he was planning to take.

These passages that reveal most clearly Lowell's personal preoccupation with the dangers of ambition were all removed from the 1849 (and final) version of the poem, but the author left enough of the original to make clear to well-informed readers of his collected works that a personal application was in his mind as he wrote. His characterization of Margaret is particularly illuminating. The images that he had applied to Maria in so many poems converged on her. She dwelt in a bright region "far aloof from earth's eternal moan" and was full of the quiet wisdom of nature. Her being was like "A new-made star that swims the lonely gloom." Her purity encircled her "like adamantine mail," and gentleness dropped from her "sky-like spirit" like "a sunlit fall of rain." And her love—like all true love, as Lowell observed in an old poem first printed in this volume—was an "humble" thing. She even discovered her emotion in a place where a brook had sung itself to sleep scooping a "well To please the fairy folk" which may not have been unlike the "fairy well" before which James and Maria had plighted their troth. However much of a not-impossible self Lowell put into, and later removed from, the character of Modred, he drew his heroine from the Maria he had so often portrayed to the world. Lowell's additions to his "grim chronicle" suggest that in some corner of his mind there lurked a conception of his story as an exaggerated, melodramatic warning against what might happen if he did not give his new ambition for power a proper direction.

The other new legendary poem in the 1844 volume dramatized a similar warning. Rhoecus, like Modred, wounded an "humble" thing—in this case, the messenger of love rather than love itself—and was left alone with remorse. Lowell afterwards revised "Rhoecus" as he revised "A Legend of Brittany" by eliminating the personal application and leaving it as a sort of moralized parody in which the hamadryad murmurs, in effect, "as ye have done it to the least of nature's works, ye have done it unto me." Originally it was much clearer and much more closely related to his own problem. His concluding interpretation of the allegory made it the story of youth which shaped its noble ends until it gained, by "haply wandering into some good deed," a momentary sight of "Truth."

> Then the sly world runs up to us and smiles,
> And takes us by the hand and cries, "Well met!

Come play with me at dice; one lucky throw,
And all my power and glory shall be thine;
Stake but thy heart upon the other side!"

The messenger came from "Truth" which would never let alone the heart that once had sought her but might be ignored by one "all fresh and burning in the game" of active life until "just too late." The final moral of "Rhoecus" was connected more precisely than that of the longer poem to the verses on the poet which Lowell was publishing in the magazines:

And so, instead of lightening by our lives
The general burden of our drooping kind—
Instead of being, as all true men may,
With grateful reverence as men who talked
With spirits, and the dreaded secret wrung
From out the loath lips of the sphinx of life,—
Instead of being named in aftertime
Part of the memory of all great deeds,
The inspiration of all time to come,
We linger to our graves with empty hearts,
And add our little handful to the soil
As valueless and frail as fallen leaves.

Lowell was warning himself not to allow his impulse toward activity and his ambition for power to become too worldly. He should not place his heart in hazard for power, not only because an exchange would be a bad bargain, as Modred learned, but because he might lose both and be left, as the Greeks in the legendary wisdom realized, completely forlorn.

Most of the other poems first published in the 1844 volume are lyrics either addressed to Maria or somewhat tenuously related to the ideas and attitudes expressed more explicitly in verses published in magazines. Lowell went back to 1840 for the blank-verse "Love" which had drawn too sharp and clear a contrast between his boyish affairs for publication in *A Year's Life,* and he also used a sonnet of the same year which paid tribute to the serene passage of Anna Cabot Lowell "Through suffering and sorrow" and had probably been omitted from his first collection because the memory of Charles's failure had then been too fresh to be mentioned. A few other sonnets published for the first time were tributes to individuals: "Full many noble friends my soul hath known," obviously written when the fury for Shakespeare's sonnets was upon him, expressed his devotion to the little "Band" of young people whose discovery of "nobility" in his "humblest verses writ and read for love" and whose "burning words of high democracy" had an influence upon his work that cannot be measured. The sonnets "Wendell Phillips" and "To J. R. Giddings" were his most direct and specific abolitionist verses up to that time. Phillips had heard the hissing of the "serpent" to which Lowell had referred in "A Chippewa Legend" and had behaved as Lowell had said in his Dedham "Stanzas" all men should behave:

> he went
> And humbly joined him to the weaker part,
> Fanatic named, and fool, yet well content
> So he could be the nearer to God's heart
> And feel its solemn pulses sending blood
> Through all the wide-spread veins of endless good.

Giddings, though not so perfect a representative of the ideal poet in action, was memorable as one who had used his tongue and pen as a freeman should; and Lowell's memorial to him, the concluding sonnet in his book, is remarkable as the first poem in which he abandoned periphrasis and indirection and used the word "Negro" in connection with his pleas for "Freedom" and "the Right." But these are exceptions to the general rule that the new poems in the 1844 volume represented Lowell more clearly as a lover admiring his sweetheart, worrying about her frailness, and distressed by absences from her, than as a man concerned with social reform.

Lowell brought the lover and the reformer together in "L'Envoi" addressed to Maria. "Less of that feeling, which the world calls love," he told her, would be found in his new volume than in the unripe firstlings of his muse which he had published too hastily three years before; but there was more of something that had grown out of his love for her—a "love of God, of Freedom, and of Man." This she would approve, for she was not one of those "niggard souls" who believed that poetry should "jingle words" and "string sweet sorrows" in order to "hide the bareness of unfurnished hearts" or to "prate about the surfaces of things."

> The day has long gone by wherein 'twas thought
> That men were greater poets, inasmuch
> As they were more unlike their fellow-men:
> The poet sees beyond, but dwells among,
> The wearing turmoil of our work-day life;
> His heart not differs from another heart,
> But rather in itself enfolds the whole
> Felt by the hearts about him, high or low,
> Hath deeper sympathies and clearer sight
> And is more like a human heart than all.

There was a theory abroad that a great land such as America should produce great poetry under the influence of her rocks and woods; but nature was not necessary to teach poets how to sing, and her outward shows seemed "small and worthless, and contemptible" in comparison with the "realities" of those central thoughts which various nations had to express for all people:

> Our country hath a gospel of her own
> To preach and practice before all the world,—
> The freedom and divinity of man,
> The glorious claims of human brotherhood.

" 'Tis the soul only that is national" and the true patriot is one who is loyal to his soul alone, he concluded, and it was his weakness that he could not be true either to those he loved or to himself—yet he had been "most true" to her and somehow hoped that having been true "in one thing" he could be "as true in all." There is some suggestion in all this that Lowell made no clear distinction between what Emerson described as being "born into the great, the universal mind" and doing exactly what Maria wanted.

The quality of dependence that makes so much of Lowell's poetry seem lacking in force and his more vigorous verses often appear theatrical is clearly revealed in the previously unpublished sonnets of the new volume. One of the earliest, "What were I, Love, if I were stript of thee," reveals that he had felt such dependence clearly in 1841 when he still believed in the primary importance of "nature's teachings," for such teachings would be entirely "fruitless" without her. In "Impatience and Reproof," written in the same year, he attributed his escape from periods of "weariness of soul" and shaken faith in man to "great, inborn thoughts" that thundered within him; but it is clear that on a majority of the occasions when he felt impelled to express such matters in verse he was inclined to look upon Maria as the lightning which brought about the thunder. As he put it in a different figure of speech in his sonnet "On My Twenty-Fourth Birth-Day, February 22, 1843," the cloudy doubts of his boyish days had been dispelled by "Love's sun" which had filled his soul with splendor and enabled Hope to become Power, Wish to harden into Will, and Longing to grow into Certainty. These notions were not mere fancies versified into conventional love poetry. Actually, the qualities of power, determination, and certainty he had acquired were emotional rather than intellectual and therefore less evident to other people, but the circumstances under which he was to lose them reveal how clearly he had identified their source. Purposefully during the latter part of 1843 and somewhat less consciously in the poems written the year before, Lowell was informing the public of his growing intention, as a poet, to take a more active part in the life of his time. His allegories of doubt and self-warning, he somehow felt, had not been appropriate to the periodical press, and he had reserved them as the mainstays for his new volume of poems. But in filling out the volume he made use of a few verses that disclose how the gentle Maria took the poet by the hand and led him down from the safety of his mountain top, through the shadows of his many doubts, and to the edge of the world's broad field of battle in which she was to engage him.

By adding to his "Ode" and "An Incident in a Rail-Road Car," by condensing "A Dirge" and "A Fantasy," and by making a few other revisions in the latter two poems and in "The Moon," Lowell showed some desire to improve his poems before incorporating them in a durable book; but except for the lines added for their substance, most of his corrections were those of a proofreader or an editor with a pair of shears. He exhibited little of the strict self-criticism that made Tennyson rewrite his early poems so completely, and he apparently had none of the concern for finish or smooth polish which he recognized and admired in his English contemporary. He probably read his own poems through an emotional haze that obscured his editorial eye. Others saw the effect of the haze upon the verse. Elizabeth Barrett, who had her own poetic license to speak about the matter, wrote of a certain vagueness and golden mistiness which she attributed to a redundancy of poetic diction. Thomas Noon Talfourd, who of course knew nothing of Lowell's early extravagant admiration for his own *Ion,* reported as publisher's reader to C. E. Mudie that the volume reflected true, although sometimes extravagant and obscure, poetical feeling in a style modeled on Wordsworth with a bit of Tennyson thrown in. Yet he recommended its publication in England as a probably unremunerative service to the lovers of thoughtful poetry and thus contributed to the beginning of Lowell's English reputation. The stylistically unsophisticated Americans were more enthusiastic, and Poe, one of the few American critics who had a flair for careful analysis, not only was personally friendly but was encouraged to publish his flattering review before he had time to make a thorough examination of those poems that would not normally have attracted his first attention.

John Owen lost no money by his "speculation" in Lowell's poems. By March 8, 1844, the author was able to report that his volume would soon reach a third edition of five hundred copies, about eleven hundred having already been sold, and that he might "get something from the book yet." He would pocket anything he got, he added, "with a free heart in spite of the shame which our anticopyright gentleman would fain lay at the door of an author who demands his wages." He received something from this final small edition, and his name also became more valuable to magazine editors as a result of the recognition achieved by a successful book. George R. Graham, who was now sole editor of his magazine, revealed one of the secrets of his success by losing no time in renewing his contacts with his old contributor. Although Charles J. Peterson was editing his own magazine, he remained in close touch with his former employer; and when he wrote Lowell on January 10 in praise of "A Legend of Brittany" and other poems in the new book, his promptness may have been stimulated by a desire to pass on the news that Graham was disturbed because Lowell had gone so long without sending any contributions for his magazine. Graham probably speeded the production of the hastily written review in the March number in which Poe declared that the "new volume of poems by Mr. Lowell will place him, in the estimation of all whose opinion he will be likely to value, *at the very head* of the poets of America"; and on February 2 he wrote directly that Poe wanted Lowell to write his biography for the "Our Contributors" section of *Graham's* and that he himself wanted a sketch of Lowell in the same "portrait gallery." He also wanted a poem and hoped that Lowell, if he wrote for any three-dollar magazine, would make *Graham's* his "medium of communicating with the public."

But Lowell, who had discovered that necessity was the mother of bargaining, was in no hurry to commit himself. Furthermore, he was "very busily employed upon a *job* article on a subject in which," as he wrote Poe sometime later, he had "no manner of interest." His reply to Graham merely offered congratulations, based on internal evidence in the magazine, upon obtaining Poe again as an editor. Graham, on March 2, assured him that he was mistaken about Poe but suggested that Poe be allowed to write Lowell's life for the "portrait gallery" and underlined an entreaty: *"Send me a poem."* Lowell at last obliged. He apparently remembered Poe's accusation in the March review that he had "suffered himself to be *coteried* [presumably by the abolitionists and the man Poe described as "that ass O'Sullivan"] into conceptions of the *aims* of the muse, which his reason either now disapproves, or will disapprove hereafter, and which his keen instinct of the beautiful and proper has, long ere this, struggled to disavow"; for the poem he sent, "A Mystical Ballad," was in his old *Graham's* manner and in the manner of the poems from his new volume which Poe had selected as representative of his indistinct feeling that "the sole legitimate object of the true poem is the *creation of beauty.*" Yet he managed to introduce into it some of his growing humanitarianism: after killing off another beautiful maiden in a way that would be wholly satisfactory to Poe, he allowed a youth in another land to wilt mysteriously as an illustration of those "subtlest sympathies" that, although "Unproved by outward evidence," exist to bind individuals together. Graham was satisfied by the combination and published the poem in his May number, writing on May 4: "I have engaged Cooper, Paulding, Longfellow, Bryant, and I *hope Lowell* for 'Graham.' *If Godey can beat this card,* I am certain he will have to hunt up new authors."

Graham had been trying to engage Lowell at twenty dollars per poem, but in frankly exposing his "card" he allowed his prospective contributor to make his own bid for a place in such flattering company. He asked Lowell to set his own fair price for a monthly poem under an agreement giving *Graham's* the exclusive use of his name and of all his works except anonymous reviews. Lowell accepted the estimate placed upon him, in comparison with other American poets, in Poe's review and set a price of fifty dollars—the amount, he had learned, that Graham was paying Longfellow. Graham did not permit himself to answer. Instead, Peterson wrote for him, explaining that his former employer was ill. As a mutual friend, Peterson undertook to straighten matters out. Twenty dollars, he wrote, was the highest price Graham "ever paid *regularly* for poems, since Longfellow and Bryant only contribute occasionally," and in that way he got the benefit of their names for a less sum yearly than was offered Lowell. Nevertheless, the magazine would stretch a point and offer twenty-five—a sum greater than that paid any other poet with the exception of Bryant and Longfellow. Lowell's reply is not available, but Graham recovered sufficiently by May 26 to express his pain and astonishment at such a response to the courteous treatment he had hitherto given his contributor. Like O'Sullivan, he was willing to put up with just so much from an author before he cracked the whip on a tender spot. "But one learns, something every day, in this bustling, jostling world," he wrote in a tone of sorrow and disillusionment, "and the most important yet hardest lesson is, to treat all men as bargain-driving sharpers. I see my dear Lowell you have learned it early." The "unkindest" part of Lowell's letter to Peterson had been his reference to the improbability of Graham wanting his portrait *"now"* and his request for the return of his most recent contribution. The businessman whose virtue had been so wounded had already spoken to the engraver about doing the portrait in his best style, and the poem had already been "printed off" for the July number.

Graham was, in fact, on a difficult spot. Whether or not the new poem, which appeared on the first sheet of the July number, had actually been "printed off," the title page for the first volume of *Graham's* for 1844 had certainly been printed and distributed with Lowell's name on the "card" of principal contributors. After all his bargaining on the basis of being unwilling to pay more than two or three hundred dollars a year for any "name" and his sanctimonious attitude toward Lowell for wanting more, he found himself in the position of having really paid only twenty dollars for the use of Lowell's name for one half year and—since the title page of one volume was an advertisement for the next—subject to the charge of taking it again for nothing. "New Year's Eve, 1844: A Fragment" was somewhat too radical in its implications to be exactly in Graham's line, but he had to have it in order to avoid listing among his own contributors a man who otherwise might conceivably appear exclusively in *Godey's*. He raised his offer to thirty dollars, and the dickering continued until August. By August 6 it was time for Lowell, annoyed at Graham's exaggerated charges of mercenariness, to be plain-spoken: "I did not expect to appear in "Graham" every month, and even if I did it would be very far from amounting, as you say, to "another $1000." The fact is that if I expect to earn *any,* even the meanest, support from my pen, it would be wholly idle in me to sell myself exclusively for between three and four hundred dollars a year." He was sensitive, however, to any suggestion that he might be mercenary, and he used Maria to protect him against suspicion by adding: "Now my purpose is to be married next January, and it is my *duty,* not my will, to make the most I can out of my wits." Although he had made Graham wait a month for his letter, he showed no indication of wanting to break off negotiations entirely and promised to talk matters over in person after his arrival in Philadelphia in the near future. He was both frank and reassuring on one point: "I have made no arrangements with any body else yet—nor have I tried. I wrote in answer to a letter from Mr. Godey, but have never been honored with a reply."

Dr. Lowell was supporting his son's judgment that it would be foolish to make an exclusive agreement with any editor, but at the same time was insisting that he would have to find some permanent situation immediately.

He was willing to spend a thousand dollars on a cottage for James and Maria on one corner of his own estate, but, proud as he was of Lowell's literary accomplishments, he evidently felt it unwise to allow him to marry and settle down under the paternal roof. Lowell's proposal to visit Philadelphia reflected his interest in the city which had been so friendly and beneficial to Maria during her visit there in the late winter and spring, and he had some hope of lecturing there. His first appearance on the platform, in Concord five years before, had profited him only four dollars, but he had gained confidence after speaking before an occasional anti-slavery or temperance audience and lecturing in general was becoming more profitable year by year. He wrote Peterson of his plans and received a sensibly qualified encouragement: he could hire a good room for ten dollars, and the Quakers would hear him as an abolitionist, several literary sets of young people would hear the poet, and a good many well-informed people would go to hear what he had to say. The project was a good one if Lowell's elocution was good, he thought, but he warned that everything depended upon his making "a hit." Emerson's experience in leaving off with better houses than he had begun with was unusual, and Peterson attributed it to the fact that "his wit did more for him, than his philosophy." But Lowell had lost his optimism and had no enthusiasm for speculation. He was already too deeply in debt to risk the expense of travel and board and of engaging a hall for a series of lectures that might fail, for, although he would have had confidence in his wit, the material he planned to use was not particularly witty and he might have experienced doubts concerning the quality of his elocution. Maria was anxious to return to Philadelphia after their marriage and inquired of friends concerning the possibility of a lecture series, or any other form of employment, but appeared to be looking for a formal engagement that would offer financial security rather than risk.

Peterson was equally matter-of-fact and even less encouraging about Lowell's prospects with Graham. He did not profess to know Graham's real attitude toward Lowell but guessed that he was probably vexed at the latter's termination of the correspondence. As a magazine editor himself, however, he was sure that Lowell was expecting too much from the profession of authorship. "The question with you ought to have been, as I said in my last letter," he wrote, *"not what I am worth, but what can I get?"* He was sure that Graham had offered as much as Lowell's poems *"were worth to him"* and that he was justified in being displeased when Lowell took exception to his paying a higher price to others. Lowell's attitude in asking for as much as Graham would pay any author instead of as much as any editor would pay him, Peterson tried to explain, was all wrong, and his final advice was: "If you could get $350.00 a year from Graham, you might get enough from prose-articles to the Democratic Review and other periodicals to eke out your income. But the fact is that literature is the worst use (in a pecuniary sense) to which a man can put his brains. I hope you may soon be rich, and I know you will be a great poet." But Lowell was not willing to limit himself to prose in his contributions to other periodicals. He had just sent the *Democratic Review* a poem "On the Death of a Friend's Child" for the October number, and he probably knew by then that the friend, Briggs, was depending upon him for poems to be published in his own new *Broadway Journal* which was to appear in January. Before the end of the year he sent Graham "To the Dandelion" for his January issue and he remained willing to do the article on Poe. But he signed no exclusive agreements.

IV

LOWELL's unwillingness to commit himself entirely to *Graham's* was a matter of general prudence rather than immediate shrewdness, for he was actually contributing very little to other periodicals at that time. His poem in the *Democratic Review* was probably the only verse aside from the two poems in *Graham's* for which he received any remuneration in 1844, and he had supplied only two periodicals with gratuitous poems. The March number of William H. Channing's *The Present* contained a little poem entitled "Winter" which dealt with the melancholy state of mind and the forced optimism of a misunderstood poet in a cold, dull world, and the same magazine had reprinted his fifth sonnet against Wordsworth in April. Circumstances had forced him into a hasty composition of a "Rallying Cry for New England against the Annexation of Texas" for the Boston *Courier* on March 19, but he made no attempt to cultivate his reputation by free will offerings as he had done two years before. He had used up his accumulated store of publishable poems for the 1844 volume, and his poetic inspiration seems to have been at an unusually low ebb during the entire year. "Winter" reveals a pervading influence of Shakespeare's sonnets which suggests that Lowell had either fallen back into his mood of two years before or had actually written the poem at that time and had given it to Channing as a means of assisting him to restore his magazine. "A Mystical Ballad" was also in an earlier manner, and "On the Death of a Friend's Child" took its blank-verse flight from the thoughts contained in a rhymed poem written in April, 1841, which Lowell had quoted to the friend a few days before as an unsatisfactory expression of feelings aroused by the occasion. Not one of his poems first published in 1844, in fact, represents a complete and spontaneous expression of Lowell's immediate sentiments, for the "New-Year's Eve" was an uncompleted fragment and the "Rallying Cry" was a journalistic effort to meet an emergency and set an example for Whittier and other poets he asked to rise to the occasion. Because of his difficulties with editors and the uncertainty of his poetic impulse, his professional income, aside from his profits from the second and third editions of his *Poems,* had been only about one hundred and twenty dollars for the year, and of that almost exactly a half had come from the "job article" for the *North American Review.* A literary man who was planning matrimony needed the security of a steady hand at prose, which would remain relatively unaffected by the vagaries of muses and editors, and in recognition of this fact Lowell turned to the rapid exploitation of some of his old material and new ideas in the form of a prose volume of *Conversations on Some of the Old Poets.*

The article for the *North American Review* had been on "New Translations of the Writings of Miss Bremer" which was published in April. It had been designed—probably at the instigation and with the help of his sister Mary—to "show up" Mrs. Mary Howitt as a translator, and although Lowell wrote Briggs that she "richly deserved it," he confessed that he had no bent for such work. His personal inclination was toward a less meticulous and more appreciative sort of literary criticism dealing with ideals rather that craftsmanship, and more discursive than analytical. The market for such commentaries, however, so far as it existed at all, was in the personalized magazines rather than in anonymous reviews, and to bring a satisfactory price it had to be signed "by the author of" a volume which proved to readers that they were not perusing the work of an amateur. Lowell must have begun work on a volume consisting of an essay on Chaucer and his *Miscellany* articles on the Old Dramatists immediately after his work for the *North American Review,* for his father was able to take a completed manuscript of that description with him in early August to Saratoga Springs where he undertook to correct and revise it and prepare it for the printer while Mrs. Lowell was under medical care. Dr. Lowell at this time, while pained by James's "radicalism" and professing an inability to understand most of his poetry, was extravagantly proud of his youngest son's literary reputation. But either the son or his publisher apparently decided that a volume of criticism would not be commercially practicable in essay form, and it was this material which, in September, Lowell was thinking of using for a series of lectures in Philadelphia. Peterson's practical comments upon the speculation involved in such an undertaking and upon the interests of a popular audience were hardly encouraging, and, although Lowell did not at once give up the notion, he may have begun in that month to consider recasting his essays in the familiar way of dialogue which, as the writers of popular textbooks used to point out, made abstruse matter easy of comprehension by the youth of both sexes.

He did not begin his actual revisions until late October, when the offer of an editorial job in Philadelphia beginning on January 1 caused him to advance the date of his marriage and settle down to the task of rewriting his book within the space of two months. He worked harder and more seriously than ever before in his life. Maria saw him only twice a week, and the book, particularly the discussion of Chaucer, grew out of control as he produced copy for three printers who gave him no time for reflection or additional revision. For the conversations on Chapman and Ford he made long extracts with few changes from his *Miscellany* essays, and for the first conversation he worked with his early commonplace book at hand as a source of quotations somewhat vaguely related to his selections from Chaucer. Yet he had much to say that was new and a good deal that indicated how his literary taste had broadened and become more discriminating during the two years since his writing for Nathan Hale. In particular, although he still refused to allow Pope the distinction of being called a true poet and was bitterly antagonistic toward Swift's verses, he was more tolerant of the eighteenth century and more willing to recognize the peculiar virtues of its poets, showing a high appreciation of "the fine imagination and the classic taste of Collins," recognizing the "originality" reflected in the "grace" of Thomas Gray, insisting upon the "sturdy English spirit" of Dryden, and discovering "a very nice ear" in Thomson and a generally "delightful" quality in Goldsmith. But most of the some four-score English authors he found occasion to mention critically were of the seventeenth and nineteenth centuries. He liked the "old" writers and was anxious to educate his readers to an appreciation of their "beauties." Concerning the moderns he was more judicious if not always temperate. He was enthusiastic over Burns, severe on Byron, complimentary to Coleridge, and uncertain about Wordsworth—very much as he had been since leaving college. His steadily increasing recognition of the importance of sensory and especially visual imagery in poetry was clearly evident in his commentaries throughout, and his expressed admiration for Keats reached its highest point in these dialogues. Lowell's published opinions of fellow poets, however, did not always represent the measure of his interest in them, for although he had words of limited praise for Shelley and Tennyson he said nothing that would indicate his indebtedness to them in his own recent work.

The incidental comments upon modern English poets in Lowell's *Conversations* did not always represent judgments that the author was prepared to stand by, but in making them he exercised the same kind of unconscious discrimination that was to make his later *Fable for Critics* a durable work. The names he mentioned so casually and in such haste all belonged to individuals whose writings possessed the store of energy necessary for survival into a later century: no matter how much he may have thought he admired such people as Henry Taylor and Thomas Noon Talfourd, he simply did not think of them when the old poets served as a touchstone of suggestiveness bringing the moderns into mind. On the other hand, he found occasion to pay passing tribute to the dramatic genius of the relatively unappreciated Robert Browning. His treatment of his fellow countrymen at this time, however, was less spontaneous and sometimes seems calculated to achieve the specific end of showing that the critic Lowell was no Edgar Allan Poe despite any suspicions that might be aroused by the anonymous review of Mary Howitt's translations. There was a self-conscious air of judiciousness in his appreciation of Longfellow; he was unenthusiastic about Emerson's "Humblebee," but he praised the latter poet for his "divine eye" and for "his deep transparency and majestic simpleness of language," and he found the "antique richness" of Charles Lamb's style comparable to Emerson's only in its "best parts." His admiration for the other Americans he mentioned was unqualified and sometimes more suggestive of an olive branch than of a critical judgment. He bowed almost obsequiously toward the irritating N. P. Willis when he called his dramas "perhaps the best in their kind since Fletcher" and apologetically toward Cornelius Mathews (who had been antagonized by reports of Lowell's private comments upon his novel, *Puffer Hopkins*) by finding "the pure Hippocrene" of his verses on the poet worthy of Collins. His comparison of Hawthorne to Collins represented a more permanent judgment, but his tribute to T. W. Parsons as "one of our most truly classic and delightful poets" certainly did not reflect the distinterested discrimination which governed his selection of English poets for comment.

Lowell's decision to present his essays to the public in the form of dialogues was probably made entirely in the interest of salability, but he had respectable precedents for his use of the form from Plato to his own contemporaries. He referred in his preface to "the Greeks and Latins," Walton, Landor, Horne Tooke, and Dr. W. C. Dendy, and he should have mentioned John Payne Collier whose *Poetical Decameron, or Ten Conversations on English Poets and Poetry, Particularly of the Reigns of Elizabeth and James I* he had read with such interest some six or eight years before. He made no attempt, however, to imitate the Socratic dialogue as a means of clarifying his ideas, and he exhibited little of the gossipy antiquarianism of Collier. Although he disavowed any "intention of giving them anything like a dramatic turn," his conversations occasionally took on the mildly dramatic quality of a man's serious argument with himself. "Philip" and "John," the two conversationalists, were not separate individuals but the spokesmen for separate impulses within James Russell Lowell. Philip was the ebullient young man whom Maria loved and encouraged, whose quick literary appreciation and sentiments of high democracy convinced his young associates that a great poet was included in their "Band." John was the son in whom Dr. Lowell placed his faith; for although his opinions hardly disagreed with Philip's, he was less effervescent in his expression of them and more conscious and respectful of the different opinions held by others. Philip looked upon him as a kind of devil's advocate:

> I know your humor for appearing what you are not, in order, by opposition, to draw out opinions upon the side which you really espouse. Such is your assumed liking for the artificial school of poetry. You are willing to assume any disguise in order to get into the enemy's camp, and, once there, like Alfred, you sing them a song that sends them all to their arms.

But actually Philip revealed a greater liking for the poetry of Gray, even when it was most artificial, than John "assumed" for that of Pope: it is a nice question which of the two voices was the voice of Lowell and whether it was John or Philip who sang songs in disguise. Philip was the man who wrote idealistically of the poet and rushed off to Philadelphia to write leaders for an anti-slavery newspaper; John was the one who lived the greater part of his life at Elmwood and became the editor of the *North American Review*. They were both combined in James, who had no philosophy by which to order his emotions and so was beginning to discover, at the age of twenty-five, that he could express himself more readily through artificially contrived characters than he could if he had to make up his own whole mind.

The *Conversations on Some of the Old Poets* by no means reveals fully the uninhibiting effect of attributing one's own tentative opinions to some one else. The gospel of sincerity had sunk deep into Lowell's soul, and he was slipping into the use of a literary device which he would have rejected had he been conscious of it. When he disavowed any dramatic quality in the book, he was trying to avoid the possibility of being "censured" for the use of a form associated with the stage. But he was also accepting personal responsibility for any of the opinions expressed, and in describing his conversations as "merely essays, divided in this way to allow them greater ease and frankness, and the privilege of wandering at will," he asserted that it had been his desire to "express his own opinions" upon matters that might not seem strictly literary. These miscellaneous matters were almost entirely related to the anti-slavery movement, the state of the church, and arbitrary conventions of public decency. Concerning the last, he did little more than repeat some earlier objections from the *Miscellany* to "French" refinements upon the good old Saxon language, amplify the criticisms of women's dress to which Peterson had taken exception in his original essay on Chapman, and defend Abby Kelly against the popular outcry that it was improper for a woman to speak in public. His words were somewhat sharper than they had been, as when he allowed John to summarize his opinions by exclaiming that "our decency is indecent," but his remarks on manners and customs were relatively inoffensive in comparison with his criticism of the church. Early in the conversation on Chaucer, John digressed into a statement of opinion which Philip was to amplify. "The world goes to church to be quiet, and takes it amiss to be interrupted in a calculation of the price of cotton by a personal reference to any of its own bosom sins." Later Philip took up the theme of a religion so refined that it could not be carried "into the street or the market, lest it get soiled," and still later worked himself up to the point of denouncing the church for selling indulgences as readily as in Luther's time and for emphasizing sectarianism while remaining indifferent to moral principles. "Christ scourged the sellers of doves out of the temple; we invite the sellers of men and women in" were his "plain words." John, in agreement, spoke like Shelley: "The church has corrupted Christianity." The more impulsive speaker renounced the institution for both of them:

Both of us, having certain reforms at heart, and believing them to be of vital interest to mankind, turned first to the church as the nearest helper under God. We have been disappointed. Let us not waste our time in throwing stones at its insensible doors. As you have said, the reformers must come from within. The prejudice of position is so strong that all her servants will unite against an exoteric assailant, melting up, if need be, the sacred vessels for bullets, and using the leaves of the holy book itself for wadding. But I will never enter a church from which a prayer goes up for the prosperous only, or for the unfortunate among the oppressors, and not for the oppressed and fallen; as if God had ordained our pride of caste and our distinctions of color, and as if Christ had forgotten those that are in bonds.

Lowell evidently considered these temperate words, however, for he allowed Philip to express a determination to ascribe what he saw of "wrong-doing to blindness and error, rather than to wilful sin," and to add wisely: "The Devil loves nothing better than the intolerance of reformers, and dreads nothing so much as their charity and patience."

Such words as these, standing alone, are bitter; but most of Lowell's contemporary readers would have considered them merely misguided. The sentiments were familiar enough to anyone who had a passing acquaintance with abolitionist literature, and anti-slavery pamphlets and reports were spread broadcast in literary circles. Lowell was explicit in expressing his own confidence in the relationship of his apparently jumbled ideas. When John accused Philip of being a reasonable fellow who went "suddenly mad" at the mention of poetry or anti-slavery, the latter replied: "You forget that I believe the poetical sentiment and what we call the sentiment of natural religion to be identical. Both of them are life-members of the New England AntiSlavery Society. You are, at heart, as much an Abolitionist as I; and if you were not, I should suspect the purity of my own principles, if they built up a wall between me and my brother." But Lowell was beginning to slip into the tacit assumption that any one who could be offended by abolitionist principles was not a brother, and he was inclined to accept membership in the New England Anti-Slavery Society as a certificate of poetical sentiment and natural religion. John Owen had urged him not to include in the 1844 *Poems* his "Stanzas sung at the Anti-Slavery Picnic in Dedham"; but the poet's reply, as he remembered the incident two years later, to the publisher's "worldly arguments" had been: "Let all the others be suppressed if you will—*that* I will never suppress." Lowell was convinced that "this was the first audible knock my character made at the door of Owen's heart—he loves me now as I him." Yet Lowell had to knock again and again in order to get his anti-slavery character admitted to the public under Owen's imprint. The practical publisher drew a distinction between the poetical sentiments to which Lowell's criticism would appeal and the sentiments that led to membership in the Anti-Slavery Society; and, since he was taking all the speculation of an edition of one thousand copies and paying the author a royalty, he naturally wanted to appeal to the wider audience. His conferences with the author on the subject are not on record, but when he wrote Lowell in April concerning the success of the edition he suggested hopefully: "While my own views in regard to most of these collateral topics harmonize with your own I have sometimes thought that not only would less enemies be made but more good accomplished by treating subjects of a nature so different more by themselves." The book had not been stereotyped, and Owen was not willing to send it back to the printer before hearing from Lowell on the subject of revisions: "If you should not decide to make important changes you may prefer on reflection to make some modifications of expression in certain cases." The only important change made was a division of the conversation on Chaucer into two parts. The criticism of the church from the abolitionists' point of view was sharpened and amplified.

The success of the *Conversations* was surprising. The author's Aunt Sally almost fluttered over the book. As Dr. Lowell described her reactions in a letter of January 24, 1845, she first looked at it and said she preferred James's poetry to his prose. A little later she repeated that Longfellow had called the *Conversations* a "gem," and still later she was saying how everybody was delighted with it and that Professor Farrar had carried a copy to Mrs. Lee. Professor Felton, although critical of the attacks on the church, was soon to announce in the *North American Review* that there was nowhere to be found so good an account of Chaucer. If the Smith Professor of Modern Languages, the former Hollis Professor of Mathematics and Natural Philosophy, and the Eliot Professor of Greek all agreed to admire young Lowell as a literary critic, his Aunt Sally was willing to change her mind. By such opinions, his talents were established locally and a successful literary career was brought closer to his grasp than it had ever been before. Owen had agreed to pay him a hundred dollars for the first edition of the *Conversations* if it sold well—which it did—and, in making a contract for a second edition of a thousand copies, he agreed to pay a royalty of ten cents per copy printed. He evidently paid the same royalty for the second and third editions of the *Poems,* and Lowell, anticipating the new edition of his prose volume, figured on March 21, 1845, that his publisher owed him three hundred dollars "at this moment." He was soon able to draw upon him in settling some of the debts remaining from the *Pioneer,* and he expected Graham to continue paying him thirty dollars per poem with no restrictions upon his use of Briggs's *Broadway Journal* as an additional source of income. The ten-dollar-a-month job he had just accepted in Philadelphia was much less important than it had been when he took it.

But while the state of his finances and of his critical talents was still unsettled, Lowell was convincing himself that as a poet he should play a more active part in life and was at last succeeding in defining the line of action a poet might properly take. The course of his thoughts is revealed in "Columbus," the third of his trilogy of blank-verse poems dealing with the relationship between poetry and action, which he had half-completed in September, 1844, and apparently had practically finished by the following January. "Prometheus" had represented the poet as the martyred prophet and friend of humanity, and "A Glance Behind the Curtain" had portrayed Cromwell as a type of poet—a man of action entitled to rank with "the true Makers." "Columbus" was the monologue of a man driven by his own great dreams toward a goal defined by the poets. There was not much difference, in nature, between the explorer and the ideal poet. Columbus possessed a vision which soared far above the imprisoning bars of the world's cold unbelief. He knew that sincerity was the key to all great success, and, by answering "God's earliest call," he had followed the genius which made "the wise heart certain of its ends." He had succeeded where Rhoecus had failed, for he had made his early hope of "love and fame" a "dryad mistress" with whom he spent his time while other youths engaged in less inspired dalliance. After boyhood visions of a land beyond the western ocean he began to "entertain the poet's song" as his "great Idea's guest"—Dante's story of Ulysses' sight of the great mountain before he died. This caused him to brood upon Plato's Atlantis and upon the Vinland of "Björne":

> For I believe the poets; it is they
> Who utter wisdom from the central deep,
> And, listening to the inner flow of things,
> Speak to the age out of eternity.

Columbus, delivering his monologue on the eve of the last day his crew permitted him to hold the helm, believing that

> One day, with life and heart,
> Is more than time enough to find a world,

was the type of active man whose feeling had been made concrete in thought by the words of a poet who thus provided a goal for his activity.

There was not much difference in Lowell's characterization of his three Chapmanesque heroes, Prometheus, Cromwell, and Columbus, who all reflected the impatience and frustrations of a young man who had not been remarkably successful in his professional career, whose home life revolved around an invalid mother, and whose emotions were controlled by a sincere desire to be worthy of a young woman with high moral principles and low physical vitality. A certain amount of emotional self-identification appeared in each of them. The three poems, however, represent a progressive dissociation of the poetic ideal from the dramatic character. Lowell had at last come around to Shelley's view—and to the not unconventional one—that the poet's business was not to kick against the pricks of compulsory inactivity, nor was it to confuse action with poetry, but that it was to guide and direct action toward a particular goal. His first major literary engagements had not been remarkably successful, but they gave him some of the experience he needed before he could make a major decision.

Chapter VI

THE SIEGE PERILOUS

I

Lowell's interest in Philadelphia was that of a young man with limited financial resources who was planning to be married and needed employment in order to provide his delicate bride with a refuge from the New England climate and himself with an escape from his unhappy responsibilities at Elmwood. Maria had found the Quaker city beneficial in the spring of 1844 and after her return talked so inspiringly of it that James became eager to take her there again. Some of her new friends were admirers of her fiancé's anti-slavery verses, and for one of them, Edward Morris Davis, she agreed to obtain an autographed copy of "A Rallying Cry for New England against the Annexation of Texas" which had been published without Lowell's signature in the Boston *Courier* in March. Lowell sent the copy on May 26, and Maria added a note about their plans and hopes. Concerning the possibility of employment in Philadelphia for three months during the following spring she said:

> I suppose the season for lectures would be over then, and I fear that Destiny has not been so kind as to arrange any exact labors for him there, simply because we wish to go. But should you hear of any situation for a literary man at that time however small the recompense, might I not depend on your kindness to let me know of it. Any temporary editorship or employment of that kind, you might hear of, while it would never reach us here.

By August the young people had received an invitation to visit the Davises and had moved up the date of their wedding to January, and Lowell was thinking of making an early trip to Philadelphia in order to look into the possibilities of lecturing. Peterson's frank appraisal of the speculative nature of his proposal, however, in September was not encouraging and apparently left Lowell undetermined, ready to grasp any opportunity that might arise out of Maria's second suggestion concerning "any temporary editorship or employment of that kind." In the meantime, the proprietorship of the Pennsylvania *Freeman* had been transferred to the Anti-Slavery Society of Eastern Pennsylvania; and although the editorial personnel remained unchanged, the responsibility for publication, beginning with the new year, rested with the Society's Executive Committee of which Edward Davis was chairman. Davis recognized the possibility of an arrangement by which the editorial columns might, "for a time at least, be enriched by the contributions of one of the ablest writers in the country" and at some time during the fall obtained Lowell's services for bi-weekly editorial leaders at five dollars each. Lowell was apologetic about accepting even such a nominal sum for contributions to a worthy cause, but the job provided the excuse and the financial margin he needed to go to Philadelphia and his wedding date was again advanced, to December 26, 1844, in order that he might report for duty at the beginning of the year.

There can be little doubt but that, whatever his primary motives may have been, Lowell was secretly relieved to have a good reason for making a formal, open connection with the abolitionist cause. For four years, as his many words on the function of poetry and the nature of the ideal poet had revealed, he had been gradually evolving a philosophy of active participation in a reform movement; and this evolution in theory had been impelled, and kept largely theoretical, by a confusion of social and political interests which had existed in his mind since he had been a junior in college. As an undergraduate, Lowell had come to a consciousness of the world about him at a time when the path of action or belief was far from clear to a young man who had been bred to ethical standards higher than those of the pocketbook. Probably at no time in the history of the United States had the political issues been so frankly and exclusively mercenary as they were during the administration of Martin Van Buren. During the course of Jackson's fight against the United States Bank, the American people had been educated to an appreciation of the close relationship between the financial structure of the country and their everyday welfare. Whether they chose to blame Old Hickory or Nicholas Biddle for their ups and downs, they became conscious that arbitrary measures affecting credit were matters of immediate personal concern; and when federal deposits were transferred to "pet banks" chartered by the states, people received further education in the inflationary dangers of an uncontrolled power to issue currency. The deflationary tactics of Jackson's efforts to make gold and silver the only legal tender for the purchase of public lands aroused the antagonism of those who were riding the wave of speculative prosperity and gave encouragement to the hard money and independent Treasury men who were opposed to all banks and, on the eve of the panic of 1837, raised a banner inscribed: "As the currency expands the loaf contracts." To make matters more complicated in Massachusetts, the group of Boston bankers headed by Nathan Appleton was demonstrating during the period of panic that the moneyed interests could operate a local business which was sounder than that of the far-flung United States Bank or of the banks receiving political deposits. The major political issues were almost entirely questions of who was to profit at whose expense.

The stream of frankly mercenary interests which dominated the channels of political expression was an offense to the inbred moral sensitivity of many New Englanders who felt obliged to rectify their self-interest with virtue before they could vote with clear consciences. Reforms of many sorts made ripples in the political stream without becoming strong enough to govern its course. Temperance was the strongest of these during Lowell's college years and abolitionism the most unrestrained; but he satirized them both in his *Class Poem,* and although he wrote of his passing notion to join the college Anti-Wine Society his most intimate friend scoffed at it as a katzenjammer impulse which was not to be taken seriously. For a whlie he alleviated his desire to do good by taking a firm stand against distant evils—against the oppression of the Seminoles and the Cherokees by the federal government, of the Irish by the English, of British factory workers by the upper classes. He was interested in reforms in France and had hopes of the liberation of Canada from British "tyranny," but at home matters were more complicated. The Whig party had adopted the temperance issue, but it was not popular in Unitarian circles, and the law passed in 1838 was a discriminatory one which split the party and lost the autumn election. As for the other reform movement, it may have been true, as Lowell noted in his *Class Poem,* that every New Englander was an abolitionist at heart, but most of those of Lowell's class found the activities of Garrison in Boston more acutely irritating than those of the slaveholders in Virginia. The older generation, which had become reconciled to the notion that virtue was a private matter and decency was the most that could be expected in public, were not so greatly disturbed by the situation, but young men—and young women—were often victims of a confused desire to do good by their votes without knowing how.

The movement which had the greatest emotional appeal to the politically minded young men of Lowell's college generation was that which called itself Christian Democracy and, under the slogan of "Equal Rights," advocated the doctrine of brotherly love that so greatly affected Lowell's conception of the ideal poet. Charles C. Shackford, the first graduate of the class of 1835 and the brother of Lowell's close friend Willam, zealously hung out "The Banner of Democracy" in a master's oration by that title at the commencement exercises of 1838. Of Christian love he said: "This is the true, eternal bond of union. All else may fail—the love of freedom, glory, country, die out—all earthly motives and all earth-formed friendships burn to the socket; but charity never faileth. The spirit of fraternal love is everlasting. Hence the banner of a true Democracy shall ever wave over a people, that are in heart united under the banner of the cross." Such sentiments were those of "Methodists of Democracy," the Loco-Focos of New York, whose opposition to all banks had been taken up by George Bancroft and the radical up-country Democrats of Massachusetts, and whose Christian principles were being used as a means of rallying support for the policies of Martin Van Buren. They bothered young Lowell, who had been bred to hold Van Buren in contempt. When his classmate Abner Loring Cushing became editor of the Boston *Reformer and Anti-Monopolist,* Lowell impulsively subscribed to the radical newspaper and then felt "like a fool" for doing so. He tried to explain himself to Loring on October 11:

> I should have cared for the agrarianism, for 'tis a pretty dream, though totally impracticable—but it is red hot V. B. and I hate politics—I have become (heaven save the mark!) a rank democrat. But of all things I do utterly detest democratic aristocracy which developes itself in two ways (especially) 1st by living in silk and luxury onesself and concealing it by raising a great dust about others who do the same, and 2nd in thinking a man a better democrat, the dirtier, more ragged, and impudent he is. In these last (as Socrates told one of his disciples, who wished to appear humble by wearing a ragged cloak,) "their pride shows through the holes in their garments."

He might have said more precisely that, although he liked the abstract principles of the Democrats and had no objection to their admirable but impossible dreams, he disliked intensely the Democratic president, the Democratic state leaders, and the Democratic rank and file. As he contemplated the political scene he found himself in the dilemma which bothered

Emerson and other well-bred and high-minded New Englanders: all the right thoughts seemed to be on one side of the political controversy and all the right-thinking people on the other.

After the November elections of 1838, Lowell's hatred of politics disappeared, and he announced to Loring that he "shouldn't wonder if the peaceable young gentleman whom you knew in college flared up into a great political luminary." He intended to vote as soon as he came of age, and he was, he reported, "fast becoming ultrademocratic." But his democracy went abroad to declare itself. He lived "in confident expectation of seeing that time when the people of England shall wake up and heave that vast incubus, which has long oppressed religion, the established church, from their breast," and he was enthusiastic about the Manchester meeting over which Ebenezer Elliott presided while the multitude of poor petitioned the government for equal representation. But although the meekness of the English poor "almost" brought tears to his eyes, and he was proud of the aggressive spirit of the Yankees of the Bay State, he had no enthusiasm for the ragged Democrats—with the capital letter—of Massachusetts who were demanding the overthrow of established banks. They were merely "impudent." He avoided the horns of his dilemma by crying a plague upon them both:

> As for the two great parties which divide this country, I for one dare to say that democracy does belong to neither of them, and certainly to neither exclusively—so I care not which whips. The V. Bs have the stoutest lungs and shout loudly of "Jeffersonian democracy," but fair and softly wins the race. A third party, or rather no party, are secretly rising up in this country, whose voice will soon be heard. The abolitionists are the only ones with whom I sympathize of the present extant parties.

What Lowell was rather unhappily seeking was a political party made up of well-bred people with democratic impulses who would apply the principles of freedom and equality to an issue less complicated and contiguous than banking.

His friend Loring, whose family was less solidified politically than the Lowells, had been old enough to vote in the election and had been obliged to choose sides. In answer to Lowell's letter, he confessed on November 22: "I came out a hot politician voting on the Democratic ticket. I am not yet an *ultra-democrat* tho' I find the foundations of my *ultra-toryism* (Whiggery is a misnomer) are fast crumbling away—I know not why; but it may be that the 'hidden virtue of *truth*' is too powerful to be withstood." He was sharply critical of the political finagling of the abolitionists with whom his classmate professed to sympathize and exclaimed "Heaven help us when this party rules." During the next few months he returned to political questions from time to time in his letters, trying apparently to break down some of his friend's prejudices. On December 10 he reported that he had listened to the Reverend John T. Sargent the day before and had "admired a pure democratic sermon" which "was a second Banner of Democracy." Charles Shackford had become a minister to the poor in Portsmouth as Sargent was in Boston, and Loring concluded of their religion: "There must be a Democratic influence in it as there is in all true Christianity. And in their pure forms they go hand in hand,—twin-brothers." Yet Loring experienced some of the same difficulties that bothered Lowell. He wrote about the problem at some length on July 12, 1839:

> I went on invitation to Groton on the fourth and heard a Democratic oration and ate a democratic dinner. The whole affair was too ultra for me and when the orator blew up our judiciary and the whole body of English law because it is English, foretelling the time when our jurisprudence would be torn from its old "Blackstone Moorings" and be free and American . . . when he traced the principles of the present Democratic party from Martin Luther . . . my blood boiled. And yet he drew a lovely picture of pure Democracy blending it with Christianity and so uniting it with good morality and learning that one could almost weep at the very thought, how very far off this Utopia. Those ideas which we have exchanged so often by letter on this subject were there, and by contrast appeared tenfold pleasing! 'Tis true one feels a thrill at seeing oppressed men rise and men, who are bowed down by ignorance and tyranny, getting a glimpse of light, but Democracy and Chartism are yet in their infancy, powerful in it, 'tis true, but as yet not lovely.

Democracy and Chartism were like Hercules who had grasped the serpent but had not yet cleaned the stables, and the question for young men was whether they should help or remain satisfied with their own condition while others labored. For himself, he admitted: "I fear I see too much of Democracy as it is to fall in love with it at present—My stomach rather turns at the thought—and when men for political views blend their cause with that of the Saviour, and by their very denouncings show how far they are from the spirit they advocate I cannot adore the sovereign people."

Exactly what answer Lowell might have given verbally to the question concerning a young man's duty cannot be determined, for the long letter he wrote in reply, on July 16, had a postscript postponing what he "forgot" to say about Democracy and he continued to forget politics while filling succeeding letters with verse and reports concerning his attempts to make his life a poem. But his actions show that he had no intention of joining in the task of cleaning the Augean stables of the Democratic party. There may be some significance in the fact that his revolt against the study of law coincided with the period of his interest in the Christian Democracy of the Loco-Focos who had passed a formal resolution "Woe unto you ye lawyers, for ye bind heavy burthens and grievous to be borne upon men's shoulders"; and there is no doubt that his poem on the Maine Boundary in the *Morning Post* for February 26, 1839, had displayed the sort of anti-British feeling which Loring found reprehensible among the Democrats. But these—despite later rumors that he had voted Democratic in his early youth—are the only signs of his possible contamination. He agreed with Loring that Whiggery was a misnomer for Toryism but disagreed that one must either work to make "beauty and strength" visible in "Democracy and Chartism" or sit quietly on the sidelines. He found it possible to rise above politics into poetry, and the pressure of the two alternatives set forth by his friend may have provided some of the impulse which enabled him to grasp the high-minded theory of poetry toward which he was reaching at the time.

During the greater part of 1840, Lowell was a resident of Boston, and whether or not he was a qualified voter he showed little of the interest in politics which he had promised to display when he became of age. He was busily writing sonnets for *A Year's Life* while Massachusetts was triumphantly removing a Democratic governor and helping overthrow the long-established regime in Washington. Had he been in Cambridge he might have found his political dilemma resolved by the new "Whig Republican Association" of young people whose constitution adopted the anti-monopolistic principles and the ideals of popular government held by the radical Democrats and used "these sound and salutary principles" to advocate a popular destruction of the selfish monopoly the Democrats held on the government. But Lowell appears to have been too high-minded to care much about reforming merely the government of the United States, and his first political act for the amelioration of the world was to number himself among those "friends of Universal Reform" who gathered at the Chardon Street Chapel a few days after the November elections in a "convention to examine the validity of the views which generally prevail in this country as to the divine appointment of the first day of the week as the Christian Sabbath, and to inquire into the origin, nature, and authority of the institutions of the Ministry and the Church, as now existing." The meeting did not reach the second item on its agenda, and when it reconvened the following March Lowell was busily reading novels as "a way of keeping all *thought* out of one's head" and probably was not among the picturesque collection of disorderly individuals described by Emerson as "Madmen, madwomen, men with beards, Dunkers, Muggletonians, Come-outers, Groaners, Agrarians, Seventh-day-Baptists, Quakers, Abolitionists, Calvinists, Unitarians and Philosophers." The people who attracted attention at the first meeting were mostly abolitionists (although it was not, in any sense, an anti-slavery gathering) and transcendentalists, and Lowell's appearance among them may have been due less to his interest in Universal Reform than to a curiosity aroused by the fact that the published "call" touched upon the problem he had recently considered in his poem "The Church."

After his engagement to Maria White, however, Lowell's interest in reform movements became less casual. The Whites as a family were interested in humanitarian, temperance, and anti-slavery societies; and Maria had received a vividly personal lesson in the evils of intemperance when she escaped from the mob which burned the Ursuline Convent in 1834. Her brother William was active in the cause, and if the two of them had not succeeded in converting James by the middle of May, 1841, they at least had been working on him enough to make him easily embarrassed by George Loring's dream of a tavern scene which he described as "being a test of your powers of drinking which were made up of your old college abilities and something which I thought assumed to keep up the dignity of the character you sustained as the Poet-wonder of the hamlet." Lowell made it clear to the world that he was not that kind of poet. His conversion was sufficiently well known by December 9 for him to make a merry "temperance address" to Maria and their little band of friends without any suspicion of satire. William, in the meantime, was visiting in South Carolina and setting a good example by refusing to attend any dinner at which wine was served, and James took the example to heart by staying away from a dinner for Dickens on the evening of January 31, 1842, when he found himself unable to persuade the "very large majority" of the "Boston Young Men" who did the entertaining that "women should take the place of wine." He was thinking at the time of writing "an American Tragedy on the trial of Anne Hutchinson, who was condemned for heresy in the good old colony times," and could probably appreciate the attraction which the temperance platform offered to the distant granddaughter to whom he himself was engaged. While the "woman question" was still a matter of debate among the abolitionists, the temperance meetings were among the very few occasions on which a New England woman could speak in public, and although Maria had too much modesty and humor to become a public agitator she was not unwilling to bear open witness to her desire for the improvement of society. "Dressed in snowy white, with a wreath of oak-leaves and water-lilies round her head, and a water-lily in her bosom," she presented a banner to the Watertown Washington Total Abstinence Society on the first Friday in July, while James listened with admiration to the "clear, silvery tones" of her brief speech. James himself spoke for ten inspired minutes before three thousand Washingtonians at Cambridgeport on the fourth, getting "many demonstrations of satisfaction and approval" for his words on the beauty and propriety of having women "at the head of the pilgrims back to purity and truth."

As the abolitionist movement increased in fervor throughout Massachusetts, however, this fine enthusiasm for total abstinence began to subside. Lydia Child withdrew from the Anti-Slavery Society in 1843 because she thought it had become too "sectarian" in character. But its sectarianism made it more exciting as a cause. William White began to devote his time more exclusively to anti-slavery politics, and the interests of his sister and of his prospective brother-in-law went with him in his activities. The speeches of John Quincy Adams in connection with the Haverhill petition for a peaceful dissolution of the Union had brought the slavery question into the open in the House of Congress at Washington, and the question of admitting Texas was henceforth publicly and actively connected with the matter of slavery. Lowell declared himself an abolitionist to Charles J. Peterson early in 1842 and began his attempts to convert his college friend from Virginia, John Francis Heath, to the cause, urging him to come home from Germany and be an "apostle" for "equality of color as well as of rank." "I cannot reason on the subject," he wrote in August. "A man in the right can never reason. He can only affirm." It was at this time that he was thinking "of writing a pamphlet on the present state of the Slavery question in this country," but in actuality he did not get around to writing anything on the subject and even the "beautiful Indian parable" to which he referred in the letter to Heath was not put into the verse of "A Chippewa Legend" until a year later. He and Loring were both working themselves into a state of excitement in their correspondence, and Lowell was keeping Heath informed of events in Boston, but he kept abolition out of his verses throughout 1842 and the period of cautious radicalism which characterized the

Pioneer. He made his Chapmanesque hero Prometheus the radical "loco-foco" he did not quite dare to be in his own person, but it was not until he included—despite John Owen's objections—the Dedham picnic stanzas in his *Poems* at the end of 1843 that he became publicly and unambiguously associated with the anti-slavery cause.

During these early years, however, Lowell refused to join either of the two anti-slavery groups which were active in Massachusetts. "He was seldom seen at our meetings" even as a visitor, Samuel J. May recalled shortly after the Civil War. "But his muse rendered us essential service." There was, in fact, no organization in which he would have felt comfortable, for the anti-slavery movement had split on matters of practical policy, and Lowell was an emotional rather than a practical abolitionist. The sonnets to J. R. Giddings and to Wendell Phillips in the 1844 *Poems* show that the strong rhetoric and violent recklessness of the Washington insurgents and Massachusetts radicals appealed to the young man who admired the heroic qualities of Bussy D'Ambois; but at the time he wrote them he was himself reckless only in his imagination, and he could not have agreed with Garrison that the Constitution of the United States was "a covenant with death and an agreement with Hell." He could even tolerate the disturbing new Liberty Party which, by preventing either major candidate for the governorship from receiving a majority, had thrown the 1842 election into the state legislature and made Massachusetts Democratic. On September 19, 1843, he advised William White:

> Do not attack the Liberty Party too fiercely. I think myself they are mistaken in many things. But one should remember that *they are only in error as to the best means of bringing about the Right,* and surely deserve more sympathy at our hands than those whose creed is *wrong*. I happen myself to know personally some very honest and very good men in that party, and belonging, as I do, neither to the old nor the new organization, I can the more easily form an unbiassed opinion.

He also advised White to be "very cautious of abusing the clergy." Such tolerance would have excluded him from formal participation in Garrison's "old" organization, whereas his conviction that political activity was an "error" would have excluded him from the "new." His inability to discover a political situation in which the good ideas and the good men were all on the same side made it as difficult for him to become an active abolitionist in 1843 as it had been for him to become active in politics a few years earlier.

Other causes also attracted his restless good intentions without holding them for any length of time. Opposition to capital punishment which gained him admission to the pages of the *Democratic Review* in 1842 had become associated with the new Democratic Governor Morton and had lost its interest—if it had ever been serious. But Fourierism caught his eye. "There is a great deal of sound philosophy mixed up with much wild deduction in it," he wrote after reading an article by Brisbane in the Boston *Courier*. "At least we ought to give a respectful hearing to anything that earnestly proposes to make man more aware of his high destiny, and show him the plainest road thereto." But he soon decided that Brisbane was not pure enough to guide man to his highest destiny and so quit listening to the Fourieristic doctrine with respect. The matter of international copyright stirred him from time to time, but his interest in that reform was largely professional although in a letter to Charles Briggs on March 6, 1844, he found humanitarian considerations that had been overlooked by the best writer he had read on the subject. There was no minor reform which could provide a sanctuary for Lowell's conscience against the rising excitement of the abolitionists who, at the beginning of 1844, were provided with an issue upon which they could all unite regardless of all internal differences.

The Texas issue was clear to every abolitionist: if the new republic were reunited to Mexico its slaves would be freed; if it were annexed to the United States its Negroes would be kept in bondage and the slave states would become stronger in their influence upon the federal government. The return of Sam Houston to the presidency of the republic had revived the question of annexation, and President Tyler was known to be conducting negotiations designed to bring a treaty of annexation before the Senate early in 1844. His Secretary of State had long been known as an outspoken advocate of such a treaty, and his position in the cabinet had been strengthened in early February by the appointment of a Secretary of the Navy who shared his expansionist views and would prepare for the war with Mexico which was expected to result if Texas were taken into the Union. It was time for all anti-slavery men, pacifists, and sectionalist politicians to unite against this imminent threat to principles, peace, and power. Lowell was an expansionist who believed that the only good thing Thomas Jefferson had ever done was to make the Louisiana Purchase and who—although he had more recently declared to Charles Peterson that he was a no-war man—had insisted that the Maine Boundary dispute be settled in America's favor by force of arms. But the attempts of wicked men to acquire territory for wicked purposes placed the acquisition of Texas on a different plane. Even the cautious defenders of the status quo could not justify it. For the first time since he had become politically conscious, Lowell had found an issue which clearly separated good and evil. The good men and the good principles were, for once, all on the same side, and in the moral scale, new territory—regardless of its ordinary importance—had no weight.

Under such circumstances he could imagine himself occupying the seat of the active reformer, toward which he had been sidling since his undergraduate years. It was a perilous position, he knew, for an ambitious young poet to take, but the peril itself may have been subtly attractive to a man who had wavered for so long between heroism and high-mindedness. Both qualities might at last be exercised in opposition to Texas.

II

A STRONG IMPULSE toward the Siege Perilous, however, came from the simple fact that Lowell himself was fidgety in early March, 1844. There was a cumulative strain in his life at Elmwood, where he was obliged to remain at home and care for a mental invalid during the four days a week that his other parent devoted to his pastoral duties in Boston. Maria had been coughing since an attack of influenza the preceding summer, and, although she had recovered from a recent set-back and he refused to believe that there was anything serious the matter, he was disturbed when he was away from her and unhappy over the prospect of a long separation while Mrs. White took her to Philadelphia in order to avoid the rigors of a New England spring. He was experiencing a reaction from the anxiety of publishing his most ambitious volume of poems and was finding no satisfaction in his current literary work for the *North American Review* or in his negotiations with Graham for the publication of the sort of work he wanted to do. The self-centered emotional turmoil in which he lived formed a whirlpool which sucked the humane imagination out of his desire to do good and left him in the worst possible state to express himself creditably on matters that affected the lives of people at a distance. At this time, the news came of the cannon which burst on the *Princeton* and killed the annexationist Secretaries of State and the Navy. It was God's vengeance upon the unrighteous, and in a letter to Charles Briggs on March 6, Lowell almost gloated over its justice:

> Was that not a strange *judgment* at Washington the other day? I cannot look at it in any other light. That Upshur and Gilmer who had been brought into the

Cabinet to second the unholy plans of Tyler in regard to the Annexation of Texas should thus have been singled out seems to mark the finger of God in the matter. Nor was his interference uncalled for. The question of Annexation is surely the most momentous of this century to the interests of Humanity and Civilization.

What a foolish fuss has there not been made because a cannon fulfilled its destiny! If it had been directed against a battalion of our poor brother Englishmen, who serve the Devil in flame-colored liveries at six pence a day, and had killed several scores of them, it would have been blessed as a public benefactor. I think it better as it is. Was it not invented and cast and pottered over for months to the express end that it might slaughter our fellowbeings? And what has it done but obeyed in its unwieldy style the instincts which man has labored to give it? If it has a soul (and some philosophers would persuade us that all matter has) no doubt it is revolving in its own mind the ambitious chance of having a monument set up for it somewhere among the other preposterous ones of the capital.

It was in this mood of insensitive righteousness that Lowell threw himself into his first active fight to accomplish a specific political end.

Since "the finger of God" had pointed to the time for action, Lowell was ready to act in "the interests of Humanity and Civilization." Although he realized that Whittier was properly the poet who should call together the forces of righteousness, he issued his own "Rallying Cry for New England against the Annexation of Texas" in the Boston *Courier* for March 19, two days before writing to the Quaker poet for other verses in a similar vein. The poem bore no relationship at all to his theory that the "true radical" should water the ground of reform rather than lop off the branches of evil—nor was it in any sense pacifistic in tone. Beginning "Rouse up, New England," it called upon the section's "old hate of Tyranny" and "deep contempt of crime" to oppose the "traitor plot" being hatched by the President of the United States who planned by "one flourish of a pen" to admit six new slave states and rivet fetters on "millions more of men" in the interest of "good democrats" and "These cotton and tobacco lords, these pimps of Slavery," who haughtily dominated the country while the silent and unprotesting New Englanders were held in contempt by the world. It was published anonymously as being merely "By a Yankee," for Lowell realized that as a propagandist he was violating his principles as poet and tried to make a distinction between the two. As he explained to Edward M. Davis when he sent the autographed copy more than two months later:

Had I entirely approved either the spirit or the execution of these verses, I had put my name to them. But they were written in great haste and for a particular object, and I used therefore such arguments as I thought would influence the mass of my readers, viz: a swinging ballad metre, some sectional prejudices and vanity, some denunciation, some scriptural allusions, and no cant. I wished *it* to be violent, because I thought the occasion demanded violence, but I had no wish to be violent myself, and therefore I let it go anonymously. Had I written aught in my own name, it would have been entirely different.

But Maria, who was convinced that she understood her fiancé better than he understood himself, believed that he was merely sensitive about the literary merit of his poem and wrote in a covering letter:

James does not at all realize how good and stirring it is, and the few remarks he makes at the end prove it. It is a war cry, but not one that of necessity appeals to bloodshed, though it has been quoted in several of the southern papers as instancing the murderous hatred of the north against them. They are too anxious to prove the warlike intentions of the North, to be very logical in their deductions.

The southerners' determination in wrongdoing was proved by their perverse illogic in pretending to find a threat in lines which called upon New Englanders, in the name of Plymouth Rock, Lexington, Concord, and Bunker Hill, to go "Forth to a nobler battlefield" and

> Shout "God for our New England!" and smite them hip and thigh
> The cursed race of Amalek whose armor is a lie!

But it mattered little if the race of Amalek were so literal-minded that they could not penetrate the surface of poetry: her James was not writing for them but for the chosen people who needed to be aroused because they, like those of an earlier generation, were placing their material interests above their duty to God.

The tone for anti-slavery agitation of the sort to which Maria was accustomed was set by William Lloyd Garrison, who had responded to a protest against the fiery language of his *Liberator:* "I have need to be *all on fire,* for I have mountains of ice about me to melt." Miss Abby Kelly had forced a similar style upon the meeting of the conservative Massachusetts Anti-Slavery Society in 1842 when, after several resolutions denouncing the church and clergy had been tabled as "not likely to gain friends to the Anti-Slavery enterprise," she made its members consider her own: "Resolved, That the sectarian organizations, called churches, are combinations of thieves, robbers, adulterers, pirates and murderers, and, as such, form the bulwark of American slavery." This also was laid on the table, but it was published as part of the proceedings of the meeting, and Lowell remembered it as a sort of poetry which he certainly did not contemplate with the literal-mindedness which Maria found so stupid among the Southerners. As Philip observed in the *Conversations,* John was commenting on Miss Kelly "favorably" when he spoke of her as one who used the English language with "its ancient privilege of thunder." A decade after her resolution, Wendell Phillips (whom Lowell also praised in his *Conversations* for his "thunder" and in his sonnets for his humility) defended such violence: "Men blame us for the bitterness of our language and the personality of our attacks. It results from our position. The great mass of the people can never be made to stay and argue a long question. They must be made to feel it through the hides of their idols." Phillips defined a republic as "nothing but a constant overflow of lava" and assumed that the business of an agitator was to preserve the republic by keeping public opinion hot. Lowell had probably not heard these exact words in 1844, but the sentiments were familiar and in keeping with his own philosophy that all thought is based on feeling. The poet expressed the thought, the agitator stirred the feeling, and the man came somewhere in between. The life which Lowell had been living in two unstable roles was becoming complicated by a third, and his literary expression became further complicated by the fact that the roles were constantly changing and oftentimes confused.

The Texas question called forth the agitator. His letter begging Whittier "to cry aloud and spare not against the accursed Texas plot" produced a poem considerably less violent than his own "Rallying Cry," but he had it reprinted in the *Courier* for April 17 with a vigorous introductory note in which he pointed out that Whittier had "not put his talent out at profitable interest by catering to the indolent and Pharisaical self-esteem of the times." Yet he did not agitate for long. Soon after the matter of annexation had been placed clearly before the public, Lowell's excitement appears to have died down. He may have decided that Massachusetts was sufficiently well united in opposition to the treaty, or he may have been simply lost in the confusion of his various roles. It was a confusing time, in fact, for many abolitionists, who were worked up to a high emotional pitch and were hopping from one side to the other of the question of disunion. At the twelfth annual meeting of the Massachusetts Anti-Slavery Society, for example, on January 26, 1844, William White had offered a resolution to petition Congress to free them "from all support and connection with slaves" or, "if this cannot be effected, a peaceful dissolution of the Union." At the meeting of the American Society early in May, C. C. Burleigh, one of the editors of the *Pennsylvania Freeman,* went on record as being opposed to the disunion movement. Yet when the question of withdrawing support from the United States government and "making the dissolution of the Union our main measure" came before the New England Society in the Marlboro' Chapel at the end of May, Burleigh was speaking in favor of the proposal and White was protesting against it. Lowell, as a man and a propagandist, managed to be on both sides at once. He had apparently joined the New England Society, and the first record of his participation in an organized abolitionist meeting shows him voting with Maria and William among the small minority who opposed the radical disunionists. But his verses in Garrison's *Liberator* at about the same time had an exactly opposite implication:

> Whate'er we deem Oppression's prop,
> Time-honored though it be,
> We break, nor fear the heavens will drop
> Because the earth is free.

As a poet, he escaped into the composition of the essays that later became his *Conversations,* avoiding the question of disunion entirely and perhaps, at first, even avoiding a criticism of the church.

In the "New Year's Eve" fragment which he sent to Graham in time for publication in his July magazine Lowell recognized his own unstable impulsiveness in a reference to his "high dependence on a higher Power" which he described as the

> Sole stay of all those restless faculties
> That wander, Ishmael-like, the desert bare
> Wherein our human knowledge hath its home
> Shifting their light-framed tents from day to day,
> With each new-found oasis, wearied soon,
> And only of uncertainty!

And the poem was broken off with a lesson against violence. Its conclusion was one of escape from the turmoil of dispute into an atmosphere too mild for men like Garrison and Wendell Phillips. But Lowell had convinced himself that the ideal poet was a man of action and had not yet, in the autumn of 1844, revised his conviction into the form it took in "Columbus." His closest personal associates were pressing him toward action, and his situation at home made him restless and eager for something to do. Yet the aim of his activity was by no means clear in his own mind. The Texas question was being fought out in the presidential election, and Massachusetts was so safe for Henry Clay that an abolitionist could vote for Birney or virtuously refrain from voting at all without affecting the important issue.

Lowell's name was on the list of Cambridge voters for the election of 1844, but he was by no means convinced that the line of political action was the best line to take: he was ready to have his mind made up for him. The prospect of an editorial job on the *Pennsylvania Freeman* probably offered more in the way of mental relief than in financial security, and the excuse of a job that would enable him to take Maria to Philadelphia was doubly welcome.

Lowell knew before he was offered a journalistic connection that he would have to follow a political line opposite to that he had followed at the meeting of the New England Society. The Eastern Pennsylvania Anti-Slavery Society had accepted responsibility for the *Freeman* in August, heard evidence of the conversion of its two editors to the cause of disunion, and approved their continuance in their positions with the determination to edit the paper according to their "New Light." The new management and policy of the paper were clearly put before the public in the issue of January 16, 1845, over the signature of Edward M. Davis as chairman of the executive committee of the society:

> The Freeman has been transferred from the individuals who have published it during the last year, into the hands of the Anti-Slavery Society of Eastern Pennsylvania, and will in the future be published by their Executive Committee. It will be conducted by the individuals who have heretofore had charge of it, and its editorial columns will also, for a time at least, be enriched by the contributions of one of the ablest writers of the country, James Russell Lowell.
>
> ... It will advocate the fundamental principles of the Pennsylvania Anti-Slavery Society—immediate emancipation, without expatriation or compensation; its measures—the preaching of truth in love, and the bearing of a practical testimony against slavery in every rightful way. It will advocate the doctrine that abolitionists cannot consistently swear to support the Constitution of the United States, or vote for officers of the government who must do this. It will teach that the guilt of slave holding rests on the north and south, and that every individual, both at the north and south, is bound to sever those alliances by which he has so long supported the national system of oppression.
>
> It will expose the unfaithfulness of the American church, and the hypocrisy of the American government relative to this subject, and aim to enlist every heart and conscience in the warfare against oppression. In short, it will strive to do its part in carrying on the anti-slavery enterprise, by the continued proclamation of uncompromising truth.

The change of the Eastern Pennsylvania Society to radical principles had been announced in the *Liberator;* and the relationship between Davis and the Whites was such that when Lowell was offered a job with the *Freeman* he could have been under no illusions concerning the propaganda line he was expected to bear in mind if not to follow. When a mixture of motives led him to preach the gospel of liberty, he allowed chance and someone else to determine the doctrines he would accept.

To a certain extent, Lowell began to preach the doctrines of the "New Light" before he took up his new job, for he "exposed" the church in his poem "The Happy Martyrdom" for the 1845 *Liberty Bell.* In it he renounced the notion, expressed in so many of his earlier poems, that martyrdom consisted of suffering "hatred, scorn, and sorrow" and found it in seeing the unwillingness of his fellowmen to experience the bliss "Of giving all to serve the Right." What greater pang could there be, he asked specifically, than

> To see the Church hold up Thy Book
> To keep Thy light from bursting in?
> To see Thy priests with patience brook,
> For the rich sinner's sake, the sin?
> To see the red-eyed vengeance creep
> Upon our nature in its sleep?

It may have been at this time (near the end of 1844) that he introduced into his *Conversations* his criticisms of the church, for his father, who begged him to remove them from the second edition of the book, would hardly have passed them over without comment had they appeared in the earlier essays he read during the summer.

James and Maria were married on the evening of December 26 and reached Philadelphia by the first of the year, settling down economically but comfortably in a third-floor room of the friendly boardinghouse where the bride and her mother had spent the preceding spring. They were charmed by their new friends, and James found no difficulty in swallowing the party line to which he committed himself when he accepted his position. In the issue that contained Davis' explanation of the paper's position, Lowell published "A Word in Season" which supported the disunion movement:

> I rejoice at the stand which has been taken by the Society. In my eyes it never looked so sublimely as now. It has refused to palter with wrong. It has refused to fling away its impenetrable *moral* buckler, and to fight the enemy with their own clumsy weapons of politics and guile, in which it has no skill, and with which it would surely be defeated. I am glad that the tree has had such a heart shaking that all the fruit in which the old worms of worldliness and respectability have laid their eggs, must needs fall.

The new employee was going to prove himself as radical as any member of the staff. He had defined respectability as "that which has in itself no essential claim to respect, but depends entirely on external and assumed ones"; and he was determined to shake off the respectable abolitionism with which he himself had been associated:

> Abolitionism has its respectable side also, in virtue of being the advocate of Freedom. The poet who can round off a couplet, and the editor who can give sound to the closing of a paragraph by some flourish about freedom and the destiny of America, claims to be an abolitionist. But let abolitionism become anything else than speculative,—let it take one step toward the accomplishment of its object,—and they repudiate immediately with indignation all sympathy with fanaticism, yet remain as good abolitionists as before.

Lowell had confessed himself a fanatic in a letter to Heath nearly three years before, but he would have said at this time that he hardly knew the meaning of the word until his own respectability had been "detected by and writhed under the Ithuriel-spear of pure abolitionism." Henceforth he would be a genuine fanatic.

His fanaticism was not sufficiently great, however, for him to send a copy of his first leader to his father, who wrote on January 24, 1845:

> I will not *say* I am sorry that you have become an editor of a newspaper, but I will caution you not to write in the newspaper style, or with the newspaper spirit, i.e., do write like yourself, kind, dignified and no personalities. I do not regret your hatred of slavery, but I do regret to have you *narrow* your mind to the abolitionism of the day, hard, dogmatical, uncharitable, *unchristian.* You will allow me to say for *once,* Do not give to party, what was meant for mankind. Be assured you can do much more good to the cause of abolitionism, if you stood aloof from party, on the broad ground of *Humanity.* This is the advice of an "old head" though there is reason to fear a young head will not take it.

But Dr. Lowell was advising his son to be like the ideal poet of the 1843 version of the "Ode" and the author of the "Elegy on the Death of Dr. Channing"—a "respectable" abolitionist of the sort that James had since been taught to despise. He had already sent to the Boston *Courier* "Another Rallying Cry: By a Yankee" for the anti-Texas convention held in Fanueil Hall on January 29 which, if not so liable to misinterpretation, was as vigorous as his earlier cry on the same subject. His article on Texas for the *Freeman* of January 30 may have been more dignified than many of the other abolitionist articles on that issue, but it was neither kind nor free from personalities, for it denounced George Bancroft and Alexander H. Everett by name and accused the Whigs of a hypocritical compromise with "the smooth devil of expediency." A "reverence for a pro-slavery constitution" was at the bottom of the failure of the anti-slavery forces to defeat the Texas resolution, and it would continue to be a source of weakness "till the utter worthlessness of that piece of parchment has been so thoroughly illustrated by the rejection of its authority by all good men, that politicians instead of asking *"Is it constitutional?* shall be compelled to ask *Is it right?"*

The "New Light" in which Lowell dwelt aroused so much heat in him that his friendship with Charles F. Briggs, who had succeeded George Loring as his closest confidant, almost became a sacrifice upon the altar of his enthusiasm. He had expected to contribute not only poetry but prose, for friendship's sake and at a dollar a column, to Briggs's new *Broadway Journal,* and his first article was sent in the single-minded "hope of doing some good" for the abolitionist cause rather than for the cause of a friend's success. It was in the form of a letter of denunciation from a countryman, "Matthew Trueman," to a member of Congress who had voted for the annexation of Texas; and the author realized while sending it in that "It may be a little too abolition for you as yet" and confessed that he was following Maria's judgment rather than his own concerning its quality. Briggs was unwilling to publish the satire—which, he wrote, "bruises instead of cutting the flesh"—without removing "certain expressions that could not be safely used in public" and eventually decided not to publish it at all. Lowell, who had urged him to "reject it without scruple" or "alter it as much as you please," was annoyed and wrote Robert Carter of his disappointment concerning the *Journal* as a possible "weapon in the hands of reform" and of his inability to write for a periodical which "shut its doors" on every subject in which he was "mainly interested." After the first outbursts following the passage of the Texas resolution, however, Lowell became calm enough to write an article on the "Pennsylvania Academy of Fine Arts" which, although hardly good-humored, was satisfactory to Briggs and appeared in the *Journal* on the author's twenty-sixth birthday. He also wrote a leader for the *Freeman* on "The Prejudice of Color" that he considered sufficiently charitable to send to his father, who found some truth and some error in it and wished that his son would send him copies of everything he wrote.

But the son's obedience to such a request would hardly have been conducive to his father's peace of mind, for on the morning of February 25, with his old habit of delaying his articles until the last moment, he dashed off a leader on "The Church and Clergy" which attacked the "third party" or political group of abolitionists for dissociating themselves from the criticisms of religion. His language was temperate, but his thesis was clear: "In this country the civilization of the people has not yet come nearly up to the political principles set forth in the Declaration of Independence, but it has already gone beyond the religious principle as now represented by the church." He was, in the spirit of Wendell Phillips, taking his stand as one of "the foremost spirits of the age" and calling the institution before him for judgment, insisting that it had become time to "protest against protestantism" and demand that "the church re-form itself so as to be the emblem of something higher and purer." He promised to take up the present condition of the church in another article, but before doing so he had to pause and consider the departure of President Tyler and the inauguration of Polk. His article for March 13 on "President Tyler's Message on the African Slave-Trade and President Polk's Inaugural Message" was temperate neither in language nor in sentiment. Slavery was a "huge ulcer which disfigures the face of our strumpet goddess of liberty," and the new president was "one of those cuttlefish politicians" whose inky message was characterized by "falsehoods" and "twaddle." His intemperance carried over into his reference to the church as "the main pillar of that hideous despotism which the Constitution has usurped over men's consciences and religion—the pillar to which Christ is bound to be scourged anew"—and the Constitution itself was "just as despicable as any other piece of cant and hypocrisy." Something of the same tone was preserved in his second article on the church and clergy which appeared on March 27. The clergy deserved more severe blame for "upholding slavery" than did the merchants, lawyers, and manufacturers because they had convinced people that the church was not merely "a part of our civilized machinery for *getting along*" but an institution of "more than human origin." Without passing judgment upon the validity of the claim, he argued:

> If the church be, then, the depository of truth, if its ministers have the sole charge of the conduit pipes for conveying the waters of truth to the rest of mankind, it is our duty to complain if they cast impure and poisonous matter into that blessed reservoir, or if they allow the pipes to be so clogged that only a few drops of the precious elixir can ooze through their corrupted channels.

"The outward form of the church is, at present, nothing but a block of wood rudely carved," he concluded, "which we shall cast away for some purer image, and it will not be long before we shall wonder at our benightedness in allowing it room on earth so long."

During these weeks of apprenticeship to the art of agitating, Lowell was doing more than adopting the journalist's conventional practice of allowing the policy of his paper to become his guide and conscience. He was living in a world of self-righteous fantasy. He was delighted and stimulated by his new friends, and Maria had adopted the policy of refusing all evening invitations in order that James might not be restrained by either her health which prevented her from walking abroad at night or their poverty which kept them from hiring a carriage. The closest of their associates were Hicksite Quakers who were not only anti-clerical and anti-church by profession of faith but spoke of their own Society in the language of Jeremiah. Yet they were the most kindly, generous, and hospitable people that Lowell had ever known, and they accepted the inner light of his ideal poet as the daily guide of ordinary persons. Poetry, the delight in ornament and imagery for its own sake, however, was not in them. Figurative language was a practical tool, and in order to be useful, it had to be strong enough to crack the shell of indifference and material interests so that the inner light might be free to shine. They held to the philosophy of the Boston radicals, with which Lowell sympathized in theory, and expressed it in a spirit, if not in the language, of a loving kindness which made it acceptable to Lowell in practice. Maria was completely at home among them; and James fell readily into their assumptions, for it was easy for him—as he had shown during the years of his apprenticeship to the art of verse-making—to see in his own words merely what they meant to himself and his immediate circle of friends and not what they might mean to an objective reader at a distance. Lowell could never have understood the allusion of one of his friends to Philadelphia as "the city of brotherly *hate*." His own adelphian love was such that he complained to Robert Carter of the restraint placed upon his expression by the "rather timid" attitude of the conductors of the *Freeman*. In the newfound vigor of his righteousness he was ready to batter mankind into a state of brotherhood.

At Elmwood, Dr. Lowell held to the old illiberal notion that you could not improve the temper of humanity by beating it with a hammer and continued to pay his son's debts and beg him to use discretion. He wrote in March expressing his regret "that you should go out of your appropriate sphere, and descend to become the editor of an ultra party press." "You are *wasting* your powers, my son," he added, "—But why should I write? You will not heed me." He wrote of his own belief in the church and made the painful query whether James could have been the author of an article on the Whigs, abolitionism, and the church which he had recently read. He was also concerned about James's literary reputation: "I am told you are writing a *book* on slavery. Let me conjure you not to publish it for two years at least. —These ephemeral essays will die soon. Do not embody them in a volume I entreat you." Dr. Lowell's disturbance was deeper than that of the respectable abolitionist to which James felt so superior. He feared that his son was writing from a spirit of hate rather than of love and knew that he was not facing the problem that bothered him in the expression of his own feelings about slavery. His own concern was practical: *"Shew how it is to be removed."*

The son was impressed by his father's attitude even if he did not show it in his editorials. He confessed to Briggs on March 21 that he did not wish to see the *Journal* "a partisan" and added:

> I think it could do more good by always speaking of certain reforms and of the vileness of certain portions of our present civilization as matters of course than by attacking them fiercely and individually. It always goes against my grain to say anything ill of a man or men, and I assure you that (minister's and conservative's son as I am) I do not occupy my present position without pain.

His last leader for the *Freeman,* in the issue of April 10, was a rambling discussion of "Our Union," satirizing the "third party" for its use of traditional patriotism as an argument against the moral assurance of his own group and for the general ineffectuality of its candidates for office. It was written after a visit to the country in Germantown with some of his and Maria's new friends and his old college friend Charles Scates and his bride. It contained some echoes but none of the consistency of his earlier vehemence. The country made him homesick. His mother had been placed in a sanatorium, and Elmwood would be more pleasant for Maria than it had promised to be a year before. Philadelphia had already become for him a place of "turmoil," and with the arrival of spring he found it a glaring city of harsh pavements, hot red bricks, and interminable white steps. They accepted the long-standing invitation to visit the Edward Davises, had daguerreotypes made, paid their farewell calls in a borrowed carriage, and by the latter part of May were ready to go home. Mr. White and Dr. Lowell were each willing to build a house for the young couple in order to keep them near by, and James was willing to shake off the obligation to write according to a regular schedule. They left on May 19, in high spirits, for a leisurely two-weeks' trip back to New England where James was to take up again the care of his chickens after the catharsis of fifteen weeks of active radicalism.

III

LOWELL HAD NOT been comfortable in the situation to which he had felt called. Whether he liked it or not, he was—by background, training, and most of his associations—respectable. He may have been able to persuade himself that it was his duty to resist the paternal advice of an older and more conservative generation, but he had no defense against his father's failure to criticize him for not earning a living. His marriage had possibly put a strain upon his belief that his love for Maria was "worthless" unless it inspired thoughts of universal brotherhood; and, in any case, the obligation to support a wife was more deeply ingrained in his consciousness than was his desire to purify the American Union. The abolitionist periodicals, unfortunately, were not sufficiently well financed to enable him to do both.

The thirty-five dollars or so that James had earned by his work on the *Freeman* would have done little more than take care of his incidental expenses during his stay in Philadelphia and was, in fact, nine dollars less than the bill his father paid for his wedding garments and the other new clothes he took with him. Income for board and lodging came from the contributions of both the bride and the groom to periodicals which had little to do with the anti-slavery or any other reform movement. He had sent Graham the substantial, innocuous poem, "To the Dandelion," for publication in his January magazine and called upon him soon after his arrival in town. The editor and publisher distressed the eager young man by remarking that he would have paid a hundred and fifty dollars for "A Legend of Brittany" without the copyright, but he was vague about future contributions and rates. Lowell had already written the article on Poe for the "Contributors" column in the February issue, however, and he may have received as much as fifty dollars for it. He wrote Carter on January 14 that he would "probably be able to make a good arrangement" with Graham after his "new book has been puffed a little more" and two days later that he would "no doubt" receive his old price of thirty dollars a poem. But Graham published only one other poem by Lowell—"An Incident of the Fire at Hamburg," in May—while the latter was in Philadelphia.

The weekly *Broadway Journal* of his friend Briggs was a more dependable if less profitable medium of publication in which either James or Maria had a poem or an article for every number except two from its beginning on January 5 until March 22. By the latter date, the Lowells had broken off their literary routine in their attic room on Arch Street and had gone visiting, but James found time to review Fitz-Greene Halleck's *Alnwick Castle, with other Poems* for the *Journal* of May 3 and Maria had a poem in the issue for June 7. But Briggs's paper was another of those journalistic ventures in which the editor's hopes were high and his cash was low, and he hesitated to tell his friend just how little he could pay for contributions. Poe, he finally wrote, was being paid at the rate of a dollar a column for prose, and contributions by Lowell at the same rate would be esteemed "capital bargain." Poetry would be paid for "separately on a different principle" which was not declared but which probably represented another bargain for the *Journal*. If Lowell wrote prose for a dollar a column, his article on the Pennsylvania Academy of Fine Arts and his review of Halleck together brought in only about six dollars and a half; and he and Maria probably received no more than fifty or sixty dollars for the five poems which Briggs printed from each of them.

Little as that was, however, they apparently counted upon it as regular income. The disappointment they revealed when Briggs was unable to print the prose satires which Lowell wrote in rustic disguise probably reflected a genuine regret that a good friend did not see eye to eye with them concerning the overwhelming importance of reform, but James's irritation when one of them was crowded out of the poetry corner had no such excuse. The reprinting of "The Raven" instead of a poem by a Lowell on February 8 occurred at a time when the young groom's relationship with Poe was already so near the breaking point for other reasons that it is impossible to determine whether resentment hastened the process. There seems to be little doubt, however, concerning Lowell's attitude toward being squeezed out by Park Benjamin's "The Belle of Broadway" on March 15. Although the first exchange of letters apparently has not been preserved, Lowell's letter to Briggs on March 21 indicates that the latter had informed his friend of some necessity for printing the poem and had referred to it somewhat humorously as a form of literary blackmail of the sort which any new journal had to pay to the various interests which might affect its success. Lowell's response had evidently been sharp, for after another letter from Briggs he replied: "Mrs. Child is my authority for my estimate of P. B.'s personal character and I think you speak quite too lightly of his levying literary black mail. I think it one of the meanest crimes a man can be guilty of, looking upon literature with as sincere a reverence as I do." But he assured his friend, in the same letter, that he understood the difficulties of making a new journal exactly what one wanted it and he also found occasion to boast that he himself was beginning "to feel rich" because his Cambridge publisher owed him nearly three hundred dollars at the moment. His royalties from Owen, although they may have consoled Briggs for passing him over for an issue, did not affect his immediate financial standing. They were being used to pay off the remaining debts for the *Pioneer*. The young couple left Philadelphia with no surplus cash for the comforts of travel, and after spending a night in New York in a room too small to hold both a bed and a chair, James wrote Edward Davis that if he had happened to have a nightmare during the night "it would have assumed the shape of a coroner sitting on my body bringing in a verdict of 'suffocated in the pursuit of economy.' "

Of the poems that sustained the Lowells in Philadelphia some were gleanings from his almost bare portfolio, the "fragment" entitled "Remembered Music" which appeared in the *Broadway Journal* for February 15 having been composed as early as 1840. Others reveal something of the immediate strain that was placed upon him by his decision to enter the active ranks of the reformers. "A Song" which appeared in the first issue of the *Journal* addressed in a spirit of glad proprietorship "To My Wife" (and later simply "To M. L.") and "To the Dandelion" in the January *Graham's* were both, of course, written before he left Elmwood late in 1844; and the latter reveals his old tendency, under emotional strain, to revert to his childhood. The sight of the flower called to mind the robin which used to sing in the old horse chestnut tree about which he had written in the days of his uncertainty before he met Maria, and in the concluding stanza, which he later suppressed, he found consolation in the notion that he would never grow old so long as the lowly flower returned annually to keep him "pure" with memories of his childhood. As usual when he let his mind dwell upon his primal sympathies with the birds and the flowers his unconscious recollections began to flow along the channels of literary precedent and intimations of Wordsworth overflowed his verses. The dandelion became

> the type of those meek charities
> Which make up half the nobleness of life,
> Those cheap delights the wise
> Pluck from the dusty wayside of earth's strife.

Its "winged seeds," like those in Shelley's "Ode to the West Wind," also became typical of "the words of poet and of sage"; and the flower generally, in the last stanza the author preserved, was recognized as one of the "living pages of God's book" of teachings. But whether or not he read the lesson right, he originally concluded, the purely Wordsworthian associations surrounding "Nature's first lowly influences" were a source of gladness, peace, and hope in days of greatest dreariness. Although the "Song" to Maria took an opposite view of the past, Lowell preferring his full-blown "woman-flower" to the "lily-bud" he had known at first, he contemplated the future in terms of her influence rather than her presence, and the suggestion of death hints at the same melancholia that touched the dandelion poem.

This wary balancing of past, present, and future in the scales of happiness was characteristic of almost all Lowell's personal poems during the first year of his marriage and of his abolitionist activities. "The Epitaph," which he selected for the second number of his friend's periodical, was dated February 7, 1844, and shows how his hopes for the future were linked with his dissatisfaction with present conditions in a manner revealed earlier by "The Shepherd of King Admetus" and other writings on the poet: instead of vain, material evidences of fame, he wanted to achieve the sort of influence that could be represented in such an epitaph as

> He came and left more smiles behind,
> One ray he shot athwart the gloom,
> He helped one fetter to unbind,
> Men think of him and grow more kind.

But he did not, in his current state of determined activity, approve either of these moods of escape nor of those heavy moods in which, as he put it in a poem for the *Journal* of January 25,

> All the present is but caring,
> All the future more despairing,
> And the past is sweet alone.

The "Dreamy river of the Past" had its Wordsworthian fascinations, he made clear; but when it came to the question of exchanging the "hard present" for it, the question of whether he was really willing to "make ease first, and labor last," he exclaimed firmly: "Out on such unmanly shirking!" And he advertised his determination by giving his poem the title "Now is always Best."

One of the troubles with Lowell was that he was haunted by visions which he described in "The Ghost-Seer" and sent to Briggs on February 25, 1845, with the note that it was "better in conception than in execution" although he had intended it to be one of the best poems he had ever written.

His visions were of a pale seamstress who might have stepped out of the pages of Thomas Hood, haunted by the lean bloodhounds Want and Sin—of a well-born, well-dressed woman suckling the hyena Pride—of a modern Judas who had sold the God within his heart for success in the market place and consequently nourished a Hawthornian snake in his bosom—and, most distressing of all, of a poet who had betrayed his trust by failing to reveal golden glimpses of the future and by refusing to be the voice of "the weak and spirit-wrung." The poet who chose to be "a bird of night" for the world's idolatry instead of "a lark of Truth's morning," he announced, with perhaps some thought of Poe, could never hope to climb the mountains where the prophets dwelt. Lowell had no doubt of his own desire to be a lark instead of a raven, but he was torn and distressed by the difficulty of finding a single song which would give "Golden glimpses of To Be" and also represent the poor and the downtrodden.

His next contribution to *Graham's,* "An Incident of the Fire at Hamburg," was an exemplification of faith in time of peril after the fashion that Longfellow had made popular by his magazine ballads of foreign cities; but in the August number, in the only poem Graham used in order to keep Lowell's name among the contributors for that volume, he returned to his familiar theme and addressed himself "To the Future." The irregular ode was the outburst of a poet who was explicitly "Aweary of the turmoil and the wrong" of his own generation and longed to gaze into the future as a "Land of Quiet" in which there would be no war, no selfishness stifling the godlike sense of man, no anger of the humble toward the high, and no unwillingness of the nobleman to recognize his brother beneath the foul rags that covered him. It was mostly an escapist poem which showed again how inevitably Lowell found sanctuary in Wordsworth when he tried to flee the reverberations of the street, but it also showed how determined he was to put down any dreamy inclination to escape his duty. The "golden gleams" of the future admittedly brought on an "agony of hopelese contrast" to the present. But the poet had made his choice and he reaffirmed it in his closing lines:

He is a coward who would borrow
A charm against the present sorrow
From the vague Future's promise of delight:
As life's alarums nearer roll,
The ancestral buckler calls,
Self-clanging, from the walls
In the high temple of the soul;

Where are most sorrows, there the poet's sphere is,
To feed the soul with patience,
To heal its desolations
With words of unshorn truth, with love that never wearies.

Although the young man, in his determination, clanged his buckler with a vigor that may have made his ancestors turn in their graves, he could not by an act of will keep his love from wearying. "Orpheus," which he sent to George H. Colton for the August number of his *American Review* in response to a request and an offer of twenty dollars, was the expression of a poet who had delighted and found satisfaction in the humblest things of nature but who had discovered that the world was a "land of shades" in comparison with the "spirit-realm" where Eurydice dwelt. His ode "To the Past" in *Graham's* for January, 1846, indicated a similar weariness, for, although it dealt with the historical rather than the author's personal past and therefore indicated no desire to escape into former days, it found the "true life" of the past still existing in the present as "the green Fortunate Isles" floating amid "the bleak waves of our strife and care." Lowell was not altogether happy about the strife to which he had dedicated himself.

The ode "To the Past" was, in effect, Lowell's temporary farewell to the general magazine public, although he wrote a few other verses during the 1844–45 period which were not related to the abolitionist cause. Occasionally, at this time and later, he contributed a poem to a worthy periodical that needed the assistance of a good name, but most of them appeared for the first time among the few new works in his *Poems, Second Series* at the end of 1847. "Hunger and Cold," which he dated 1844, was another expression of his sympathy with the poor and downtrodden, suggestive of the earlier "The Forlorn" and of the personification of Want and Sin in the later "The Ghost-Seer," but remarkable for its hint of a bloody class revolution unless the world could "be by pity led To Love's fold." "To a Pine-Tree," which he wrote after his return to Elmwood and sent to the newly established *Harbinger* for publication on August 2, 1845, indicates a certain amount of reaction against reform, for it ignored the "unity of Man with Man" in which both the poet and the editor of the Brook Farm periodical were so greatly interested and also ignored man's union "with Nature and with God" despite the fact that ordinarily such a theme would have flowed from his pen as readily as his rhymes.

The other two poems that can be dated from this period were in substance somewhere between the purposeful social consciousness of "Hunger and

Cold" and the Shelleyean ode "To a Pine-Tree." "To the Memory of Hood" was a tribute to the author of "The Bridge of Sighs" and "The Song of a Shirt" rather than to the punster whom Lowell must have appreciated even though he did not admire him as he admired Hood as the voice of freedom and of the poor. "Eurydice" was of them all the most personal and the most closely related to Lowell's greatest emotional problem at the time. Although Lowell dated the finished poem 1845 when it was printed in 1849, the date probably referred to the fragment in his private journal or some other draft which related the theme more clearly to his own experience than is apparent in the published version. He identified himself more definitely with the forlorn lover than he had in his poem for the *American Review* but made less use of the myth: Eurydice became a symbol of his lost joy in the "outdoor influences" to which most of the poem was devoted and which, at the end, faded away into something vaguely better while leaving the poet too melancholy to affirm the "joy" that Wordsworthian precedent called for.

That Lowell was neither entirely happy with his situation nor given to spontaneous overflowings of reform verse, however, is indicated by a letter he wrote from Elmwood in July, 1845, in response to a request from the editor of *The Missionary Memorial: A Literary and Religious Souvenir.* "The piece has no particular fitness for a missionary memorial, nor had I any that had," he confessed with reference to "The Captive" which he was enclosing, "but it has a moral and that perhaps brings it within the pale." The story was a repetition, in oriental costume, of the one he had used in "The Ballad of the Stranger" in which a maiden gladly gave up her ghost to meet in spirit the lover that she could not meet in the flesh; and the moral was simply that heaven is better than earth—a not uncommon observation that might be produced either by enchantment with the former place or disenchantment with the latter. The moral of "The Captive" was the result of disenchantment, one can be sure, for not only was it in keeping with Lowell's prevailing mood of unhappiness over the turmoil of contemporary life but it revived one of the most persistent symbols through which he expressed his unfulfillment: in the middle of the poem up cropped Coleridge's solitary date tree "yearning for its mate afar." Lowell would neither confess nor permit himself to believe that he had made a mistake in taking up the cudgels of reform. On the contrary, these poems in which he expressed his own emotion instead of attempting to influence the emotions of others often show a persistent determination to assert the rightness of his action. But it is difficult to read them without believing that James found what Emerson would have called one of his "own rejected thoughts" in his father's distressed pride and affection, "You are *wasting* your powers, my son."

The source of Lowell's unhappiness during this period, however, is not to be found entirely in his uneasy fear that propaganda might not be the highest calling of a poet. He was being forced toward the realization that his position as a professional magazinist was not nearly so strong as he had liked to believe. A writer who expected to make his living from the American magazines of the 'forties had to have most of the qualities of a politician who had mastered the art of give and take and had acquired flexible standards and a thick skin. Lowell was temperamentally unfitted to such a career, for he gave too impulsively and demanded too much, and he was as sensitive about himself as he was critical of other people. Even his natural friendliness, considered as a professional asset, was often neutralized by his intractable wit. The attraction he felt toward many of his fellow authors was spontaneous and apparently genuine, and although he was often blind to their failings he was never wholly so for long—and when he made a penetrating observation on their works it was frequently in language too sharply pointed to be dulled by repetition as it made its quick way to their ears. His extant letters from the period before the middle of 1845 contain comments on Graham, Emerson, Mathews, O'Sullivan, Willis, and Griswold, among the editors who had published his poems, which would have rankled had they been repeated to them. Some of them certainly were, for Mathews had been deeply offended by Lowell's reported comments upon his novel *Puffer Hopkins,* and Lowell several times felt obliged to explain himself to Emerson and, through Peterson, to Graham. Nor was his erratic attitude toward his literary friends and acquaintances revealed entirely through gossip. Lowell was modest enough about his work when he judged it by absolute standards of what it ought to be, but he was sensitive and quick to take offense at any critical comment implying that he was in any way inferior to the "empty rhymers" who were his rivals in the magazine columns. He regularly encouraged editors to criticize or reject his contributions and was regularly offended when they took even the most hesitant and apologetic advantage of the privilege. The personal friendship of Briggs or the desire of Graham to keep him on his list of contributors may have prevented his direct protests from giving offense, and N. P. Willis' suave worldliness was of the sort that could hardly be penetrated by Lowell's indignation at his review of the 1844 *Poems;* but Lowell could hardly have had the reputation of being an easy person with whom to deal.

Furthermore, he had, in Poe's phrase, "coteried" himself into a professional corner. When he joined the Philadelphia abolitionists he found himself moving in circles quite different from those of his old friend by correspondence, Charles J. Peterson, who had no interest in the reforms with which Lowell had become so preoccupied. Following the course of an increasing specialization in the magazine business, Peterson had become the editor of a ladies' magazine designed to rival Godey's, and both he and his rival were stimulating the growth of a boudoir literature in which an active abolitionist could have no part. Lowell's disunionist affiliations also placed him at odds with the principles of the *Democratic Review* and probably qualified the desire of the *American Review* to have him as a regular contributor. His complaint to Carter concerning the *Broadway Journal*—that it had shut its doors on every subject except those in which he had no interest and therefore could not treat well—could have been made with reference to all the other periodicals to which he had contributed with the exception of the Boston *Courier* and those publications formally issued by the more radical section of the abolitionist press.

Had Lowell's fellow magazinists been as sensitive as he was during this period he would have returned to Elmwood with no literary friends at all. But fortunately Briggs was patient and loyal despite Lowell's momentary petulance over the rejection of his satires, and Evert Duyckinck, who served as an intermediary for Lowell's vain attempt to get back into the pages of the *Democratic Review,* was tactful; and there were few others who had to deal critically with his work at this time. Poe's was the only literary friendship which was unmistakably sacrificed to his ill humor. His article on Poe for the February *Graham's* had been the means of interesting Briggs in the brilliant and versatile journalist as a possible associate in his new periodical venture, and Briggs's first meeting with Poe dissipated all that remained of prejudice inspired by the "shocking bad stories" told of him by Griswold. He liked him, he reported on January 6, "exceedingly well" and apparently was immediately moved to share the editorship of the journal with him as soon as practical details could be arranged. Lowell should have been delighted at the association of his two greatest admirers, but his response was, in actuality, sour. Although he admired the article about Elizabeth Barrett which Poe had contributed to the first two numbers of the *Journal,* he was driven to add: "From a paragraph I saw yesterday in the Tribune, I find that Poe has been at me in the Mirror. He has at least that chief element of a critic—a disregard of persons. He will be a very valuable coadjuter to you." His tone was neither just nor fair. In his review of the *Conversations* for the *Evening Mirror* of January 11, Poe had been generous to the point of extravagance in his praise and had exercised remarkable self-control in ignoring the abolitionism and social puritanism which undoubtedly was offensive to his personal prejudices and his artistic theories. His only adverse criticism consisted of a disagreement with an opinion that literary success was more likely to be achieved by artlessness than by art—and even in his disagreement he was sufficiently tactful to attribute the opinion to one of Lowell's characters rather than necessarily to Lowell himself. But Lowell was not interested in the fact that Poe was less critical of him than he had been of Poe in the forthcoming biographical article: he was in the ungenerous mood which caused him, in the same letter, to call William A. Jones (whom he had been anxious to get and found too expensive for the *Pioneer* and who was the first subject of the *Journal's* series of "Sketches of American Prose Writers") "a dull and second rate writer." Graham had apparently lost interest in publishing the sketch of Lowell that he had planned so long before, and there can be little doubt but that Lowell, having chosen to eat the bread of abolitionism, was finding some bitterness in comparing it with the cake of praise and publicity which was being awarded to less virtuous literary rivals.

The feeling of self-imposed but unwilling exile from literary fame continued to rankle, as time went on, beneath the surface of Lowell's consciousness. One of the opening volleys of Poe's "Little Longfellow War" made a casual hit at the poet's wife, and Lowell (who admired the former Miss Appleton enormously) was perhaps more offended than Longfellow himself. Yet he tried to be fair. Although he received without enthusiasm the news that Poe had been made an editor of the *Broadway Journal,* he admitted his ability and merely questioned the wisdom of having "more than one editor with any proprietary control over the paper"—an arrangement which had been satisfactory enough between himself and Carter. After the new editor's name had been announced and he had begun to fill the pages of the *Journal* with the critical charges of his "war," Briggs himself became worried and wrote Lowell regularly and at length of his dislike for Poe's "hobbyhorse" of plagiarism, the wisdom of letting him ride it to death, and the possible value of the attention it brought to the paper. The whole business was embarrassing to Lowell, for he was aware of his own lack of enthusiasm for Longfellow's verse, feared that his Cambridge neighbor would associate him with Poe's attacks, and realized that he was largely responsible for the connection between Briggs and Poe which might prove troublesome to the former. Briggs tried to reason with his friend concerning the impersonality of Poe's allusion to Mrs. Longfellow, but perhaps did little to ease Lowell's mind when he continued to insist that his good opinion of his associate was no more than a verification, by personal acquaintance, of the opinion he had formed in September when "my love for you and implicit confidence in your judgment led me to abandon all my prejudices against him when I read your account of him." Lowell insisted as late as March 21 that he was still of the opinion he had expressed in his article and that the stories told by the Reverend Mr. Griswold were the untrustworthy gossip of an "ass" and a "knave." But when he called on Poe for their first meeting face to face, on his way home from Philadelphia, he was no longer anticipating the realization of the close spiritual intimacy he had felt earlier.

The meeting was not a success. Poe had certainly possessed every reason to expect an expression of appreciation for his generous notice of the *Conversations,* and even if he had not heard from Briggs that Lowell was unreasonably annoyed he was acutely aware of the fact that Lowell had quit writing to him while corresponding regularly with Briggs—and he probably suspected that he did not go unmentioned in these letters. Yet he was anxious to make a good impression. His own state of mind as the interview approached was one of hurt self-consciousness and anxiety. He fortified himself for the occasion, and Mrs. Clemm remained anxiously in the room while the two men talked. In his stimulated dignity, Poe impressed his visitor as being pompous in manner and clammy in appearance, and the stubby, chin-whiskered Lowell turned out to be not half so noble-looking as Poe had expected him to be. They parted with the young temperance reformer ready to believe the worst of his erstwhile admirer, who, in turn, was left with the sort of nagging conscience and offended self-respect that normally seeks relief in self-assertion at the expense of one to whom no explanations or apologies are possible.

Lowell went on to Elmwood and helped dissociate himself from Poe in his own mind—and in the minds of his local friends—by cultivating more friendly relations with Longfellow, discussing frequently and at length those coincidental resemblances between poets that Poe called plagiarisms. In the meantime, Briggs was losing his good opinion of Poe and seeking a new publisher for the *Broadway Journal* with the intention of removing from the masthead the name of the man who had "latterly got in his old habits" and was causing alarm. In the shuffling about, however, Briggs either lost or gave up the *Journal,* and Lowell's lines "To the Memory of Hood" failed to appear in its columns where he had expected to print them in July. Whether this failure was the result of Poe's or of Lowell's action is uncertain, but Poe had already begun his self-assertion at the other's expense, reprinting the objectionable paragraph from the review of the *Conversations* among his marginalia in the August number of *Godey's* and adding a new characterization of the author as "the Anacharsis Clootz of American letters." In his review of the August number of *Graham's* in the *Journal* for August 16 he called attention to a "palpable plagiarism" of Wordsworth in the concluding lines of Lowell's poem "To the Future." This was too much for Lowell, who indignantly wrote Briggs that Poe was "wholly lacking in that element of manhood which, for want of a better name, we call *character."* He had made Poe an enemy by doing him a service, he asserted, and Poe had falsely accused him of plagiarism and, furthermore, had misquoted Wordsworth to prove it.

But Lowell, professing accuracy in his own defense, misrepresented Poe much more seriously than his critic, professing to quote approximately and from memory, misrepresented Wordsworth's lines; and he evidently missed the entire point of Poe's charge, which was simply that the American was imitating the English poet's pathetic fallacy in attributing the desire and power of action to inanimate armor. Poe should never have used so offensive a word as plagiarism in connection with Longfellow or Lowell when he really had reference to something that might better have been described—in a word that Poe actually did use occasionally—as imitation in a somewhat Platonic sense. Had Lowell focused upon his admirer (who called the poem in question "altogether a noble composition") any portion of his enlightened sympathy for humanity he might have observed that Poe was engaged in a sort of critical strutting, preening his intelligence and rather pathetic virtue while stridently calling attention to another poet's lack of well-informed, objective editorial judgment concerning his own work. If the charge had been made less stridently but more often during the preceding six years, Lowell might have become a better poet. But its tone and timing only aroused resentment. He forgot the encouragement he had received from the former editor of *Graham's* and the generosity of the impoverished contributor to the *Pioneer,* and, remembering only that he had introduced Poe to Briggs, wrote to the latter:

Poe wishes to kick down the ladder by which he rose. He is welcome. But he does not attack me at a weak point. He probably cannot conceive of anybody's writing for anything but a newspaper reputation or for posthumous fame which is but the same thing magnified by distance.

"I have," he added, "quite other aims."

IV

Exactly what his aims were is not clear from this long letter of an earnest but fretful young man. But they may be inferred from the nature of his succeeding activities. Except for the single poem in *Graham's* for the following January, he was not to make his appearance with a new poem in a well-established popular magazine for nearly five years. He was to print five poems in such relatively unknown periodicals as the *Harbinger*, the *Young American's Magazine*, and the *People's Journal* in 1847, but otherwise he dedicated his muse exclusively to the group of reformers who read the *Freeman*, the Boston *Courier*, the *Anti-Slavery Standard*, the *Liberty Bell*, and the new *Liberty Chime*. He continued, after his return to Elmwood, to make occasional, unidentified contributions to the *Freeman* and to accept compensation for them; but his career as a professional magazinist was temporarily at an end. The local *Courier*, which could print his verses while they were still hot from the occasion which inspired them, became his favorite medium of communicating with his readers, who, if they chose to lionize him, had to enter the anti-slavery tent to do so.

The first occasion to call forth Lowell's fighting muse after his return to Elmwood was that which produced his "Lines on reading of the capture of certain fugitive slaves near Washington" which appeared in the *Courier* for July 19. It was another "rallying-cry," but, as a call to the spirit of New England to sympathize rather than to act, it was less violent than the two earlier poems upon which it was modeled. Like its models, it was written in the old stirring ballad stanza of *The Day of Doom* and "Yankee Doodle," but it was evidently hastily done and in it Lowell occasionally slipped into the more forceful trochaics of "A Psalm of Life" and "Locksley Hall." A single couplet in which he followed, at once, the new doctrines of the abolitionist party line and the old philosophy of Sir James Mackintosh can illustrate his metrical indecision between a fourteen-syllable iambic and a fifteen-syllable trochaic line:

> We owe allegiance to the State; but deeper, truer, more,
> To the sympathies that God hath set within our spirit's core.

The greater part of the poem is in the iambic measure, but occasionally he caught the true swing of Longfellow and Tennyson and found it fitted to the exclamatory expression of his most vigorous ideas:

> Man is more than Constitutions; better rot beneath the sod,
> Than be true to Church and State while we are doubly false to God!

The poem, as a whole, was one that could not have been read aloud without an awareness of its metrical conflicts; and Lowell doubtless made a choice between his two rhythms with little if any conscious reference to the fact that one of them had been used for "Locksley Hall." Lowell's literary imitations at this stage of his career—like the numerous echoes of Wordsworth that Poe never caught—were not intentional but were the result of what Poe called a "keen sensibility of appreciation" which led "inevitably to imitation," especially, he might have added, when the possessor habitually followed the theory that a poetic style should grow wild rather than suffer the drastic pruning of a heartless gardener. Thus, although Lowell's verse always showed the unfortunate results of inadequately controlled cross-pollination, he was ready for his next literary occasion with a new meter which had been discovered in his own practice rather than in that of any of his contemporaries.

Before the next occasion arose, Lowell was able to relax. The quiet life at Elmwood, with his chickens, his garden, and his field of marsh hay as his only responsibilities, was an agreeable change from the turmoil of Philadelphia; and Maria's expectation of motherhood by the end of the year gave the young couple an adequate excuse for the quiet life which they both enjoyed. The unexpected death of Mr. White in September gave Maria the further expectation of a considerable fortune when the estate should be settled, and they talked of spending the spring in the South in order to avoid the east winds and of going abroad to Italy for two or three years beginning in the autumn. The anti-slavery impulse was not strong in New England that year, and Lowell, though disapproving of what Maria called the "taint of indifferentism" around him, did not have the sort of inner enthusiasm for the cause which would take the place of external stimulus in driving him to activity. He was exchanging long letters with Charles Briggs (who never approved his devotion to a single cause) on the subject of reform in general and some with Longfellow, diversifying his impulse to do good into expressions of distress over white slavery in the cities, over the absence of true Christianity in the church, and over the evil of war and the inheritance of acquired lusts. There was also time for self-analysis, for remembering the beginnings of his career as a poet, and for speculation concerning his future prospect of doing something worthy of the poetical abilities he was conscious of possessing. Even his plans to write further on the subject of slavery were dispassionate, for Charles Dickens and John Foster, who wanted him to do articles on liberal terms for the newly founded London *Daily News,* specifically did not want him to write under his own name or in the tone of an abolitionist. With quiet surroundings, congenial and profitable immediate employment, and no worries about the future, Lowell spent the latter part of 1845 in a rare state of peace.

The two poems that he published in anti-slavery annuals during the early winter reflect his state of mind by a quiet earnestness which showed neither a desire to escape from his feeling of moral responsibility nor an excessive assertion of it. He described himself, in a poem by that title for the *Liberty Bell,* as "The Falconer" who hunted error and the uncleanly birds that "preyed" in the temple, without molesting the harmless and the innocent; and of his symbolic hunting bird he wrote:

> His eye is fierce, yet mildened over
> With something of a dove-like ruth;
> I am his master less than lover,
> My brave sun-seeker's name is Truth.

It was a different falcon from the one he had loosed in Philadelphia, and "A Contrast," written for the *Liberty Chime,* was in the same spirit of one who thought of himself as the lover rather than the master of "Truth." In this poem, however, he did not write in his own proper person but in the role of someone who, like Rhoecus, did not recognize God's messengers—although in this case they appeared as "the poor, the outcast, and the black." But neither poem suggests anything of the unhappiness and divided purpose which was so evident in the author's work during the earlier part of the year: for a while, at Elmwood, the poet Lowell was a whole man.

It was during this while that the Congress of the United States met in December and received President Polk's message that the terms of annexation had been accepted by Texas and that her formal admission to the Union awaited only the passage of a joint resolution to that effect by the two houses. Its passage was inevitable, and even the Boston *Advertiser* and Nathan Appleton had expressed the opinion that matters had gone too far for further opposition. Lowell, with no immediate abolitionist pressure upon him and no hope of affecting the issue by any sort of propaganda, sat down to compose a poet's elegy upon the spirit of magnanimity in Congress. The emotion which moved him was a profound one, for he had decided a year before that the Texas question was the one great issue in his immediate experience which brought about a clear division between the right and the wrong; and his mind had been long stored with thoughts and figures and images which were now ready to array themselves in the strong trochaic measure which he had used for part of the lines on the capture of fugitive slaves—his third "Rallying-Cry" to the forces of right. His new theme was the triumph of life over apparent death, the ultimate survival of good beyond the immediate victory of evil. He had written several times in his letters of the man-child—he hoped—who was stirring beneath Maria's heart and often, in his verse, of the terrible birth pangs of freedom in which all humanity was shaken by the struggles of the few. A belief in the slow but inevitable progress of mankind toward ideals born of suffering and the martyr's fire had been his constant consolation during periods of distress, and his belief had been strengthened by a conception of the unity of all human beings through a sympathy of which they might not be entirely conscious. There was nothing, really, to lament in the anticipated behavior of the Congress: the unbelievers and the Judases of the market place always outnumbered the true apostles, but it was the latter who marked the way for other generations to follow. So his poem touched lightly upon the conventional elegiac chord and stressed the major theme of triumph and faith:

> Hast thou chosen, O my people, on whose party thou shalt stand,
> Ere the Doom from its worn sandals shakes the dust against our land?
> Though the cause of Evil prosper, yet 'tis Truth alone is strong,
> And, albeit she wander outcast now, I see around her throng
> Troops of beautiful, tall angels, to enshield her from all wrong.

But Lowell did not place his faith in beautiful, tall angels. Nor did he, for all his belief that all "mankind are one in spirit," base his hope upon the common sentiments of humanity. His philosophical universality decreased as time went on, and his call was upon "that great Impulse" which had driven the Pilgrims across the sea and which should enable their descendants to realize that "New occasions teach new duties" and that the door to the future could not be opened by the rusted truths of the past.

These "Verses suggested by the Present Crisis" were published in the Boston *Courier* for December 11, 1845—on the day, whether by accident or design, that the news was received of the favorable report on the Texas resolution by a House committee and the introduction of a similar bill in the Senate. They represented Lowell's nearest approach, if the term may be applied to a work so local in its emotional appeal, to a great poem. He was to write in the future with more humane sympathy and with a more discriminating everyday wisdom, and with a greater perfection of craftsmanship. But not even in his "Commemoration Ode" was he to achieve such a combination of vigor and memorability upon a theme so elevated. Rarely was he in the fortunate position of being able to concentrate his undivided self upon the composition of a single poem, and rarely has any American poet been so genuinely inspired to rise above the occasion that moved him. For Lowell did not, of course, mention Texas in "The Present Crisis"; and, by the accident of a typographical error, the poem is ordinarily dated December, 1844, and thus dissociated from the actual events that produced it. The nearest he came to a direct and ungeneralized allusion to the admission of the new state was in his question concerning the blind Cyclops slavery: "Shall we guide his gory fingers where our helpless children play?" But that query is strangely put for a reference to Texas, and, in the light of his letters to Briggs, is more probably a reference to slavery to the passions—for Lowell, at the time, agreed with Mr. Shandy concerning the pre-natal influence of circumstances, "though Sterne," he declared, "was unconscious of the truth he preached." The poem is to most readers exactly what Lowell felt the action of Congress called for: an expression of faith in the common spirit of mankind which could be inspired to moral progress by the impulse of those who were willing to place virtue above expediency.

Lowell's tendency to withdraw his confidence from the universal impulses common to all humanity and place it in the peculiar "Impulse" which he attributed to Oliver Cromwell and to the early New England Puritans was illustrated not only in "The Present Crisis" but in "An Interview with Miles Standish" which he printed in the *Courier* for December 30. The poem was in the light humorous verse of Herrick's "Gather ye rosebuds" and represented a whimsical dream of Miles Standish escaping from the threadbare speeches of the annual forefathers' celebration at Plymouth where men who habitually compromised with the right in their own days boasted of their holy birthright from uncompromising ancestors. It was another serious, although by no means solemn, appeal to the people of New England to show the blue in their blood by being true to the spirit of 1620 and 1776 rather than to such compromises as the Constitution. Miles was tempted to use violence upon the "painted sticks" who held the offices dignified by Winthrop and Vane but, instead, sheathed the ghost of his broadsword and prophesied. He was created in Lowell's own image and merely following his creator's example, for the poet seemed to be giving up all attempts at direct action in the anti-slavery cause.

In fact, Lowell wrote little of anything during the early months of 1846. Blanche—a ten-pound girl-child—had been born on the afternoon of December 31, and the new father dithered around the house upsetting everybody's routine in his attempts to be useful. He had sent off the first of his articles for the London *Daily News* and was not ready to begin another until he learned whether the first was acceptable, and he had cashed his thirty-dollar draft on Graham for his poem "To the Past" without being urged to make further contributions. There was no pressure upon him from outside and no impulse within him to compel composition. He was spending a good deal of time practicing French, walking into Boston and back for every lesson, but he soon found himself back in his college habit of cutting classes and gave his lessons up before the end of February. "I never write (whether prose or verse) when I have *occasion,* but when I *feel like it,*" he wrote Briggs, more apologetically than accurately. "I am Quaker enough always to *follow* the Light, never Quaker enough to imprison it in the strait drab coat of compulsion." Instead, he tried to put his anti-slavery principles in practice around the house. He heard the "faint tinkling of chains" whenever he saw Maria mending his stockings or Ellen bringing the water for his showerbath in the morning, but when he threatened to learn darning and tried to bring his own water he merely succeeded in amusing his wife and shocking the maid—although the latter eventually agreed, unwillingly, that he might carry his own coal upstairs. His daughter alone was tolerant of his eccentricities, and he became expert with a diaper and convinced that she preferred his attentions to those of any one else. These were happy months, for Maria's health had been better than at any other time during the preceding two years, and all the fears concerning her confinement had proved vain. They had decided that it was unnecessary to go south again for the spring and had given up, at least temporarily, their plan to go abroad after discovering that more than half of Maria's inheritance was in unproductive real estate which could not be advantageously sold at the time. Her income-producing property, however, was estimated at being worth five hundred dollars a year, and they believed that, with the addition of Lowell's earnings, they could live comfortably at Elmwood with their own servant and without imposing upon the generosity of Dr. Lowell.

In this new atmosphere of domesticity and independence, Lowell got out of touch emotionally with the more violent abolitionists. When Sydney Howard Gay inquired whether he had spoken too harshly in the *Standard* of Longfellow's omission of his anti-slavery poems from the Carey and Hart edition of his poetical works, Lowell replied, through Briggs, quite frankly that he had. The poet was the only judge of the quality of his works, and Lowell, who had found this group of Longfellow's poems inferior when he reviewed them three years before, placed the responsibilities of the poet unquestionably above those of the propagandist. Furthermore, he was falling away from the notion that the unrighteous should be assaulted with indiscriminate violence. He explained at length on February 18:

In a country like ours where we have Texas annexations and Park Benjamins and some three hundred members of Congress, besides I know not how many office-seekers and -finders, I think it behoves the wise Editor to keep in view that baseness is not merely positive, but that it is *declinable* and has its comparative and superlative degrees, for the proper use of all which he will have so many occasions that the most concentrated wormwood of language comes at last to lack gall. He must therefore be judicious, and neither waste mere vinegar on the rhinoceros-hide of a politician, while he empties a whole carboy of vitriol on the bare nerves of a poet to whose compulsory Marsyas Poe has played Apollo, and I think with the rusty hoop of a barrel for a scalpel. The truth probably is, as I remember to have said when these poems first appeared, that they were written from *without* and not from within. Though Longfellow held the pen, yet Public Opinion guided it, and it is impossible for a man to love these bastards of his muse as if they were his own begotten children. He must forever be tracing in them one resemblance or another to that adulterous father of theirs, at whose door nine tenths of the looselimbed spawn which pass for the genuine offspring of American Authors might justly be laid. Longfellow would write better Anti-slavery poems now, for he has climbed now in fact to where he then stood in fancy, but he has not the nerve to sing under the shadow of the singing arrows of the battle. He is cast in a gentler mould, and to him the hoarse trumpet of the onset whose shrill peal seems to rend asunder the clouds and let in the full light of heaven upon my soul, must be softened by distance, till one should scarce know it from the pipe wherewith the shepherd marshals his timid hosts. All men are not meant for Reformers, else some one or other would be pulling down every-body's house about his ears, and we should have at last a new social order where men's only occupation would be to kick about the *debris* of the old. Longfellow has his vocation, and it is as good as that of any of the rest of us, as there is no gradation of rank in the offices to which the Good father calls us—Only be sure that he *does* call us. Longfellow is no coward, but only a gentle, shrinking nature.

Like Emerson in his "Ode" to W. H. Channing, Lowell was falling back into the old ethical pattern of Puritanism which held that no man should be expected to labor outside the established limits of his vocation unless he had an unmistakable call to do so.

Judged by the old standards, Lowell was more culpable for his sins of omission than Longfellow was. His own "calling" was "clear" to him. He should fill the great office of the poet by "pouring out one glorious song that should be the gospel of Reform, full of consolation and strength to the oppressed, yet falling gently and restoringly as dew on the withered youth-flowers of the oppressor." But there is no evidence that he attempted to obey it. Inspired by "the first real Yankee" he had seen in print, Deacon Ramsdill in Sylvester Judd's *Margaret,* he was thinking of writing a New England novel that would astonish his friends "if it ever gets delivered." His intention to write articles on the history of the anti-slavery movement for the *Daily News* evidently had caused the old idea of a novel to stir again in his mind, for Wendell Phillips, in sending some printed material which Lowell had requested from Garrison, had referred obscurely to his planned "sketch for the 'young abolitionist' to bring him up even with his times." The note-book in which he jotted down his earliest plans and occasional scraps of conversation is undated, but the suggestions of a plot show clearly that he was thinking in terms of story based upon his own experience as a New Englander and a reformer which would be in keeping with Phillips' reference. The full history of Lowell's attempt to become a writer of fiction is a later story, but it seems apparent that he began making notes in that direction at a time when he was able to be objective, if not amused, at his own enthusiasm for reforms, and when he was so excited over babies that he thought the use of baby talk in a novel would be an amusing literary device. The thing he had in mind would have been a cross between *Margaret* and *Tristram Shandy.*

The only immediate literary stimulus which affected Lowell, however, came from John Foster, who wrote on February 3, 1846, that the first of his papers for the *Daily News* was acceptable although its style was perhaps more suitable for a review than for a newspaper. Nevertheless, he agreed to pay a generous two and a half to three guineas per column for essays that would deal not only with slavery but with "the society manners and policy of the several States of the Union (especially in their relation to and action on Foreign States)" and for news of particular interest to England. As soon as Lowell received the letter some three weeks later, he began work on further papers dealing with the anti-slavery movement and eventually published, at monthly intervals, three additional ones which were restrained and historical in tone, with few outbursts of his own feelings. But a decrease in size in the *News* supposedly brought the series to an end, and, in any case, Lowell mailed the last of his published contributions before the first of May. The literary tone of an interested spectator, rather than an active participant in the anti-slavery cause, also marked his "Lines on the Death of Charles Turner Torrey" in the Boston *Courier* for May 23. Although Torrey had founded the Massachusetts Abolitionist Society in opposition to the radical activity of Garrison, his death while serving a sentence in the Maryland State Penitentiary for assisting fugitive slaves made him a martyr to the cause, and his funeral in Boston on May 18th was made the occasion for a public meeting in Faneuil Hall. The affair was so well planned in advance that Lowell was actually asked, six days before the martyrdom occurred, to write his poem in anticipation of it. He did his duty and the poem was read, but the circumstances and the subject stirred his emotions so little that, for once, he was able to write according to what he had described as his own clear calling: he consoled the oppressed and dealt gently with the oppressor—and seriously disappointed the committee which had arranged for his performance. The doctrine of mercy to the oppressor, wrote Dr. Henry I. Bowditch in protest, will never be appreciated until a new and lovelier race of beings settles on this earth.

To all appearances, Lowell had fallen into indifference concerning the sort of beings really settled on the earth. The unofficial beginnings of the Mexican War failed to stir him from his literary lethargy, and the formal declaration of May 11 did not stimulate him to the point of making so much as an allusion to it in the poem on Torrey which could so easily have provided the means for public expression of any feelings he might have had. The flattery of Garrison, Mrs. Chapman, and Sydney Gay could enlist his name for the *National Anti-Slavery Standard* but could get little service from his pen. He missed his friends in Philadelphia and wrote longingly of them to Davis (with whom he was investing the four thousand dollars which formed the liquid portion of Maria's inheritance) and was reading the *Freeman* regularly although he had no feeling that he would "do any good" by writing for it. He professed to feel at work in his vocation only when he was writing a poem such as the one "To the Past," but the spirit moved him rarely. As a reformer, he seems to have become limited almost entirely to a concern for the virtue of Massachusetts—for the spirit of the Old Bay State upon which he had called so often in his verse and in which Emerson and Whittier also took such pride.

Accordingly, the only new occasion which aroused him to a really spirited undertaking of new duties during 1846 was the assault on Yankee virtue by the recruiting officers who attempted, with flag, fife, and drum, to get the spirit of '76 involved in Mr. Polk's unholy war. His first "squib" on this subject was fired anonymously from what he called "the ambushment of the *Courier*" on June 17 and was reprinted upon a hint from the author, without signature, in the *Standard* for the following week. This, however, was the first of the group of poems that were to become the *Biglow Papers,* and an account of its genesis is a part of their revealing history. The attitude it represented is equally well reflected in the prose editorial, "Daniel Webster," published in the *Standard* for July 2, for the appearance of Edward Webster in Boston, with his father's approval, as a recruiter, turned on the inner light which convinced Lowell that he would not be wasting his time with prose. The article itself was no squib against the recruiter but a blast at the rhinoceros hide of the politician with an occasional shot at Governor Briggs (one of the "painted sticks" of "An Interview with Miles Standish") for his "eminent faculty" for inconsistency of "that singular kind which is uneasy till it escapes from right to wrong" and for "bringing himself into disgrace with all honest men." Sending his son to Boston to recruit a company for the Mexican War was, to Lowell's mind, only the last proof of Webster's "subserviency to the slave power" and failure to rise to the great occasions of his age. As an example of "great faculties debased from their legitimate function," he reminded Lowell that "there is no sadder sentence than *'might have been'*"; and as "an eagle turned buzzard," he forced Lowell to ask: "Shall not the Recording Angel write *Ichabod* after the name of this man in the great book of Doom?" It was a violent article, for even Whittier (who agreed with Lowell concerning the saddest words of tongue and pen) waited four more years before writing "Ichabod" after Webster's name. It was Lowell's last outburst until near the end of the year. After it, he went on a vacation from both propaganda and spirited poetry.

V

It had been a mistake to trust Maria's constitution to the east winds that swept through the bare boughs of Elmwood, for her cough returned and lingered until Dr. Lowell was sufficiently disturbed to urge James to take her to Stockbridge where she could avoid the midsummer heat. The trip meant that he would have to contribute to the young couple's support, but he urged his son to forget his determination to be entirely self-sustaining after his marriage and accept his small gift with no feeling of dependence except upon a kind Providence. In the quietness of the village among the mountains, Lowell was able to produce one set of verses for the *Standard* in which he tried (after the manner of his earlier poem, "The Heritage") to console the oppressed by insisting that "The Royal Pedigree" of the poor included "hero-spirits plain and grand" who handed down the acquired characteristics of "godlike patience" which was greatly to be preferred over the blood of "sceptred brutes" and wealth resulting from the "passion of two title-deeds" in a marriage of convenience. It was, as its author recognized, a not very good poem, but it was the best he had at the moment, and he had none at all for his customary offerings to the various worthy annuals that wanted the use of his name. It became necessary for him to spend a couple of weeks on Staten Island while Maria was under the observation of Dr. C. W. Eliot, who had treated James's eyes during the death struggles of the *Pioneer,* but they were back in Cambridge by the end of September, in time for Lowell to make his customary contribution to the local *Liberty Bell* and to go on with his project of issuing a new volume of poems at the end of the year.

But before the end of the year, his publisher, John Owen, had failed, leaving Lowell with the expectation of receiving only ten cents on the dollar for the one hundred and sixty dollars he had advanced toward the publication of his book and in no position to seek another publisher. The misfortune probably did his reputation no harm. He had neglected the muses during the greater part of 1846, and to get out a new volume he would have had to yield to the urging of one of his friends who wanted him to reprint "The Two" and other poems that he had left out of the 1844 *Poems.* He came home with a great deal of new energy but with hardly enough to make up for nine months of relative indifference to his vocation. He had also neglected reform and apparently had the unhappy feeling of having deserted the turbulent waters of abolition without soaring very far on the wings of song. Henceforth he would be both fish and fowl. When Dr. Oliver Wendell Holmes delivered his "Urania" at the Tremont Temple on October 14 without exhibiting adequate signs of excitement concerning the great issues of the day, Lowell felt called upon to take him to task. The doctor, he charged, was indifferent to the evils of war and of slavery, to the cause of temperance and the claims of the poor, and to reform in general, and he ignored the existence of conscience in the spiritual organization. Holmes defended himself in a long letter, answering his young friend's accusations one by one from the same point of view that Lowell himself had adopted for his defense of Longfellow during the preceding February. It was the proper business of a poet to follow his own judgment and his own taste rather than mold himself upon those of others, and as for the specific question of slavery he was able to cite, discreetly, Longfellow's little volume as an illustration of the fact that "nothing is so flat and unprofitable as weakly flavored verses relating" to a subject which had been treated with so much of "the cloacae of vituperative eloquence" for which the doctor obviously had no liking or talent.

In addressing his bill of complaints to Holmes, Lowell was moved by a sort of frenetic impertinence that made him feel obliged to disturb the complacency of his own social class which included the "little club of ten physicians" among whom Holmes could describe himself as occupying "the extreme left of the liberal side of the house." It was a disturbing obligation, for his friend's goodness was beyond question, and it was against his own principles to nag the good for not being better while allowing the wicked to stand ungoaded. Nor could he be entirely sure of his own superior wisdom. Holmes believed that the Mexican War was a "poor" one, but he was also convinced that disunion would mean "a future of war and bloodshed" which was "frightful" to contemplate. And as a practical man he saw no virtue in inviting a catastrophe by vain protests against a misdemeanor. The warning from Holmes, emphatic though it was, was probably not enough by itself to make Lowell reconsider his position as a reformer; but he received others of the sort, and something, after the first of *The Biglow Papers,* caused him to change his mind about disunion and the virtue of standing aloof from political action.

Had Lowell been less enthusiastic about his "bale of isms" he would have been less quick to pass arbitrary judgment upon a fellow poet, for he was still upset by what he considered a perverse condemnation of himself in a recent article on "American Literature." Margaret Fuller had never appreciated him, but he felt so much at peace with her that he had protested, less than eight months before, when Briggs had been "too hard" on her in his mildly satiric "Pinto Letters." Consequently it was almost like feeling a stab in the back when he found himself reading her opinion that he was

> absolutely wanting in the true spirit and tone of poesy. His interest in the moral questions of the day has supplied the want of vitality in himself; his great facility

at versification has enabled him to fill the ear with a copious stream of pleasant sound. But his verse is stereotyped; his thought sounds no depth, and posterity will not remember him.

He tried to be amused by the succinct damnation, but when he touched upon the subject in a letter to Davis on September 26, 1846, he was incapable of passing it by with a smile—and almost of passing it by at all:

I suppose you have seen the brief and decided manner in which Miss Margaret Fuller disposes of me in her new book. I believe it has given less pain than amusement to my friends as it certainly has to me. Fortunately I have many more important matters to think about than whether I am a poet or not. As a question of fame I thank God it never entered my head or heart, and even did I write with no worthier motive than desire of reputation (which Miss F. seems to think the end and object of authorship) I still have common sense enough to see that the world has many concerns of rather more weight—and that such things are always settled as they should be at last. Whether that great monster Posterity ever [will] think of me or not—I shall at least leave a good name of my own, and Blanche shall have the satisfaction of remembering a father who always acted and thought and spoke up to his convictions of right and duty.—Yet though I feel all this I must confess that the baser nature in me rebels at Miss F.'s arrogance and conceit, and that my sense of the ridiculous is somewhat vividly impressed by her follies and impertinences. I leave time to settle my account with her, however, strong as is the temptation to a little retaliatory satire where so large a target is offered to its shafts.

His irritation, however, could not be soothed by the nobility of his final resolution, and within two years he had drawn the bow upon his target with not one pleasant but two sharp satires.

The Lowell who sat down, some time in October or November, to compose his annual poem for the *Liberty Bell* was something less than a happy man. The call of duty was in his ears, but he was not sure of the direction from whence it came. His father had boasted, during the son's absence in Stockbridge, that he had "almost" succeeded in making an abolitionist out of a young woman visitor to Elmwood without saying anything against the church or state, and the younger Lowell had already revealed in his letter to Briggs and his lines on Torrey that the ideal of reform without scandal (which he had adopted as the motto for the *Pioneer*) continued to appeal to him whenever he dwelt in the atmosphere of Elmwood. On the other hand, he had recently accepted an obligation to the publishers of the *Standard;* and, although he had carefully retained his privilege of writing when and what the spirit dictated, he was bound in association with such aggressive radicals as Wendell Phillips and Edmund Quincy, who had no patience with generosity toward oppressors. But, even granting them the wisdom of action, he was not nearly so sure as he had been in Philadelphia that their line of action was the wisest which might be adopted. In contrast to all these anti-slavery impulses, he was ridden constantly by his fear that the poet was being lost in the propagandist and he was torn between the high desire to abandon everything in the pursuit of his calling and the lower inclination to turn upon those who, like Margaret Fuller, claimed that he had lost it.

The effect of these conflicting impulses may be seen in most of the poems produced in the minor surge of creative energy that Lowell experienced near the end of the year. They reflect his determination to fulfill his proper destiny and his uncertainty concerning what it was. He was clearest about what he was not going to be: the retrospective monologist in "Extreme Unction" had been "called in many ways" but at the end of fourscore years could only offer "gold" when asked for an accounting. In his youth he had possessed an Ideal, sympathy for his fellow man, receptiveness toward God, and a generous share of Heaven's instincts. But he had used the light to find a track "Whereby to crawl away from heaven." Any one who bought the *Liberty Bell* at the annual December Anti-Slavery Bazaar might discover that James Russell Lowell was determined not to commit the unpardonable sin that prevented the old man with a "snake-turned nature" from receiving the last rites of forgiveness. Yet no one who followed his contributions to the *Standard* and other journals through the middle of 1847 could guess whether he would follow any particular gleam of the light. There was no more fine theorizing about the ideal poet. On the contrary, the little poem "Above and Below" which he sent to the *Young American's Magazine* for January, had as its theme "they also serve who work in the valley"; and although he began his verses by talking down to the workers, when he drew his contrast between them and his conventional ideal poet, the "Lone watcher on the mountain-height," he spoke of "we, who in the shadow sit." The most definite implication he could make concerning his own position appeared in "The Oak" in the *Standard* for December 31: he would be one of the "true hearts" who draw sturdiness "from the pinched soil of a churlish fate" and stand with simple greatness "somewhere between earth and heaven" bearing "some message" of God's truth.

The "Letter from Boston" which he sent to James Miller McKim in late December in response to an old request for a Boston newsletter for the *Pennsylvania Freeman* gave further evidence of his difficulty in settling upon his message. Although he had contributed to the *Liberty Bell* and attended the Bazaar on December 22 and was reporting upon his visit for the benefit of the sympathetic readers of both the *Freeman* and the *Standard* for early January, he made his report in humorous verse which revealed his lack of agreement with some of the abolitionists he admired and his lack of admiration for others who probably found it hard to tolerate his sense of humor on so serious a subject. He respected Garrison and admired Edmund Quincy and Wendell Phillips; but his own "heart" explicitly refused to approve Phillips' condemnation of Judge Story for enforcing the Constitution, and there was a certain amount of ambiguity in his comments upon the willingness of "our Edmund" to throw the pipe of peace at the leader of the political-action group of abolitionists and "scourge him with the olive branch." He had no admiration at all for that grim and "kind of maddened John the Baptist," Stephen S. Foster, and although the portrait delighted Garrison, it probably had no appeal to the subject, who had suffered the stones that amused Lowell because of their appropriateness to the latter-day martyr's Christian name and to the accusations of blasphemy which were so frequently directed against him. Lowell obviously found the abolitionist ranks, at their best, full of excellent ladies, admirable friends with whom he occasionally differed in his heart and about whom he had the shadow of a doubt in his head, and rude enthusiasts who were neither to be admired or liked although they might possibly be respected at a respectable distance.

There was a good deal of humility and soul searching in Lowell's writings at the beginning of the New Year. With the Psalmist he prayed for sincerity, and, despite his awkward efforts to identify himself with laboring men and women in such poems as "The Royal Pedigree" and "Above and Below," he realized that there were many dreary-spirited persons from whom he was far removed by birth and circumstance. For such unfortunate and guilty souls, "wandering dim on the extremist edge Of God's bright providence," he found consolation in the faith of the one hundred thirty-eighth Psalm: "If I descend into hell, Thou art present." He used the Vulgate Latin of that fragment of a verse as a title for one of the most imaginative and personally unpretentious of his poems, "Si descendero in infernum, ades." Even in those who had fled God's presence he found some relics of their childish "recognition of the all-ruling Grace"; and, searching his own heart in turn, he discovered wickedness which was "the worst man's mate." The difference between the sunshine in which he dwelt and the darkness of so many of his fellow men could be attributed to nothing more than the thin fence of "station, chance, or prosperous fate" which had preserved him from the "clutching waves of sin." Like Emerson in the little poem "Grace," when he contemplated corrupt men, he was willing to attribute his own purity to the influence of his environment. But, also like Emerson, he dared to be true to the God within. Although some parts of wayward humanity might be "Self-exiled to the farthest verge of night," they could not break the force which united them with the source of light: still subject to the laws of divine gravity, such prodigal comets might find their perihelion in the very bosom of the sun.

"Si descendero in infernum, ades" was published, somewhat inappropriately, in the *Harbinger* for January 16, 1847, and was followed in the *Standard* for February 25, by "The Search," a complementary poem on a theme which was more personal and perhaps more troublesome to the poet. For Lowell, in his letters for nearly two years, had been declaring his "infidelity" to institutionalized religion and, to the regret of his father, had persisted in his criticisms of the church, going so far, in his recent "Letter from Boston," as to accuse the organized church of making an infidel of Christ. Yet he asserted his own piety and seems to have felt the need, while being so distressingly critical of organized religion, to state his personal beliefs as a sort of simple, primitive Christianity entirely free from the transcendental heresies which had attracted him a few years before. His new poem dealt with his search for Christ through nature and through the wealth and power of the world and with his disappointment until he was led by Love to find him among "the outcast and the weak"—among the least, as the New Testament taught, of his brethren. The doctrine of humility that Lowell was preaching before the public was also being taken privately to heart during these first two months of the year, for two companion poems in his notebooks—one a letter to a friend and the other entitled a "Dedicatory Hymn" though apparently another letter—show him disclaiming any "care" to make his mark upon his age. Both were written in the stanza so frequently used by Robert Burns, and the "Hymn" shows Lowell placing his own poetic ambition not on the level of prophecy but upon that of Burns's achievement—comforting "poor old Humankind" and binding "Men's hearts together."

The distress aroused by the death of Blanche on the morning of March 10, made doubly poignant by the lisping affection with which she had been so generous during her brief illness, was also humbling. Lowell had been convinced that his baby daughter had brought out something new and fine in his character, and his sense of sudden loss was too deep for immediate expression in verse. He was not able, in fact, to write much of anything during the months that immediately followed, and his plan for publishing a collection of poems on the first of May was abandoned. Most of the work he accomplished during the next half year was done in disguise, in the anonymous character of a critic or in the rustic pose of the *Biglow Papers,* for Lowell was discovering that a man's complicated life could not go into a poem as wholly as he had thought it could when he was a youth. The two little poems that he did manage to publish in his own proper person were both thoughtful and somewhat melancholy considerations of the problems he personally faced as a poet. In the first, "Hebe," published in the *Young American's Magazine* for May, the traditional cupbearer of the gods carried not youth in her bowl but a "godhood" which was apparently the fulfillment of ambition. The poet had tried to grasp it too quickly, spilled the nectar, and broke the vessel. The moral was precise:

Coy Hebe flies from those that woo,
And shuns the hands would seize upon her;
Follow thy life, and she will sue
To pour for thee the cup of honor.

Yet for all Lowell's apparent feeling that he had been too eager for greatness, he continued to feel that the life he should follow was that of the poet. As the manager of Maria's real property (which, incidentally, brought in a very poor rate of income) he balanced the occupation of master of rents against that of maker of verses in "The Landlord" for the *People's Journal* of September 4 and came to the conclusion that the poet not only drew more income from the fields than did their owner but became at last the lord of thoughts which were both almighty and immortal.

Lowell was to print one other poem in a magazine before he got at last to his collected volume. His "Study for a Head" (second of the two such "Studies" in his collected poems) appeared in the October number of the *Young American's Magazine* which delighted in satirizing the transcendentalists after the fashion that Lowell adopted for that poem. But this portrayal of Bronson Alcott, like the companion "Study" of Margaret Fuller which immediately preceded it in his notebook (with the date September 4, 1847) and in his published works, was not originally designed for his new volume of *Poems.* For Lowell's original intention had evidently been to get out a volume of recent magazine verses and old poems from his portfolio without drawing upon the results of his current interests. He was playing, in different moods, with satire and with reminiscent descriptive verse during the autumn of 1847, and the long specimen of the latter sort in his notebook consisted of an unfinished lot of heroic couplets presenting mellow recollections of his boyhood in Cambridge and sensuous descriptions of the New England "Indian Summer." His satire and his treatment of the seasons, however, belonged to some future plan. Lowell was in the process of shifting his conception of the art of poetry from the category of the active to that of the intellectual powers—of renouncing, in terms of his college philosophers, Sir James Mackintosh for Dugald Stewart—and his new book was supposed to get his accumulation of older poems out of his mind by putting them between boards. He intended to use all but four or five of the poems published under his own name since he returned from Philadelphia and five previously unpublished ones (in addition to an introductory sonnet to Maria): the descriptive "Summer Storm," which had been written in 1839; "Columbus," the third of his 1843 trilogy dealing with the poet and the active life; "Hunger and Cold," which he later dated 1844; and "The Birch Tree" and a fragment called "The Growth of the Legend," which are undated. He apparently expected to use few if any of the verses published in 1844 and none of the early magazine verse, such as "The Two," which friends had urged him to include in the volume he had planned to issue in 1846.

But when the printer's proof came through, Lowell made the curiously belated discovery that he had overestimated the amount of space these poems would take up and that they would make a volume smaller than the one for which he had contracted and too skimpy for a favorable impression upon the public. Accordingly, in late October, he set about increasing its size to precisely twelve sheets, apparently going so far as to tailor one of his new poems to fit the printer's form. He added "Anti-Texas" from the *Courier* and "The Falconer" from the *Liberty Bell* to the collection (leaving out only "Now is always Best" and "Orpheus" among his non-satiric verses printed since his return from Philadelphia) and went back to 1844 for "On the Death of a Friend's Child," possibly because it made a good companion poem to the two little elegies on Blanche, Maria's "The Morning Glory" and his own "The Changling," which he had decided to include. He also used the satires on the two transcendental conversationalists he had written in September as a single poem entitled "Studies for Two Heads" and added a new non-satiric study of a third head, "On a Portrait of Dante by Giotto." Three other new poems, "An Indian-Summer Reverie," "The Pioneer," and "Longing," completed the volume.

Of the new poems, the "Studies for Two Heads" became available for the collected volume after Lowell's satiric impulse found a more promising outlet in *A Fable for Critics,* and the three shorter poems were all in the old familiar vein of self-pitying melancholy that found Dante more interesting as an outcast than as an immortal poet. "An Indian-Summer Reverie," however, represents a new Lowell. Its seven-line stanzas were put together by craft largely from the couplets of the manuscript poem "Indian Summer" which dealt with his memories of Cambridge and was to be used again in part in the introduction to the first series of *The Biglow Papers.* For ten years, of course, it had been an inevitable tendency of Lowell's mind to escape from present melancholy into recollections of childhood. But the new Lowell, while letting the present fade in memory's glow, avoided his customary use of the language of Wordsworth's Intimations Ode and used instead the language of the sense, dwelling upon the visionary tints of the autumn and admitting frankly for perhaps the first time that the sensuous delights of nature meant as much to him in maturity as they had in boyhood. When he refashioned the descriptive and some of the reminiscent parts of the poem into "An Indian-Summer Reverie," it is true, he adopted a semi-Spenserian stanza which may have been suggested to him by the last three strophes of Coleridge's lament on his solitary date tree, for that portion of the familiar poem would normally have come to his mind often after Blanche's death; but the exact stanza he used was of his own devising, and neither in that nor in the language did he imitate the English poet. Poe's accusation that he had plagiarized from Wordsworth, Bryant's suggestion that he might be indebted to him in part for "To the Past," a suggestion from Briggs that he might have noticed the green ice of another poem in Coleridge rather than in nature, and his various exchanges with Longfellow on coincidental resemblances in their own verses—all tended to make him more self-conscious in his editorial proofreading, and the fact that his "Reverie" was the product of craftsmanship rather than the result of dreaming enabled him to be more objective than he normally was. It was to be some time before Lowell became sufficiently skilled to make a patchwork poem that succeeded in appearing spontaneous, but "An Indian-Summer Reverie" shows that when he quit trying to be a poetic Maker and was content to be a maker of verses he was able to escape his unconscious imitation of nineteenth-century English poets and exhibit a sensuous richness of style which, while revealing a certain temperamental kinship to Keats, was peculiarly his own.

Although Lowell was paying for the plates of his new book, he yielded unenthusiastically to the urging of his publisher, George Nichols, to take advantage of the artificial seasonal demand and get it out by Christmas. As usual with his publications, however, it appeared late and was a holiday volume only for local Christmas Eve shoppers and for the greater number of New Englanders who gave their presents on New Year's Day. Charles Peterson wrote enthusiastically from Philadelphia on January 10, 1848, that his old friend had "improved greatly" in the quality of his poetry and cited the descriptive "Summer Storm" among other poems as evidencing the improvement. The compliment was unconsciously ironic, for Peterson might have had the poem at any time for *Graham's* and Lowell might have exhibited such improvement six or seven years earlier had not Peterson and Poe encouraged his development in the opposite direction and left his more sensuous verse to the unprofitable appreciation of Nathan Hale. The public which had bought three editions of the 1844 *Poems,* however, showed considerably less interest in the *Poems, Second Series,* and Lowell seems to have been able to meet his note for publication costs only with difficulty and there was no call for a second edition. The author himself apparently had little interest in his book, for he wrote Francis Bowen on November 18, 1848, that it had passed out of his mind "so entirely" after publication that it had not occurred to him to keep a copy for himself or to acknowledge the notice it had received in the *North American Review*. At the time he wrote his letter the volume was still in print, and he professed to have been unable, when he got one three weeks before, to remember "the titles even of three quarters of the poems contained in it."

Such a profession of indifference, made in a letter which was written for the purpose of preserving friendly relations with an editor who was then Lowell's employer but whose review undoubtedly gave offense to his sensitive spirit, cannot be taken entirely at face value; but it is true that by the time he had his book ready for the printer he was actively engaged in other literary interests, and was primarily concerned with getting a thrice-planned volume off his mind. There were signs of improvement in it, but Lowell was living in the future rather than in the past. "I am perfectly conscious in myself (I may be allowed to say it to you)," he wrote Briggs in a moment of relaxation when he had got ahead of the printer while working over the final proof, "of finer powers than I have ever exercised or perhaps ever shall."

But these powers, though suggested in the book, were only then in the process of development. He had several projects under way and more energy than he had had to spare in a long time. His distress over Blanche had been softened and his natural anxiety concerning Maria had been relieved by the arrival of his second daughter on September 9, 1847; and while he was delighted with the new child, she was not so much of a novelty and he considered Mabel "less spiritual" than Blanche and was more willing to leave her in the care of a nurse. Furthermore, although he had not yet reached the state of being able to get through a year without going in debt, he had made a favorable investment of part of Maria's fortune in stocks and could look forward to a steady income of three hundred and twenty dollars a year in addition to the uncertain returns from farm rents and literary sales.

He had tried earnestly to sit in the seat of the idealistic reformer but had found it inadequate to his material needs and unsuitable to the development of his highest literary powers. Having once occupied the Siege Perilous, he was committed to the quest for a particular symbol of a better world. But his energies and his ambitions needed more outlets than the abolitionist movement provided. A belated recognition of his own talents was driving him in directions that turned away from the anti-slavery party line and prevented his devotion to a single cause.

Chapter VII

KNIGHT-ERRANT

THE MOST remarkable quality Lowell demonstrated during his "marvelous" year of 1848 was his ability to ride off—with almost equal enthusiasm—in three or four directions at once. He wrote Briggs of his "way of looking on the Poet Lowell as an altogether different personage" from the man; and he observed that his complicated literary "self," in addition, was "very curiously compounded of two utterly different characters." One he called the "clear mystic and enthusiast," and the other was the "humorist." Had his self-analysis gone further, he might have found that he was even more curiously compounded. His nature and state of mind were such that he was ready to do battle in a variety of inconsistent causes while also trying to follow a disciplined crusade guided by leaders with a single aim. At the same time, he could tilt vigorously and often maliciously with the entire field of contemporary authors while cherishing, between engagements, a vision of inactive magnanimity. The enthusiastic dreamer and the shrewd humorist may have alternated in their control of his many activities; but *The Biglow Papers,* his editorials for the *National Anti-Slavery Standard, A Fable for Critics,* and *The Vision of Sir Launfal* represented the disintegration of that carefully unified poetical and personal identity which he had tried to achieve during his early search for the "heroic" life. In his letter to Briggs and in his devotion to such a variety of major interests, he accepted the fact that he was better suited to knight-errantry than to the sort of heroism which pursued a single great aim.

The earliest and most memorable of the Biglow Papers, in fact, were hardly the products of any sort of heroic aim. They grew out of his desire to write effective political satire, for its own sake, and out of a serious ambition which had affected him ever since he had written his "Ode" on the poet in December, 1841—the ambition to get closer to common man in a way that was hardly possible to the young gentleman who had been offended by the personal habits of the good people of Concord and who had written so much poetry from on high. He had admired the common touch in the poetry of Burns and had paid tribute to it in "An Incident in a Rail-Road Car." Yet he himself had never been a genuinely popular poet. His own efforts to put the common feelings of humanity into memorable words had never been successful until one of his anti-slavery poems managed, whether by accident or by design, to follow Burns in his use of the language of common men to express sentiments which—if not timeless and universal—were at least momentarily popular in certain circles. The language, of course, was not the Scots which he had imitated from Burns in his early youth but the Yankee dialect which was as familiar to Bostonians as Scots was to the people of Edinburgh. This dialect exercised the same secret charm upon people who knew it and held those who did not in a similar state of uncritical suspension between curiosity and dissimulation.

Lowell's first "squib" in the Yankee dialect (published in the middle of June, 1846, as "A Letter from Mr. Ezekiel Biglow of Jaalam to the Hon. Joseph T. Buckingham, editor of the Boston *Courier,* inclosing a poem of his son, Mr. Hosea Biglow") may have been the result of a suggestion made more than a year before by Charles Briggs when he urged his friend to put his abolitionism into verse rather than adopt the disguise of a countryman in prose. But it was more probably the accidental result of the desire to avoid the appearance of repeating himself on an occasion which happened to arise while he was playing with the idea of a New England novel and while he was impressed by the "real Yankee" quality of Sylvester Judd's Deacon Ramsdill. For Lowell had promised occasional contributions to the *National Anti-Slavery Standard,* and his conscience was sensitive concerning his recent neglect of the cause. The attempt to recruit a Massachusetts company for service in the Mexican War was the first occasion for another "rallying-cry" after his conscience had been aroused from the unsatisfactory torpor exhibited in "Lines on the Death of Charles Turner Torrey." The Texas issue had been settled, but the same forces of unrighteousness were trying to lug California into the Union for the same unrighteous purpose of spreading slave territory; and, more than ever, the Old Bay State was being insulted by an attempt to divert its militant spirit from its traditional path of virtue.

The occasion was perfect for another set of lines that followed his formula for influencing the mass of his readers: "a swinging ballad metre, some sectional prejudice and vanity, some denunciation, some scriptural allusions, and no cant." As he had told Edward Davis two years before, he would not have written that way under his own name; but by this time the formula itself was almost a signature, for he had used it in four poems in the *Courier* and his authorship, especially after "The Present Crisis," was freely admitted and well known. The first two poems in which he had followed this formula had been signed by an anonymous "Yankee" who had been identified. For his fifth, he would create another Yankee, give him a name and personality, and allow him to speak in his own dialect. The device had the advantage, as Lowell explained to Sydney Gay when suggesting that the anonymity be preserved when the poem was reprinted in the *Standard,* of causing "Slavery to think it has as many enemies as possible"; and it also solved the problem of his own divided mind by permitting him to write "in character" and therefore perhaps more freely and strongly than he could otherwise.

The poem, as shown by the trial efforts in the author's "Private Journal," went through two experimental stages before reaching its final form. Lowell first tried it in the iambic meter of his first and second "Rallying-Cry"—fourteeners with feminine endings—although he divided the long lines, introduced a middle rhyme, and put them on paper in the stanza form of the published poem. Its second metrical state was one of iambic pentameter quatrains with feminine endings for the even lines. His countryman also went through an evolution before he became the Hosea who was primarily opposed to committing murder and only incidentally anxious to save himself for Nancy and home consumption: in the first metrical experiments he was disturbed in the opening lines by the fear of bullets and bayonets, and in the pentameter version, by the low wages for the risk he took not only from enemy weapons but from the yellow fever. It is obvious that not until Lowell settled upon the trochaic meter and syncopated rhythm that had been so successful in "The Present Crisis" did he settle upon a hero who might properly speak in a rustic parody of the tones of that high-minded poem. Hosea was only the better half of his first Yankee spokesman. The original suggestion of mercenary cowardice was left out of his character.

The noble Hosea of the first published "squib" expressed, in his peculiar way, the local patriotism and the humanitarian philosophy of the poet Lowell and the strict orthodoxy of an abolitionist of the non-resistance group. As a representative of the poet, he was concerned not only over the enslavement of Negroes in the South but over that of whites in the North, and he managed one of the most direct, though limited expressions Lowell ever achieved of his belief in the common nature of humanity:

> Laborin' man an' laborin' woman
> Hev one glory an' one shame.
> Ev'ythin' thet's done inhuman
> Injers all on 'em the same.

He also shared Lowell's somewhat contradictory notion that despite the common nature of humanity there was a peculiar virtue in the North, particularly in Massachusetts, which was justified in laying a special claim to the spirit of 'seventy-six and should be expected to hold up the beacon to the oppressed. As an abolitionist, Hosea expressed the orthodox creed of the group with which Lowell had been associated in Philadelphia and which had recently taken over the *Standard:* he believed in the grasping nature and diabolical cleverness of the slaveholding politicians, in the sacrilegious wickedness of war (conducted in the spirit of 'forty-six), and in the slogan "No Union with Slaveholders!" Hosea closed on the last note, and although he did not go so far as to follow Garrison in calling the Constitution "an agreement with Hell," he did justify his preference for separation with the suggestive declaration that "Man hed ough' to put asunder Them that God has noways jined." If Hosea could only have spelled better he would have been more satisfactory than Lowell as editor of either the *Pennsylvania Freeman* or the *National Anti-Slavery Standard.*

Despite the fact that the poem had "struck the old hulk of the Public between wind and water" and had become an undoubted popular success, Lowell made no further attempt at Yankee verse for fourteen months. The dialect had not come easily and consistently to his pen on the first occasion, as he had recognized when he looked over Hosea's production and, instead of making it uniform, had Ezekiel explain that "the parson kind o' slicked off sum of the last varses" but had not wanted "to put his ore in to tetch to the Rest on 'em, bein they wus verry well As they wuz." When Lowell did bring himself to take it up again, in a second number for the *Courier* of August 18, 1847, he revived the other half of his original experimental Yankee, gave him the name Birdofredum Sawin, and represented him as having been gulled into enlisting before he discovered the dangers the manuscript Yankee feared in anticipation. For Lowell evidently went directly back to his "Private Journal" for guidance in his second paper: Birdofredum wrote of the dangers of bullets, bayonets, and yellow fever, of the low wages of ninepence a day (although he made them for killing folks rather than for being killed), and of the ease with which he could imagine himself being led to the gallows—of all the matters, in short, that had been brought up as objections to enlistment in the fragmentary experiments toward the first paper. Hosea also versified the letter in the meter with which Lowell originally experimented, although it was printed in long lines and without the middle rhyme.

The new satire appeared at a time when there was still a serious need of replacements for the twelve-month volunteers of the year before, and Lowell's representation of the life of a soldier stationed in Saltillo was certainly not the sort which would encourage recruiting. But the Massachusetts men of Birdofredum's regiment had been mustered into active service only seven months before, and there is no evidence that Lowell was inspired by a new recruiting drive or by any other external occasion. Most probably he was stirred by his antagonism toward a newly popular idea which was a particular abomination to most abolitionists—the notion of Anglo-Saxon racial supremacy that he represented as having been preached to the recruits in Faneuil Hall and as having been expounded by Colonel Caleb Cushing to the troops in Mexico. Lowell had ventured a tentative satire upon racialism in his article, "D'Israeli's *Tancred,* or the New Crusade," in the *North American Review* for the month before. In *Tancred,* he recognized, D'Israeli had "interwoven a kind of defense of the Jewish race against the absurd prejudices of a so-called Christendom—a purpose which led the reviewer himself to play with the idea "that the pleasurable sensation of pedigree has somewhere its peculiar organ in the human frame." His first reaction was fanciful rather than bitter:

> With proper deference to the opinions of other physiologists, we should be inclined to place the seat of this emotion in the Caucasian race near the region of the toes. Tribes of this stock, at least, have always seemed to consider the keeping of somebody or other to kick as at once a proof of purity of lineage, and a suitable gratification of those nobler instincts which it implants. In Europe, the Jews have long monopolized the responsible privilege of supplying an object for this peculiar craving of the supreme Caucasian nature. The necessity of each rank in society found a vent upon the next below it, the diapason ending full in the Jew; and thus a healthy feeling of dignity was maintained from one end of the body politic to the other. In America, the African supplies the place of the Hebrew, and the sturdiest champion of impartial liberty feels the chromatic scale of equal rights violated when the same steam is employed to drag him and his darker

fellow-citizen. Civilization has made wonderful advances since the apostle Philip mounted the chariot of the Ethiopian eunuch. It must be remembered, however, that Ethiopians do not keep chariots nowadays.

The comment in his *North American Review* essay, however, was only a casual example of a characteristic digression introduced into his review of a book for which he could not "see any use."

He was more serious—if not more solemn—in his verse. "I confess I think that Birdofredum's attempt to explain the Anglosaxon theory is the best thing yet," he wrote to Briggs on November 13, after the third paper had been published, "except Parson Wilbur's letter in the Courier of last Saturday (today week)." Birdofredum's attempt obviously took its departure from the sentences in the *North American Review,* for the fictitious hero represented himself as having got an idea before he left home (presumably from the supposed tribute to the Anglo-Saxon race in Faneuil Hall) that the Mexicans were a sort of subhuman race who could be slaughtered without regrets—for, he explained in a couplet that summarizes Lowell's observations in the *North American:*

> I'd an idee thet they were built arter the darkie fashion all,
> An' kickin' colored folks about, you know, 's a kind o' national.

But the statement of "the Anglosaxon theory" of which Lowell thought so highly appeared in Birdofredum's version of Caleb Cushing's remarks to the troops and forms perhaps the least outworn piece of satire in *The Biglow Papers:*

> Thet our nation's bigger'n theirn an' so its rights air bigger,
> An' thet it's all to make 'em free thet we air pullin' trigger,
> Thet Anglo-Saxondom's idee 's abreakin' 'em to pieces,
> An' thet idee's thet every man doos jest wut he damn pleases;
> If I don't make his meanin' clear, perhaps in some respex I can,
> I know thet "every man" don't mean a nigger or a Mexican;
> An' there 's anuther thing I know, an' thet is, ef these creeturs,
> Thet stick an Anglosaxon mask onto State-prison feeturs,
> Should come to Jaalam Centre fer to argify an' spout on 't,
> The gals 'ould count the silver spoons the minnit they cleared out on 't.

In the more particular parts of his satire, however, Lowell was either grossly uninformed or extraordinarily irresponsible. If he was acquainted with the facts of the case, it made no difference to him that the troops stationed in Saltillo were kept out of town and subjected to strict discipline in order to prevent further scandalous mistreatment of the natives with whom he was so sympathetic: restraint represented a brutally enforced distinction between the privileges of a misguided volunteer and those of his commander, and discipline became the abuse of "ossifers" acting in a typical "Anglosaxon" manner. It made no difference that Saltillo itself, with its fields of grain and orchards of fruit, reminded the first Americans who entered it of New England: he took a big leap at the derivation of its name, identified it with "Saltriver," and described it as "about the meanest place a skunk could wal diskiver" in which a man found such "trash" to eat that he would give a year's pay for the smell of "one good blue-nose tater." It made no difference that the Massachusetts regiment had been raised by proclamation of the Whig Governor Briggs and its officers commissioned for service abroad despite his promise to the contrary: two Democrats, John A. Bolles and Robert Rantoul, Jr., had made speeches at the time of their departure; and although both were well-known anti-slavery men, they were held responsible for the doctrines of racial oppression. It is unfortunate that one of the few outstanding men of letters in the English-speaking world who attacked the doctrine of Anglo-Saxon racial supremacy in the nineteenth century did not achieve his admirable distinction in an atmosphere of greater fairness and candor.

But the time for the annual political conventions was approaching, and Lowell had become interested in politics. As a further consequence, he sent Hosea through a quick but unrecorded conversion from the non-political, disunionist principles of the radical abolitionists whose orthodoxy he had followed in his first attempt at "pottery," and brought him into action with no signs of his former attitude except the wholly negative one of absolute indifference to the politically active abolitionists of the Liberty party. The Democrats nominated Caleb Cushing, who had become a major general in Mexico; and, although the Whigs in convention rejected a resolution denying support to any presidential candidate who did not oppose the extension of slavery, Hosea became a "Conscience" Whig. The "vartu" of the Bay State demanded the defeat of any gubernatorial candidate who went in for war and took the side of President Polk. And when John P. Robinson, of Lowell, published his last-minute decision to support Cushing, Hosea Biglow, of Jaalam, hastily took up his pen to balance accounts. Governor Briggs, to whom Lowell had referred as a "painted stick" in "An Interview with Miles Standish" and to whom he had attributed an "eminent faculty" for inconsistency in his *Standard* editorial in July of the year before, was described by Hosea as "a sensible man" who "draws his furrer ez straight ez he can"; and, whatever his real feelings may have been on the matter, the author of the poem certainly gave the impression that he was going to "vote fer Guvener B."

By this time, Lowell was ready to accept the credit and responsibility for Hosea's writings and opinions. The day after "What Mr. Robinson Thinks" appeared in the *Courier* on November 2, the Democratic *Post* appeared with a paragraph attacking the rustic effusions and attributing them to Lowell, who immediately wrote the *Courier* under the name of Homer Wilbur and denied the attribution in a way which brought public attention to it and amounted to an open confession. After this letter (which was later combined with the poem to make the third of *The Biglow Papers*) appeared on November 6, its author could no longer enjoy the ambiguous satisfaction of overhearing someone insist that Hosea's verses were too good to be Lowell's. He had acquired a public character as a popular comic writer, and he immediately became self-conscious about it. It was a week later that he wrote to Briggs of his assorted personalities, but he had already displayed his self-consciousness in the Wilbur letter which he thought superior to his Anglo-Saxon satire and the best thing he had done in the series. For the parson took pains to represent Hosea as being dissatisfied by the paragraph in the Boston *Post* which, on the basis of "What Mr. Robinson Thinks," "classed him with the Whig party" and by implication made him a friend of the protective tariff. Master Homer Wilbur rather than Hosea was Lowell's picture of a conventional Whig—a "respectable Christian," proud of his connection with Harvard College, whose sympathetic interest in such an admirable youth as Hosea did not prevent him from combating the "heresies" of Garrison's *Liberator* ("of which," he thanked God, he had "never read a single line") and keeping his own sentiments acceptable to all his "people (of whatever political views), except the postmaster" who as a Democrat "dissented *ex officio*." The public misunderstanding of Hosea appears to have been an embarrassment to Lowell, who wrote Briggs after the third paper: "The only further use I shall put Hosea to will be to stir up the Legislater at the next session on the subject of allowing women to retain their own earnings, etc." Actually, it is difficult to say precisely what Lowell did do with his hero: he kept his signature for his dialect verses, but the personality of Hosea vanished after the charge of Whiggery and remained in hiding until 1857.

Parson Wilbur apparently superseded his young protégé as the character who dominated Lowell's mind, and the change not only gives a further indication of the author's self-consciousness but perhaps explains why he thought the letter better than the verses. The shepherd of the flock at Jaalam was not merely a satiric portrait of a Whig but a deliberate attempt at humor—as opposed to wit and satire—in that he was dramatically conceived as an individual who had an eccentric personality of his own and who would always speak and act in character. Lowell was brooding over the humor of Fielding and Dickens at the time Parson Wilbur came into being as a personality, and he seems to have tried to combine in his own creation the better *"conception* of humor" he found in the earlier novelist with the better *"observation"* he found in the later, giving Wilbur something of the goodhearted simplicity of Fielding's Parson Adams while portraying him with the careful attention to eccentricities of expression which was characteristic of Dickens. The goodheartedness was appropriate to and the eccentricities were typical of the Yankee parsons with whom Lowell was thoroughly familiar from his early visits to country parsonages with his father and from the sort of ministerial stories that are common in the household of every clergyman with a sense of humor. At first, Parson Wilbur himself appears to have possessed a considerable amount of dryly ambiguous clerical wit which disappeared as the author grew tired of his creation. Without much doubt, he was drawn largely from Lowell's observations of life, but the persistent report that he was modeled upon the Reverend Barzillai Frost, who was young enough to have been a senior in the Divinity School while Lowell was a freshman at Harvard, is hardly plausible.

If Parson Wilbur possessed any particular hidden antecedents, they might be traced through his Shandyism. For there can be little question but that he and the pedantic care ultimately devoted to him were the results of a critic's suppressed desire to be a novelist. The evolution of the novelist's ambition in Lowell's mind is impossible to trace through the number of notebooks—some mutilated and fragmentary, and all, with the exception of the last, undated—that record it; but as the plan gradually took tentative shape the suggestions concerning the plot show that Lowell was combining incidents from *Tristram Shandy* with those of his own life and planning to use them in connection with such major characters as an unworldly father, an eccentric uncle, and a child whose career was to be traced from before birth to the maturity of a young reformer. A shadowy mother, Yankee nurse, more than one college professor, and a conservative minister were in the background; but whether Parson Wilbur represented the conservative minister, allowed to creep Yorrick-like into the family circle, or whether he combined the characteristics of the father and uncle is not evident. Yet the connection between *The Biglow Papers* and the meditated novel is clear from the appearance, in the midst of one set of preliminary notes on the plot, of one of Mr. Wilbur's "entirely fragmentary" notes on Hosea's pedigree as a note for the novel. The young man whose "life at college—Father's letter—Professor's lectures" were to be written up had no connection with the semi-literate Yankee poet. But the "P. W." who appeared immediately after these brief notes and " 'thought some' of having his effigies prefixed to the work as likely to make it sell better" was imagined while Lowell's mind was actively playing with the idea of becoming a writer of fiction.

The character of Parson Wilbur was to grow—or, perhaps more accurately, expand—slowly in Lowell's mind. At first, he did little more than provide his creator with the thrill of his first purely dramatic creation. Hitherto, Lowell's characters had been projections of himself, distorted by his habit of seeing himself in the mirror of other men's writings, but never entirely dissociated from the personality of the author. For even the first letter of Birdofredom Sawin had been so ambiguous in tone that the reader alternates between contempt and sympathy for the gullible Yankee who had to learn by experience what the shrewd Hosea realized in advance. There is no such ambiguity in the succeeding Papers. Lowell was discovering that irony and the superior delights of omnipotence were more exciting than argument and the possibility of frustration. He was learning to fashion his own opponents and let them destroy themselves by the words he put in their mouths. It was the kind of satire which delighted those who shared his opinions and made no new converts to his side, but he only knew at first that it pleased him and later that it pleased his readers. By the time he published the first versified result of his new discovery he had given up his notion of getting rid of Hosea by sending him to college although he did carry out his intention to improve his spelling to the extent of making it phonetic rather than merely bad. Some of his self-consciousness remained in the new poem, for he referred to the criticisms of the *Post* (especially to the charge of blasphemy, to which he seems to have been especially sensitive) and took occasion to clear Hosea of sympathy toward the Whig tariff policy; but practice in irony soon relieved him from the demands of consistency. Hosea's future role was merely that of imitating "the historians of antiquity, who put into the mouths of various characters such words as seem to them most fitting to the occasion and to the speaker." He had to commit himself to no positive opinions of his own.

The new product of his new freedom filled Lowell with enthusiasm. He considered it "the best" he had done and planned to indulge his fun in "a volume of H. Biglow's verses" which he would edit "under the character of the Rev. Mr. Wilbur" with an essay on Yankee dialect and perhaps a "complete natural history of Humbug" in Latin, all to be published at Jaalam on old-looking paper with old-fashioned decorations. The new poem, "Remarks of Increase D. O'Phace, Esquire," which appeared in the *Courier* for December 28, was an improvement upon the prose Wilbur letter in its attempt to correct any wrong impressions that the hasty "What Mr. Robinson Thinks" may have given concerning the author's sympathy for the conservative Whig party. For the speaker (who owed his name not to an Irish ancestry but rather to the use of the slang term "doughface" to signify a Northern politician with Southern sympathies) was represented as a good party man who, shocked to the core of his being by the refusal of Whig Representative John G. Palfrey to cast the deciding vote for the Whig candidate for the Speakership of the House, delivered himself of a spontaneous overflow of candor in State Street. It was Lowell's version of an honest statement of the Whig position and the politician's attitude. The party tried to be on both sides of the fence at once, opposing wrong in the abstract while remaining tolerant of particular sins. The politician was the party in miniature, frankly placing opportunism above principles and freely admitting that

> every fool knows thet a man represents
> Not the fellers thet sent him, but them on the fence.

Palfrey's unpardonable crime was that of violating, in the interest of his anti-slavery principles, that party regularity which enabled the successful politician to sit profitably on both national and local fences. His critic revealed what was wrong with the Whigs who could never take advantage of the moral strength offered their party by men who would place principles above the wishes of their Southern "masters" and thus show its superiority to the Northern Democrats.

Whether the reading of Robert Browning suggested to Lowell the device of dissociating oneself from a character who reveals his secret self in monologue is a question—like that of the relationship between Tennyson and *The Vision of Sir Launfal*—which cannot be settled without the benefit of direct testimony. But Francis Bowen, the editor of the *North American Review,* had written Lowell in April, 1847, of his inability to locate a copy of Browning's latest book and of his desire to have Lowell review Miss Barrett's unknown husband if he happened to possess his works. The review was not written until the following February, but when it did appear it took particular notice of the qualities in Browning that Lowell was putting into his own satires: the self-revelation of his characters by what they leave unsaid and undone as well as by what they say and do, his ability to create persons who are "above all . . . not the mere mouthpieces for the author's idiosyncrasies," and his high dramatic faculty which "lies not in a knowledge of character, so much as in an imaginative conception of the springs of it." He also questioned in the review whether verse was "the proper vehicle for humor at all" and, in general, showed that he was thinking of Browning's work along lines that ran parallel to his thoughts of his own. But whether he was learning from Browning or was learning from his own experiments to read Browning is not to be settled by the date upon which he finally got around to reviewing the works of a man whose dramatic genius he had praised in his *Conversations* three years before and whose poems he had been one of the few persons in America to buy.

The first four Biglow Papers were consistent neither in point of view nor in purpose. They were all written before Lowell became an editor of the *National Anti-Slavery Standard* in 1848, and they represent a high-spirited indulgence of the dramatic faculty which Lowell recognized in Browning and discovered in himself when he turned to dialect verse. In them he could follow his humor while tilting with various aspects of public opinion with his visor down. The last five of the series, however, were different. They were contributions to a campaign, closely related to his editorial activities and the abolitionist party line.

II

Lowell agreed in March, 1848, to become a corresponding editor of the *Standard* at a salary of five hundred dollars a year. He wrote Briggs on March 26 that he did not like to take money for his contributions to the cause and, with a curious lack of self-consciousness about the inconsistency of his statement, that he did not "agree with the abolitionists in their disunion and non-voting theories." He was also critical of Garrison, who was by that time in the midst of an effort to engage the abolitionists in anti-sabbatarian activities. But despite the income from Maria's property, he had spent more than he had received every year since his marriage and, believing that his abolitionism had cut him off from the magazine world, he felt justified in taking the job offered to him. The commitment to regular contributions, however, was a strain upon him, and he often used the same material in both prose and verse with the result that *The Biglow Papers* (which went over to the *Standard* after one more appearance in the *Courier*) became rather intimately connected with his editorial activities. Yet his new position could hardly have been an unpleasant one, for the group managing the *Standard* was not nearly so single-minded in its anti-slavery activities as the board of the *Freeman* had been, and the managing editor, Sydney H. Gay, gave his contributing associate free rein to deal with any of the exciting events of one of the most exciting years in the nineteenth century.

The event that interested Lowell most during the first month of his editorship was the new revolution in France. His first contribution, for April 6, was a long "Ode to France" which shows signs of the haste in composition made necessary by the narrow interval between the time the news reached America and his first deadline. He had evidently known of the opposition aroused by Louis Phillipe's attempts to extend the influence of the Bourbon dynasty and had anticipated some trouble for the king in his Biglow Paper of December 28, but he knew little of the actual events of February 24 when he wrote his poem and assumed that the populace was more bloodthirsty than it actually was. There was a distinction in his mind, though, between the actions of such ignorant brutes as Birdofredum Sawin who were deceived into murdering Mexicans and those of "that maenad throng" of "Brutes with the memories and desires of men" whose

despair of trampled centuries
Leaped up with one hoarse yell and snapped its bands,
Groped for its right with horny, callous hands,
And stared around for God with bloodshot eyes.

The latter represented "the Spirit of the Age" (interpreted, apparently, as a desire for abstract freedom for its own sake and for work as its own reward) as opposed to the spirit of trade personified in the "Broker-King" who had been dethroned. Quietly interpreting the events in France as a parallel to the struggle between the abolitionists and the Boston merchants, Lowell rejoiced in the triumph of the "invisible Spirit" and out-Emersoned the author of the recent "Ode to W. H. Channing" in his contempt for "chattel":

Nay, what though
The yellow blood of Trade meanwhile should pour
Along its arteries a shrunken flow,

And the idle canvas droop around the shore?
These do not make a state,
Nor keep it great;
I think God made
The earth for man, not trade.

"The French Revolution of 1848" was also the subject of his prose article in the next issue of the *Standard,* and he treated it in essentially the same way, although after a week's thought—and perhaps after receiving more information—he decided that it seemed "less a revolution than the quiet opening of a flower which, before it can blossom, must detrude the capsule which has hitherto enveloped and compressed it." By this time it was the first and not the second French Revolution which "was only the natural recoil of an oppressed and imbruted people." The more recent insurgents had formed merely a so-called mob which was inspiringly "satisfied with the hope of work"; and he made as much as he could of the conservative sympathy for Louis Phillipe in America and of the theory of "the divine right of *institutions*" which had superseded that of kings and hedged "pauperism, slavery, and other such blotches of our self-satisfied nineteenth century." The violent climax of the reform movement in France was still in his mind when he wrote an editorial for the *Standard* of April 20 with the title "Shall we ever be Republican?" His attitude was not hopeful: Americans blinded themselves to the quackery of their democracy by transferring the government at intervals from one great party to another which was equally corrupt, whereas they could never really achieve "that inward fortunateness, without which all outward prosperity is a cheat and a delusion," until they uprooted the "deadly Upas" of slavery "no matter with what dear or sacred things its pestilential roots may be entwined." But unfortunately the Northern Democrats were not as opposed to the revolution in France as Lowell had represented them, and their illogical refusal to sympathize with the "Broker-King" inspired him to use again his device of irony in the next of his Biglow Papers for the purpose of exposing their "insincerity." "The Pious Editor's Creed" in the *Standard* for May 4 presented the Democratic "doughface" who did believe in Freedom "Ez fur away ez Payris is" but was convinced that it was the sort of thing "Thet don't agree with niggers." His reverence for Uncle Sam's pockets also led him to believe in excise taxes, but he was quite ready to advocate free trade if he could remain in his customhouse office, and hard money if he could get his own easily. Lowell allowed him to summarize his creed in one fervent ejaculation:

I *don't* believe in princerple,
But oh, I *du* in interest.

But he closed with a return to the hypocrisy of the Democratic attitude toward affairs abroad—the talk of "peace" and the conduct of the Mexican War under the assumption that the Mexicans could be thrashed into a state of "brotherly kindness." The new poem was "not so humorous as some of Hosea's productions," he wrote Gay on April 27 (for humor required a certain amount of sympathy with the character portrayed) although he described it as "by far the wittiest."

The wit might have taken on the characteristic of a boomerang had Lowell not been too busy to stop and think. For he had certainly been thrashing away at almost everybody outside his own narrow group of reformers as though he himself believed that by such means he could arouse the feelings of brotherly kindness upon which, he had so often insisted, true reforms must rest. Only a few months before, he had advised his fellow abolitionists, through "An Extract" in the 1848 *Liberty Bell,* that "Force never yet gained one true victory" whereas "An olive-wreath, stretched harmlessly across, . . . enchants all enemies." But the pressure of his literary engagements, within a month of his employment by the *Standard,* had forced him back into the role of the agitator who divided humanity into groups on his right hand and on his left, dealing gentleness to the sheep and violence upon the goats, although his only rational hope of achieving practical results lay in arousing an exactly contrary reaction among them. Even among the anti-slavery agitators, though, Lowell's position was not in the front line with Garrison and Wendell Phillips but always with the supporting troops. Although the *Standard* had been established as a paper published by abolitionists for the general public from which they hoped to draw recruits, it was being sustained at the time Lowell joined the staff by loyal devotees to the cause, and it seems never to have occurred to the corresponding editor that it was part of his job to make converts. His job was to keep those who were already stirred up from settling down, and it is not always possible to tell whether his journalism was pushing or riding the cause. So long as he identified its opponents, he had the privilege of trying to touch their hearts in one issue and of taking their skins off in the next. When he sent Gay "The Pious Editor's Creed," he gave him the choice between that and a better but less "taking" serious poem in which he attempted an affecting indication of what man had done to man. But in "A Parable" (the second of his poems with this title) he was undecided whether the most effective preaching should appeal to pity or to fear, for although he represented men and their institutions as having changed the image of God into a haggard artisan and a starving motherless girl, he portrayed the institutions as shaking and splitting apart because they were founded upon the "bodies and souls" of such oppressed beings.

Few of Lowell's journalistic writings, however, dealt with such serious matters as the foundations of society. He needed the stimulation of immediate events in order to keep up his schedule. And so far as *The Biglow Papers* was concerned, he had found the device of stultifying an opponent by making him a ventriloquist's dummy so simple and satisfying that he used it for all the rest of the series. When Senator John P. Hale set off a furor in the Senate on April 20 with a resolution sympathetic toward the slaves that Drayton, Sayres, and English had attempted to abduct from the District of Columbia, Lowell had a chance to use his trick upon real people instead of the types who had previously been its victims. John C. Calhoun, harried by the prospect that the Mexican War might add more territory to the union than the South could control, allowed his temper to overcome his political judgment; and Lowell, with a variation of his successful John P. Robinson refrain, emphasized and magnified the indiscretion of his remarks by having "The Debate in the Sennit" "sot to a nusry rhyme" by Hosea. The jingle of his rhyme also encouraged brief attentions to eleven other senators, eight of them Southerners and the other three Northern "doughfaces" including Hale's senior colleague from New Hampshire and General Lewis Cass who, as one of the leading Northern Democratic politicians, had attracted Lowell's notice before and was here singled out for special irony. He also let his Southern senators express the sympathy for the "wise" aristocracy of France which his pious Democratic editor had perversely avoided.

"The Debate in the Sennit" was sent to the *Courier* in order that it might appear as quickly as possible after the event satirized, and, by virtue of the fact that the Whig paper was published a day ahead of the abolitionist *Standard* which printed "The Pious Editor's Creed," the "Debate" became the fifth rather than the sixth of the Biglow Papers as they were arranged in the published volume. It was Lowell's last attempt to do good through the columns of the *Courier,* for he was already finding it difficult to keep up with the demands of his regular job, and he wrote Briggs on May 12 that although he could interest himself in general ideas, he wearied of applying them to the present. Yet he was having trouble with his farm tenants and needed the *Standard* salary—especially since he had not yet paid his note for stereotyping his *Poems, Second Series.* He got by, at times, by making the same material do double duty in prose and in verse, and of his two new prose editorials, one was to provide the seventh Biglow Paper and the other had grown out of the fifth. The latter, which was published in the *Standard* for May 25, was "An Imaginary Conversation" by Senators Calhoun and Cass and Henry S. Foote of Mississippi in which they reviewed their debate on the Drayton and Sayres incident, admitted their mistake in providing fuel for the abolitionist fires, and made some of the same errors again. In this, Lowell transferred his poetic device of irony to his prose and again attempted to make his Democrats associate themselves with Louis Phillipe, getting around the difficulty of doing so by having General Cass correct a reference to his "friend" into his "late friend" and allowing Calhoun to remark sympathetically: "The unfortunate are never the friends of the wise man."

But the "Conversation" was a more thoughtful and skittery document than the "Debate." By 1848, the abolitionists had fairly well accomplished their aims in arousing popular interest in the slavery question and had reached a time for decision concerning practical procedure in the future. The believers in political action were on the verge of combining their differences and uniting in the Free Soil Party, and even Garrison, although holding to his old principles of political non-intercourse, was growing tolerant of the kind of conscience that would permit an anti-slavery man to vote. A decision to fight the battle on political rather than moral grounds, of course, would involve the more radical abolitionists in a complete change in attitude toward the Constitution; and Lowell, without attempting to analyze the way matters might be going, was sensitive to Senator Foote's expression of the Southern Democrats' desire to dissolve the Union. He allowed the Senator to hint faintly that his expression was an insincere threat designed to keep certain economic elements of the North in line, but he showed signs of his own concern by making his Southern politicians admit more disadvantages in secession than they ever thought of admitting in reality—the impossibility of establishing an alliance with republican France or with England after the inevitable success of the reform movement there, and the certainty of the South becoming a "Black Republic" within "a fearfully short time from the period of rupture."

Lowell (whose own attitude seems to have been that all politicians were probably blackguards but the Democrats certainly were) was quite ready to maintain the superiority of the moral principles of the Declaration of Independence over the political compromises of the Constitution, even though it involved him in his old problem of what to do when he found good words coming from the mouths of bad men. He resolved his dilemma easily, however, on this occasion and corrected any impression of admiration for Jefferson that he might have given in his editorial on the French Revolution by representing the author of the Declaration as a typical politician whose words elevated him to the presidency while his works should have elevated him to the gallows. The hodgepodge of his satire also included an ironic defense of the religious sentiment of the North as a bulwark of slavery and a statement, by Calhoun, of a doctrine of instinctive class consciousness closely akin to the "Anglosaxon idea" which had been ironically presented in the first letter by Birdofredum Sawin.

The editorial that grew into a Biglow Paper was one on "Presidential Candidates" which, although it represented a later interest, was published two weeks before "An Imaginary Conversation." One of the weakest of Lowell's satiric papers, it maintained the thesis that the best way to become a President was to refrain from writing letters and is perhaps most interesting as an indication of how impossible it was for the abolitionist group to agree upon any candidate for office. Among those who had committed themselves to an anti-slavery course, Gerritt Smith was too good for the people, Senator Hale received only ambiguous approval for his "common-sense" and refusal to write, and Van Buren (whose current letter making him acceptable to the Free Soil Party had not yet been published) had made "for himself a political winding-sheet out of a single sheet of medium foolscap" in 1844 and presumably was a failure not worth considering. Lowell had positive objections to most of the prospective candidates from the two major parties, although he seemed cynically reconciled to the possibility of Zachary Taylor, "whose claims," he said, "may be very shortly summed up. He is a general, a slaveholder, and nobody knows what his opinions are." The seventh of the Biglow Papers, published as "A Letter from a Candidate for the Presidency" in the *Standard* for June 1, was Hosea's versification of just the sort of communication such a candidate might have penned. Admitting that he was "a kind o' peri-Wig," he was on the fence about everything except the settled issue of "a Bank" and his willingness to get Hosea into the Jaalam Point lighthouse if Hosea got him into the White House in Washington. Lowell was not sure how good it was when he sent it in on May 19, but, as he had written Gay the week before, he had "got the *hang* of the treadmill" and was able to give his irony an amusing bite even on those mornings when he confessed feeling "rather stupid."

Lowell kept his journalistic treadmill going most smoothly in ironic prose in "The Sacred Parasol" for June 8, in which he represented the Constitution as a parchment shade designed to protect the people of the United States from "the sun of a new political truth" that had "got quietly above the horizon in our Declaration of Independence." He did not maintain his ironic tone for long, however, and in the poem "Freedom" for June 8 he fell back into the sort of solemnity which was characteristic of his more youthful treatment of future prospects. When the political conventions finally did meet and nominate Generals Taylor and Cass, he summarized some of his earlier comments on the Whig candidate in the form of an imaginary conversation between "the thinking portion" of the party and the practical politicians (whose words were, in part, parodies of remarks he had previously attributed to Abbott Lawrence) but the greater part of "The Nominations for the Presidency" was an exposition of the solemn opinion that "both parties have done their worst"—although he quoted and agreed with the general opinion "that anybody is better than Cass," who made up for his failure to hold slaves by being one. He had no hopes for the ability of the dissenting members of the two parties to agree upon a mutually acceptable candidate and was cynical about the durability of their dissent.

Lowell had got himself into a bad state of petulance. In a series of editorials during the following two months he expressed his annoyance with people who sympathized with the current rebellion in Ireland (which appealed to racial prejudice) while doing nothing to encourage a revolution against racial prejudice in the United States; with people who kept asking "What will Mr. Webster do?" and with the Yankee Achilles himself who, lacking a tent to skulk in, sat on his fence at Marshfield; and with the bourgeoisie of France whose blind stupidity, as he interpreted "The News from Paris," was responsible for the new outbreak of violence among the workers. He was trying to follow the philosophy to which Emerson gave such succinct expression in his "Ode to W. H. Channing": "Let man serve law for man ... The state may follow how it can"; but he was unwilling to admit, with Emerson, that his was "the day of the chattel" or to see any virtue in the materialistic "law for thing." On the contrary, he continued to insist that the spirit of the age was high-minded rather than materialistic and that every man was "furnished with an inward consciousness which distinguishes right from wrong as infallibly as the electric spark selects the iron and shuns the glass." Why men possessed of a common moral sense could, in a high-minded age, so persistently concern themselves with questions of practical expediency rather than of right and wrong puzzled and irritated him. According to his philosophy, the state, directed by the sentiments of the mass of men, ought to follow closely at the heels of those who pursued the humanitarian "law for man." But, according to his observation, it refused to follow at all, and the only explanation he could see was that the politicians ignored their "inward consciousness" and tried to cultivate the masses—whom Lowell quite obviously distrusted despite his philosophy. He could neither ignore the evidence of his observation nor give up a belief that went contrary to it, and the conflict between the two disturbed the equanimity with which he played his literary role and made him display in print his personal petulance and lack of balance.

The lack of balance that Lowell often displayed in his more unhappy moments was clearly revealed in the unseemly and grotesque humor of the sixth Biglow Paper, "A Second Letter from B. Sawin, esq.," which appeared in the *Standard* for July 6, 1848. The Mexican War had come to an end and many of the troops were already on their way home when peace was officially proclaimed on the national holiday of July 4. The occasion inspired Lowell to be funny—with a more extravagant array of puns than he had ever before put into print—about the returning soldier, and he allowed Birdofredum to report from Vera Cruz on his military gains. The elaborately detailed joke was on him: he had lost a leg, an eye, his left arm, and all four fingers of his right hand; and he had acquired six broken ribs, a permanent case of malaria, a memory of hardships and abuse, and nothing in the way of financial security except the possibility of a pension and a nickname ("Old Timbertoes," or "the one-eyed Slarterer," or "the bloody Birdofredum") which might prove a political asset. It was less than the gallows that Lowell had earlier suggested as the proper desert of a man who would go off soldiering in an unholy war, but he seems to have thought it funnier; and he was not yet ready to kill off his hero, who was left, for the time being, begging that a subscription be taken to buy him "a low-priced baby" in order that he might become a slaveholder in the South and thus qualify himself to become a presidential candidate. For those people who did not have wounded friends or relatives returning from the war it may have been extremely comic, but, in any case, it is probably the one of Lowell's poems which gains most by being disassociated from the occasion that inspired it.

In the meantime, he had written and sent to Gay on June 29 a poem which had the "benefit" of his own "approbation"—as indicated by his willingness to go against the customary practices of the paper and sign it with his initials. It was the ode "To Lamartine" which, although not printed until August 3, complemented "A Second Letter from B. Sawin" as an indication of Lowell's state of mind during the month of June. The poet who had written nobly and who by giving "politics an epic strain" had also succeeded in touching "the bard's true lyre, a nation's heart," with his doctrines of reform and peace was one who had fulfilled Lowell's own ambition; and the fact that the "crowd" had more recently turned against and rejected him somehow consoled Lowell for the fact that he had himself begun to feel rejected before he achieved fulfillment. Falling into his old habit of believing that, despite appearances, the pure in heart were blessed in a world where men said all manner of things against them, he was able to find words of sympathy for a new martyr poet whose "Cross" was to have his advice ignored by a country that had not yet become worthy of him.

It was Lowell's habit, in times of uncertainty and distress, to alternate between exaggerated considerations of inner virtue and of the wickedness of the world; and it was probably not long after signing "To Lamartine" that he wrote "A Dialogue (Author and Friend)" in which he expressed his feelings with too great a frankness for publication. Done in the tone and manner of an eighteenth-century satire, it began with the friend's surprised question "Not vote for Taylor?" and with Lowell's customary objections to the candidate:

> The coarse old Zachary, till a year agone,
> Just whipped his slaves, and hied his bloodhounds on,
> Swore much, went dirty, and his cotton raised,
> By Whigs undeified, by Choate unpraised.

He had no use for Taylor and little more for a considerable number of other public figures. He was especially bitter about the "mercenary" Horace Greeley and sad over Webster who had been first "bought" and then "betrayed" by those who bought him. Among the great men of Boston, "descended" Winthrop, the Speaker of the House for whom Palfrey had refused to vote, was damned for allowing his actions to be governed by the desire to "follow cunning Bancroft to St. James," and Rufus Choate was described as being merely "windy." The editors of the two local Whig papers, other than the *Courier,* were little better: William Schouler of the *Atlas* was a peddler, and the author's old friend Nathan Hale, Sr., of the *Advertiser* was in his dotage. After such an outburst, the Friend's concluding exclamation was more pointed than Lowell intended it to be:

> Enough! such accusations are too base.
> You're either mad, a Garrisonian rank,
> Or else you want no discounts at the Bank.

For a person who had disavowed Garrisonism and had an eight per cent interest in matters of financial policy, Lowell was behaving in a way which suggests the methodless madness of a person who had lost his balance and was striking around at anyone who maintained any judiciousness concerning the practical problems of the time.

Before his interest in the eighteenth-century literary manner had left him, however, he had got a grip upon himself, and when he appeared in public in the literary dress of Prior and Gay, he was dealing with fundamental issues rather than with personalities. "Leaving the Matter open, a Tale by Homer Wilbur, A. M.," which appeared in the *Standard* for July 27, was a clear-cut statement of Northern objections to the defeat of the Wilmot Proviso, made with humor and good sense and with little suggestion of violence except for the somewhat ominous conclusion which hinted of the strain placed upon the North's self-control and perhaps of some future breaking apart of the American "farm." This settling upon a major issue after a period of random frustration also settled Lowell's political mind for the time being, for while the poem was being transferred from manuscript to print, the "Conscience" Whigs (with whom Lowell had been associated through the *Courier*) were meeting in Cincinnati and deciding to secede from the party on that issue and call a convention in Buffalo on August 9 for the purpose of trying to get together with the Democratic "Barnburners" and the Liberty Party on the platform of forbidding slavery in the new territory acquired from Mexico whether or not it might lie south of the Missouri Compromise Line. In the *Standard* for August 10, Lowell hailed "The Buffalo Convention" as "the most important event in recent American politics" and cheerfully anticipated its action in nominating Van Buren for the presidency as naming "fully as much of an Abolitionist as any other candidate who is likely to be proposed." The Free Soil Party, he made clear, was "not an Abolition party in any sense of the word," but it was one made up of people who had "at last satisfied themselves of the existence and necessity of Conscience"; and Lowell, although believing that the Wilmot Proviso was "inadequate," had come to the conclusion that it was a "forward step" into which the politicians were forced by the people and had renewed his faith that the "fresh instincts of the popular heart clearly tend to a point above and beyond" the leaders of the Free Soil movement. The nomination at Buffalo had no personal interest for the non-voters among the abolitionists, he admitted, but it pointed out the best course for "any Anti-Slavery man"; and it seems reasonably clear that it pointed out Lowell's own course for him and relieved him of the disturbing irritation that had been caused by his earlier uncertainty.

With a steadier mind concerning the political situation—for the Buffalo Convention did follow his expectations by nominating Van Buren and offering a threat to the major parties—Lowell was able to recapture some of the matter-of-factness and irony which had enabled him to walk easily on his *Standard* treadmill. His editorial on "The Irish Rebellion" for August 24 was written from the point of view of practical expediency, and those on "Fanaticism in the Navy," "Exciting Intelligence from South Carolina," and "Turncoats," in successive weeks, were all lightened to a greater or less extent by an air of humorous detachment and so relieved of the quality which made his preaching heavy when he was less sure of himself. Parts of the last germinated into "A Third Letter from B. Sawin, Esq." which was printed two weeks later in the *Standard* for September 28. In it, Birdofredum withdrew from the presidential race and, although he had been a Democrat for years, announced for Taylor with a tribute to Webster's lukewarm speech from Marshfield and assurances of the ease with which one could agree with a man who had expressed his opinions on nothing. Like other riders on Old Zack's bandwagon, as Lowell had portrayed them in his editorial, Birdofredum ridiculed the Free Soil nominee as not being the sort of man he had previously voted for and as not being "half antislavery 'nough"—although veteran Sawin did not profess anti-slavery principles himself (except in the abstract) and thus did not reveal the hypocrisy which the prose account of "Turncoats" attributed to so many of Taylor's followers. On the contrary, since this was to be the last of the first series of Biglow Papers and Lowell had a humorous conceit that he did not want to leave out, he attributed to Birdofredum a recent and peculiar experience as a slaveholder which frankly convinced him that "renegader slaves" such as the ones who stole his wooden leg and forced him into servitude were not "fit fer being free." As he brought his series to an end, Lowell found that satire and humor were making conflicting demands upon him; and, in yielding to both, he showed that it was not always easy for him to hold his impulses to the party line.

III

During September and October, Lowell was busy with printer's proof and finding difficulty in meeting his obligations to the *Standard*. On September 21, he published the verses "To the Memory of Hood" which had missed appearing in the *Broadway Journal* when Briggs turned its editorship over to Poe, and his three prose editorials in October were all uninspired comments upon things he had read rather than articles with their own excuse for being. His one prose composition of that period which appeared to stand alone, "Calling Things by their Right Names" in the *Standard* for November 9, also really belongs in that category, for although it was probably written after he had finished with his proof and shows his old ironic sparkle, it represented no new thought but was an amplification of the comments he had made five weeks before on a letter from a Reverend Dr. Bullard of St. Louis. Two of his poems were similar reflections of a spontaneous reaction to the words of somebody else. When former Mayor Harrison G. Otis, in October, published his letter supporting Taylor for the presidency, Lowell seized upon a casual digression concerning the humble origin of the *Liberator* and responded first with "The Day of Small Things" (later "To W. L. Garrison") in the *Standard* for October 19 and a week later with "The Ex-Mayor's Crumbs of Consolation: a Pathetic Ballad." The latter was an unfortunately timed satire, for Lowell did not know that Otis was desperately ill at the time it appeared and would die two days later, and perhaps is most interesting as an example of how the author was making a single casual inspiration do double duty and of his economy in using the conclusion of his editorial on "The Buffalo Convention" as the conclusion of his poem. His other contribution in verse, "To John G. Palfrey" on November 2, had been in his notebook as a serious but unfinished companion piece to the fourth of the Biglow Papers and was probably finished and used at that time because of the pressure of his immediate journalistic need.

While doing the best he could on his "treadmill," Lowell was driving himself through an almost overwhelming job of more ambitious writing, editing, and proofreading. He had thrown himself into the business of editing Hosea's poems (which were to be published locally, in Cambridge) as soon as he had thought he had finished the manuscript of *A Fable for Critics* in August, and by September 2 he was able to report to Gay that there were "between twenty and thirty pages already printed." His statement, of course, represents a technical impossibility and cannot be taken literally, but he probably had corrected the newspaper versions of the first two numbers and had added Parson Wilbur's commentary and may have seen the results in type. If such early corrections and annotations kept him "more employed" than he cared to be, it is probably well that he could not foresee what lay before him. For the good parson, who was responsible for only five of the thirty-one pages devoted to the first two numbers, had taken up a pen which was eventually to produce more than three-fifths of the finished book. The chore of correcting the dialect and preserving uniformity in his semi-phonetic spelling was in itself "no easy task to perform properly," as he confessed to Briggs on the following day, and at some time later in the month he wrote Gay of being "so wearied out with Mr. Biglow and his tiresome (though wholly respectable) friend Mr. Wilbur" that he had to get his contribution for the *Standard* (apparently the poem to Hood) from his "coffers" rather than from his head.

If Lowell had started out with some notion of being a Yankee Burns, he had found, in Parson Wilbur, his bogle. The Jaalam pedant seized upon his brain and could not be shaken off by any form of abbreviation. For the character caught at the imagination of the man who had thought of being a novelist and practically chased Lowell's original purpose out of the book while he exhibited his humors in longer and longer commentaries and demanded an elaborate Introduction in which to reveal peculiarities that could not be related to Hosea's verses. On October 4, Lowell told Briggs that he was *"druv like all possessed"* while "keeping up with the printers with Wilbur's notes, Glossary, Index and introduction," supplying one set of hands with the body of the book and one with the extremities. Yet he found a stimulation in being "druv" and two days later wrote his friend that he had added some amusing preliminary "Notices of an Independent Press." The addition of a liking for parody to his parson's variety of humors was merely another example of how *The Biglow Papers* grew until by the time Lowell had finished reading the page proof, on November 4, it had become fifty pages longer than he had "expected" it to be "and so took longer" to get out.

Such passive submission to the arbitrary demands of his long-winded editor is indicative of how completely the author had forgotten his original purpose of political satire. The printer's schedule had probably been originally set in order to get the work out before the national election—which it might have been expected to influence—on November 7; but it did not appear until at least three days and possibly as long as two weeks later, for although Lowell wrote Gay on November 10 that he supposed it would be published that day, he told him on November 25 that the first edition was "nearly exhausted" and on December 20 that it was "all gone in a week." G. P. Putnam had taken a third of the first printing of fifteen hundred copies for distribution in New York and an additional one hundred for his London branch, and the others were apparently handled not by the publisher George Nichols (who was actually one of the proprietors of Metcalf and Company, the printers, rather than a distributor) but by the Cambridge bookseller, John Bartlett, who was also responsible for the second edition of two hundred and fifty copies run off before Christmas from the same stereotype plates.

The hurried attempt to get the book on the market in New York and New England in time for the election—or, when that proved impossible, before the political excitement had entirely died down—resulted in a certain madness in its printing which has been the source of later bibliographical confusion. It also was the source of a strange confusion between the author and the fictitious editor which makes it sometimes impossible to tell which is which. In his annotations of the first four papers, Parson Wilbur kept fairly consistently to the literary character he had established for himself in the first letter to the editor of the *Courier*. He was a rather pompous and pedantic country parson with Whig principles, a certain amount of dry humor, a considerable store of out-of-the-way learning, and a tendency toward periodic displays of clerical rhetoric. As Lowell began to send copy irrevocably to the press, however, he lost the opportunity for review and perspective; and when the printers began to close upon him, he let the literary personality of Homer Wilbur break down under the pressure and occasionally speak with the voice of his creator. In his annotations for the fifth of Hosea's poems, the parson used a long passage from the editorial "Exciting Intelligence from South Carolina" in the *Standard* of September 7, and he later used passages from "An Imaginary Conversation" and from "Presidential Candidates" and frequently expressed sentiments that came strangely from the pen of one who professed neither to read nor to approve of the "heresies" of the *Liberator*. Some of the acknowledged quotations were imbedded in the parson's own eccentricities; but the eccentricities themselves took on a new character, with suggestions of Sterne cropping up among the hand-me-down relics of seventeenth-century periods until Lowell himself realized that his creature had got out of hand. Somewhat apologetically, he allowed his editor to defend his prolixity in the last paper; but the author never seemed to realize that by making his own vice a characterizing humor of Parson Wilbur, he had permitted the latter to take on something of the author's personality.

When Lowell reached the extremities of his book the parson had his revenge. The inconsistencies in dialect and spelling which he discovered while making the glossary and index might not have been out of character as the mistakes of the uneducated Hosea, but they were intolerable to the pedantry of his spiritual and grammatical mentor—and so Lowell, who never spent much effort correcting his own poems, revised the verses of Hosea until corrections for the stereotype plates increased their cost by almost fifty per cent and consumed more than the entire profits of the first edition. In the prefatory and introductory parts of his book, Lowell stepped in and out of his clerical character so often that he appears to have assumed that the two personalities were interchangeable. The "Notices of an Independent Press" reflect the author's own and peculiar annoyances: the demand for nationalism in literature, the political bias frequently found in journalistic criticism, the finicky attitude toward vulgar diction in poetry, and the general meaninglessness of the silly verbiage which characterized so many reviews. The long passage in Carlylese attributed to the pseudo-transcendental *World-Harmonic Æolian-Attachment,* in particular, would have been impossible to the fictitious character who was supposed to have composed it. On the other hand, the "Note to Title-Page" is faithful at least to Lowell's original conception of the character who would list his "prospective" academic honors with a thoroughness which was somewhat more than exhaustive. The fragment of a Latin treatise on humbug was also a part of his original plan, but if its "Proemium" was in character, the two specimens of the work itself (dealing with military and critic classes) hardly were, for the description of the critics was in the current humor of the author who was even then publishing an anonymous poem which he hoped would put them to flight.

The Introduction was probably the greatest hodgepodge of any of the fragments that made up the finished book. For Lowell started it with the parson in his old literary style and soon allowed it to degenerate into a collection of odds and ends thrown together as a memorial to his own literary plans rather than a finished accomplishment by his editor. He gleaned from his notebook two unused fragments of the poem "Indian Summer" which had first been harvested for "An Indian-Summer Reverie" in his *Poems, Second Series,* and he carried out a sort of private joke with his father by giving his parson the image of Dr. Lowell in a paragraph alluding to the "very near ancestor" who had contributed to *Pietas et Gratulatio* and describing the differences in opinion over the poetry of Pope which existed between the older man and his surprisingly successful young protégé. He began but succeeded neither in finishing nor in getting into Mr. Wilbur's usual style the planned essay on the Yankee character and the Yankee dialect. It is probable that in the middle of it the printers caught up with him, for he was forced to put his familiar character to bed with a "dangerous fit of illness" and create the shadowy Reverend Columbus Nye to explain the "fragmentary and disjointed state of his manuscripts" and finally the "entirely fragmentary" state of those that in some cases came directly from the author's notebooks. Some were notes originally intended for Parson Wilbur and some—especially those dealing with genealogical matters—were for his projected novel. They all became filler as Lowell reached his deadline, and his most ambitious character fell to pieces in the fragmentary notes that the author had no time to adapt to his personality.

The most important piece of filler in the early (but last printed) section of *The Biglow Papers* was a bit of new verse by Hosea from which the printers used six stanzas in order to fill up a blank page among the "Notices of an Independent Press." When new plates were made for the 1857 edition, another blank page was filled with six additional stanzas, and the lengthened poem attracted so much attention that Lowell was compelled to finish it as "The Courtin'" and the most popular of all his rustic verses. On the same occasion he also revived, and inserted in the Introduction, Parson Wilbur's fable "Leaving the Matter Open" from the *Standard* of July 27, 1848, and added a parallel poem with the same moral in dialect that he had written in early December of that year. But he was never so interested in consistency of characterization as he had been in consistency of dialect, and he made no effort to change his first hurried and unsystematic portrayal of the character who had initially fascinated him and then caused him so much toil and expense before going to pieces in his hands.

By publishing *The Biglow Papers* with the names "Meliboeus-Hipponax" at the top of the title page, Lowell publicly confessed to the acrimonious quality of his rustic verse. Through his use of dialect he had achieved something of the homely humor and the common touch of the pastoral poetry of Bobbie Burns, but the Hipponactean tone of his satire, as he himself realized, was the mark neither of the humorist nor of a man filled with that all-pervading love which placed Burns in the front ranks of genuine poets. The

Biglow Papers were all a part of his activity as a political propagandist, and most of them were intimately connected with his duties as a paid employee of the American Anti-Slavery Society which published the *Standard*. The original leading character, Hosea, had been relegated to the background after he deviated from the abolitionist party line; and his successor, Parson Wilbur, had not been able to retain his complete individuality as a "respectable" abolitionist and a conventional Whig. The disintegration of Parson Wilbur's character was, in part, the result of Lowell's having undertaken so much, in his contribution to the *Standard* and in his composition of *A Fable for Critics* and *The Vision of Sir Launfal,* that he could not spend his time and his imagination freely upon *The Biglow Papers*. In part, it was the result of a disintegration of Lowell's own personality which enabled him to write too easily as a politician and as an abolitionist rather than as a whole man. "As we grow older," he wrote Briggs on September 3, 1848, while the collected Papers were being printed, "Art becomes to us a definite faculty, instead of a boundless sense of power." The man who had once determined to live the heroic poem he hoped to write had finally come to dividing his "power" by keeping his various literary impulses separate. He used one "definite faculty" for humor and another for political satire in *The Biglow Papers* and in his editorials. But at the same time he was exercising his wit and his critical faculty in *A Fable for Critics* and his faculty for dreamy idealism in *The Vision of Sir Launfal.*

IV

By dividing his "power," Lowell really conquered some of the worst faults he had developed in his youthful attempt to be the artificial man who had been created by Maria White and transcendental literature. Part of his achievement at this time may be attributed to his release from artificial restrictions upon his literary talents, and part to a temporary release from the nervous strain which affected his personal life. He and Maria were living quietly at Elmwood, and their second daughter, Mabel, who was born on September 9, 1847, was a healthy child who gave them little worry and whose care James was willing to leave to a nursemaid. During the year that followed, he had an excess of energy which he would have had difficulty in restricting to a single line of literary production, and although the two new poems appear to bear only the most incidental relationship to his other work, they actually complement and supplement it. For his political writings could hardly have been as vigorous as they were had he not been able to divert what he called the "mystic" side of his nature into the channel of his *Vision,* nor could he have held so closely as he did to abolitionist principles in his satire had not the waywardness of his high spirits sometimes found release in his *Fable.* Both poems were written in fragments and as the spirit moved him toward solemnity or toward drollery, but in each case away from the aim of purposeful amusement which characterized *The Biglow Papers.*

Of the two poems, which are even less closely related to each other than they are to *The Biglow Papers, A Fable for Critics* seems to have been the earlier in its inception and in its actual beginning. It was started at some time between early September and late October, 1847, when Lowell let himself go in a riot of punning and Byronic rhymes which became some five hundred and forty-four lines of comic mythology, of satire directed against a "representative" critic and against particular editors who had disappointed his expectations, and of half-comic and half-satiric treatments of the transcendentalists who were so often and so easily made the subjects of laughter. He was writing primarily for his friend Charles F. Briggs, who had also turned humorist, but he delayed sending him the manuscript until it was "finished"—a delay, as it turned out, which was prolonged for more than a year while the poem grew through varying moods of good humor and irritation into a survey of contemporary American letters.

The precise reason for Lowell's original outburst (which he spoke of, from the beginning, as a "satire") is obscure, but it seems to have been stimulated by the irritation against Margaret Fuller he had revealed in the first of his "Studies for Two Heads" during the early part of September. Some connection between the *Fable* and the "Studies" may be found in the fact that the surviving fragment of the first draft of the former immediately follows the latter in an old composition book which contains these and no other poems. And it is hardly an example of mere coincidence that the critic portrayed in the opening part of the *Fable* had so much in common with the former editor of the *Dial* who was notorious for her erudition and tactlessness, who not only would but had written up her visit to Wordsworth, who had worried in public over the poor rewards of authorship and had been enthusiastic about Cornelius Mathews' "American Drama of Witchcraft," and who was then in the midst of giving her "first impressions of Rome" in the columns of Greeley's *Tribune.* Nor is it certain that she did not appear more directly in the initial part, for, although Lowell was nearly halfway through the poem before he made up his mind to put her in as an unmistakable character, it is possible to fill out the couplet in which he sentenced murderers (to make them "grow wiser and cooler") to "hard labor for life on the works of Miss ———" with a bad rhyme and a good indication of the source of his irritation.

Nor is it also entirely a coincidence, perhaps, that most of the individuals satirized in the original passages were included among those praised by Miss Fuller in the essay on American Literature which had condemned Lowell. The most vicious lines of his survey dealt with the man to whom she had given the most space and praise—Cornelius Mathews, toward whom Lowell had once felt so friendly and whose verses, *Man in the Republic,* he had praised so highly in his *Conversations.* Although Lowell went back over this section before publication and interpolated a parenthetical couplet praising this volume of poems, he left the "small man in glasses" no other reminder of his former friendship: he condemned him for his aggressive nationalism and for his efforts to receive favorable notice from Britain and for trying to be an American Dickens, and he charged him with a hysterical sensitivity to criticism—apparently because Lowell never quite forgave him for being hurt by his own reported wit at the expense of *Puffer Hopkins.* With Evert Duyckinck, who had recently failed to get one of Lowell's essays accepted by the *Democratic Review,* the satire had less to do except imply that there was something ridiculous about carrying the "soul of a gentleman" through Grub Street, considering New York "the New World's metropolis," defending his friends, and offering to get book notices in the periodical to which Lowell was no longer a welcome contributor. The satirist also corrected Miss Fuller's judgment upon Emerson's poetry and philosophy before turning to such imitative transcendentalists as the short-legged Ellery Channing (for whose verses she had expressed a particular admiration) and the quicker Thoreau and to the dreamy Alcott whose "head" had been one of the two "studied" in early September. These might all have been called, in one sense or another, members of "the Margaret Fuller clique"; and they received most of Lowell's attention during his first outburst. Of the other four individuals who were the objects of his original satire, "Tityrus Griswold" was, like Miss Fuller, a protégé of Horace Greeley and a critic who had failed to appreciate young Lowell, and Orestes Brownson had once been a transcendentalist and, like Duyckinck, a member of the staff of the *Democratic Review.* George B. Cheever, a recent defender of capital punishment on Biblical grounds, and Charles Astor Bristed, who was removed from the poem before it was published, appear to be the only persons mentioned who are not known to have been somehow included in Miss Fuller's orbit.

Yet Lowell insisted in his prefatory note to the second edition of his *Fable* that his critic was "a character drawn in pure fun and condensing the traits of a dozen in one," and it is true that he was meditating the critical talents of his fictitious Parson Wilbur at the time he drew the character. With his remarkable capacity for self-deception, he may have been able to convince himself (while denying the portrayal of Francis Bowen with perfect honesty) that he really had not been inspired by any single individual. But it is difficult to believe that Lowell would ever have begun *A Fable for Critics* if Miss Fuller had not first written her essay on American literature.

Whatever his stimulus might have been, however, the form Lowell gave his poem was an old one to which he had been attracted by Leigh Hunt's *The Feast of the Poets*—a relatively mild satire in which Hunt adopted the frequently used convention of having Apollo hold sessions and pass judgment upon contemporary poets. Lowell adopted the convention from Hunt together with "those touches of painting and combinations of the familiar and fanciful" which the English poet added to it, and he also borrowed Hunt's meter as a good jangling tune with which to ring in American authors as Hunt had "rung in" the "bards of Old England." He broadened the plan to cover as great a variety of authors as were included in Byron's *English Bards and Scotch Reviewers* and seems to have hoped to achieve some sort of characterizing humor that he did not find in his two English models. The necessity of finishing his *Poems, Second Series* forced him to lay his satire aside for the time being, but he brooded over it while developing the device of ironic self-revelation for *The Biglow Papers* and for a while had some notion of modifying the first plan to the extent of including parodies of the poets he was satirizing. "It is a rambling, disjointed affair and I may alter the form of it," he wrote Briggs on November 13, 1847, "but if I can get it ready I know it will take." At the moment he was thinking of giving it "some serial title" and publishing it "at intervals," possibly as Poe had republished his "Marginalia" in *Godey's,* but he was too busy with his new collection of *Poems* to make any definite plans.

He was to discover soon enough that his *Fable* was not the sort of poem that could be continued by an exercise of the will. When he attempted to return to it after the publication of his new volume, he realized the difficulty of recapturing the enthusiastic mood with which he began it and made up his mind to quit worrying about its publication. He would write for Briggs alone and allow his friend to dispose of the manuscript as he saw fit. And it was not until near February 1, 1848, that he was able to make a new start by rounding out his criticism of Emerson and writing additional passages on Longfellow and N. P. Willis. His mood had changed noticeably. It was less rollicking but considerably better than it had been at the beginning, and, as was proper for a man then engaged in reviewing Tennyson and Browning for the two leading New England reviews, he had become more seriously critical. To his original lines that severely criticized Emerson's verse, he added the tribute to the "rich matter" that might be found in even the worst of his friend's poems, and he concluded with a serious comment upon the necessity for unity in poetry. To his remarks upon the Emersonian philosophy he also added the brilliant afterthought of the comparison with Carlyle. His treatment of Longfellow was a wholly generous one in which he deliberately avoided the sort of "characterization" which would inevitably have involved either satire or a misrepresentation of the less generous opinions he had so freely expressed in his letters. It was impossible for him to be so impersonal about the irritating Willis, but his criticism was mild and his satire mellow even when he touched upon such a gossipy matter as Willis's eye for a barmaid. Edgar Allan Poe profited most from Lowell's new mood, however, for although the reference to him was irritatingly brief and casual, it was, in comparison with Lowell's antagonistic feelings at the time, generously free from a characterizing satire which could have hurt the author of "The Raven" more seriously than anyone else mentioned in the *Fable*. When he reported to Briggs on his burst of progress, Lowell was sure that the whole poem would be finished within the month.

As the month wore on, however, he made no further progress, and on February 26 he was protesting that he needed "pleasanter weather in order to finish it." He wanted Briggs to give him "a spur" in the form of a specific suggestion or a set deadline, and he may have had some fear that the composition might outlast his spell of good nature. Wherever she might have been at the beginning, Margaret Fuller certainly kept creeping into his mind as the poem progressed and he began writing of her to Briggs as a "fair target" and a "very foolish, conceited woman" with a "great deal of information, but not enough *knowledge* to save her from being ill-tempered." Maria thought he really "ought to give her a line or two," but he himself, although tempted, was determined to show his generosity by leaving her out altogether. His good intentions were weakened by the mood with which he contemplated the Democratic Senators and the "Pious Editor" of the fifth and sixth Biglow Papers, however, and before the middle of May he yielded to his temptation and introduced her without any possibility of mistake as the vain and spiteful Miranda. The nature of his mood may be judged by the fact that although he later tried to remove the specific remarks on her spite and vanity, he nevertheless described them as "perfectly good-humored." William Cullen Bryant and Lydia Maria Child also suffered from the same sort of "good humor." His comments on the latter, he was sure, would make her friends laugh, and they were relatively harmless, if not charitable, in their characterization of a person whose feelings toward him and toward Maria were so kindly. But his jealousy of a man who could write fifty-dollar poems, which he had curbed in his consideration of Longfellow, cropped out in his treatment of Bryant—who was, after all, a newspaper editor in whom Lowell may have seen some resemblance to the "pious" one that he had so recently satirized in *The Biglow Papers*. While insisting that his lines were "funny" and, as far as he could make them, "immitigably just," he recognized that they were not entirely so. A rumor that Bryant believed himself Lowell's creditor for certain of the younger poet's expressions concerning "the past" made him remark that he "might have knocked him into a cocked-hat" in his satire, but, instead, he waited for "a happier mood" than the one in which he had written "the comic part" and added the complimentary lines with which the section now concludes. Before the happier mood arrived, however, he received a visit from James B. Hirst of Philadelphia with a prospectus for his new nationalistic magazine and from J. T. Fields and Edwin P. Whipple which provoked him to the "trifling digression on bores" attached to his comments on Margaret Fuller.

The nationalism talked so tediously by Hirst was an old irritation to Lowell, who was inspired within the following week to deal with his country's three leading nationalist writers—the muscular patriots John Neal and James Fenimore Cooper and the unaggressive Hawthorne for whom Lowell had a more profound admiration than he had for any other American author, although he did pay John Sullivan Dwight, the music critic of the *Pioneer* and Brook Farm, the tribute of comparison with him. He probably wrote his plain words to patriots, which immediately followed, at the same time; and he also versified, for the preservation of his anonymity, some of the familiar criticisms of himself which the new poems in his most recent volume partially discounted. By this time he believed that his poem was almost finished and would not be more than twelve hundred lines in length. But he was not keeping a careful count, and the work had now reached a stage of growing almost of its own accord. He had added extra lines for Apollo in order to get a faint suggestion of a plot, and if he had written the sections on Theodore Parker, Whittier, the elder Richard Henry Dana, and "Harry Franco" Briggs in one of his good-natured moods before May 19, the poem had already gone beyond the length he told his friend to count on. It was all finished, he informed its owner, on August 22, and he was reading proof on September 3. But he could not stop writing. While it was too late on October 4 to remove the offensive lines on Miranda, it was still not too late to add criticisms of Irving, Sylvester Judd, and—last of all—Holmes, who could hardly have been left out of the survey of contemporary American literature into which the *Fable* had evolved and who might have been suspected as the confessed son of the Bay State who wrote it. His problem of welding together his various moods "without making an ugly swelling at the joints" had been solved by distributing the various passages without much reference to the moody serial of their composition. The comments upon himself were placed toward the end of the volume next to the reflections upon Halleck, which, if his statement in the poem itself can be trusted, were made in early May before the visit by "two honest fellows" (not counting, presumably, his friend Fields) put him out of humor and made him dwell upon the general subject of bores. The poem also contains a number of undatable passages of miscellaneous criticism and closes with a suggestion concerning George Washington Peck's inability to appreciate a man who "has anything in him peculiar and strong," and a final, unifying reference to Apollo's escape from Miranda. Through the very multiplicity of its joints, it managed to disguise its swellings of anger and made them almost indistinguishable from its rolling good humor; and there is little on the surface of the published poem to indicate how accidental some of the author's judgments were.

Unlike *The Biglow Papers,* Lowell's *Fable* profited by a haphazard method of composition, for the distinguishing characteristic of the poem as a work of criticism is a lively impressionism which resulted in more human and hence more lasting critical judgments than may be found in the more rational opinions expressed in Poe's "Marginalia." The least interesting parts of the work are those in which Lowell tried to attain some sort of unity of plot and consistency of humorous tone. Throughout most of it, his ill-natured moods added salt to his prevailing drollery, and he was responsible enough, in such important cases as those of Emerson and Bryant, to supplement his original acerbity with high and judicious praise. He also showed discretion in refusing to "characterize" Longfellow. But the work, as a whole, was not particularly judicious: had Lowell happened to consider Lydia Child in February and Poe in early May, his reputation as a judge of contemporary literature might have been somewhat different from what it is today.

The little book was issued on October 25, 1848, four days after the date advertised, and immediately fulfilled the anonymous author's expectation of making a "hit." The first edition of a thousand copies was sold out within about three weeks and a second was set and stereotyped. Lowell was able to correct the title page and other errors of typography for the second printing but made no attempt to remove the remarks on Margaret Fuller about which he had qualms in October, for it was not until he had heard from his friends the Storys in Rome that it seems to have occurred to him that she might be materially hurt by his satire or that she might deserve consideration of any sort. Some of his friends in America protested against and some were particularly pleased by "Miranda." Holmes, who knew little or nothing of the feeling that lay beneath the portraiture, was almost as delighted with it as with the comparison between Emerson and Carlyle. "I have heard of a peg to hang a thought on," he wrote before the second edition was published, "but if I want a thought to hang a Peg on I shall know where to go in the future." There were rumors of retaliation from other *literati,* for neither Lowell nor Briggs had been very serious in attempting to preserve the secret of authorship, but Lowell was not disturbed and rather regretted that he had been too busy at the proper time to expand some of his criticism. He was worried, however, over the "Public's" blunder of identifying the editor of the *North American Review* as the critic, for the identification was not only unjust but was a possible threat to a promising source of income. He attempted to set his readers right in "A Preliminary Note to the Second Edition" which was elaborately padded in order to fit the pagination of plates already stereotyped. This was an afterthought, though, of which he was able to send Briggs only a "taste" as late as December 18; and ten days later he wrote that since part of the edition had already been "struck off" it might be well to leave out the new preface—unless it would sell more copies if advertised. Actually it was printed as three separate leaves after some copies had been distributed (probably for the holiday trade) and others were in the process of being bound, for the extant copies of the second edition which contain the "Preliminary Note" show that in some cases it was pasted in after and in some inserted before the volume was bound.

The satire probably gave its author a number of other doubtful moments before he convinced himself in his old age that it was a *jeu d'esprit* extemporized for his own amusement and with no thought of publication. For a while he would confess to liking only the tribute to the Bay State with which he interrupted Apollo's judgments of Judd and Holmes. But the *Fable* seems to have aroused little resentment, and instead of being "put in the shade" by *The Biglow Papers* (as Briggs feared) it quickly exceeded the political satire in popularity. A third edition of a thousand copies was printed within three and a half months of the original issue and exhausted by the end of November; and a fourth was printed after Putnam had moved to his new place of business on Park Place the following year. Outside of New England *A Fable for Critics* seems to have sold better than *The Biglow Papers* and all Lowell's earlier volumes of poems combined, and there is some irony in the fact that the man who introduced his review of Tennyson's *The Princess* with an attack upon modern critics—and concluded his *Fable* with a versification of some of the same material—should have achieved his greatest victory on the field of literature in his critical rather than in his creative role.

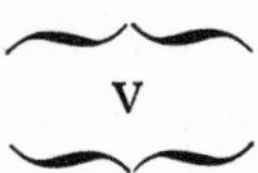

WHILE LOWELL was breaking a lance with contemporary politicians and his fellow authors, he did not forget his visionary idealism. But it became separate from his practical efforts at social reform and occupied a smaller part of his mind. He spent less time in the composition of *The Vision of Sir Launfal* than upon his other major works, and he had less to say about it to his friends. Yet it is an important poem in the continuity of his early literary career. The idealistic quality of his writing which had been so pronounced during the first decade of his activity was almost entirely lacking in his critical satire, and it had taken on such a sardonic disguise in his political verse and miscellaneous contributions to the *Standard* that it was effectively concealed if not lost altogether. But the serious-minded young poet had not lost sight of his ideal in his excessive attention to the obstacles to its attainment. On the contrary, it had become simpler and clearer to his "mystic" personality: it was less complicated by the emotionalism of Sir James Mackintosh, by the transcendentalism of Emerson and Carlyle, or by the theorizing that had affected him earlier. As he expressed it in his *Vision,* it was Christian rather than Loco-Foco, and the dream of the medieval knight taught a simple lesson for every man rather than a peculiar one for the ambitious poet. Lowell's newly acquired ability to separate his different personalities allowed him to achieve a greater simplicity in his literary themes than had been possible to him before.

Although *The Vision of Sir Launfal* is simple in theme and reflects none of the emotional ups and downs that may be seen in *The Biglow Papers* and *A Fable for Critics,* it is, in some respects, a less coherent poem. For in it Lowell brought together three separate lines of interest that had been developing in the *Poems, Second Series,* and however organic their relationship may have been to him, emotionally, they seem to have been united with a more obvious "swelling of the joints" than is noticeable in the *Fable* about which he was so worried. "The Growth of the Legend" had given evidence of his intention to treat some sort of legendary material in his own variety of the irregular, four-stress measure of "Christabel"; and while the publication of that poem as a fragment in his collected volume indicated that he no longer expected to deal with an Indian story, the notion of doing something of the sort still remained in his head, and he found occasion to drag into the early part of *A Fable for Critics* a humorous allusion to Coleridge's poem. It was easy enough for him, perhaps, to create his own legend and make it a parable after the manner of the Hawthorne whom he so greatly admired, for he had already acquired some experience in mixing his interest in narrative with his interest in morality. But it was more difficult for him to blend with them the new enthusiasm for sensuous description which he had displayed in "An Indian-Summer Reverie" and other poems in his recent collection. It is in this connection that the swelling joints of *The Vision of Sir Launfal* are most apparent, and as a result of the awkward union of description, narration, and didacticism, the story itself loses its clarity of outline so that a casual reader might take the vision of a single night for a narrative of events actually occurring in June and December.

Lowell had an artistic theory to justify his lack of clarity and precision of outline, but whether his poem grew out of the theory or the theory out of the poem seems impossible to determine. The theory is suggested in the seemingly irrelevant lines on the organist with which the poem opens but is clarified only in the review of Tennyson's *The Princess* which Lowell wrote for the *Massachusetts Quarterly Review* for March, 1848. "The growth of the poem is as natural as its plan is original," he declared in partial explanation of the extravagant admiration he had for the English poet's new work: "The gradual absorption of the author in his subject, till what was begun as a song 'turns out a sermon,' the growing predominance of the poet over the mere story-teller, as the higher relations of his subject matter appeal to him, and the creative faculty feels itself more and more taxed, are exquisitely true to the intellect and the heart." And as he tried further to explain the progress of the poem and the modulation of its movement forward he drew the analogy suggested by the opening lines of his own poem:

It is as if some composer, in a laughing mood, had seated himself at the organ to *fantasy* for the entertainment of a few friends. At first, he is conscious of their presence, and his fingers run lightly over the keys, bringing out combinations of notes swayed quaintly hither and thither by the magnetism of the moment. But gradually he becomes absorbed in his own power and that of his instrument. The original theme recurs less and less often, till at last he soars quite away from it on the uplifting wings of his art.

Lowell had seated himself at his own organ in a more serious mood and soared less ambitiously, but when he began his own poem with a reference to the musing organist who approached his theme through a "wavering vista," he had in mind the plan of achieving unity through absorption which he found so "natural" and "original" in Tennyson.

Yet he could hardly have read *The Princess* before he began *The Vision of Sir Launfal,* for the English poem was not published until about Christmas time in 1847. Nor is he likely to have written the four lines which immediately follow those on the organist when he still believed, as he wrote Briggs so late as September 3, 1848, that "it is far behind us in the wilderness, in the early time of struggle, that we have left our Sinais and our personal talk of God in the bush." The passage denying that heaven lies around us only in our infancy and affirming that daily "we Sinais climb and know it not" was not only a contradiction of Wordsworth's Intimations Ode but a correction of his own statement to his friend, added to his poem as an introductory afterthought which may have included the opening lines as well.

But, whether this particular theory of "organic" unity was conceived before or after the inception of the poem, Lowell certainly did not pull the stops of his varied interest according to the exact order in which they are recorded in the published work. His moral was the theme in which he lost himself and, variously decorated, was one of the oldest themes in all his poetry: "Inasmuch as ye have done it unto one of the least of these my brethren, ye have done it unto me." Indeed, one of the early entries in his "Private Journal" (which was begun in 1840) when he was concerned with the Chapmanesque idea of the great soul was one which contained the germ of the legend he created to illustrate his text: "It is the stamp . . . and seal of a great soul to know . . . an angel when His brightness is concealed with rags [—] to know all men are angels." He had used the theme itself for his poem "The Search" in the *Standard* for February 25, 1847, and repeated it in the same journal nearly fifteen months later as part of the moral for "A Parable" of which he had a curiously high opinion. If he had any bad conscience at all about his anti-slavery writings it was over his neglect of the simple gospel of brotherly love in his concern for the complications of practical politics, and it is hardly probable that he mused his way into his major theme instead of starting with the theme and devising new decorations with which to make it attractive.

The decorations, in fact, may have been composed without reference to the moralized legend at all, for they reflect the preoccupation with seasonal descriptions which first appeared in the manuscript "Indian Summer" and was to bulk so large in his notebooks and future published writings. The brook in the "Prelude to Part Second," he declared later, was drawn from observation of the little stream between Elmwood and Watertown which could never be stopped by the first big December freeze; and if this bit of description was the product of immediate observation it was written during late December of 1847. The tribute to June, which forms the greater part of the "Prelude to Part First," was probably also written during the same winter; for whatever Lowell's youthful preference in seasons might have been, after his marriage he always looked forward with relief to the end of the east winds and a renewal of hope for the improvement of Maria's persistent cough. A series of octosyllabics in his "Private Journal" which were written before Blanche's death in March, 1847, and later formed into "A Day in June" (or, in his published works, "Al Fresco") shows that the first month of the New England spring had become to him a symbol of relaxation from "manhood's tenser strain"—as he put it in lines added later—and a return to the relatively carefree mental state of boyhood. When the halls of Elmwood were no longer dark and draughty and Lowell could open an upstairs window and watch a robin building its nest where one had built every spring that he could remember, he usually found a new energy and desire to be up and doing; and his lyric appreciation of the season in *The Vision of*

Sir Launfal was probably composed in anticipation of it rather than in the midst of his recovery in the June of 1847 from grief at Blanche's death or amid the irritation which characterized all his other work during that month of the following year.

In any case, the "new poem" seems to have been largely completed when Lowell described it to Briggs on February 1, 1848, as "a sort of story" of which Maria thought "very highly" and which he intended to print by itself during the following summer. It was probably written in parts during or near the Christmas season of 1847 and put together while the author was composing his review of Tennyson in January and finding in *The Princess* the sort of organization which encouraged him to look upon his own poem as a work of art. For *The Vision of Sir Launfal,* despite the fact that its hero went to bed and arose again on one of those rare days when "the soul partakes the season's youth," was a Christmas poem. Christmas was the proper time to think of wanderers discovering Christ, and Lowell, regretting New England's indifference to the day, probably let his mind dwell with more than ordinary seriousness upon the religious traditions that justified its celebration. Sir Launfal's vision was of a bitter winter day which was spiritually rarer than the day in June celebrated by the poet, and the poem, with its luxurious anticipation of warm weather and its vivid portrayal of the cold, presented a new Christmas story in a setting appropriately designed to make the reader enjoy the fireside. It was not published during the summer as Lowell had inappropriately planned but was kept—with probably some revisions and additions—until December 18 and became, of Lowell's many efforts, the one which came nearest to making the Christmas market on time. As usual, however, Lowell and his local publisher thought only in terms of New England—where there was little demand for Christmas books—and *The Vision of Sir Launfal* did not break the author's record of reaching the New York booksellers at the worst possible season for distribution.

Yet the book fulfilled Lowell's expectations of being popular in a modest way, and the first edition of five hundred copies was exhausted and a new edition of the same size was issued during the following year. New editions succeeded annually, proving that Briggs was right when he observed that "its merits are of a kind that can be appreciated by the superficial as well as the thoughtful readers," and Lowell was soon more widely known as the author of *The Vision of Sir Launfal* than as the writer of any other single poem. It also, to its author's disgust, eventually became the first of his volumes to be glorified with illustrations; and, in the end, it proved to be the poem around which his reputation revolved, for he never managed quite to live up to it in the opinions of his more superficial readers or quite to live it down in the eyes of the more thoughtful.

In his various writings between the autumn of 1847 and the winter of 1848, Lowell had gained in literary assurance and in general popularity by the separation of his artistic personalities and the exercise of different poetic "faculties" in different works. He was a more competent poet than he had been. But he was giving up, in effect, the notion of achieving a whole-souled poetic greatness which had been his ambition in his youth. His gains from following this sort of literary knight-errantry were real, and for a while he was to find satisfaction in following different banners to the sound of various trumpets. But it was to be only for a short time.

Chapter VIII

THE LAST TOURNAMENTS

I

LOWELL'S PROLIFIC and popular literary output in 1848 had also been unprofitable. He had given away the anticipated royalties on his most successful book, *A Fable for Critics,* which should have earned slightly more than one hundred and fifty dollars for the first three editions. He had cleared \$12.78 on the first two editions of *The Vision of Sir Launfal* and \$1.64 on the two printings of *The Biglow Papers*—although, for the latter, he had spent sixty-six cents on better bindings for gift copies and so had a net profit of only ninety-eight cents on the 1720 volumes sold. The *Poems, Second Series* apparently did not sell well enough to pay for the plates, for he was worried all during the first part of the year over the note he had given his publisher and had to use his salary from the *Standard* in order to meet it when it came due in early June. The *North American Review* had either reduced its regular payment for articles or Lowell was a cut-rate contributor, for he expected only "twenty odd dollars for the article" on Browning, or apparently fifty cents a page for the forty-four page review. The only other periodical for which he wrote, the *Massachusetts Quarterly Review,* paid nothing. Briggs had planned to invest a third of the proceeds from *A Fable for Critics* for the benefit of Mabel on her eighteenth birthday, and it might be said that the Lowell family as a whole could have expected almost to break even on the four books James had published in a year. But unfortunately James himself had been made over-optimistic by the first evidences of popular success and, in anticipation of his profits on *The Biglow Papers,* had run up a bill of \$55.32 and accepted a sixty-dollar cash advance from John Bartlett; and his accounts show that the year of his greatest literary success left him indebted to his publisher for $81.56, which he finished paying off on July 7, 1849. As a professional poet, brilliantly rounding out his first decade of versemaking, he was not doing so well.

Had it not been for his five hundred dollars a year from the *Standard,* an equivalent income from Maria's property, and a rent-free home at Elmwood he would have been in desperate straits. As it was, he was living from hand to mouth during the entire period of his wonderful year, counting his pennies as he had counted them when he tried to smoke cigars on a fifty-cent weekly allowance in college; and although Briggs sent him a ticket to New York in June, he had to wait a couple of months for his long-delayed payment from the *North American Review* before he could afford to use it. Even his regular sources of income provided him with financial worries, for the rents on the farms Maria had inherited were uncertain and sometimes uncollectable and he suspected that Sydney Gay occasionally had to put off his own landlord in order to pay his corresponding editor on time. He was not at ease about his position with the *Standard,* nor was he entirely happy about the situation at Elmwood where his father, although inactive as a minister, was prevented from resigning part of his pastoral salary by the son's inability to bear his proper burden of household expenses. As his thirtieth birthday approached, Lowell thought of himself as entering upon middle age, and with a wife and child, and another baby expected, he found it hard to hold on to his old hope of writing great poetry now he had learned that even popular poetry would barely pay the cost of publication.

The *Standard* made him most uneasy, for Lowell was not entirely sure of his judgment concerning the prose articles he wrote with one eye on the abolitionist party line and so often without inspiration from within. He was aware that his contributions varied greatly in quality, but Gay gave him no instructions and printed without criticism whatever Lowell sent. The freedom which he had demanded when he accepted the job was so conscientiously allowed him that it made him uncomfortable. Lowell was not the sort of person to borrow trouble just in order to worry, but he could not have avoided occasional consciousness that Stephen Foster and Francis Jackson were among the dominating members of the executive committee which controlled the *Standard* and that their practical and unsympathetic eyes evaluated every paid contribution. Although the corresponding editor wanted every one of his articles to be worth more than ten dollars to the cause, he was incapable of weighing moral or even literary values in the scale of dollars and cents and was never entirely sure that he was earning his keep. He tried to reassure himself by an expression of determined energy, writing Gay in October that as soon as he finished his glossary and index to *The Biglow Papers* he would "go into the *Standard*" with his "coat off"; and after clearing up a few miscellaneous obligations, he did devote himself to that periodical with an exclusiveness which would have doubly satisfied George R. Graham, for he published no poetry and only one prose article through any other medium for more than a year.

He had already taken time off from proofreading in order to write an "Ode" for the school children of Boston to sing when the city celebrated the opening of its new supply of Cochituate water on the day *A Fable for Critics* was published in New York, and he had written a review of the works of Walter Savage Landor which the *Massachusetts Quarterly* had wanted for June and actually got at the end of July although it did not appear in print until December. Writing the review probably helped Lowell clarify the relationship between his own work and some of the ideas he had expressed in his reviews of Tennyson and Browning, for he found the elder poet clearly opposed to his two younger contemporaries in two crucial respects. Despite the fact that he had agreed with Browning in calling Landor a "great dramatic poet," he did not find in the author of the *Hellenics* or of the *Imaginary Conversations* the sort of dramatic genius he found in *Bells and Pomegranates*. "He translates everything into Landor" and so, as a dramatist, resembled Chapman rather than Shakespeare. Browning he had praised for not making that mistake, and in his own "Imaginary Conversation" for the *Standard* of May 25, 1848, as in the last six of the Biglow Papers, Lowell had followed Browning. As a poet, Lowell found Landor "too minutely circumstantial" with a mind cramped by that "careful exactness in particulars which gives finish to his prose and represses any tendency to redundance." For the young critic insisted that "in poetry, it is necessary that each poem should be informed with a homogeneous spirit, which now represses the thought, now forces it to overflow, and everywhere modulates the metre and cadence by an instinct of which we can understand the operations, though we may be unable to define the mode of them." This was the sort of thing that he found in Tennyson's *The Princess* and had nudged the reader into expecting in his own organ poem on Sir Launfal. The unqualified admiration he had held for Landor in the days of his youth was gone, and the new edition of his *Works* served to impress upon Lowell the fact that his own place was with the more modern school of Browning and Tennyson. His only other publication outside the *Standard* for this period was "The Burial of Theobald" in the *Liberty Bell* for 1849, which may have been inspired by the melodramatic picture of the Renaissance given in the seventh number of *Bells and Pomegranates;* but the poem turned out to be nothing more than a more vigorous revival of the old *Graham's* manner which Lowell had outgrown, and it struck the author as so nearly ridiculous that he "half-parodied it" to himself as he went along, and he probably would not have published it had he allowed himself sufficient time to compose another before the volume went to press in early December.

The first of Lowell's shirt-sleeve contributions to the *Standard* was a poem, "The Sower," for November 16, 1848, in which he vigorously turned away from the emotional attraction of the past which he had revealed in so much of his own earlier verse. The deaf and blind, soulless dotard who sowed again the "holy Past" dropped germs of truth, but each was "mated with a dragon's tooth" and the crop was strife and bloodshed. The moral was plain: the necessity of progress and the dangers of dwelling upon "The happy days when I was young." Lowell applied it to current history in an editorial for the following week. "If, as it has been often said, America be a kind of posterity in relation to Europe," he argued, "it will follow that Europe must in some sense be a past to us." And despite the proverbial fact that men refused to learn from the past, he drew the lesson pointed out by the recent revolution in France: "when social disorganization has reached a certain point, there is a natural union of all except the highest class, not only against that highest class, but against the system whose necessary tendency is to divide men at last into a highest and lowest with no intermediate grade." Because the distinctions in America were drawn along lines of both race and class, he believed, "The causes . . . now producing anarchy in Europe may be expected to combine in bringing about yet more shocking results here." The only hope of avoiding the fruit of the dragon's teeth lay in doing away with the distinctions—particularly racial—that were characteristic of the past and in progressing to the point of doing away with "imaginary boundary-lines" by admitting all people "to equal privileges."

The new cogency that appeared in Lowell's writings as a result of his determination to put more effort into his work did not last long, for he soon slipped back into his old habit of writing—apparently with little forethought—on Thursday night what had to go into the mail on Friday. His editorial on "Irish and American Patriots" for November 30 was a rambling comment upon the news that the English government had decided not to execute the sentence of death upon the leaders of the Irish revolt, and he permitted himself the illusion that he could write his contribution for the following week during the evening after a big Thanksgiving dinner. The burning of Willard's great stables provided him with an exciting diversion until nearly midnight, however, and he was able to save his bacon (as he wrote Gay) only by a Friday morning inspiration which enabled him to compose the parable "Ambrose" in a couple of hours. The inspiration was probably made possible by the fact that he had recently been reading proof on *The Vision of Sir Launfal* and had the rhythm and the tone of that poem filling his mind. The result, in any case, was happy: eleven stanzas that preserved the feeling of spontaneity while effectively presenting Lowell's old objections to formalized creeds and summarizing, with unusual neatness, his own philosophy. The holy Ambrose sincerely built "a perfect faith" according to his own measure and insisted that others fit themselves to it, only to be taught by the youthful angel that the Water of Life could go into many different vessels from which it could take various forms without being changed. But the author made no attempt to make the lesson of tolerance which his "parable" taught compatible with his own contributions to the *Standard,* nor did he attempt to adjust his new contributions to his lesson, for his editorial on "The President's Message" for December 14 was a nagging indication of the inconsistencies and ironies in the communication of a man who could write in praise of freedom only a few hours after having been shaved by a slave.

Yet Lowell was more generous and tolerant than his associates, and when he reviewed Whittier's poems in the same issue of the *Standard,* Gay felt it necessary to cool his generous praise by an introductory note explaining that the reviewer could not have been aware of the fact that "in the struggle of 1840, which was a struggle of life and death to the anti-slavery cause, Whittier the Quaker was found side by side with men who would have sacrificed that cause, to crush, according even to their own acknowledgment, the right of woman to plead publicly in behalf of the slave." Such an unforgiving attitude toward any deviation from the Garrisonian line was not the kind of thing about which Lowell could make an issue, but it could easily moderate his enthusiasm. There was the sort of undercurrent which exists in most "goodnatured" jokes in the letter of December 22 which informed Gay that he was "sending something this week rather alien (in appearance) to your denouncing and excoriating columns"—an attack on the proposal to erect the Washington Monument, made on the grounds that heroism should be celebrated in song and deed rather than in marble and that the slaveholding Washington was less "our representative American man" than Daniel Boone. Furthermore, the drawing for an obelisk five hundred feet high "does not," he declared, "strike us favorably," for it had neither utility nor significance, and he saw no need for "any monument at all, least of all in such an out of the way place as the city of Washington." He was quibbling as he always did when he had nothing he really wanted to say. He admired himself, as he admitted a week later, for his ability to "sit down and write a poem for the *Standard's* order so resolutely." But "The Mill" or "Beaver Brook" (as he later called it) did not have its origin entirely in journalistic resolution: it rose from a simile in his notebook which compared the forces of action to the many forgotten brooks contributing to the mill stream, and it was probably brought to mind by his experience of pausing on a hill and listening to the unfrozen tinkle of the little brook he had described in *The Vision of Sir Launfal* and heard again as he walked over the snow to Watertown on the night his sister-in-law Lois was married to Dr. Estes Howe.

In the first two of his editorials for the new year, Lowell occupied himself with pointing out the failures of the Whigs to keep their preëlection promises, but in his third, "Politics and the Pulpit," he returned to his old criticism of the church and revealed again the incompatibility between the lesson of his parable "Ambrose" and the abolitionist line he followed in his articles. Instead of being readily adaptable to vessels of many sizes and shapes, the Water of Life froze under the northern blast of abolitionism. The truth of Christian revelation became "a standard which cannot warp or shrink, and which indicates with impartial indifference every deviation from the immutable line of right and duty." His objection to the church was not (as it had been in the poem) that the "doorway's size" was fitted to one who

> knew, by a sure and inward sign,
> That the work of his fingers was divine

or that the light inside was meted to the eyes of its builder. On the contrary, his criticism of the church was that it allowed its members to see according to their own lights; and he found his own ideal pastor in the man who, as a lad, had tagged along behind him while he discoursed on *The Faerie Queene*—the T. W. Higginson of Newburyport whom he thanked "for rejecting this eclectic vicarship of Bray, and for giving us not merely the exact measure of duty, but for giving it pressed down and running over." His spokesman angel in the poem had aroused Ambrose to holy wrath by maintaining "a dividual essence in Truth" with his insistence that

> To each in his mercy hath God allowed
> His several pillar of fire and cloud.

The corresponding editor of the *Standard* demanded the "God-sent pillar of flame by night and a cloud by day." If the poet spoke with the tongue of an angel, the abolitionist wrote with the zeal of Ambrose.

Yet the poem and the prose article were not so completely contradictory as their language seems to indicate, for in the first Lowell was thinking of religious creeds, and in the second about social philosophies. He was exemplifying in his own writings a phenomenon illustrated on a larger scale by the New England reform movement as a whole: the identification of religion with morality and the transfer of the puritan impulse from the church to the state as an institution which had grown corrupt. The result was a tendency away from religious and toward social sectarianism. The movement was as confused as the puritanism of the seventeenth century had been, for there was a difference of opinion whether the institution should be used or abused by the righteous. Lowell was in the difficult position of being a son of Massachusetts Bay who had found employment in Philadelphia and in a spiritual Plymouth. He agreed with his fellow abolitionists in their subordination of theology to sociology, in their "demand of the Clergy that they no longer organize sects, but society." But no such agreement was possible concerning the way to use or change the existing social organization in order to achieve "a pure Ethical Idea," as he capitalized it in "The Moral Movement against Slavery" which was published on February 22, 1849, his thirtieth birthday, and the day of his entrance upon what he called "middle age." Although he regularly denounced "the middle course as the path of wisdom" and fence sitters of any sort, he found himself incapable of getting off the fence between the free-soilers who wanted to capture the state and purify it and the disunionists who wanted to separate themselves from the corrupt part of the nation. Privately leaning toward the one side and professionally toward the other, he perched between them with little comfort but as philosophically as possible. He explained "the popularity of Taylor" and "the power of Garrison" on the grounds that "Two things especially absorb the admiration and sympathy of men—practical success and that weariless devotion which does not need the stimulus of success." The fact that currently the "Free Soil Party lacks any attraction which might arise from success" meant that some of its newspapers were failing and giving the impression that the movement was transitory, but he looked upon this as part of "the natural reaction which has followed a crisis of extraordinary anti-slavery excitement in politics" and "shows not only the policy but the absolute necessity of a distinctly moral organization against slavery." The article was a curious one which, in effect, defended the disunionist movement on the grounds of expediency while leaving the way open for later support of the free-soilers on the same grounds. With a poet's ability to write better than he knew, he had expressed his own situation in a poem "The Parting of the Ways" in the *Standard* for two weeks before: he was aware that pleasure was the false Florimel and that duty was a truly beautiful maiden—but exactly what she looked like he did not know.

In the meantime, he was trying to follow the lesson he had consciously set for himself as the moral of "The Parting of the Ways": "Thou seest no beauty save thou make it first." He was ready to seize upon any argument that came to hand with the promise of hurrying the attainment of his "pure Ethical Idea." He had already borrowed, for an article on "Ethnology" in the *Standard* for February 1, arguments for the original unity of all races from a report on James Cowles Pritchard's *Researches into the Physical History of Mankind* which had appeared in the *Edinburgh Review* for October, 1848; and if he stultified the argument by naïvely simplifying the evidence offered in proof, it made little difference, for he was writing for readers who judged the evidence by the direction in which it pointed rather than by its scientific plausibility. He praised Dr. Pritchard as "a man of great learning, and apparently of an honest and well balanced mind, not likely to be led astray by theory, nor to form his conclusions in advance of his facts"; but he was impressed by the learning because it offered an unexpected scientific support to the "truth" already established in his own mind by those "feelings" that he considered more trustworthy than any science. He kept editorializing against Calhoun, against Taylor, against Henry Clay, and against Horace Greeley as he saw them obstructing, in various ways, the ideal road which he wanted to follow but somehow never seemed to see very clearly when it was not marked out by obstacles. He was pursuing his duty by trying to make a more beautiful society but obviously finding little inspiration in it.

Some members of the Executive Committee of the American Anti-Slavery Society were not finding his work very inspiring either, and he was allowed to keep writing beyond the end of his agreed term of employment while the Committee debated his worth to the cause. The editor of the *Standard* took pride in the literary value of his contributions, but such men as Stephen Foster, Francis Jackson, and Samuel Philbrick, who were responsible for the finances of the profitless journal, had no interest in mere literature so long as Captain Drayton languished in the Washington jail and three million Negroes remained in bondage. They were less interested in an "Ethical Idea" than in freeing slaves and frequently found it difficult to understand what Lowell was "at." Lowell himself was somewhat confused about what he was supposed to be doing. "Poets prophesy what is right," he had written in his article on "The Moral Movement against Slavery," "philosophers see it, fanatics accomplish it." But such words evidently had little meaning for him even while he wrote them. He seems to have been impressed by an article by Theodore Parker in the *Massachusetts Quarterly Review* for December, 1848, which suggested that "the American Idea" had so far found expression in action rather than in literature, and he had made a note to the same effect in his "Private Journal": "New England has written her Epic in railroads and commerce." He was developing a greater appreciation for practical action than he had ever possessed before, and the moral of "The Parting of the Ways"—"Thou seest no beauty save thou make it first"—appears to indicate that he was working toward a justification of his own recent career by developing a new theory of poetry which called for a poet who neither prophesied nor merely guided active men but who participated directly in the affairs of the world and reported upon them. The philosophy of the abolitionist leaders was exercising an influence upon him, but it was so cloudy in its immediate results that they could not recognize it and, if they had known what was happening, probably would not have been willing to pay him ten dollars a week for his compositions while their influence was slowly precipitating. The best they would do after two months of delay was to compromise with the wishes of Sydney Gay and place Lowell on half-time and half-salary, hiring the more vigorous and direct Edmund Quincy to alternate with him in the columns of the *Standard*.

The action of the Executive Committee gave Lowell an opportunity to escape from the peculiar kind of self-deception which he had been practicing—at least on Thursday evenings—and open his mind in a long letter to Gay on May 21, 1849. He confessed that all during the year he had felt that he worked under a disadvantage:

I have missed that inspiration (or call it magnetism) which flows into one from a thoroughly sympathetic audience. Properly speaking, I have never had it as an author, for I have never been popular. But then I have never needed it, because I wrote to please myself and not to please the people; whereas, in writing for the "Standard," I have felt that I ought in some degree to admit the whole Executive Committee into my workshop and defer as much as possible to the opinion of persons whose opinion (however valuable on a point of morals) would not properly weigh a pin with me on an aesthetic question. I have felt that I ought to work in my own way, and yet I have also felt that I ought to *try* to work in *their* way, so that I have failed of working in either.

He exempted "some two or three of the poems" he had written from his over-all confession of inadequacy and actually seems to have felt that in keeping his eye upon the Executive Committee he had gone against his better judgment on political and humane questions more than in any matter of aesthetics—as in fact he had, for the story of his connection with the *Standard* makes it clear that if he published anything in it against his own aesthetic judgment, the act was a result of his own dilatoriness rather than of any desire to please Messrs. Foster or Jackson. On the other hand, he wrote Gay more emphatically than he had written Briggs the year before:

You know I never agreed to the Dissolution-of-the-Union movement, and simply because I think it a waste of strength. Why do we not separate ourselves from the African whom we wish to elevate? from the drunkard? from the ignorant? At this minute the song of the bobolink comes rippling through my open window and preaches peace. Two months ago the same missionary was in his South Carolina pulpit, and can I think that he chose another text or delivered another sermon there? Hath not a slaveholder hands, organs, dimensions, senses, affections, passions? fed with the same food, hurt with the same weapons, subject to the same diseases, healed by the same means, warmed and cooled by the same summer and winter as an abolitionist is? If you prick them do they not bleed? If you tickle them do they not laugh? If you poison them do they not die? If you wrong them shall they not revenge? Nay, I will go a step farther, and ask if all this do not apply to parsons also? Even *they* are human.

Despite the literary flourish of his parody of Shylock, Lowell was in earnest. This was the attitude he had constantly set before himself in his poetry, and although he often departed from it in his varying moods of literary excitement, he was irked by the expectation that he should abandon it in cold blood. It was apparently not very difficult for an occasion to work him up to the point of abandonment in consideration of the humanity of slaveholders, parsons, and politicians. But the question of disunion—on which he had touched frequently in his editorials, with never a suggestion of disapproval—was a less emotional one, and it must have been something of a strain for such an apostle of sincerity as Lowell to be consciously insincere on that subject for a salary.

If he had made any such compromises with his aesthetic conscience, he would hardly have printed all but one of his contributions to the *Standard* (and that one was a duplicate treatment of a theme which was preserved) prior to May 1 in his *Collected Poems,* leaving out so many that he wrote as a free man in order to do so. As a matter of fact, his complete indifference to the literary prejudices of the Executive Committee probably gave its more critical members a new reason for their dissatisfaction. "A Day in June," which appeared on March 8, was put together by craft from lines written in his "Private Journal" at a time when he had little interest in taking an active part in the abolitionist cause; and although the "Lines suggested by the Graves of Two English Soldiers on Concord Battleground" pointed out a relationship between the American Revolution and the abolitionist movement (as successive battles in the conflict between past and future) the suggestion was neither sufficiently direct nor forthright enough to be very impressive to Stephen Foster. And the publication of "An Oriental Apologue" on April 12, while the Committee was debating the fate of the corresponding editor, was simply foolish. It took up about five times as much space as any of Lowell's other poems at a time when the value of every inch of space in the *Standard* was being weighed in the cold scales of practicality, and the more hard-headed members of the Executive Committee probably found it about as pointed as a feather duster. It was a satire against religious fanatics, and, although the lesson of the fable was that people would continue to encourage fanaticism no matter how much hardship it caused, Lowell introduced into it some good advice that his practical critics would have approved:

> creating is man's work
> And that, too, something more than mist and murk.

But he put his apologue in *ottava rima* with a Byronic tone and comic rhymes that obscured the seriousness of his teaching even to those who might find the oriental allusions amusing rather than mystifying. It is not surprising that some of his employers found the young man puzzling if not definitely queer. Lowell himself knew that he had not been fighting a good fight in the anti-slavery cause, and he may have realized that he had just about finished his course as a reformer without having been able to keep any consistent faith.

II

Lowell's failure to make a satisfactory show in the columns of the *Standard* was undoubtedly a blow to his vanity. The financial loss was also a serious one, for his father had resigned five hundred dollars of his annual salary less than a month before and James was acutely conscious of the necessity of bearing his part of the family expenses. He had been unwilling to liquidate Maria's inheritance of real property because he did not want the responsibility of trying to keep it intact in a less solid form of investment, but he determined at last to do so and seek a larger income from the capital. His need was not only genuine but also embarrassing, for it was bad enough to have to count his pennies without having people think such behavior by the son-in-law of the late and wealthy Mr. Abijah White was mere miserliness. His mind also naturally turned to a new source of literary income. Mrs. C. M. Kirkland had only recently been begging him to "learn to put a price" upon himself and contribute to the *Christian Inquirer,* and, although she expressed a willingness to take the same sort of material he had been giving the *Standard,* Lowell was unwilling to take on a new obligation and during the entire year actually published only one commercial article—a review of Longfellow's *Kavanagh* in the *North American* for July, 1849.

Except for its damage to his vanity and his financial situation, the new arrangement with the *Standard* was a relief to Lowell. Not only was he freed from half his weekly articles but also from the feeling that he had to allow the Executive Committee to peer over his shoulder as he wrote. By offering to resign entirely from the paper he had achieved the position of writing once a fortnight by request rather than by tolerance, and his editorials became less tortured in their efforts to keep at least within sight of the party line. Having confessed to Gay that he did not agree with the disunion movement, he felt no obligation to try to justify it on the grounds of expediency or by any other arguments; and during the year that followed he ignored both it and its advocates, making a defense of the Wilmot Proviso his major concern until he became, in effect, the spokesman for the free-soilers in the columns of the *Standard*. When he touched upon the matter of disunion at all, it was as a Southern "threat" rather than as a Northern hope; and although he looked upon an expression of devotion to the Union as being, in practice, a protest against the Wilmot Proviso, he made no secret of his feeling that if the Union had to be sacrificed in order to prevent the spread of slavery, the sacrifice would be a matter for regret rather than for rejoicing. He remained as willing as ever to attack Calhoun as a reactionary and Southerners in general for their bad grammar, but his most vigorous words were directed against those politicians who were willing to compromise with the extension of slavery in territory acquired from Mexico. Henry Clay was the object of his most consistent scorn, and Webster's seventh of March speech provoked his longest and evidently his most carefully prepared editorial as the second year of his employment drew toward a close.

Some of the fifteen prose articles he wrote during the course of the year were brief and casual almost to the point of indifference, but, on the whole, Lowell did his duty by his employers with the apparent ease of a man who had acquired facility in the journalistic field and had learned not to take his job too seriously. Since he had quit trying to compromise his own point of view with that of the Committee which paid his salary he had become more consistent in his attitude and more relaxed in his style, for he allowed his humor to play freely over his subjects without getting out of control, and he rarely gave the appearance of struggling for something to say. He also felt free to let his attention wander away from the anti-slavery cause, and as the year wore on he gave evidence of increasing concern for the revolution in Hungary and the treatment of the exiled patriots—probably because his elder sister, Mary Putnam, had taken up the Hungarian cause and he himself was growing tired of abolitionism and welcomed a new interest.

Of all his prose writings during the year 1849, he put the most thought into his essay for the July number of the *North American Review* and in doing so began to reveal his first signs of maturity as a literary critic. Hitherto, it might have been said of his criticism what he had said of Landor's: that his remarks were "valuable as far as they go" but were "commonly fragmentary"—at least when they were dealing with a specific piece of literature rather than with the nature of poetry and the function of the poet. It may not have been precisely true to say of Lowell, as he had said of Landor, that "he perceives rather than conceives," but, as a critic, his perceptions were a great deal clearer than his conceptions, and his literary essays had been more notable for their penetration than for their breadth. His new assignment for the *North American,* however, had been a peculiarly fortunate one which came at a time when he had every practical reason for doing his best with it. Bowen, who had been after him to do an article on American poetry, sent him Longfellow's new *Kavanagh, a Tale* for review; and although the volume itself proved too slight for any elaborate commentary, the gentle satire of the chapter in which Churchill exchanged sentiments with Mr. Hathaway on the subject of a national literature inspired Lowell to an essay on a subject which had long been a source of irritation to him. For Longfellow's attitude was Lowell's own, and Mr. Hathaway was the sort of casual visitor who had inspired the digression on bores in *A Fable for Critics.* He had the occasion for a new treatment of an old subject; he had the leisure and the financial incentive for establishing himself as a solid critic; and he also had acquired some new ideas concerning the matter at hand.

Earlier, Lowell's quarrel with the proponents of a distinctly national literature represented the conventional quarrel of the transcendentalist who believed in intuitions of absolute beauty with the associationist who thought that the mind formed its ideas of beauty by combinations of sensory impressions. To the latter, literature had to be national or without power, whereas to the former, power was universal or it was not power at all. Yet the matter was not nearly so clean-cut in Lowell's mind, for he was not a proper transcendentalist, and his over-soul, as a source of universal feelings rather than of ideas, could hardly support a system of aesthetics which could withstand the appeals of the nationalists on the one hand and uphold the sensuous imagery of his own more recent verse on the other. Furthermore, the inherent antagonism between a transcendental and an associationist aesthetic was weakened by the peculiar attraction which "the doctrine of correspondences" held for the former. It would be difficult to maintain, on the grounds of a transcendental correspondence between the ideal and the real, that a poet's verse could take on beauty from a buttercup without acquiring majesty from Niagara Falls—although Lowell had, in effect, made the one contention in his own verse and ridiculed the other when he found it expressed by someone else. The ease with which he slipped from a mood of sublimity to one of ridicule and his habitual indifference to logic and intellectual self-criticism had made such inconsistency possible. They had also kept him from becoming a very substantial critic.

But more recently Lowell had been thinking about his own literary career, and if his tentative efforts to justify it in such poems as "The Parting of the Ways" and "An Oriental Apologue" did not result in a new defense of his own poetry, they did help him along the road to becoming a more respectable commentator on other writers. Parker's article on "The Political Destination of America and the Signs of the Times," which had already impressed him with its exposition of "the American Idea," was in agreement with Longfellow that a national literature was the product of a slow growth:

> Hitherto, in spite of the great reading public, we have no permanent literature which corresponds to the American Idea. Perhaps it is not time for that; it must be organized in deeds before it becomes classic in words; but as yet we have no such literature which reflects even the surface of American life, certainly nothing which portrays our intensity of life, our hope, or even our daily doings and drivings, as the Odyssey paints Greek life, or Don Quixote and Gil Blas portray Spanish life.

Lowell did not entirely agree, for soon after reading the article he had written Briggs in a letter of December, 1848: "I am the first poet who has endeavored to express the American Idea, and I shall be popular bye and bye." But despite such occasional spasms of egotism he adopted Parker's point of view for his essay and urged patience upon those who demanded a national literature, pointing out, as he had pointed out six years before in grieving over Wordsworth's betrayal of his calling, the long intervals between great poets. American literature was a continuation of that of England, just as Chaucer and Spenser were continuations of a Norman rather than of a Saxon tradition, and the "most truly national epic" of the English was "the colonizing of America." The people of the United States had inherited the genius for "practicalizing simpler and more perfect forms of social organization" and it had not yet found its perfect expression: "We have yet many problems of this kind to work out, and a continent to subdue with the plough and the railroad, before we are at leisure for aesthetics." Whether it was to be the country's "destiny to produce a great literature" he was not sure, but he was convinced that a better literature would come in due time. "Our spirit of adventure will first take a material and practical direction, but will gradually be forced to seek outlet and scope in unoccupied territories of the intellect."

It can hardly be doubted that an important but immeasurable element in this theorizing was the desire of a man to justify his own sacrifice of a poetical calling to his active efforts toward "more perfect forms of social organization." It was less probably motivated by, yet equally in accord with, Lowell's mature habit of writing out of his experience rather than out of his dreams—with his acceptance of the fact that flowers were merely flowers and that the business of the poetic imagination was not to dematerialize the world of the senses but to rearrange it in a way that would arouse the sympathetic imagination of someone else. It was not that Lowell had come to believe that the poet should be nothing more than a describer or a reporter: "There is a vast difference between truth to nature and truth to fact," he wrote; "an impassable gulf between genius, which deals only with the true, and that imitative faculty which patiently and exactly reproduces the actual." But he no longer believed that one could express the truth simply by looking in his heart and writing. "With us introspection has become a disease," he said in comparing his own time with the "more purely objective age" of the Greek dramatists, "and a poem is a self-dissection." His impatience with critics who insisted upon classifying everything as either objective or subjective—which he had expressed in *A Fable for Critics* and in his review of *The Princess*—was almost as great as his impatience with those who insisted that literature should be national. Good literature should be both. In the language of Dugald Stewart, whose half-remembered ideas were the matrix in which Lowell's were taking form, it was created by the combining power of the Imagination and out of materials that Fancy had selected from the external world. Thus nationalism was not a virtue but a fanciful restriction upon material that the imagination should use freely. "Human nature is everywhere the same, and everywhere inextinguishable. It we only insist that our authors shall be good, we may cease to feel nervous about their being national. Excellence is an alien nowhere."

There was much in this essay that Lowell had said before. The new quality in it is the existence of certain solid assumptions concerning literature which formed the common law to which more explicit canons of criticism had to conform. Prometheus could no longer be the prototype of his ideal poet, for the poet must have experience as well as forethought—fancy as well as imagination. Nor could Cromwell, the man of action, be identified with the poet; for, although action might be called epic and poetry might be found in it, the action provided merely the materials for literature and provided an escape for an energy which had to occupy the "territories of the intellect" before it could become poetry. A great poet could not come into being solely through the force of his own will. Time and circumstance had to give him the right materials for his genius to use. And Lowell, unlike his contemporary who also set himself up as the "Bard of the great Idea," apparently came gradually to the conclusion suggested tentatively in his essay: that the time was not ripe for a great American poet. His ambition, in any case, eventually shifted from poetry to criticism instead.

The energy for this shift, however, came from the force of other circumstances which were to affect Lowell much later. At the time, although

Bowen paid promptly for the article on *Kavanagh* and suggested other subjects on which Lowell might write, he did no other criticism for the *North American*, and the proportion of poems to prose included in his contributions to the *Standard* increased. But even these show a lessening of his ambition to be a great poet and a growing indifference to reform. The one exception, "King Retro," published on May 10 while his new relationship to the paper was still undetermined, was an allegory in ballad stanzas which represented slavery as a Trojan horse with a tendency to run away from the retrograde kingdom where it was being preserved as an "institution." Its moral was convenient to the "cause" but based upon the very notions Lowell was denying at almost exactly the same time in his essay on nationality in literature: no prohibitive tariff on free speech and thought, the Bible, and "Light" could keep the slaves inert so long as they were exposed to the teachings of nature and could learn "Hope, courage, and devotion" from the stars. Lowell had dipped back into the philosophy of his youth to get material for his propaganda. But it was an unusual procedure, at this stage of his life, for most of his poems that were at all philosophical kept pace with the ideas that affected his criticism. "Bibliolatres," which appeared on May 24, was addressed to those people (among whom he included himself in *The Vision of Sir Launfal*) who daily climbed Sinais yet knew it not because they, like Ambrose, looked upon the law as once revealed and forever after unchangeable. In it, Lowell held to his old conviction that the pure in heart could hear God speaking with more authority than could be contained in any book of revelation at secondhand, but he brought his belief up to date intellectually by a concluding stanza which paid tribute to the accumulated experience of the past as something which should be valued as well as supplemented by each generation. His book worshiper was not to be condemned entirely because he followed the past to the exclusion of the present, but in part because he bound himself so rigidly in one fragment of the past. Sectarians in religion made the same mistake in time that the nationalists in literature made in space: they placed arbitrary restrictions upon materials which had to be used freely in the search for truth.

The philosophy implicit in the essay and poem was put more directly in a letter Lowell wrote to his nephew Charles on June 11. Study, observe, and learn as much as possible about everything was the burden of his advice, for knowledge is power in the noblest sense. School furnished the mind from books and trained the intellect, and the country was the "great school of the senses."

Train your eyes and ears. Learn to know all the trees by their bark and leaves, by their general shape and manner of growth. Sometimes you can be able to say positively what a tree is *not* by simply examining the lichens on the bark, for you will find that particular varieties of lichen love particular trees. Learn also to know all the birds by sight, by their notes, by their manner of flying; all the animals by their general appearance and gait or the localities they frequent.

"We ought to be as familiar with every object in the world" as with the "name and use of every piece of furniture in the house," he wrote with an enthusiasm which might have been more readily expected of the boy of fifteen than of the man who confessed middle age at thirty. The author of *A Year's Life* and of "Rosaline" and "A Legend of Brittany" had developed a quality which he was later to find in Keats: a passion for "something less ethereal than culture."

During the months which immediately followed the composition of his essay on nationality in literature and the poem "Bibliolatres," Lowell apparently let his mind lie fallow. He had hay to cut during the hot days of June while he was awaiting the birth of his third child, and, although he was able to write with some copiousness for the *Standard,* the "best" which he skimmed off for publication was not the result of any long or strong working of the intellect. The poem to which he later gave the title "Trial" was actually a tribute to culture, as the word was generally used in Lowell's day—to the lifelong effort to build human nature into "a temple fit for Freedom's shrine" which was a greater privilege than freedom itself. But in his next poem, "Eurydice," published eight weeks later on August 23, he paid a contrasting tribute to the less ethereal "outdoor influences" that quickened the senses and made his pulses burn "with olden heats" and restored his "childhood's hopes." Yet the poem was not very coherent. To produce it, he had gone to his "Private Journal" for a fragment written during his unhappy period of four years before, which began with the Wordsworthian question "Why am I changed?" and lamented the loss of

> That undesigned abandonment
> That rash unquestioning content,
> Which could erect its microcosm
> Out of a weed's neglected blossom,

and could herald each change in existence with the glow of some "goddess-hiding haze." For publication he changed the question to the observation " 'Tis we are changed," made the content "wise" instead of "rash," added literary illustrations of his youthful imaginative activity, and slightly revised the epithet describing the "haze" with which he surrounded his youthful anticipations of the future. But even in the published poem, the abandonment was to what Dugald Stewart and Coleridge would have called "Fancy" rather than to the "shaping spirit of Imagination" or to the sensuous joy in nature which the new context of the fragment might imply. The Lowell whose early volumes had reflected his notion that sensuousness was permissible only in early boyhood, and who had so often longed for his childish days in the language of Wordsworth and Coleridge, was again trying to fit his experience into the pattern set by the Intimations Ode and the Ode to Dejection. The facts borne out by his actual writings, however, do not correspond to his thinking. Sensory perception was always strong in him, however unwilling he was for a period to admit it to his poetry, and when he began to relax freely under the influence of something less ethereal than culture, he was not recapturing his youth but acknowledging his maturity.

The acknowledgment was not made with entire gracefulness, however, for after paying tribute to Kossuth as an ideal hero in a poem for the *Standard* of September 6, Lowell returned to the theme of his lost youth. The verses "To ——" which appeared on October 18 may have been addressed to the favorite nephew in whom Lowell saw a renewal of his own boyhood and to whom he had written the letter of good advice during the preceding June. It was an admission that he had reached the cold autumn of his life when it was necessary to light his "sullen fires" with the driftwood beached in his spring tide. He was, as he put it in another figure of speech, stitching the shroud of his youth "By the pinched rushlight's starving beam." And out of his mature wisdom he was able to give clear advice which apparently contradicted the assumptions found in his essay on nationality in literature and in "Bibliolatres":

O thou, whose days are yet all spring,
  Faith, blighted once, is past retrieving;
Experience is a dumb, dead thing;
  The victory's in believing.

Wordsworth's "Expostulation and Reply" and "The Tables Turned" were probably in the back of his mind as he wrote the poem, and he was perhaps even more consciously aware of the Intimations Ode and Coleridge's Ode to Dejection. For the "driftwood" which kept his fires lighted in age was the "primal sympathy" which remained behind in Wordsworth's life after the glory and the dream of youth had departed, and his "rushlight" was probably the scholar's candle by which Coleridge had stolen from his own nature all the natural man—since Lowell also accepted Dugald Stewart's notion that the habitual use of words as instruments of thought destroyed the imagination.

But what Lowell was lamenting was not the loss of impulses from the vernal wood or from a peculiar tint of yellow green in the western sky. What he missed so painfully was the confident faith that the "earth could be remade tomorrow," and the "experience" he disavowed was synonymous with disillusionment. He was not lamenting the loss of wisdom but the acquisition of it. He was not regretting the loss of an excitement which came from clarity of perception but that which came from being misty eyed—from the ability to face each successive stage of existence, as he had put it in "Eurydice," through a "goddess-veiling haze." Herrick as well as Wordsworth had contributed to the tune of his little lyric, and Lowell was advising his young kinsman, in the spirit of the older poet, to gather while he might the rosebuds of impossible hopes and aspirations. Such prizes, he had begun to realize, were not for a weary knight-errant who had reached the age of thirty.

III

By this time, Lowell was ready for another assault on the book-reading public with another collection of his poems which he hoped and trusted would be more successful than the unfortunate volume of two years before. The new edition was to be published in two volumes by Ticknor, Reed, and Fields under an agreement which would, for the first time, give him a profit of a hundred dollars or more for the first edition with, perhaps, twice that amount for each successive edition of the same size and price. Since the new collection was to be reprinted with such frequency that it practically established the approved canon of Lowell's early work and became the final version of the poems included, it was peculiarly unfortunate that an agreement with his new publishers should have been made at a time when he was more interested than usual in the proceeds that might be available for the annual settlement of his debts on January 1. For his anticipated profits were not to come from any unusual generosity on the part of his publishers, but from their willingness to combine old and new plates for their edition and allow the author the proceeds of the economy achieved by their willingness to place their imprint upon a slightly peculiar specimen of typography. Lowell suffered more than they did, however, by their tolerant attitude. There were few of his poems which would not have been improved by an editorial scrutiny and minor revisions; but when the revisions had to be chiseled out of stereotype plates at a stated cost per change, the editorial eye became less sensitive than usual and the delicate balance of taste was disturbed by the price of zinc. It was cheaper to use the shears than the blue pencil, and the poems fell by the requirements of economy into three general classes: those that were so poor that it became worth-while to replace them by others of approximately the same length, those that could be improved by excisions (especially at the end), and those that would do all right as they were. The only poem to receive any considerable revision was the "The Falconer" from the *Poems, Second Series* which was changed to "The Falcon" by the removal of five stanzas and some of its egotism. It apparently was completely reset, and Lowell was enabled to make in it, at no extra expense, a few changes in diction and punctuation of the sort that would have improved a number of his other poems.

But the others that were changed at all from their appearance in the 1844 and 1848 volumes were revised by the carpenter, who sawed off the plates at the designated places and sometimes made whole new pages by nailing two old halves on a new block. Lowell managed to keep such patchwork at a minimum, however, for in cutting down "A Legend of Brittany," he usually dropped out his stanzas by pairs (or whole pages) and whenever it was necessary to eliminate a single stanza he was always able to find another close by that he could sacrifice to the trouble of cutting and nailing. Yet the fact that he mutilated his poem in order to avoid mutilating more than the minimum number of plates is not particularly evident. The "Legend" originally contained a lot of stanzas that were less closely related to the narrative than to the author's personal problems at the time they were written, and while removing them and reducing it in length by almost one-third, he found it necessary to reset only one line in order to preserve the continuity of his story. The revisions of "A Chippewa Legend" and "Rhoecus" were made by the simple process of sawing off their conclusions, and the moral earnestness with which he ended both poems was melted up as scrap. The moralizing in each case was too elaborate, and in the former it was no longer as appropriate as it had been to conditions in England and to Lowell's own attitude toward America. But in abbreviating the latter poem he was casting aside a serious statement of the same moral he had made less earnestly in his most recent poem for the *Standard* and was doing so at the cost of almost the only extra trouble he caused the printers in making the new book: in order to get a minimum of four lines on the concluding page of the new version, they were forced to the expedient of cutting each of the two preceding plates one line short and thus adding another peculiarity to a volume which is more nearly a model of economy than of perfection in bookmaking. Lowell tried to extend his economies by keeping the same pagination for the first volume that he had used for the 1844 *Poems;* but the effort became too complicated when he was little more than half way through, although he did succeed in making the pages of the second volume correspond in number with those of the 1848 collection as far as the latter went. He could not avoid being billed for some corrections in the plates, but except for the single line in "A Legend of Brittany," they seem to have been almost entirely corrections of the page and stanza numbers for that poem, for renumbering the sonnets, and for changing the page numbers in the latter part of the first volume.

The carpenter was also called upon for help in revising "L'Envoi" which Lowell directed with such neatness that it was necessary only to saw two plates and cut the tail off a comma in order to remove four full pages of material, most of which was not as relevant to the new issue as it had been to the 1844 volume. Among the deleted lines were those that had once been salvaged from the poem on Cromwell and some of those on the nature of poetry, although he left that part of the discussion which was close to his recent essay on nationalism in literature. His other major changes were accomplished by dropping out entire poems and substituting others for them. Most of these omissions were apparently made in an effort to eliminate the haziness of poetic diction which Elizabeth Barrett had found an objectionable characteristic of the original volume, for of the seven entire poems discarded, three of the longest ("A Dirge," "In Sadness," and "A Reverie") were characteristic of his early contributions to *Graham's* and a fourth ("Fantasy") was in the same manner. The other three, a "Song," "Forgetfulness," and "Silence," were short lyrics. To replace them and the omitted parts of "A Legend of Brittany" and "Rhoecus," Lowell had recourse to *A Year's Life* although he appears to have had little enthusiasm for the quality of the poetry in that volume. His first selections of "Threnodia," "The Sirens," "Serenade," and "Irenè" were rather obviously made because three of those particular poems had some peculiar association that made them especially attractive to his own mind, and the "Serenade" may have been included among them because it was the sort of poem that should have been addressed to Maria and was of the appropriate length. "With a Pressed

Flower" and "My Love" also were attached to the canon of Lowell's *Poetical Works* for sentimental reasons which he was able to indulge because he wanted to escape the signs of his *Graham's* manner exhibited by "A Dirge" and "In Sadness." The only other poem he included from his first collection was "The Beggar," which was certainly more clear-cut in style than was the dirge it partially replaced, but it had little other claim for preservation than its convenient length and actually represented a curious revival of the point of view which he had so recently satirized in his essay on *Kavanagh*. The other gaps in the pagination were filled with the abbreviated version of "The Falconer" and by the recently composed poem the "Trial," both of which were out of place in this volume of early poems. After he gave up the effort to preserve the original page numbers, he showed less evidence of straining to fill up space. He added "To the Memory of Hood" and three bits of unrelated verse under the title "Thistle-Downs" to the poems and felt it necessary to substitute only three sonnets—two of them from *A Year's Life* and a third, the introductory sonnet to Maria in *Poems, Second Series*—for the thirteen that he omitted. The sonnets he left out, on the whole, seem to have been removed on the grounds that they revealed too much of his youthful wavering of purpose, although he also left out the advice to reformers and the tribute to Pierpont he had originally printed in the *Liberty Bell* for 1842. The most interesting of his omissions, however, was the sonnet in which he urged his readers to look for a double meaning in his writings—the "outward grace" of color and form and the inner meaning of the "spirit." His recent tendency had been to portray nature for its own sake, and he may have wished to give his readers no reason to look for anything deeper.

For the second volume of his collection, Lowell reprinted the entire *Poems, Second Series* with the exception of "The Epitaph, "The Royal Pedigree," "Anti-Texas," and "The Falconer" which had already gone into the first volume. For these he substituted "The Sower," "Ambrose," "Eurydice," "The Day of Small Things" under its new title "To W. L. Garrison," and the only previously unpublished poem in the entire collection, another little memorial poem to Blanche entitled "She Came and Went." The new volume was enlarged beyond the limits of the earlier one, however, by the addition of *The Vision of Sir Launfal,* the Cochituate Water "Ode," and all the remaining poems he had contributed to the *Standard* with the exception of the unfinished "A Day in June," "The Parting of the Ways," and "An Oriental Apologue" (all three of which were to appear in later collections) and the only two poems of that period which were never collected, "The Ex-Mayor's

Crumb of Consolation" and "King Retro." It hardly bore out his contention that he had compromised his aesthetic standards in a desire to please the members of the Executive Committee of the American Anti-Slavery Society, for the untimely poem on Otis was too close in substance to the poem on Garrison for both to appear in the same volume, and "King Retro" was written after he had made his complaint and when he was in no mood to care what the Committee thought. Yet, on the other hand, there is little probability that Lowell made his selection of poems for this edition on aesthetic grounds or after any complete review of his poetical works. He was careless about keeping copies of his writings, and some of his contributions to periodicals may never have been considered for this collection. Of those that were considered, his selections were influenced by sentiment and by arbitrary considerations of space, apparently with little, if any, suspicion that he was establishing the basic canon and permanent text of his early works. Few poets have ever staked out their claims on posterity with greater carelessness.

Lowell wrote Briggs on November 25 that he expected his new edition to be out about December 10, and it probably appeared near that date for the printer billed him on December 5 for stereotyping and correcting the plates and some copies seem to have been issued in a red binding and gilt edges for the holiday trade. His new publisher was more energetic than any he had dealt with directly before and sent out seventy-five copies to editors for review. By June 22, 1850, a total of 917 copies had been sold, and it was probably time for the first of the new editions that were to appear almost annually until another collection was made in 1857. Lowell had suffered little in popularity—although he had not been helped—by his abolitionist activities, for if the new work did not sell quite so rapidly as the 1844 *Poems* had, it sold for twice as much in the cheapest binding and the difference in price should share the responsibility for the difference in sentiments in an accounting for the slower sales. By his ingenuity in making revisions he had succeeded in keeping the cost of the plates and corrections to $107.97, or less than one-third his royalties at thirty-six cents per copy, but he had other expenses greater than he had anticipated. For he was obliged to pay for John Bartlett's and perhaps the publisher's equity in 346 copies of the *Poems, Second Series* which had remained unsold and were made valueless by the new edition, and he actually cleared, on his first accounting, only $62.89 instead of the hundred dollars he anticipated. But the subsequent editions, as he anticipated, were "clear gain"; and with the 1849 *Poems* he achieved, for the first time, the position of being able to expect a fairly steady, though small, income from a published book.

Getting out his new edition of poems was less harrying than usual to Lowell, and while working on it he had time not only to keep up his writing for the *Standard* but to engage in other miscellaneous literary activities. Theodore Parker had asked him on June 14 to write a notice of from four to six pages, including extracts, of Thoreau's new book, *A Week on the Concord and Merrimack Rivers;* but Lowell appears to have been slow in getting started and to have had some difficulty in settling upon the right approach to his subject. The article, which finally appeared in the December number of the *Massachusetts Quarterly Review,* was written in the high spirits of *A Fable for Critics* and ran to four or five times the length that Parker had requested. But the approach remained ambiguous. Lowell regretted the loss in modern travel literature of that element of wonder which was characteristic of the older voyagers, for, as he made clear in "A Day in June" and in the poem on the autumn of his days, he envied the person who could approach each new experience through a "goddess-veiling haze" and who habitually felt that the "earth could be remade to-morrow"—or, as he put it in this essay, who possessed the conviction that "a bird in the bush is worth two in the hand." Thoreau, of course, could not have the exact quality that went with the naïvete of youth or of the days when men were less well-informed about the world they lived in, but he did reveal the quality which Lowell was to prize so highly in himself when he wrote the first of his own travel essays: the imaginative ability to see what other people could only look at, the faculty for finding poetry in objects which to other observers were merely "items." To find this rare quality in a man remembered as a ridiculously green-coated satellite of Emerson who had not even been elected to the undergraduate literary society of Alpha Delta Phi, however, was somehow funny. After his essays on Browning and Landor, Lowell could not avoid looking for this quality, and he was sufficiently honest to recognize it in Thoreau. But he could not take it seriously. If his old schoolmate showed a sympathy for nature beside which Walton had "but an extraqueous and coquine intimacy with the fishes," it was not necessarily a sign of wisdom but possibly that "his memory is better, and can re-create the sensations of that part of his embryonic life which he passed as a fish." On specific points of style and form, Lowell balanced praise and blame in a way which was fairly just though not generous, but his treatment of the man was in a vein of satiric mockery which reveals the subordination of his critical judgments to his emotional impressions, and helps explain why the best of his criticism was to be that in which a personal recollection of the man did not get between him and the printed page.

The power of Lowell's prejudices over his criticism was unconsciously dramatized by the contrast between his review of Thoreau and that which he wrote of the Reverend Sylvester Judd's *Philo: an Evangeliad* for the *Standard* on January 24. The poem was not altogether "fortunate": it lacked the cathedral-like construction one expected of a poem, and Lowell could not fail to recognize that the "author lights somewhere short of the height of his great argument." "But the book is genuine and sincere," he added in compensation for its faults, and it contained some fine "conceptions." The story of *Philo* was one that he was so strangely unable to find in Thoreau's books—"that of a spiritual Don Quixote" in reverse, ridiculing society by showing that reality is with the enthusiast. "In it the Church, the State, the Press, the Politics, and the Social Life of the country are subjected to the biting test of Christianity. And not only is each brought to judgment, but to condemnation, albeit in a spirit of love and faith which holds out hopes of a final regeneration and reconcilement." It also had a lesson for abolitionists, for if clergymen were to engage in self-examination one could not be too sure that the lecture and Lyceum had taken the place of the church. That a pencil manufacturer should exhibit a quixotic concern with higher utility, however, was another matter. "We were bid to a river party, not to be preached at" was the impatient reaction of the author of *The Vision of Sir Launfal* to the didacticism of Thoreau's *Week*. At a time when his personal feeling was running so high, it was probably well that Lowell allowed Griswold to reprint the old *Graham's* article on Poe rather than a new one which Poe's executor wanted him to compose. If the sins of omission in the reprint are Lowell's (which is by no means certain in view of the rapidity with which the edition was turned out) they are insignificant in comparison with those he would have committed had he written on Poe in the mood with which he dealt with *A Week on the Concord and Merrimack Rivers.*

Lowell wrote little poetry for immediate publication during the latter part of 1849. "Yussouf" (which he wrote only after repeated requests from the *Liberty Bell*) was perfunctory, and the three little poems that did appear in the *Standard* were all touched by a certain melancholy retrospection. "The Lesson of the Pine" on November 15 advised against the sort of preoccupation with the past which Lowell exemplified in "The First Snow-Fall" and which was sent to Gay on December 22 with the instructions: "Print *that* as if you loved it. Let not a comma be blundered." The latter poem was the product of the emotion aroused in Lowell annually by the coming of winter, but this year he thought of Blanche's lonely little mound in Mt. Auburn rather than the unfrozen brook that he had crossed so often between Elmwood and Watertown. He forced himself into an expression of optimism for "New-Year's Eve, 1850"—a somewhat preliminary celebration of the passage of "the midnight of the century" in the *Standard* of January 10—but his inspiration was less the belief that "the sorest trial" had been passed than the recurrence to his mind of a figure of speech that he had thought of three years before at the time of the winter solstice: no matter how far human beings move away from the sun they will swing back, willy-nilly, by the law of heavenly gravitation. His artificial optimism not only echoed "Si descendero in infernum, ades" but also "Above and Below" which had been written at the same time.

IV

The fact is that Lowell was weary in well-doing and wanted a change. He was tired of anti-slavery and was gathering his resources for a revolt against reform. But before he revolted, he plunged once more into the field of controversy on a matter which had come to arouse a more stimulating interest in him than did the old question of slavery. The concern he had shown over the Hungarian exiles in the *Standard* during the month of December had overflowed into the pages of the Boston *Courier* for January 3 where Lowell, in a plea for financial assistance for the exiles, explained his support of the Magyar cause on the curious grounds—for the Corresponding Editor of the *Standard*—that the revolution would be kept orderly "by the independence of a people habituated to respect constitutional forms,—forms many centuries old, but which proved their vitality by a tendency to adapt themselves to the requirements of the time." Lowell urged the collection of funds for the exiles as the payment of a "debt" owed by the lovers of freedom to those who had fought for it, but simultaneously with the appearance of his appeal in the *Courier,* the *North American Review* appeared with an article which cast serious doubts upon the claims of Louis Kossuth and his fellow Magyars. In preparation for a review of Auguste de Gérando's *De l'esprit public en Hongrie, despuis la révolution française,* Francis Bowen had been prompted (as he put it later) by some evil genius "to give the leisure of a few weeks to an investigation of the causes and nature of the war which was then raging in Hungary," and had come to the conclusion that it was less a revolution for liberty than a war of races in which the Magyars had declared their independence of Austria only after the new Emperor had granted the country a liberal constitution allowing the Croatians and other races privileges equal with those of the Magyars. The Hungarian Declaration of Independence, Bowen pointed out, had made Kossuth a dictator. Lowell was indignant at the reflection upon his latest cause and most recent ideal hero. He had been planning a new volume of poetry, which would have nothing whatever to do with social questions, for May, but he was always ready to put off an old plan for a new one and so wrote Briggs on January 25:

> I am not certain that my next appearance will not be in a pamphlet on the Hungarian question in answer to the N. A. Review. But I shall not write anything if I can help it. I am tired of controversy, and though I have cut out the oars with which to row up my friend Bowen, yet I have enough to do, and, besides, am not so well as usual, being troubled in my head as I was summer before last. I should like to play for a year...

Before he had time to begin any serious work on a pamphlet, however, his baby daughter Rose died after a brief illness, and he had less spirit than ever for controversy. He missed his bi-weekly contribution to the *Standard* after her death on February 2, and, soon after he began writing again, he was under pressure from all sides to deal with Webster's seventh of March speech and spent most of his energy on the long editorial which appeared on March 21. At the time he sent it in, he wrote Gay of his strong inclination to resign his position on the paper: "It seems to me as if I have said my say—for the present, at least—and had better try silence awhile. I am sick of politics and criticism." By April 17, he was aware that his resignation had been " 'accepted,' like that of a vizier, by a couple of mutes with a bowstring"; and he was sending in "one last poem" in order that he might, "like that famous ghost of Aubrey's, vanish 'with a melodious twang.' " The poem, "Mahmood the Image-Breaker," was an appropriate, if not perfectly melodious, valedictory from a man who had denounced Webster as being influenced by self-interest in his attempts to preserve the idol of the Union, yet who had himself about decided to accept the world without trying to change it: Mahmood, refusing to sell his "truth" to the Brahmins who tried to ransom their idol from his hands, smote the image in twain and found fifty times the ransom concealed in its hollow core. Lowell had descended from his high moral position and, for those who understood his allegory, had begun to argue that the greatest material benefits were not those visibly offered by the proposed compromise of 1850. He set essentially the same moral of long-term profit before Webster and his fellow compromisers in another eastern poem, "Dara"; and he occasionally made other contributions to the *Standard,* which kept his name at the masthead for a year after his resignation from the staff had been accepted, sending Gay a poem, "The Northern Sancho Panza and his vicarious Cork Tree," in July, a prose article, "Pseudo Conservatism," on November 14, and another poem, "A Dream I Had," two weeks later in which he represented himself as Crito and Daniel Webster as Socrates talking "cheerfully, bravely, and wisely" of hemlock—and making Ellen Graft drink it. He had hoped after the passage of the Fugitive Slave Bill to write something in the "Hosea Biglow vein, with a *refrain* to it that would take hold of the popular ear," for, he explained to Gay early in November:

> I should like to tack something to Mr. Webster (the most meanly and foolishly treacherous man I ever heard of), like the tail I furnished to Mr. John P. Robinson. But I wish to be sure that it is good enough before I try it on in public, for a failure in such a case would be disastrous. I walk about crooning over various ridiculous burthens and cadences, and am not without hope that he may catch it yet.

He also went to such an extreme in his reaction against the Whig compromisers that he voted for Democrats when the Free-Soil ticket had gaps in it, but he never found his popular cadence for Webster, and his "dream" was too discursive and too sophisticated to attract much attention to its damning criticism.

As a matter of fact, Lowell apparently could not feel the spontaneous flow of moral indignation against Webster he had felt two years before when he had prophesied that "Ichabod" should be written opposite his name as a sign of his departed glory. Whittier was the recording angel who fulfilled the prophecy a half-year before Lowell began to croon over his possible burthens. The burst of energy and righteousness which marked the end of a late summer and fall of intellectual hibernation was inspired by Francis Bowen. For while Lowell was trying to work himself up to the proper heat to deal with Webster, his sister Mary Putnam (who was the *North American Review*'s authority on Hungarian literature) and his friend Robert Carter (who had been serving as secretary to the historian Prescott) had undertaken to answer the article on "The War of Races in Hungary" which had so stimulated Lowell in January. Kossuth (who was so popular in America that his full-whiskered tour of the country two years later gave him the reputation of being the Johnny Appleseed of the bearded age) had other defenders, and Bowen was bombarded by anonymous threats through the mail and public denunciations in the press. But Mrs. Putnam's article, "The North American Review on Hungary" in the *Christian Examiner* for November, was the one he chose to answer—apparently because it was the most impressive reply to his own and because it touched upon the factual crux of the difference in opinion by denying that there was or had been any racial discrimination in Hungary "since the reign of St. Stephen." He replied through the columns of the Boston *Daily Advertiser* for November 28 and 30 in a tone which, on the whole, was good humored and temperate although he may have been indiscreet in the implications of his charge that the *Transcript* had urged readers of the *North American* to cancel their subscriptions as a protest against the appearance of his article before it was published. Yet he certainly was reckless in his concluding summary, when he charged Mrs. Putnam with ignorance and possible misrepresentation where he had earlier recognized nothing more than a difference in nomenclature, and, as a reply to a lady with the best Boston connections, his answer was not a model of tact.

The most serious mistake that Bowen made, however, was to follow the forms of classical rhetoric and include in his reply a formal "ethical" argument. He had recently received a tentative appointment as McLean Professor of History at Harvard which had not been confirmed by the Board of Overseers, and he held himself up before the public as a persecuted man of learning whose livelihood—and whose children's welfare—was being threatened by persecutions inspired by questionable motives. Had Bowen, as tutor of sophomores, disciplined Lowell more thoroughly in the conventions of classical rhetoric instead of tolerating him until his senior year and then sending him to Concord to gain confidence in his emotions, his former student might have responded differently to the form of this later debate. As it was, Lowell was raised by his indignation to the highest level of industry he had reached since the month he had seen two books through the press at once and to a higher level than he had perhaps attained at any other time in his life. He had a great deal of respect for the linguistic attainments of his sister, who was one of the few Americans who professed to be able to converse in Magyar and who was supposed to know ten other foreign languages and twice as many more modern dialects. He had never had much respect for the intellectual or any other attainments of his former teacher. The suggestion of the latter that his sister was either ignorant or had misrepresented her sources made Lowell (who was always both energetic and irritable at the approach of fatherhood, and whose only son, Walter, was to be born on December 22) more angry than he had ever been at Webster or even at John C. Calhoun. The rhetorical self-portrait of the learned father of a family being damaged by malicious persecution was sufficiently artificial to destroy any humane feelings Lowell might have held toward the person who drew it. He set out to tear up the picture by wrecking Bowen's claim to learning, satirizing the professor who would hide his ignorance behind his wife and children, and challenging the honesty of a man who would use the prestige of his professorial chair to support his errors as a journalist.

His article was entitled "Mr. Bowen and The Christian Examiner" and appeared in the *Advertiser* on December 28 and January 2. "It was the severest job I ever undertook," he wrote Gay the day after the second part had appeared. "I believe I was longer at work in actual hours than in writing all Hosea Biglow and the 'Fable for critics.'" Its fifteen thousand words certainly incorporated the results of more extensive reading and research than he had done for anything else he had written, and he must have had the assistance of materials collected by Mrs. Putnam and Carter. He accused Bowen of avoiding the point at issue in his reply to the *Examiner* and stated it to his own satisfaction, not as the question of fact concerning the racial situation in Hungary and the effect of the Magyar Declaration of Independence upon it, but as a question of the accuracy with which Bowen used his sources and of his general qualifications as a historian. Lowell's answer was that Bowen had treated his authorities as the Irish first treated potatoes, gathering their tops while leaving their roots underground as worthless, and few Puritan divines ever worked more vehemently through a maze of citations than he did in an effort to support the truth of his contention. And in addition to making a meticulous examination of the authorities Bowen cited, Lowell constantly threw at him the "authority" he did not cite—the *Penny Cyclopaedia* of 1838 on which, he charged, the Harvard professor of history based his generalizations concerning conditions in Hungary a decade later. So far as he dealt with Bowen's main contention at all, the Corresponding Editor of the *National Anti-Slavery Standard* simply appealed to the good sense of the public against the radicalism of the Editor of the *North American Review:*

> We think that he will not damage the cause of the Magyars much by proving that they were so conservative as to wish rather to adapt their existing institutions gradually and safely to the requirements of the time, than to resolve all parts of

their social system at once into one element of confusion, and trust that some natural process of crystalization would combine them again into the best and wisest form. It is to us a proof of sound judgment that they did not look upon the human mind as a slate from which the character inscribed by centuries of custom and prepossession could be rubbed out at one brush, and new ones put in their stead by the pencil of theoretical statecraft. The ideas of a country-village cannot be remodelled in a day, much more those of fourteen million people differing in religion, in race, in language, and in tradition.

Lowell had evidently not forgotten that Bowen had sent him to Concord nearly twelve years before in order to learn to answer Locke on such "controverted points" as the *tabula rasa;* but it is also evident that as new fires kindled old embers, Lowell forgot the answer he had learned at Concord and put out of mind all that he had been preaching and writing since.

To what extent they were affected by Lowell's article is unknown, but the Harvard Board of Overseers did not approve Bowen's appointment, and he acquired the unappreciated distinction of being the first professor of history in the United States to lose his post because the conclusions to which he was led by his historical perceptions did not correspond with those indicated by popular prejudice. His opponent doubtless had the momentary satisfaction of feeling that not even the Harvard Corporation could boil a pot when the Lowells disturbed the fire, but the episode was one he avoided recalling afterward; and it probably served, in the long run, to give him a lasting distaste for personal controversy. Harvard made up for its injustice to Bowen by offering him the Alford professorship of Moral Philosophy when it became open a few years later, and he, in turn, welcomed Lowell into the Smith chair of Modern Languages shortly afterward. The two men became occasional smoking companions and apparently let bygones be bygones. But the affair broke off Lowell's connection with the *North American Review,* and it remained broken for a decade after 1853 when Bowen gave up the journal.

It also practically broke off his connection with the *Standard,* for the two contributions he had made in November were to begin a series of unscheduled offerings and he apologized to Gay early in January for interrupting them. He attempted to begin again with "Anti-Apis," a somewhat generalized attack on the Fugitive Slave Bill which he had partly composed while lying in bed one morning "studying the rime upon the windows." Starting as a conversational argument on the theme that although the love of law is an admirable thing a person must select the law to love, it soon fell into the swing of "The Present Crisis" when denouncing those who preserved the letter of one law while dashing to pieces the spirit of a better one and all the time secretly worshiping a calf of gold. In places it showed the spirit of the Lowell who had rushed to the *Courier* the hot expressions of his reaction to contemporary events:

> Give to Caesar what is Caesar's? yes, but tell me, if you can,
> Is this superscription Caesar's here upon our brother man?
> Is not here some other's image, dark and sullied though it be,
> In this fellow-soul that worships, struggles God-ward even as we?

But he had to pump his inspiration to get the whole poem on paper: the tune was an old one, and its revival was accompanied by too many old words from his anti-slavery editorials for his new singing to have any effect of spontaneity. He promised more, but his only other contribution consisted of some verses "On Receiving a piece of Flax-Cotton" which he sent Gay on April 20 and which were published ten days later. A specimen of flax treated by the Claussen process, then on display at the London Exhibition, gave him the notion that if flax could be given the peculiar properties of cotton by chemical treatment there would be no further excuse for Southern plantations. The new discovery had "fairly taken the oxygen out of the air on which slavery (and proslavery) lives," he wrote Gay with enthusiasm; and his poem paid tribute to the scientists as "God's passionless reformers" who quietly and unobtrusively accomplished what people of his sort attempted "with human rage and heat." The poem ended with an appeal to "happy change" to come quickly and bless "Our longing sight before we die." But nothing more was heard of the process, and Lowell made no attempt to preserve the poem with which he brought his anti-slavery writings to a close.

His name was to become more prominent in the abolitionist organizations, for after having been a counsellor in the Massachusetts Anti-Slavery Society from 1847 to 1851 (and one of its "agents" in 1850) he became a vice-president in 1855; and for an anniversary meeting held in Stacy Hall on October 21, 1855, he wrote, to the tune of "Scots wha hae," a short hymn beginning "Friends of Freedom! ye who stand." The cause could claim his name, three stanzas of indifferent verse, and a small amount of his time and money perhaps, but it could no longer stir him into a burst of activity. He was ready to quit both the anti-slavery and the literary field.

When Lowell at last made his long delayed trip abroad in 1851, he left home with no change in the attitude he had expressed when he announced his plans to Gay on the November before: "The farther I can get from

American slavery the better I shall feel." He was to express similar sentiments when he went abroad again in 1855. Such enormities as the Fugitive Slave Bill, he believed in 1851, weighed him down, made him unhappy and too restless to work in his "own special vineyard." Yet he could not write about the "kidnapping" of Thomas Sims and his return to Savannah: the affair was too "atrocious." Or perhaps, for all the scandal it caused, it was not atrocious enough. Lowell depended, by habit and by faith, upon his emotions, and the emotional spring of abolitionism had been stretched so often and so regularly that it had been wearied into a constant state of low tension. An event that lowered his spirits could not raise him again to the point of spontaneous expression. Furthermore, his poem against the golden calf had shown that he found it hard to avoid repeating himself, and he had the sort of critical conscience that discouraged a career of self-imitation. Circumstances had demanded, and he had cheerfully given, more to the anti-slavery cause than he might have offered voluntarily, and he was tired and ready for a change. His resolution had been made in the autumn of 1849, and in 1851 he carried it out by selling some of Maria's land and sailing with his family for Italy.

Chapter IX

THE WASTE LAND

WHEN LOWELL set sail for Europe in the summer of 1851 with his wife, two children, nurse, and (having sought in vain for a servant with all the qualities necessary for Walter's happiness) a nanny goat, he abandoned a literary plan which otherwise would have eased his transition from the active to the passive life of letters and preserved the continuity of his career as a poet. More than a year and a half before, he had confided to Briggs his intention of calling his next volume "The Nooning" and had evidently discussed with Maria, who suggested the title, his plan to dissociate his muse from the anti-slavery cause and devote her to a pursuit of the languid beauty of summer afternoons when workers lounged around the cider jug and gossiped until the midday heat was dissipated from the hayfields. The reapers in his poem were soon replaced by a more variegated group, for his "plan," as he explained it to Briggs in a letter of January 23, 1850, was "this":

I am going to bring together a party of half a dozen old friends at Elmwood. They go down to the river and bathe, and then one proposes that they shall go up into a great willow tree (which stands at the end of the causey near our house, and has seats in it) to take their nooning. There they agree that each shall tell a story or recite a poem of some sort. In the tree they find a countryman already resting himself who enters into the plan and tells a humorous tale with touches of Yankee character and habits in it. *I* am to read my poem of the Voyage of Leif to Vinland in which I mean to bring my hero straight into Boston Bay, as befits a Baystate poet. Two of my poems are already written—one "The Fountain of Youth" (no connection with any other firm), and the other an address to the Muse by the Transcendentalist of the party. I guess I am safe in saying that the first of these two is the best thing I have done yet. But you shall judge when you see it. But Leif's Voyage is to be far better. I intend to confute my critics, not with another satire, but by writing better.

He thought of himself as still serving his apprenticeship to the art of poetry, and as he entered upon the new year of his service he momentarily forgot the feeling of middle age that had oppressed the Corresponding Editor of the *Standard* and confessed to being "very young for a man of thirty." His intent was to renounce reform altogether, to seek "more *wholly* after Beauty herself," and, if he lived, to "try to present Life" as he had seen it. The muse of reality, which he had so casually hailed in his *Class Poem,* was being gradually revealed to him in his maturity; and with the revelation came the consciousness that his youthful poems of love and freedom were less than he had thought them at the time. "What I have written will need to be carried down to posterity," he admitted, "on the shoulders of better poems written hereafter, and strong enough to carry the ore in the stone which imbeds it."

There were public inducements for Lowell to carry out his plan, for after his year of popular success he was in demand as a poet. Not only had Mrs. C. M. Kirkland asked him to contribute to the *Christian Inquirer,* but other magazines had indicated a willingness to support him in a revolt against the sort of writing he had been doing for the *Standard.* John S. Hart had urged him to put a price upon his work and write for his *Union Magazine,* and Mrs. Sarah J. Hale offered higher rates from *Godey's* than were paid to the successful N. P. Willis. George R. Graham, too, had regained the control of the magazine that bore his name and immediately turned to his former contributor for help. Godey's interest was proof enough that Lowell's anti-slavery activities had not injured his reputation beyond repair, and had the magazine editors of the country been able to read the current indication of his "mental and moral latitude and longitude" in his letter to Briggs, they would have been even more eager to lay claim to his future services. With a magazine market that could be so easily cultivated without strain upon his conscience, with a new and energetic publisher of his books in the person of W. D. Ticknor, and with promising signs that the lecture platform was ready for him, Lowell might have turned again to the career of a professional man of letters with a fair promise of success.

Yet he would have had to gamble the welfare of his family and his obligations to the household at Elmwood upon an even flow of poetic inspiration which he had begun to lose. He had been obliged to pump the well of his imagination for some of his verses in the *Standard,* and as his critical ability matured he could no longer feel the enthusiasm for second-rate poetry which had so automatically raised his feelings to a state of spontaneous overflow in his youth. He was also preyed upon by emotions that were too complex to be indulged and too serious to be repressed. The death of Rose, whom he and Maria thought "the loveliest of our three" and for whom he "would have no funeral," left him with an emptiness that argued down all the wisdom of his philosophy; and although the death of his mother, less than two months later, may have been more of a relief than a desolation, the two events together made Elmwood a sad house of memories during the spring of 1850. Nor was the birth of his son, before the following Christmas, as joyful an event as it might have been had his other children all been able to survive infancy, and his sister Rebecca seems to have been already showing signs of the darkened mind which he later described in a poem that has been interpreted as a reference to the similar condition of his mother. Recent sorrows cast their shadow over a future which showed visible signs of repeating the past. The conflicting purposes which Lowell had exhibited in his contributions to the *Standard* and the unbalanced anger of his attack on Bowen could not be overcome and reduced to the calm pursuit of beauty by mere resolution. They required an emotional relaxation which circumstances did not permit or a control that the poetic impulse could not overcome.

Furthermore, the magazine offers with their promise of public success were not in themselves a sufficient stimulus to any great activity. Lowell's inability to look upon his work as a commercial product made him consider each proposed honorarium a judgment upon his merit, and the periodical market which was open to him had fallen off from its peak during the early rivalry of Graham and Godey. The former was willing to pay only forty dollars for his "very best poems," and the special rates offered by the latter were ten dollars less, although he was ready but by no means anxious, to pay fifty for a "long" poem. To Lowell, who had put aside the memory of his own experience with the *Pioneer* and consequently had not yet acquired the editorial point of view, their offers represented a lower estimate of his powers than Graham had held some years before, and he seems never to have realized that a successful publisher was obliged to steep his literary appreciation in business caution. Yet he did acknowledge his old association with Graham by extracting from his "Private Journal" some verses which had not been used in "The Ghost-Seer" and sending them to him for publication, under the title "Out of Doors," in his magazine for April, 1850. He allowed Graham, in December, to publish a poem "To J. F. H." which he had written in July as a personal letter inviting his old friend Frank Heath to "revisit all the old places" with a group who were going to the Isle of Shoals. But Graham had wanted a humorous poem, in the vein of Lowell's best-selling works, for his Christmas number, and the verses to Heath, although light enough, were hardly an adequate substitute. Lowell was finding it difficult to undertake "humor by contract," the quarrel with Bowen was driving him beyond the normal limits of his intellectual energy, and the only poem he wrote specifically for *Graham's,* while dated in December, 1850, was not finished at that time and so was put off to an untimely appearance in April. In the meantime, he consoled his publisher with a fragment "Appledore" from the unfinished pictorial poem he was composing for "The Nooning." Such a method of dealing with his most liberal editor was not one which would have encouraged Graham or anyone else to continue baiting him with the prospect of professional success.

Nor was "The Unhappy Lot of Mr. Knott" any considerable literary success when it finally appeared. The subject of spiritualism which Lowell had in mind when he made his contract for humor was one which superficially attracted his eye for the ridiculous without arousing enough genuine interest to provoke the awareness of details and implications necessary to a successful satirist. For Lowell, despite his many references to his own "visions," had little patience with those who confused the experiences of a heightened imagination with the phenomena of nature, and the spirit rappings that began in Rochester in 1849 and spread excitement all over the United States during the following year, attracted less serious attention from him than they did from so sane a man as Robert Browning when they were heard in Italy a few years later. The "raps that unwrapped mysteries" inspired him to the sort of ingenious rhyming that the rats of Hamelin had inspired in Browning, but his comic story of Mr. Knott's medieval mansion haunted by the poltergeist of Eliab Snooks contained none of the bitterness that was to appear in Browning's portrayal of "Mr. Sludge, 'the Medium.' " Lowell, of course, had none of the personal incentive to satire that affected Browning's treatment of the same subject, and without it he was not a very successful humorist.

Yet all the while Lowell was working at intervals upon poems for "The Nooning." According to his letter to Briggs he had already written, by January 23, 1850, "The Fountain of Youth" and the transcendentalist's address to the Muse and was in the process of composing his account of the voyage of Leif to Vinland. But before he had finished "Thorwald's Lay" from that poem (which, as "The Voyage to Vinland" eventually became the story of Biörn rather than of Leif) he wrote most of his "Pictures from Appledore" and some nine manuscript pages of blank verse that were to be partially printed first as "A June Idyl" and later as "Under the Willows." He also had apparently composed a considerable part of his countryman's tale "with touches of Yankee character and habits in it" before he went abroad, for he later assigned "Fitz Adam's Story," in which the narrator finds the countryman in his memory rather than under the tree, to the period of his original plan for "The Nooning." In any case, he was sufficiently far along for Ticknor to announce in the early autumn of 1850 that the book was "forthcoming," and in an undated letter probably written before the following Christmas, he assured Fields that he would finish the manuscript during the winter—that two more poems, in addition to the first two completed, were already "partly written and long ago wholly thought out." But his promise was made in the midst of the excitement caused by his recovery from a period of mental hibernation, and after his attacks on Bowen in the *Advertiser* and the comic poem for Graham he was taken up with his plans for going abroad and had no time for the sort of drudgery required to drive a book through the last half of its passage from the bright nebulosity of an idea to the ink-stained reality of proof sheets. He could manage an occasional poem for the *Standard* and a few verses that were to remain in his notebook for further revision and later publication, but he could not go abroad and have his "Nooning" too. The latter, he decided, could wait.

Lowell's trip abroad was, in fact, an undertaking too serious to permit any sort of dalliance with the muse during the fifteen months he allowed himself. The doctrine of self-culture which was explicit in his serious poems placed a solemn obligation upon him to make the most of the experience to which he had been looking forward for more than a decade. Living for two months in Florence with his friend William Page and spending the winter in Rome with the Storys, he studied Italian manners and customs, the language and the art of the country, and the observances of the Roman Catholic Church. In his leisure time he attempted to keep a journal, but the expatriate company in Rome (which included a number of old friends and at least seven other Lowells who were not members of his immediate family) was good, and even the journal was unsystematically kept although it did provide material for three prose articles in *Graham's* two years after he returned. He learned to distinguish the leading Italian painters by their several styles, and under the direction of Page he cultivated his enthusiastic fondness for the paintings of Titian; but the only verses that came to him were those found in occasional letters, in a little comic "parable" eventually published in 1888, and in two punning prologues written for amateur performances of the comic interlude in *A Midsummer Night's Dream* in which he took part.

The sorrows of Elmwood also followed him on his vacation. News that his father had suffered a paralytic stroke reached him in the autumn and kept him uneasy in conscience during the first half of the winter until he received some evidence of his partial but unmistakable recovery. Mabel's measles kept her parents in anxiety during the spring, and although Walter escaped that disease, he caught another after a brief visit to Naples, and the little family spent an unexpected, harried, extra three weeks in Rome before he died and was left behind in the Protestant Cemetery there. Maria's own health had been only slightly, if at all, improved by the winter abroad, and the cold feeling of mortality lay heavy on James's mind during the summer. Yet they conscientiously made their planned tour of Venice, Switzerland, and the south of France, and Great Britain before taking ship—with Thackeray and Arthur Hugh Clough—for home at the end of October.

The varied emotions and new experiences of his trip placed a long gap between Lowell and some of the old interests from which he was already drifting at the time he left. He found the modes of life in Europe agreeable to him in many respects, he wrote his father on January 12, 1852, but he had found nothing which would replace Elmwood as a place of permanence. It was to Elmwood rather than to the field of controversy that he wanted to return. As the time approached, on October 1, he wrote his father again, urging him to avoid "all extremes of mental condition, whether of excitement or of depression," and added without any consciousness of irony:

> I say this because I find that you have been writing about the slavery question, or rather I surmise that you have from something I saw in an Antislavery journal. You know that I would be the last to counsel any supineness in regard to that horrible iniquity, but I look upon you as one who has done his duty in the particular function to which he has been called, and who is now fairly entitled to his retiring pension of quiet fireside offices and enjoyments. . . . I feel a particular gratitude for having been withdrawn to such a distance from our politics that my eye has acquired practice in looking at generals instead of particulars, and the ability to compare masses instead of getting bloodshot in straining at minute and worthless details. One may be as far off from them at Elmwood as in Europe.

Upon his return, the son found his father still partially incapacitated, almost stone deaf, and full of recollections of things past. "Little Bec," too, was settling into her speechless retirement; and James and Maria had more and more of the responsibility of Elmwood where little Mabel wandered alone over the ground that had felt so many childish footsteps.

Lowell himself was ready to begin a new phase of his literary career, skipping the search for poetic beauty which he had begun before he went abroad and turning instead to his notion of writing of life as he had lived it. His friend Charles F. Briggs had fine plans for a new magazine of original American literature and was anxious for Lowell to revive "The Nooning" for serial publication in the first numbers, but the poet seemed incapable of recapturing the muse he had left behind when he sailed for Europe. The best he could do for the first number of *Putnam's Magazine* was to extract "The Fountain of Youth" from his portfolio and print his description of the "woodland enchanted" with a concluding question which was peculiarly apt to his new situation of increased responsibility and enforced maturity:

Dare I think that I cast
In the fountain of youth
The fleeting reflection
Of some bygone perfection
That still lingers in me?

He did not, it seems, dare to enter the enchanted woods and look over his whiskers for the reflection of a childish face in the fountain. He would write out of his experience rather than out of the enthusiasm he had lost. On November 29, Longfellow met him on the street near Craigie House: he was on his way home from John Bartlett's bookshop where he had bought a blank book in which to write his novel.

The book had cost two dollars, and its substantial binding and sturdy pages indicated more calculated determination than Lowell had exhibited in any literary plan since he began keeping his scientifically arranged "commonplace book" in college. Two weeks later, Longfellow noted in his diary that Lowell had begun his novel. The author's notebooks bear out his statement made nearly thirteen years later that he "had sketched the characters, and even written the first chapter," for he seems to have gone back to the notes he had probably made while composing *The Biglow Papers* and penciled in additions. The dates of these fragments are by no means certain, but some bits of wisdom he derived from life as he had lived it reveal that he was by no means so free as he had been to run the literary race he was again undertaking. The new deafness of the uncle who interrupted the hero's fine remarks with "How much did that pig weigh?" was perhaps an indication that he bore the burden of Dr. Lowell's irrelevances with more strain than Arthur Hugh Clough had observed when he noticed them while dining with the family. But more surprising are the numerous references to women's temper. There was "No such conductor of feminine electricity as a husband," noted the husband of the gentle Maria, and added immediately afterward: "There are two quarters of the female mind in which thunder and lightning are brewed. The Western of positive storm and the Southern of meekness." Lowell was learning with Longfellow at about the same time that "as one grows older," even though his children did not multiply, "the time is broken up; and household cares usurp the place of poetic dreams and reveries." They evidently interrupted novel-writing as well, for although he made a neat copy of the first chapter of his novel on December 16, he never got any further with it despite the fact that, contrary to his usual practice, he kept the rest of the book invitingly blank for its possible continuation.

Nor was his career as a magazinist getting underway with perfect smoothness. When he sent "The Fountain of Youth" to *Putnam's* he hinted that it should be worth a hundred dollars, but after receiving Brigg's startled reaction he quickly agreed that half that sum was a proper remuneration for his contributions. Yet even after reaching a financial agreement which he considered generous on his part, and which was certainly liberal on the part of the magazine, he became involved in embarrassing difficulties. For the pressure of his annual New Year's settlement put him in too great a hurry for his money, and his draft upon Putnam (who had adopted the new practice of paying by check) was protested. The publisher immediately sent his check, but the poet's tender feelings had been injured to such an extent that he tried to withdraw his second contribution from the hands of the editor. Nevertheless, "Simpkins on his Baldness" (which seems to have been the poem in question, although it was only tentatively attributed to Lowell by his literary executor), appeared in the March number along with Maria's more serious poem "Necklaces," and Lowell, unable to write seriously, offered to continue in a comic vein. But "Our Own Correspondent," as he wanted the magazine to style him, was not altogether sure of himself. On February 17 he promised Briggs five pages by the following Monday and added:

I wrote one hundred and fifty lines yesterday, and it is thought funny by the constituency in my little Buncombe here. I have hopes that it will be the best things I have done in the satiric way after I once get fairly agoing. I am thus far taking the run back for the jump. I have enlarged my plan and, if you like it, can make it run through several numbers. It is cruel impudent,—sassy, I meant to write. Some parts of it I have flavored slightly with Yankee—but not in dialect. I wish to make it something more than ephemeral, and shall put more thinking into it as I go along. My idea for it is a glass of punch, sweetness, sourness, spirit, and a dash of that Chinese herb favorable to meditation.

In short, he did not know exactly where he was going to land when he made his jump; and, like a small boy with more determination than confidence, he was making a long run because he was afraid of the leap. The assurances he put on paper were the protests of one who had no genuine confidence in his success, and when he sent the manuscript three days later, he exhibited both his determination and his diffidence: "I think it will get good as it goes along," he declared with an air of conscious understatement. But he could not conceal his anxiety. "*Is* there any fun in it?" he asked: "Or am I a fool?"

The appearance of such doubts after a man finishes his work is normal. But their persistence throughout the period of planning and early stages of composition was indicative of a state of mind in which neither fun nor satire could flourish. Briggs was probably troubled to find a reply to Lowell's questions. He knew, from his experience with the prose satire that Lowell had contributed to the *Broadway Journal,* that the distinction between editor and friend was not very clear in Lowell's mind, yet he apparently tried to make it in this case by assuring his sensitive contributor that he found the work amusing while indicating by his actions that he feared a contrary judgment from the public. To Lowell's annoyance, he divided the preliminary run into two installments and "diplomatically" ignored the author's several inquiries for advice concerning its continuation. Briggs had reason for suffering the distress of a divided mind which was hesitant about committing itself to one clear-cut opinion. He had a warm and sincere appreciation of Lowell's ability and perhaps an exaggerated notion of his potential value to the magazine. But no editor could be so misguided by his inclinations that he could see much good in the first part of "Our Own." The poem contained nothing of general interest in its subject matter; it got nowhere even as a preliminary "run"; and even the little movement that it possessed required the assistance of such incongruous crutches as a parody of Spenser's doggerel "arguments" in *The Faerie Queene* and an imitation of Byron's manner in *Don Juan*. Friends who were primarily interested in James's cleverness might have praised numerous neat allusions, striking phrases, and ingenious comic rhymes; but only a single-minded desire to admire the author could hold the reader's attention through even the first short installment Briggs decided to print. Unfortunately, however, the editor could not depend upon that slender means of attracting readers to his magazine, for it was the policy of *Putnam's* to offer its substance on its merits and without signatures.

But despite the lack of forthright encouragement, Lowell was going ahead with a continuation of "Our Own," which was so far from clear in his own mind after he sent the first parts to Briggs that, lacking a complete copy, he hardly knew where to take it up when he began again in the latter part of March. He was also nervous about a review of his literary career which Briggs was planning for the May number as a companion piece to the series on young American authors which had begun briefly with Donald Grant Mitchell in January and been continued more pretentiously with Herman Melville in February. Let a man of sense say what he will, he urged Briggs on March 24, but don't give a fool a staff to knock down a friend. He was still insisting that "Our Own" would *"get good"* in time but continued to be doubtful of his ability to write seriously or to feel very free about writing anything "while Mrs. Grundy is criticizing what has gone before." In April, Briggs was forced to admit frankly that the public did not like "Our Own," and Lowell learned from some other source that the author of the review was to be a young man whose judgments would certainly not please Maria and whom he himself considered more pert than wise. He showed an inclination to be nasty but no intention of giving up. "I am sorry the public don't like it, because it is good and is going to be better," he wrote, and added with a design to hurt: "Perhaps I had better try my hand at a tragedy?"

Lowell's jump into the real matter of his poem for the June issue of *Putnam's* was, in fact, considerably better than the preliminary sections. In it, he finally turned to a loose narrative which was supposed to reflect his recent travels. He satirized the discomforts of contemporary railroad journeys and some of those found on shipboard, and two of the passages he considered good enough to include in his poetical works as "Fragments of an Unfinished Poem" and "Aladdin." But Briggs was forced to cry quits at the end of the installment. Lowell continued to assert his own belief that "there is good in it" and also claimed that some things he heard had given him reason to hope that it was becoming popular; yet he generously accepted his friend's judgment on the ground that Briggs owed a greater duty to the financial interests of his employer than to those of a mere friend, and he agreed to wind up the whole business with the return of the unpublished portion of the manuscript and upon payment of fifty dollars for each of the three unsuccessful numbers for which Briggs apparently had never formally contracted. He spoke of the possibility of printing the finished work with the notation "as it was d——d in Putnam's Magazine" on the title page and implied by the general tone of his long letter of June 10 that he would send Briggs no more poetry. Yet the only additional part which appeared in print was incorporated—with many apologies by the author—into "Cambridge Thirty Years Ago" and thus perforce published by Briggs the following year as the work of "a satirist of some merit, whose works were long ago dead and (I fear) deedeed to boot."

II

HIS FAILURE to get back into the routine of writing successful magazine verse affected Lowell deeply. Although his annoyance at the circumstances relieved him of some "imaginary stuff" that was darkening his mind at the time, he confessed his discouragement in the long letter of June 10, 1853:

> Authors ought certainly to be as sensible as shopkeepers, and to know that if the public does not want their wares, it will not buy them any the sooner for being called fool and blockhead. There may be a satisfaction in it, but it will not help pay a quarter's rent. The best way is to take down sign, shut up shop, and go Westward where there are fresh fields and pastures new, and both fortune and health to be dug from the soil. *My* West is to be found in a course of lectures, which I have already been paid for, and which I am to deliver before the Lowell Institute next winter. I dare say they will be all the better for my having some of my conceit knocked out of me, and I can revenge myself on the dead poets for injuries received by one whom the public won't allow among the living.

He was already working on his lectures, expecting to finish his novel, and planning to complete "The Nooning" which, he was determined, *"shall* turn out well." But, as his notebooks show, he was not able to settle down consistently at anything; and in August he gave up and took a vacation by going moose hunting in Maine with a party which included his young nephew Charles. He failed to shoot a moose, but he did hit upon a fresh field of literary endeavor which would help pay a quarter's bills. He kept a journal in which he not only recorded his experiences but his interested observations of Down East characters and conversations, and the document proved to be such a successful combination of "a little nature, a little human nature, and a great deal of" himself at his light-hearted best that he sent it to Briggs for publication.

Briggs apparently thought the journal too discursive, and Lowell was again annoyed at the criticism for which he had asked. But he was not nearly so tender about his prose as he was about his poetry and finally admitted:

I believe all you say is true and if you will bring the 'darned thing' on with you, I will show that I learned some woodcraft down East by cutting it down. But I think the principle you go on is a wrong one. I don't mean in this particular case. But I doubt if your magazine will become really popular if you edit it for the mob. Nothing is more certain than that popularity goes downward and not up (I mean permanent popularity) and it is what the few like now that the many have *got* to like bye and bye.

The notion that a magazine should be edited for a few immediate readers who would be followed by the mob "bye and bye" is so peculiar that it shows, rather conclusively, that despite his denials Lowell was brooding over his own "particular case"; and the wording of his added, unnecessary protest indicates his state of mind: "I have pretty much given up the notion that I can be popular either upward or downward, and what I say has no reference to myself. I wish I could be." But "A Moosehead Journal," when it appeared in the November issue addressed to "Edelmann Storg" (a Swiss hotel-keeper's misreading of William Story's signature, when the Storys and the Lowells were traveling together the year before), did prove popular, and the author was encouraged to write again after the same fashion for *Putnam's* and to print parts of his Italian journal in *Graham's* for the following year.

While busy preparing his Journal for publication and working on his series of lectures, Lowell had little time for other activities. The Reverend Thomas W. Higginson tried to interest him again in reform by asking him to address a temperance gathering, but the young man who had discovered more to admire in the wine-drinking temperance of Europe than in the abstinence of his native country replied: "I should not have the least notion how to address the Whole World's Convention even if I had anything to say to them. I can only declare that I sympathize heartily with any movement that shall promote temperance or shall elevate man or woman socially or morally. The *How* must be left to the case of individual experience." As a poet, he was giving way to Maria, whose verses were being published in *Putnam's* and whose "Necklaces" he learned with delight had been attributed to Tennyson by Oliver Wendell Holmes. "She is quite cutting me out as a poet—though she laughs when I tell her so, God bless her!" he wrote Briggs in September. Yet he found that he could write prose in his spare time, and although Briggs had "deferred" publication of a sketch of Allston he had written for *Putnam's,* Lowell went ahead during September with another sketch of the Cambridge he had known as a boy and eventually incorporated his memories of the painter in it. His new literary experiment with "A Moosehead Journal" had, of course, not yet appeared and received its popular acclaim, and Lowell, as he had done so often before, was summoning up recollections of his childhood as a relief from uncertainty and worry over his immediate future.

By the end of September, however, all literary plans and professional worries were driven out of his mind. Maria had been ill and he had gradually realized that she apparently did not have enough force left for her customary recovery. During the first week of October he was beginning to anticipate her death; and, although such friends as Edmund Quincy refused to "admit the idea" which he apparently broadcast, his expectations proved true for the first time since he had returned from Europe, and she died on October 27. For nearly a month Lowell was completely desolate. One period of his life had come to a close, and he spent his time going through his papers, sealing up his old letters with black wax and filing them away. Yet he was unwilling to wear his grief upon his sleeve, and it was not until the day after Thanksgiving that he was able to unburden his soul to Briggs, who was then his most intimate confidant:

> I keep myself employed most of the time—in something mechanical as much as possible—and in walking. I have been horribly nervous sometimes. I could not keep myself warm, and then sometimes my thoughts all became external to me somehow, and talked to me and talked faster and louder till my head would get confused and I had to go out and walk all the morning. But I have the most beautiful dreams and never as if any change had come to us. Once I saw her sitting with Walter on her knee and she said to me, "See what a fine strong boy he is grown!" And one night as I was lying awake and straining my eyes through the gloom and the palpable darkness was surging and gathering and dispersing as it will, I suddenly saw far far off a crescent of angels standing and shining silently. But oh it is a million times better to have had her and lost her, than to have had and kept any other woman I ever saw.

He felt in himself "an indefinable sense of having begun to die" which had nothing to do with the fact that his body might live on for fifty years longer: the blood was no longer a pleasure to him running in his veins, and he was perpetually weary without any physical cause. He tried to express the same idea in a poem, using a sheet from the block of blue paper on which Maria had pathetically attempted to write her will, but he was not able to finish it; and the first version of his "Ode to Happiness" as he had possessed it when his

> blood would dance and run
> As full of morning as a breeze

contained none of the consolations of the infinite shoeblack philosophy which appeared in the additional lines he was to print in the *Atlantic Monthly* for April, 1858, nor did it contain any of the "Tranquility" he celebrated in the finished poem. His agony was unrelieved.

Yet in the midst of his Gethsemane he experienced a stronger desire to express his grief publicly than he was willing to admit. Francis H. Underwood had been after him to contribute to a new literary and anti-slavery magazine which he planned to begin in January, and while going through his papers Lowell found an old poem which he sent to him on November 23, two days before he wrote to Briggs. "The Oriole's Nest" (which became simply "The Nest" when, after Underwood's magazine failed to materialize, it was finally printed in the *Atlantic Monthly* for March, 1858) seemed to him then, he confessed, perhaps better than it really was because "an intenser meaning" had been "added to it" by his own desolation. Whether or not the poem was as good as he thought it, its revival stimulated him to an effort to express its "intenser meaning" more directly in another poem in which the empty oriole's nest reappeared and in which the author again made use of the device of a "palinode" to draw a contrast between a cherished memory and a bitter sorrow. The notebook version of "Auf Wiedersehen" shows that the memory came easily to Lowell but that he had to wrestle with his sorrow before he gave it the controlled expression which he revealed in the pages of *Putnam's Magazine* a year later. One of his rejected stanzas was apparently revised and used to give greater pathos to the little poem on Blanche, "After the Burial," before it was eventually published in 1868, and almost half of that poem may have been written out of his grief for Maria rather than with emotional reference to the owner of the "little shoe in the corner." But Lowell's impulse was to suppress entirely the first desperate expressions of his emotion, and the fourth stanza of his published "Palinode" reflects a more confident, if still searching, Christian faith than did the cry for hope which he first put on paper in his notebook. A few years later, when Lowell had mastered the art of meeting a deadline and had settled down to being primarily what he called "a good provider" rather than a poet, he exploited unused portions of his notebook rather thoroughly; and the objectivity which accompanied his acquisition of a certain amount of professional craftsmanship usually enabled him to revise the spontaneous expression of his most powerful emotion. The ten lines beginning "We, who by shipwreck only find the shores Of divine wisdom" near the conclusion of "Under the Willows," for example, appear in his notebook just after "Auf Wiedersehen" and were written soon after Maria's death. But they originally began: "I who have just been shipwrecked on the shores Of Divine Wisdom." The mature craftsman could change the direction of the ways of God to man and improve the meter of its description with nothing more than an editorial pencil.

But during the winter of 1853, Lowell showed few signs of the emotional restraint that he was to achieve later. He apparently found another old poem, "The Singing Leaves," for publication in *Graham's Magazine* for January, and he drove himself to the task of preparing selections from his Italian journal for publication in the same periodical for April, May, and July and eventually, he hoped, in a book. He also worked on his Old Cambridge essay which appeared in *Putnam's* in April and May under the title "Fireside Travels." But when he tried to make verse of his broodings before his hearth, he was ill at ease and uncertain. He had not only lost contact with the public; he had lost his private audience, the one person to whom every one of his earlier poems had been submitted for approval before it was allowed to take its chances with the world. His first attempt to strike "the unused chords" of poetry for a public audience after Maria's death was in "A Winter Evening Hymn to my Fire," which he sent to Briggs on February 8 with the comment:

> I send you a poem which I have just written and which I should be glad (pecuniarily) if you would like for your Magazine. There must be something wrong somewhere when an author of fourteen years' standing is doubtful whether a contribution of his will be acceptable or not. But if the Public don't want one's wares, I am not so void of commonsense as to grumble or hold my head higher as a blessed martyr. It is more reasonable to suppose *one* fool than twenty millions. I am trying to employ myself, but vainly, I fear. This is the first poem of mine which Maria never saw. Do you understand that?

In order to make his friend understand, he laid bare all the agony he kept concealed from such newer friends as Charles Eliot Norton, to whom he had sent a gay ode of thanks for a gift of cigars only a week before:

I am very unhappy sometimes. It is worse than lonely here, with my father per fectly deaf, and often alarmingly excitable, and my sister who never speaks for a week together. And if I go into society, I despise myself when I come back. I am trying to make a book out of my Italian Journals and letters. I am going to print a bit of it in "Graham" and when it appears, I wish you would tell me your opinion of it. You see I have not a single *old* friend near me, nor within reach of me. It would do me good if I could only unload my heart now and then. It *is* lonely and bad is it not? But I have learned to pray and I try to keep my soul pure and sweet, and sometimes I feel as if something were near me, but oftener not. And then I lie awake for hours thinking of my razors and my throat and that I am a fool and a coward not to end it all at once. I am not an ass and never could deceive myself. I know perfectly well that my nature is naturally joyous and susceptible of all happy impressions. But that is the very reason why I am wretched. I am afraid of myself. I dread the world and its temptations for I do long to keep myself pure enough to satisfy her who was better than all I can say of her. I often troubled her while she was here, but I cannot bear to now that she is in entire felicity. Do forgive me. I know that all this will seem exaggerated to you there in your office surrounded by all the bustle of life and its thousand healthy distractions. But I cannot help getting rid of it now and then. Tears come hardly and hot after thirty, but I have found the secret of them and something seems to catch my throat as I am writing. Remember that you are an old friend and that I love you and do not despise me for uncovering that dear dead face for I cannot help it. I cannot talk about it. I cannot write it in my journal to be found perhaps hereafter and pried into by dry executorial eyes. But do just bear it as one of the incumbrances of my friendship and burn this letter and my last one which I am afraid is as bad.

Lowell's distress was caused not only by grief but by the feeling of having more responsibility than he could bear. Dr. Lowell had set his mind that year upon resigning the whole of the salary paid him by the church he could no longer serve, and his alarming excitability may have been caused by his son's anxious efforts to dissuade him from making the offer which the church, generously and fortunately, declined to accept. For Lowell's own income from the property Maria left was only six hundred dollars a year, and although he was fortunate in obtaining a good governess for Mabel in Frances Dunlap, the sister of one of Maria's Portland friends, he was made desperate by the fact that half his income had to go to pay her salary. It was "absolutely necessary" that he should earn money somehow, and he was anxious for Briggs to commission him to finish the account of Cambridge thirty years ago which Maria had liked in the part she had seen before her death. Graham was only buying his name, he suggested, and Briggs could have the "best" of his prose. He also promised to send more poems, but, although he could not have helped being hopeful, he was timid about them and accompanied "A Winter Evening Hymn to my Fire" with an interpolated comment: "(don't tremble—not to be printed)."

The prospect of being deluged by the literary works of a close friend who was desperately anxious to sell his wares apparently did make Briggs tremble. He could hardly have failed to be aware of Lowell's ability to send his manuscripts to a friend and expect a reply from an editor. He knew that the poet needed friendly encouragement, but his position made it impossible for him to supply that need without obligating Putnam to follow his kind words with a check. He seems to have hinted that the "Hymn" was too late for the March issue of the magazine and quite evidently failed to grow enthusiastic about its quality. Lowell, whose own doubts had given Briggs the cue for his editorial reaction, characteristically achieved a state of confidence as soon as he received the criticism he invited: "But you are all wrong in the matter," he declared; "It *is* good and you will think so one of these days." He also continued to ask for the return of the unpublished parts of "Our Own," by which he was still willing to "stand" and which he was determined to finish according to the original plan and print. "I have got enough left in me yet," he announced, "to float that even were it heavier." His momentary self-assurance gave him a lordly indifference to the fate of his poem: "as it is too late for March I care no more about it," he proclaimed—Briggs might "give" it to Sydney Gay for the *Standard*. Toward the end of his long letter he rose above the editorial judgment of *Putnam's Magazine:*

> I shall send you nothing more. If you want anything write, as Graham does and I will give what I can, and there an end. Only I shall judge myself whether what I send is good enough to print. Don't think me annoyed about the poem. I truly am not. But I *will* be popular with myself, if with nobody else and I am old enough to judge for myself. I had another poem which I knew to be better than that I sent, but I would not send it, because I would not do it the wrong to put to any one's judgment whether it would *do* or no. I am as good natured as Punch, but as proud as Lucifer and can't help it, if I were taken down once a week all the rest of my life. I am sure that there are better things in my poems than you think, and that the world will acknowledge it one of these days. My only fault is that I have written *too* sincerely but I am not a fool and am quite willing to wait till my turn comes. My poems are not so good by ever so much, as they ought to be. But I will write better ones yet; strong fellows that can bear the weak ones on their shoulders.

Under such pressure, Briggs, who genuinely sympathized with Lowell in his morbidly excited state of mind and who prized him as a friend and as a contributor, managed to get the fireside hymn into the March number of the magazine.

Lowell's letter of February 15 was almost as excited as the one of the week before, and although he described the earlier one as reflecting "a state of morbid excitement" and apologized for his "silly" reference to "those Sheffield instruments" as a "cry of pain" coming from a long suppressed "agony of mind," he showed no real signs of being much calmer. He was obsessed with his own failure to achieve "popularity" and felt that if it had been his fortune to achieve it, he could have written "with the force of all his admirers." While asserting his indifference to any good opinion other than his own he was, in fact, explaining his literary failure on the grounds of his inability to gain the good opinion of a large public. He declared that he had been "only a learner" when he had written his earlier criticism and would write no more, and in the next paragraphs he promised to try to write something about Clough (whose *Bothie* he had wanted to review before Maria's death), damned Alexander Smith, and launched into a whole series of critical comments on other authors. Incoherent, erratic, and uncertain, he was in a miserable state of mind.

He got out of it by working like the proverbial dog on his Italian journal, his essay on Cambridge, and on some uninspired verses—and by receiving some flattering attention from *Putnam's* which asked for a daguereotype for publication, a notice which the magazine had not yet paid to any other contemporary author. The request put him in a good humor, and, having received a check from Graham, he offered to make his pose either "respectable or authorlike." By the last day of February he was eagerly writing Briggs for a report on some verses he had sent and was recognizing that the "dreary collapse of doubt" into which he had fallen was a normal reaction to "the enthusiasm of writing anything." He was taking a new interest in the world about him and seems to have been rather pleased, despite his professions to the contrary, at having been made a director of the New England School of Design for Women with the responsibility of assisting in the award of prizes that was being made in Boston. If James was not wholly himself again, he showed unmistakable signs of his old self when he exclaimed: "I meditate an edition of Shakespeare! and a life of Dean Swift!! I meditate everything, for I must keep busy at work."

Yet the new poetry which aroused his enthusiasm for composition was far from being strong enough to compensate for the weakness he saw in his early verse. The contrast between the first part of "Without and Within" and the first half of his "Fireside Travels" reveals the truth, so far as he was concerned, of the observation he had made in his notebook not long before: "The Death of a beloved one, at least, does this for us—if it takes away the present it gives us back the past in its entirety and sacredness." The historical essay was rich in humanity. The contemporary poem showed no signs of the imaginative sympathy that Lowell had learned to admire in other writers and had managed to some extent to get into his own verses. Looking through the glass of a restaurant door at his freezing coachman waiting outside, the purported author of the verses could see no difference between the coldness of the winter wind and that of the bright smiles of his female companion; and he could see no difference between well-fed and hungry boredom. A second poem with the same name and a sub-title "The Restaurant" which appeared the following month was a semi-humorous variation on the same theme: this time Lowell balanced the good teeth and sound digestion of the hungry outsider against the ills of the wealthy diner within, and the minor worry over the source of the next meal against the major problems which beset the man of affairs. Both poems were dramatic, of course, and in neither did the author represent the diner's point of view as necessarily his own; but there was an insensitive complacency in both that Lowell had occasionally exhibited in his most youthful poetry but from which he had been free for a decade and a half. It was to grow as time went on, yet it is evident from these verses that if Lowell felt a sort of spiritual death creeping upon him (and twenty-five years later he wrote Charles E. Norton that he had originally ended the poem with the author in his grave still "feeling dreadfully bored") it was the kind of disease that dulled his imagination enough to let him die in comfort.

But Lowell was unable to attain anything like a steady feeling of complacency. He was keeping himself occupied in part by preparing editions, with introductory essays, of Wordsworth, Keats, and Marvell for Professor Child's series of *British Poets,* and he was filling his emotional vacuum with new friendships—most notably with Charles Norton and his sister Jane, and, a few months later and to a lesser degree, with William J. Stillman who visited him in the interest of a new periodical *The Crayon.* He had determined during the spring to solve his immediate financial difficulties by selling some of his land, and he found a great delight in little Mabel who was then approaching her seventh birthday. But he could not settle down to one literary plan. His notebook and a letter to Fields show that he was restlessly playing with the idea of reviving Hosea Biglow, but his new notes were only variants upon sentiments already expressed in print by Birdofredum Sawin in the last of the printed *Biglow Papers:*

> Whenever an Amerikin distinguished politishin,
> Gits kind o' oneasy and begins definin his posishin
> And to the suvrin people takes the tallest kind o' shine,—
> Wal, I fer one, feel sure he aint got nuthin to define.

The new Democratic federal administration had apparently begun to annoy him, and as he contemplated his own financial situation he seems to have allowed himself to brood jealously upon the fortune of his friend Hawthorne whom he had seen off with such sincere good wishes a year before. There was, of course, no allusion to Hawthorne in the reference to speeches in the *Morning Post* in his draft of a prose sketch, "My Cousin's Family Portraits," written at about the same time. The opening sentences, however, were rather curious in view of the fact that Hawthorne had once occupied the Boston Custom House and was then Consul at Liverpool:

> "You are a furious radical, my dear sir, and, if I may credit your speeches (which I always read in the Morning Post with delight and instruction) perfectly sincere in that way of thinking. You believe that all men are born equal with each other, and a little better than anybody else, but with different *adaptabilities,* your own being clearly for an inspectorship in the Customs or the consulate at Liverpool.

The sketch itself had enough of Sterne in it to show some anticipation of Holmes's later "Autocrat" and to be reminiscent of Lowell's own efforts to write a novel, and it seems to have been designed as a prose adaptation of the "sincere journal in a picture gallery" which he had planned to include in "Our Own." It was never finished, however, with sufficient completeness to reach its intended destination in the pages of *Putnam's*. Nothing seemed to go well that spring: even the "Leaves from my Italian Journal" halted and then broke off after three installments in *Graham's*.

Maria was too much with him. She inspired him to the best poetry he did write at the time, but successful magazine verse was not written according to the sort of inspiration she provided. He described his search for a proper pipe on which to play in "Invita Minerva"; and his draft of the concluding stanza of that poem, as it appears in his notebook, reveals both his emotional state and his consciousness that his efforts were not in accord with the art of poetry. The true poet he portrayed did not seek but was sought by the "mighty Mother" of his inspiration, who exclaimed:

Thou who dost my harmless subjects wrong
Learn that 'tis not the singer makes the song,
The rhythmic beauty wanders dumbly long
Nor stoops to any daintiest instrument———

But he could not finish. He managed the last line as it appears in the published version, but the next to the last would not come. The page is filled with doodlings of initials, names, and drawings of leaves, and the poem reveals his difficulties. "But matches some poor reed," he wrote, crossed out "and then" which followed without getting anywhere, and left the rhyming word "consent." A new attempt produced "Till found its mated voice" with "the two" crossed out and the original rhyming word left untouched. Then his mind wandered into the past. "Darling Molly—Maria Lowell," he wrote—and followed the exclamation triumphantly:

Till, found its mated lips, their glad consent
Makes mortal breath than time and fate more strong.

It was only necessary to change "glad" to "sweet" in order to produce the final version.

Lowell spent the greater part of the summer of 1854 with his brother Charles at Beverly, and there, although his forthcoming lectures were occasionally on his mind and he was working on his introductions to the *British Poets* and planning an edition of Maria's poems, he rested. The woods and the sea, he wrote Norton, formed a lotus land: "It does not make us forget, only memory is no longer recollection, it is passive, not active, and mixes real with feigned things." Sometimes, though, his memory was active enough, causing him to write in his notebook:

Weeping beside my Past's unburied corse
Which I with every choicest flower have strown,
Alone as only he can be alone
Who feel[s] through body and soul the harsh divorce
From what made solitude society
And crowds a solitude for thee and me...

But immediately after this he wrote the little poem, "Seaweed," in which he found an image of hope in the inevitable turn of the tide that, like the orbit of the comet in one of the poems of an earlier despondency, would bring him again in touch with divine consolation. It was probably at about the same time that he wrote "The Windharp" which he sent to Briggs (in answer to a letter received in Beverly) with "Auf Wiedersehen" on October 4 with instructions to print them or not as he saw fit. They appeared in the December *Putnam's* opposite the portrait which, since Lowell never managed to have a new daguereotype made, was badly engraved from Page's portrait and formed the fifth of the magazine's series of authors. With the next issue *Putnam's* changed owners and editors, and these were the last contributions Lowell made to the journal.

As the end of the year approached, Lowell was working on an edition of Donne and perhaps of Shelley, but was obliged to devote himself primarily to the composition of his lectures. They did not come easily to him, for he had no critical system into which he could fit his discourse and he was nervous about his first formal appearance before a large audience. He managed to write only six before the series began on January 9, 1855, and the effort kept his mind so occupied that he had little time for correspondence and practically none for poetic dreams and reveries. He printed a considerable amount of poetry during 1855 but little if any of it was new. "Hakon's Lay," which appeared in *Graham's* for January was the part of the unfinished "Voyage to Vinland"; and the long "August Afternoon" section of "My Appledore Gallery," which was printed in Stillman's *The Crayon* for January 3, was taken almost entirely from the notebook poem out of which he had made a selection for Graham before he went abroad. There is no evidence concerning the age of the last "Appledore" selection published in the same magazine four weeks later, but it could hardly have been written during the busy December that immediately preceded its publication and was probably composed not long after the earlier sections. Lowell also sent Stillman his "Invita Minerva" for *The Crayon* of May 30, but by that time he was on his way to New York and his second trip abroad. It was to be nearly two years and a half before he published another poem.

III

LOWELL HAD reached only the half-way point in his life in 1855, but, as a poet, he was never wholly to recover from his passage through this wasteland of emotional aridity and public indifference. Of his poetic career, little remained except for a few periods of occasional inspiration, a certain amount of philosophy, and an accomplished craftsmanship which enabled him to exploit fully those relics of youthful enthusiasm still left in his notebooks. Instead of writing strong poems in his maturity that could carry his early writings down to posterity on their shoulders, as he had promised, he found that his early verses often had to be used to sustain his later productivity and reputation. Without the occasions which inspired the second series of *The Biglow Papers* and his Civil War poems—especially his great Commemoration "Ode"—and the philosophy he called upon during the summer of his disappointment when he wrote *The Cathedral,* he would never have received the modest competency of his old age when his publishers guaranteed him an income of two thousand dollars a year from his books. But he could never have written the most memorable of the later Biglow Papers or kept his name so regularly before the readers of magazine verse had it not been for the early notebooks he exploited so craftily.

For the mature Lowell, working with the sort of craftsmanship he condemned in his youth, was able to put together from the rejected material of his younger days a body of poetry at least as substantial as that produced by particular occasions or by meditative philosophy. The notebooks themselves are so mutilated that it is impossible to discover the full extent of his use of them, because the pages he tore out to copy, or to use in order to avoid the labor of copying, have of course disappeared into the wastebasket in his study or in the composing room. Yet abundant evidence remains that he did draw upon them frequently during the first twelve years of his work for the *Atlantic Monthly,* for the volume *Under the Willows,* for *Heartsease and Rue,* and even for the writings that were given to the public posthumously as his *Last Poems.*

Perhaps the best illustration of his economy and workmanship may be given in an account of the fate of the "June poem" which he had intended to use as an introduction to "The Nooning." The precise date of its composition is not altogether certain, for Lowell (whose memory on such matters was never very accurate) attributed some of it to a period of "twenty years ago" in a letter to Jane Norton in 1867, to 1848 in a letter to James T. Fields written on April 9, 1868, and to 1851 or 1852 in a later letter to J. B. Thayer. There is some internal support for the earlier dates in the close and evident connection of the imagery used in it and that of the June verses in *The Vision of Sir Launfal,* but the fairly clean copy found in his notebook contains clear indications that it was made between the death of his daughter Rose on February 2, 1850, and the birth of Walter on December 22 of the same year—and probably immediately after receiving a letter from Friedricka Bremmer, describing the Middle West in terms of Norse mythology, written from Cincinnati only ten days before Walter's birth. It was, in any case, an old poem when, in 1857, he became editor of the *Atlantic Monthly* and faced the problem of getting out a journal which required three contributions from the editor for its first number. Lowell probably culled his portfolio and notebooks in search of something which would do for the occasion and read again the nine pages of blank verse from which he had already extracted some lines on the bobolink and June for his "Fireside Travels." The immediate result seems to have been that a few lines stuck in his memory and inspired him to a sonnet which he later called "The Maple" while the poem as a whole was put aside for more effective and conscious exploitation first five and then eleven years later.

His procedure during those years was so complicated that it can be described with reasonable clarity only by an illustration of what happened to a specific section of the poem in his notebook:

First all the willows swarm with saffron blooms
The caterpillars plump with fleece of gold;
The gray horsechestnuts open myriad hands
Drooping and soft as callow hands of babes
Just born; all down the loose-walled lanes, high-arched,
The barberry hangs in curves its strings of flowers
Grapelike, whose shrinking hearts the schoolgirls try
With doubtful thrust of pin; then, at a touch
All orchards turn to drifts of rosy cloud,
Every tenth crotch a robin's log hut shows,
Licensed preëmptioner, beneath barn-eaves.
Strange migrants, who eastward make remove,
Cliff-swallows cling and glue their gourds of clay;
'Twixt tree and tree the oriole flushing swift
Lightens, or like a sailor climbs the shrouds
Of many an elm ere, whistling, he elects
The happy bough to swing his hammock in.
From post to post, along the sunny fence,
The bluebird shifts his little load of song,
The blackbirds creak and clatter in tall elms,
Holding their windy parliament prorogued
By some young Cromwell with his grandsire's gun
Decrepid now, and doubtful in its speech
Swift of retort enough at Concord Bridge;
But oh winged rapture, feathered soul of Spring,
Blithe voice of woods, skies, waters, all in one,
Pipe blown through by the warm mild breath of June
Shepherding her soft flocks of wooly clouds,
The bobolink has come! With white pole thrust

> Through crowding appleblossoms on topmost spray
> He sings, or rather like the very soul
> Of liquidness imprisoned in a bird,
> Bubbles and gushes out we know not what
> Of lyric witchery, rises, without pause
> In that delirium on, 'twould seem, is lifted
> By some pent force of native lightsomeness
> With tremulous wings, or yielding to its will,
> Runs down, a brook of laughter, through the air.
> June is the pearl-month of New England's year . . .

The flow of unconscious recollection or of inadvertent repetition between this section and the June part of *The Vision of Sir Launfal* is perhaps less clear than may be seen in other parts of the poem, but there is some connection between the robin's finished "log hut" here and the "house" the same bird was "plastering" in the earlier poem, and between the last line of this selection and his earlier description of June as "the high-tide of the year." The sonnet in the *Atlantic Monthly,* however, brings the two poems together by representing the robins as "Plastering new log-huts" in the branches of the maple. Nor did Lowell have occasion to observe in the manuscript of the June poem that "The Maple puts her corals on in May." But the observation did occur to him in connection with his later use of this section of the manuscript and is a part of the complexity which has to be dealt with in any consideration of his mature craftsmanship.

These somewhat tenuous connections are matters of memory about which a later reader may speculate without being able to analyze their precise significance. The author's procedure is clearer on the other occasions when he obviously had the manuscript before him when he wrote. The first and least important of these came during the composition of "Cambridge Thirty Years Ago" when he quoted from both his Indian Summer and his June poems. From the latter he took the fourteen lines on the bobolink quoted above and reduced them to eight for purposes of quotation. The reduction is of some significance, for it shows in general that Lowell was less inclined toward expansiveness in his maturity than he was in his youth and, in particular, that he was more precisely realistic when he changed the fanciful "pent force of native lightsomeness" within the bird to the external force of "the wind." He used some images from the poem in his Lowell Institute lectures in 1855 and some others in "The Power of Sound: A Rhymed Lecture" two years later. But he read it again most carefully in the winter of 1861–62 and, according to his letter to J. B. Thayer, adapted the passage beginning "O strange New World" in "Mason and Slidell: a Yankee Idyl" from it. The only connection between the above selection and that second number of the new series of *Biglow Papers,* however, is to be found—and then barely possibly—in the "grandsire's gun" which spoke at "Concord Bridge" and may have reappeared to Hosea among the "ghosts o' guns" he saw while thinking of his grandfather and of the same fight. It was probably after this reading that Lowell decided to adopt a suggestion which had been made to him by Arthur Hugh Clough and turn a considerable part of the poem into dialect verse which would be more truly an idyl than was the Mason and Slidell poem. At any rate, he composed "Sunthin' in the Pastoral Line" in time for an appropriate appearance in the June number of the *Atlantic Monthly* for 1862.

One passage from the pastoral will illustrate the efficiency with which Lowell used part of his manuscript poem (while, incidentally, remembering his related sonnet on "The Maple") and the ingenuity with which he translated it into dialect and rhyme:

> Fust come the blackbirds clatt'rin' in tall trees,
> An' settlin' things in windy Congresses,—
> Queer politicians, though, fer I'll be skinned
> Ef all on 'em don't head against the wind.
> 'Fore long the trees begin to show belief,—
> The maple crimsons to a coral-reef,
> Then saffern swarms swing off from all the willers
> So plump they look like yaller caterpillars,
> Then gray hossches'nuts leetle hands unfold
> Softer'n a baby's be at three days old:
> Thet's robin-redbreast's almanick; he knows
> Thet arter this ther' 's only blossom-snows;
> So, choosin' out a handy crotch an' spouse,
> He goes to plast'rin' his adobe house.

The "log hut" of the original which had been plastered in the sonnet became adobe, of course, for the sake of the rhythm, and the "callow hand of babes Just born" may have become those of a baby "three days old" merely from the need of a rhyme; but the published version as a whole shows the greater precision of observation and statement which accompanied the ingenuity of Lowell's mature workmanship. The same qualities are perhaps even more evident in another passage in which he restored the bobolink to his original place among the appleblossoms while keeping the realism of the lifting power of the wind (transformed, more appropriately, into a June "breeze") that he had introduced into the extract used in "Cambridge Thirty Years Ago":

> Gladness on wings, the bobolink, is here;
> Half-hid in tip-top apple-blooms he swings,
> Or climbs against the breeze with quiverin' wings,
> Or, givin' way to 't in mock despair,
> Runs down, a brook o' laughter, thru the air.

If Lowell had been able to preserve all his early verses, unpublished, for this sort of working over he might have been a great poet.

But there was little unpublished material left in his notebooks, and he had to rework the same veins of early inspiration again. Six years after the pastoral number of the second series of *Biglow Papers,* for another June issue of the *Atlantic,* he made still further revisions of the old manuscript and produced "A June Idyl" which, after hearing a rumor that Whittier was planning to print "A Summer Idyl," he renamed "Under the Willows" for publication in the volume by that name. For the later poem he transcribed, in general, unused passages from the original poem with relatively few revisions; but he also sifted some of the well-worked sands for their remaining streaks of color. June was restored as "the pearl of our New England year" with some improvement in rhythm; and lines from the sample passage which he had admitted from "Sunthin' in the Pastoral Line" were carefully extracted and embedded in a new context. He revived

> The bluebird, shifting his light load of song
> From post to post along the cheerless fence;

and, with his mature use of more concrete imagery, he revised his comparison of the oriole to a sailor:

> *Heave, ho! Heave, ho!* he whistles as the twine
> Slackens its hold; *once more, now!* and a flash
> Lightens across the sunlight to the elm.

He also used the lines on the bobolink which he had skipped while writing "Sunthin' in the Pastoral Line."

> Shepherding his soft droves of fleecy cloud,
> Gladness of woods, skies, waters, all in one,
> The bobolink has come,

he announced, changing the original "Blithe voice" to "Gladness" because the bird had been "blithe" twice before when springing from these manuscript lines into print. The mystery of his bubbling and gushing becomes slightly clearer when he,

> like the soul
> Of the sweet season vocal in a bird,
> Gurgles in ecstasy we know not what
> Save *June! Dear June! Now God be praised for June.*

Lowell had used other lines from the quoted passage in "Sunthin' in the Pastoral Line" and perhaps had found in the reference to "some young Cromwell" the suggestion which grew into Hosea's vision in that poem; and the total result was that he managed to make some economical use of every line in this specific passage during the course of his later career as a poet. He improved the original while doing so, but, as he himself recognized in his letter to Fields, he could not do work of the same quality when he did not have some early verses to improve.

The other verses designed for "The Nooning" which still remained unpublished in 1855 had a similar, though not so complicated, history of a revision to which the author was forced by a conflict between the compulsion to publish and his inability to recapture the enthusiasm of his youth. When he decided to complete "The Voyage to Vinland" for the *Under the Willows* volume, as he wrote Norton on October 7, 1868, he had "clapt a beginning on it, patched it in the middle, and then got to what has always been my favorite part of the plan"—which, incidentally, turned out to be a prophecy of the New World rather than an actual venture into Massachusetts Bay. For the beginning, he certainly let his mind play back over his earlier writings and probably got out the "Private Journal" in which he had jotted down fragments of blank verse inspired by his Chapmanesque mood of the early 'forties and which he had used in part for such heroes as Prometheus, Cromwell, and Columbus. In any case, the heroic Biörn represented a revival of the sort of character Lowell held up before himself in his youth. When "the heart within him seethed with blood That would not be allayed with any toil," his desire for "some joy untried" becomes reminiscent of the young poet who admired Tennyson's "Ulysses" and wrote in his notebook:

> The blood that makes
> The tough cheek ruddy and the warm heart light
> Is noblest;

and the effect upon him of the Promethean dreams that came "To strain the lagging sails of his resolve" may also have been suggested by such youthful words as "the sail of my desires doth strain" from his notebook. Perhaps more definitely, however, the effect of these dreams in making Biörn decide that youth was too valuable to be staked in a shoddy gambling game for everyday rewards when he had the power to make himself a part of "the dreams of later men" is suggestive of the scrapped moral of "Rhoecus." How much memory and how much review there was in this "clapt-on" beginning of "The Voyage to Vinland" is uncertain; but it seems reasonably clear that, in some respects, the new part of the poem was really the oldest; for the introduction to "Gudrida's Prophecy" was based on Lowell's observation of whales and phosphorescent water recorded in the journal of his trip abroad in 1851, and the prophecy itself was an entirely new composition which merely incorporated some old thoughts on the new world.

The fate of his "Transcendentalist's address to the muse," which Lowell had described as one of the first poems completed for "The Nooning," is less certain, for no complete manuscript version appears to be extant. But his notebooks contain some lines used in "L'Envoi: To the Muse," which he printed in the *Atlantic* for March, 1860, and used as the conclusion to *Under the Willows;* and the moral of that poem is Emersonian enough to suggest that it was originally designed to be a transcendentalist's account of how he learned that a true poet was a passive "Listener" rather than an active "Singer." If it was the poem planned for "The Nooning," it also was revised before publication, for it contains an arresting image of the cathedral at Milan which hardly could have been composed before the author's trip abroad and an adjoining reference to the Maine woods that probably was suggested by his moose-hunting expedition after he returned. They were probably introduced when he used it to close his Institute lectures. But there is nothing in it to indicate that it went through any extensive revisions or received the substantial additions that he gave to his June poem or "The Voyage to Vinland."

"Fitz Adam's Story," according to a letter to Norton, received extensive additions before it was published in the *Atlantic* for January, 1867, growing so nearly out of hand in fact that the countryman's tale "with touches of Yankee character and habits in it" became almost lost in the description. How much of the poem was written at the later date is undeterminable, but the later composition, in accord with Lowell's habits, probably consisted of the sketch of the narrator, of his "prelude," and of some revision in the tale which was almost certainly written earlier. Fitz Adam himself was not the original narrator but apparently a character salvaged from the unwritten story in which Lowell reviewed his early love for Hannah Jackson. His notes for it show that the young man (who "was not of strong character") was to pursue the young lady (who was "a blonde" in the poem) to California and there "Find her married to a stick" but with "no children." Lowell bought a guidebook to California from John Bartlett on February 2, 1849, wrote the lines on love in a village which have been quoted in connection with his own affair, jotted down some indication of the gentleman's restraint when he found his lady on her western hill, and concluded the notes with an ambiguous comment which probably was supposed to characterize his disappointed hero: "Fitz A. Hating mankind, he would not hurt a fly." Such was the Fitz Adam of the later poem, who was "not precisely" a "cynic" but one who was forced to cultivate an attitude which would protect "a heart too prone to love and trust." Fitz Adam is one of the most interesting and provocative of Lowell's characters, for although he is by no means a self-portrait, his origins lie deep in his creator's own personality and experience. The other poems designed for "The Nooning" are of less interest: "The Fountain of Youth" was reprinted in *Under the Willows* with no significant changes from its appearance in *Putnam's,* and the "Pictures from Appledore," although considerably rearranged when its various sections were put together for the same volume, was not rewritten.

The unfinished poems of "The Nooning" did not provide all the material for later use which Lowell found in his notebooks. One of the volumes supplied him, from the period of about 1849, with part of the first and all of the second sections of the poem which he elaborated into "In the Twilight" for the *Atlantic Monthly* of January, 1868; and if "The Finding of the Lyre," which was one of the few poems published for the first time in *Under the Willows,* was not an old poem, it grew out of one of the earliest entries in his "Private Journal" when he noted "The invention of the lyre" as a subject for a poem. "The Dead House" was actually written just before it was published in 1858, but that, too, had its origin in an earlier fancy about "dead houses" which he had developed rather fully in a letter to Mrs. Francis Shaw on January 11, 1853. The extant manuscript of "The Darkened Mind" (which was considerably revised for publication in *Under the Willows*) gives no indication of its date, but it was most probably written during the period of deep emotional distress revealed in the letter of February 8, 1854, to Charles F. Briggs in which he spoke of his "sister who never speaks for a week together."

Of the poems collected in *Under the Willows* which did not have their origin in whole or in part before 1855, ten (including the introductory one "To Charles Eliot Norton") were minor occasional poems, five were "Poems of the War," and only seven were poems that might have just come to the author as so much poetry came to him in his youth. "The Nomades," "Self-Study," "Fancy's Casuistry," "Gold Egg: A Dream Fantasy," "An Ember Picture," and "The Foot-Path" provide weak evidence, indeed, that the muse visited Lowell with any regularity during the thirteen years in which they were presumably written. He produced the second series of *Biglow Papers* in that time, of course; and they, like his Civil War poems, show that a particular stimulus could still arouse in him the excitement of poetic creation. But even the best loved of the later *Biglow Papers* represent a skillful treatment of an earlier inspiration: the origin of "Sunthin' in the Pastoral Line" and, to a lesser extent, of the "Mason and Slidell" idyl has already been mentioned; and "The Courtin'," as is well known, grew by demand and the accident of available space from its original six stanzas into a complete narrative for the 1857 collection of *Poems* and, finally, was rounded out with sentiment in 1864 as an autograph for the Baltimore Sanitary Commission by the author who feared that he had "spoiled it." The ability to produce poetry spontaneously and for the sake of poetry alone had been lost to Lowell after Maria's death and the excitement which immediately followed; and he thought poorly of that which he did write *invita Minerva,* on occasion or by industry, for he wrote the mother of Charles and Jane Norton that he would never have been able to publish the *Under the Willows* volume had she not made copies of the many poems he had not bothered to preserve.

While going through his notebooks just before publishing *Under the Willows,* Lowell found in the mutilated book that contained his unfinished poem for "The Nooning" another suggestion which he worked up into verses for the *Atlantic Monthly* for January, 1868: "As the flying Dutchman hails vessels and puts on board letters addressed to people long dead, so some poets who find no inspiration in the world about them and seek it in bygone forms and thoughts seem to direct their poems to the departed." The conception tickled him, he wrote Thayer, but for once his craftsmanship failed and he felt that he had spoiled it in the finished poem, "The Flying Dutchman." He wrote Fields to the same effect—that the conception of the verses was good but the verses themselves were bad. Yet he collected them along with "Fitz Adam's Story" and "The Origin of Didactic Poetry" (in which he had set forth his anti-moralistic resolution of 1849 for the first number of the *Atlantic*) among the poems of "Humor and Satire" in *Heartsease and Rue,* which appeared in 1888 and bore further witness to the poverty of his later inspiration. For this volume was made up almost entirely of purely occasional poems supplemented by a few gleanings from the almost-exhausted notebooks and magazine pages that reflected the better half of his poetic life. From the *Atlantic Monthly* he took (among many other poems) "The Nest" which he had sent to Stillman in 1853 and the sonnet on "The Maple"; and from the notebook containing the Flying Dutchman suggestion he took the two couplets which were dated "1853" in the manuscript and formed the first of the "Sayings" included under the general heading "Epigrams." The other three "Sayings" and "A Parable" beginning "An ass munched thistles" came from another section of the same book, although the last was revised before it was printed with the date "Colonna, Italy, 1852." There was not much left for him to use except occasional bits of light verse, and he probably drew upon them for autographs, for one of them entitled "A Valentine" (included in a notebook between part of "Our Own" and "Auf Wiedersehen" and thus probably written on the February before Maria's death) somehow got copied toward the very end of his life and so was inadvertently included in the posthumous little volume of *Last Poems.*

It was the "Superstition of old man, maid, poet, and lover," Lowell remarked "In the Halfway House," "That cream rises thickest on milk that was spilt." But as he grew older and as his muse became more and more inconstant in her visitations, he may have realized that the belief was not entirely superstitious. At any rate, his later poetry would have been less in quantity and poorer in quality had he not spilled his surplus of youthful enthusiasm into his notebooks and left it there for later skimming.

Chapter X

THE FLOWING WATERS

I

JAMES RUSSELL LOWELL probably accepted the commission and the advance payment for his Lowell Institute lectures with little hesitation and with no doubts concerning his ability to do justice to the family name. The notion to lecture on the English poets had been in his mind for a decade, and from time to time after publishing his *Conversations on some of the Old Poets,* he had been jotting down notes on what he might say about their successors. Yet when he realized that he had committed himself to twelve hours of discourse before an audience which was accustomed to hearing the best speakers and scholars of the time, he became conscious of the fact that a miscellaneous collection of shrewd comments and witty illustrations would not be enough to uphold his responsibility. As a long poem required a narrative upon which the reader could coast between his periods of active responsiveness, so a series of lectures needed some systematic point of view which would give coherence to the comments, point to the wit, and aptness to the illustrations. Lowell had in his notebooks and in his head an abundance of bright verbal beads but little intellectual thread upon which to string them. And he knew that if he went before a Boston audience and merely scattered his pearls they would be outraged. He was obliged to be more systematic than he had ever been before in his criticism.

Lowell evidently had been invited, or had expected an invitation, to deliver the series of lectures some months before he informed Briggs of the fact on June 10, 1853, for one of his notebooks shows that he was working on them before he wrote the third installment of "Our Own" in the latter part of March. Some of his brief notes for the introductory lecture also reveal his difficulties in getting started. "Shakespeare's dramatic imagination passions," he jotted down; "Chaucer's narrative imagination things." Three other attempts at classification followed: "The poetical Spenser"; "Imagination Shakespeare human"; "Imaginative Milton." And these in turn were followed by a despondent note, "Definitions lost between brain and paper," amplified in the margin with the comment: "Smothered in featherbeds of words."

He was probably still acutely conscious of his obligation to get out of his featherbed and find a critical line to adopt when he wrote Briggs on February 15, 1854, that he had been "only a learner" in his earlier efforts and added, without meaning it, that he would never write any more criticism. He had learned to appreciate the sort of sympathetic, dramatic imagination which he found in Shakespeare and Robert Browning, missed in Landor, and laughed at in Thoreau; and he had learned to make distinctions in greatness among the English and some continental writers without very much conscious analysis of the reasons for those distinctions. His long youthful thoughts about the nature of poetry and the poet, which he had expressed so often in his own verse and early essays, apparently were of little use to him as a critic, for the poets he most admired unfortunately did not fit the notions he had once held of what a poet should be. Shakespeare and Chaucer were not reformers, either directly or indirectly; and of the third English poet, he had already written in his notebook that "Perhaps the sole advantage of Restoration was that it took Milton out of politics." Lowell himself, of course, had tacitly given up his early poetic ideals when he retired from the *Standard* and determined to write only of beauty and of life as he had lived it; and about the only important element in his early theorizing that survived his change of mind appears to have been his insistence that the imagination was unlimited in its field of operation—that "The poetical has nothing to do with morals," as he put it in his notes for his lectures, "but imagination *has*."

All of these attitudes were to appear in the scheme of reference which he eventually worked out and laid down in the first of his Institute lectures, but they did not, by themselves, constitute anything like a complete system. It is apparent from his notebooks that Lowell read Gray's letters in search of help, and from the lectures themselves that he read Johnson's *Lives of the Poets* and Coleridge's *Biographia Literaria* and other critical writings; and he undoubtedly consulted other critics including possibly Schelling and almost certainly Emerson. But none of them, with the exception of Coleridge, did him very much good. Gray provided him with only incidental assistance and Johnson merely gave him a point of departure; and although both Coleridge and Emerson supported the distinction between the Fancy and the Imagination, Lowell professed to find Coleridge's treatment of the latter faculty too narrow, and his critical purpose was too specific for him to make much use of the soaring generalizations of the contemporary who had, in any case, made so many of them before practically the same audience. Yet his own attitude toward literature had been transcendentalized in his youth, and the tendency of both Coleridge and Emerson to relate "Imagination" to transcendental "Reason" probably supported him in his assumption of a similar connection in his lectures. Coleridge may have given him additional help in his discussion of poetic diction during the course of his lectures and he echoed Emerson's *Nature* on language, but neither the English nor the American critic could provide him with the system that he needed.

Certain coincidences of illustration suggest that Lowell may also have turned to his old college textbook—Dugald Stewart's *Elements of the Philosophy of the Human Mind*—for such help as it could provide; but whether he did or not, it seems reasonably certain that he ultimately decided to ignore his reading and be "original." He had to have a system of critical reference which would enable him to say something coherent about such literary subjects as "Piers Plowman," "Metrical Romances," "Ballads," and "Poetic Diction" and to pass relative judgments upon such authors as Chaucer, Spenser, Milton, Butler, Pope, and Wordsworth as well as upon their less important contemporaries and intermediaries. All the critics he had read possessed limitations, for his practical purpose, and he could not avoid the imminent necessity of creating some sort of system of his own. Yet it is obvious to the reader of his first lecture, that, however much Lowell may have believed in the power of intuition or inspiration, his critical "originality" was achieved by a combination of many old ideas and the invention of a few new terms while he was engaged in the process of rationalizing common judgments. And it also appears obvious that the ideas he used with the most assurance were those which he had acquired earliest in life and possibly by this time simply took for granted, without any clear awareness of their source in the writings of his father's old teacher whose textbook he himself had studied in college. For if Lowell had looked anew into Stewart's *Elements,* he had certainly done so with such casualness that the rather dry book made no verbal impressions upon him which would make a fresh use of it demonstrable. It was the pattern of Stewart's aesthetic thought, rather than the specific expression of his ideas, that dominated the approach to literature which may be found in Lowell's lectures.

When Stewart had made the sharp and frequently reiterated distinction between the subservient Fancy and the higher Imagination which had caught Lowell's attention in his youth, he made a somewhat elaborate analysis of each of these two faculties. The former was distinguished by the fact that it dealt entirely with the material world—largely with externals—and should properly be described with reference to its materials as "rich" or "luxuriant." It depended upon the associative powers of the mind and therefore, with reference to the quickness of the association, could properly take the further adjective "lively." It was closely connected with Wit (which also depended upon the power of association and bore a relationship to Humor that Stewart clearly implied but did not analyze) and with "invention" in science (which Stewart opposed, again not too clearly, to the "discovery" of scientific truths). Because of these relationships and the ambiguity which might result from using the general term "Fancy" in a restricted sense, Stewart was normally careful to speak of "poetic Fancy" in his discussions of literature and in doing so added another element to his definition. For the "poetic Fancy" was not only "luxuriant" or "rich" in its possession of materials, but it presupposed a peculiar sort of mind which was abnormally sensitive to them. "According to this limited idea of Fancy," he wrote, "it presupposes, where it is possessed in an eminent degree, an extensive observation of natural objects, and a mind susceptible to strong impressions from them." Thus the poet almost always possessed "an exquisite sensibility to the beauties of nature."

All of this was in Lowell's first lecture as a scheme of reference which he used in the discourses that followed. Fancy was "a frailer quality" existing on a lower level than the Imagination, he told his audience, "which in combination with sentiment produces poetry, with experience, wit." Both "Fancy and Wit play with what is outward and finite," and, especially, "Fancy takes delight in life, manners, and the results of culture, in what may be called *scenery*." Like Stewart, Lowell found the relationship between Wit and Humor comparable to that existing between the Fancy and the Imagination; and he, too, classified Donne's imagination, in a loose use of the term, as that of a man of "science" who "solves problems in rhyme, that is all." Lowell did not always agree with Stewart in the relative amount of emphasis he placed upon all these elements in his discourse, for in his introductory lecture at least—except perhaps by implication—he did not stress the desirability to a poet of a rich and luxuriant Fancy and he paid much more attention to the "exquisite sensibility" which a poet was supposed to possess.

Lowell himself had been praised by Poe in his youth for his phrenological "ideality," and, although he clearly indicated his lack of sympathy with the "system" of phrenology in his lecture, it was probably inevitable that what Stewart considered a susceptibility of the mind should have become in Lowell's terminology a "poetic sense" or a "poetic sentiment" (as Poe had also described it) which combined with the Imagination or with Fancy to produce poetry. But whether it was a "sense," a "sentiment," or Dugald Stewart's "sensibility," it was clearly "exquisite" when it existed to a degree sufficient to make a man a poet: the quality that primarily distinguishes such a person, he made clear near the beginning of his discussion, "is not merely a sense of the Beautiful—but a so much keener *joy* in the sense of it (arising from greater fineness of organization) that the emotion must *sing* instead of only *speaking* itself." By definition, "the poetic sense is a joyous feeling of the Beautiful, arising from greater fineness of organization." From whatever source this emphasis upon the poetic sense may have taken its origin, however, Lowell undoubtedly adopted it because it helped him solve the practical problem of having something to say about some of the more difficult material he planned to deal with in succeeding lectures.

Stewart was much less comprehensively satisfying on the Imagination than he was on the Fancy. He was not only inconsistent in his classification of it as a passive "intellectual" power while treating it as "the great spring of human activity, and the principal source of human improvement"—an inconsistency which had been resolved for the youthful Lowell by the influence of Mackintosh—but he was undetermined about its relationship to "the fundamental laws of belief." He seemed at times to think of it as being a power comparable to the "reason," but when he was forced to commit himself specifically to an opinion about the matter, he was extremely cautious. It was clearly a creative power; but on one occasion, at least, he thought of it as being determined by the cultivated "power of Taste" and said explicitly that "the power of imagination, is not the gift of nature, but the result of acquired habits, aided by favourable circumstances." Yet on another occasion, he implied that these habits and circumstances were those which controlled the lower impulses and so left the explicitly undefined imagination free to develop on its own accord:

> One of the principal effects which a liberal education produces on the mind, is to accustom us to withdraw our attention from the objects of sense, and to direct it,

at pleasure, to those intellectual combinations which delight the imagination. Even, however, among men of cultivated understandings, this difficulty is possessed in very unequal degrees by different individuals; and these differences (whether resulting from original constitution or from early education) lay the foundation of some striking varieties in human character.

The nature of the imagination, in short, he left ambiguous; but concerning its extent as well as its importance he was clear. He objected strongly to those critics who had limited it to perceptions of sight and insisted that not only the other senses were included within its bounds but that "All the objects of human knowledge supply materials to her forming hand."

Lowell seems to have supplemented this broad but indefinite conception of the imagination with ideas derived from Coleridge and Emerson. It was under their influence that he regularly contrasted it with the "Understanding" in his lectures, thereby tacitly identifying it with the transcendental "Reason," and defined the highest form of poetic imagination as "intuitive reason infused with humanity." He also defined it, in one of his high-flying passages, as "the continual resurrection of the soul in the body"; but he recognized that his extremely transcendental accounts of its nature were not of much practical use to the critic. As he came down to earth, he wrote "more seriously":

Imagination, then, as applied to expression would seem to be that breadth of sympathy which can include the emotion of some other person with its own, and that energy which can then condense this emotion in a word or phrase so vivid that it shall reproduce the same emotion in the reader.

Coleridge, he added after some further discussion,

borrowing a term from Schelling called it the *esemplastic* power, that is, the pressing together in one, a long word which defines well enough the condensing operation of the faculty in expression. Elsewhere he calls it the translation of man into nature, a very happy phrase for labelling its action in a mind like Wordsworth's, for example, but still not inclusive enough. I think the difficulty with Coleridge's definitions is that he unconsciously based them too much upon an analysis of poetic minds. But it is to be found in all great minds which possess breadth rather than force or acuteness.

He himself found it in philosophers and (scientific) discoverers, in fanatics and reformers; and his own practical definition of it might be described, in terms of its sources, as a mixture of Stewart and Coleridge, flavored with Mackintosh and Carlyle and subjected to the practical test of its ability to provoke a reaction in someone else. But when he considered it apart from the problem of expression, he always restored the conception of its transcendental nature:

> I think that pure Imagination is the intuitive conception of a universal law, and a tendency to confound one's own individuality with it, or to state it in a way that expresses the mode of its operation, it is the so entire loss of self in the object contemplated as to be conscious of that particular thing's relation to the law to which it is at that moment subject.

As an example of it, he added an illustration which had occurred to him before he had composed his definition: "It was not merely seeing the apple fall that gave Newton a clue to the law of gravitation. It was because his mind fell with it."

But Lowell did not trust the transcendental element of intuition which he kept attributing to the imagination. Like Stewart, he was later to discuss Rousseau as a dupe of his ill-regulated imagination; and, although he touched with approval upon the organic theory of unity in his lecture, he was not at all sure that the creative power of the imagination could regulate itself. Stewart had possessed a traditional regulator in the eighteenth-century "Taste" and had defined "Genius in the Fine Arts" as "a cultivated Taste, combined with a creative Imagination"; for "without taste," he explained, "imagination could produce only a random analysis and combination of our conceptions." The word "Taste"—especially if capitalized—was too suggestive of the eighteenth century for a man of Lowell's prejudices, and he found a substitute for it in "the poetical *faculty,*" which he distinguished from the poetic "sense" and identified as "the *shaping* spirit." Yet his discussion of it shows that his "faculty" was practically indistinguishable from the Scottish philosophers' "sense" of Taste:

> But some degree of this instinctive sensitiveness to order and proportion, of this natural incapability of the formless and the vague, seems not only natural to the highest poetic genius, but to be essential to the universality and permanence of its influence upon the minds of men. The presence of it makes the charm of Pope's Rape of the Lock perennial; its absence will always prevent such poems as The Faery Queene, Hudibras, and the Excursion (however full of beauty, vivacity, and depth of thought) from being popular.

The "poetical faculty" and the "poetic sense," he observed, were rarely united in the same person; but either, apparently, could combine with either the Fancy or the Imagination to produce poetry. Alone, the Imagination was "dumb," and in combination with other senses and faculties, it produced achievements outside the realm of poetry.

Despite Lowell's criticisms—both explicit and implied—of Coleridge on the Imagination, however, he found the *Biographia Literaria* illuminating and useful on the distinction between Shakespeare and Milton which he himself had "lost between brain and paper." Coleridge had made it clearly in connection with his analysis of Shakespeare's narrative poems:

> While the former [Shakespeare] darts himself forth, and passes into all the forms of human character and passion, the one Proteus of the fire and the flood; the other [Milton] attracts all forms and things to himself, into the unity of his own ideal. All things and modes of action shape themselves anew in the being of Milton; while Shakespeare becomes all things, yet forever remaining himself.

A similar observation appeared in the *Table Talk:* "Shakespeare's poetry is characterless, that is, it does not reflect the individual Shakespeare; but John Milton is in every line of the Paradise Lost." Lowell rounded out his critical theories by accepting this distinction between two types of imagination and escaped from his "featherbeds of words" by giving each of the types a name which had not appeared in Coleridge. The loss of a poet's self in his subject matter and its relationships, as he put it, was an operation of the "dramatic" imagination which was characteristic of Shakespeare and of the highest poetic genius. The absorption into one's self of the subject matter until it became colored with the one's own personality was an operation of the "narrative" imagination characteristic of Chaucer, Milton, and the second order of poetic genius. Had Lowell been able to look back critically over his own early efforts at criticism, he might have realized that this was the distinction he had once tried to make between Browning and Landor and had vaguely made between Keats and Byron before he added the clarifying, third-to-last paragraph which distinguishes his essay on Keats from his 1854 introduction to the poet's works. The two forms of the imagination were different in kind and in degree, but they both were responsible for poetry infinitely superior to that produced by the lowest level of "poets who have properly no imagination at all but only a pictorial power" such as might be found in the "oriental poems" of Southey.

Lowell's stage direction at the end of the manuscript of his first lecture was "A very magnificent bow!" He deserved to take it. For he had made his entrance into the brotherhood of professional critics by discovering how always to have something to say. His arrangement of ideas did not constitute a formal critical system so much as it represented a series of definitions, a formality of relationships, and a hierarchy of values which could guide his thoughts toward fresh critical opinions even though he might not directly apply them. They referred primarily to the capabilities of a writer, who was required to possess such fundamental qualities as an active "fancy" and a factual "understanding" in order to collect and use the materials from which literature was formed. These materials might be shaped by the structural "poetic faculty" or informed by the "poetic sense," but before they could be turned into the highest form of literature they had to be transformed by an "imagination" which could be either "narrative" or, at its best, "dramatic." No single work of literature could be characterized by a display of all six of these qualities, but a consideration of any piece of writing with reference to them would enable the critic to make a thorough diagnosis of its merits and shortcomings. These terms and the various synonyms which Lowell used for them, in short, formed what the older rhetoricians would have called the "commonplaces" which enabled him to achieve copiousness without chaos as a lecturer in 1855 and also during his later years as a space-filling editor or as a contributor paid at journalistic space rates.

In his series of lectures, as in his later essays, Lowell was both a diagnostician and a judge—and, except when occasionally bothered by personal problems, he was usually a kind and understanding judge who rendered opinions only with reference to a proper diagnosis of the case in hand. By considering the possible combination of qualities a poet might possess, he classified his subject and considered him within the limits of that classification, appreciating him for what he was rather than condemning him for what he was not—or fairly condemning, if condemnation were due, with reference to a just expectation. There was no need to blame Chaucer for not being Shakespeare: his imagination was of a different kind, and, although it was admittedly of a lower order, it could be praised as the best of its kind. Nor was it necessary to bother overmuch about the relative merits of Milton and Chaucer: the personality into which each poet absorbed his materials was different, and any man could have a legitimate preference in personalities. Even Lowell's old difficulties with Wordsworth yielded to his new method of analysis, for Wordsworth's writings revealed a rich vein of the highest form of imagination which came and went at various moments and was often lost in a vast amount of dross. Spenser combined imagination and the poetic sense (which was usually allied with the mere fancy) rather than the "poetical faculty" and therefore did not belong in the same category with Milton and Chaucer. On the other hand, it was possible to say a good word for Pope, who, in one poem at least, exhibited a rare combination of Fancy and the shaping "faculty." Samuel Butler lacked either of the poetical qualities, yet his rich and lively Fancy, qualified by the Understanding, resulted in a Wit which was not to be surpassed despite the fact that it did not rise to the Humor so often found in Marvell.

These classifications provided the critical point of view from which he approached each of the six poets who were the primary subjects of his succeeding lectures, and they formed the intellectual background of others. The metrical romances represented a flourishing of the poetic sense with only rare touches of the imagination found in Spenser; and the old ballads, somewhat less clearly, perhaps, represented a naïvely imaginative poetry stripped of its superfluities by a process of oral transmission to which the art of printing had brought an unfortunate halt. *Piers Plowman* was inferior poetry because its allegorical personifications represented "pinchbeck substitutes for the imagination," and its value, lying in the insight it gave to the life of the times, was human rather than poetical. The lecture on "Poetic Diction" attacked the artificial school after Pope as representing "a decline from imagination to fancy, from metaphor to simile, and then a further decline to arbitrary rules that shut nature out altogether." Lowell depended, to varying degrees, upon learning, apt illustrations, and witty comments in these lectures and sometimes failed to get entirely out of his featherbed of words; but he could hardly have produced the whole series had he not been successful in achieving the combinations of critical ideas with which he began.

The last lecture of the series, delivered on February 16, 1855, was different from those that had gone before and, in some respects, rather pathetic. For in his discussion of the Poet as the Seer, Lowell returned to the old notions he had developed when he himself had hoped to become a great poet: "He it is who discovers the truth as it exists in types and images; that is the spiritual meaning, which abides for ever under the sensual." He did not have very much to say on the subject, and he said it twice—once in prose and once in verse, concluding his address by the poem addressed to the Muse which apparently was the one he had prepared for "The Nooning" as an expression of "the transcendentalist in the party." The pathos may be found not so much in what he actually said as in the wide gap it revealed between the conceptions of poetry he had reached by a study of the great poets and the conception he had developed in his own search for a guiding ideal. It was a decent tribute of a high-minded man to the art to which he had devoted himself, and, as such, it deserved the applause it received. But it was also a tribute to the ideal which had led Lowell into a poetic wasteland.

In the other lectures, however, Lowell found the secret of his later critical success. His six critical terms or categories were the secret words which released the discursive waters and allowed him, in later years, to fill his allotted pages in the *Atlantic Monthly* and the *North American Review* and without too much mental strain and without being wholly commonplace. They enabled his pen to become, at least commercially, fruitful.

II

The series of lectures was also a personal success. It is true that the audience which had demanded so many tickets that Lowell had been forced to repeat the series in the afternoons thinned out before he had finished, but the friendly reporter for the Boston *Traveller* had suggested that inclement weather had been responsible for the poor attendance on at least one occasion, and the people who counted were faithful. By the time the series was half delivered, moreover, the Harvard authorities had been so impressed by his learning and his performances that they had decided to skip over the six candidates for the Smith chair of Modern Languages and offer the position to Lowell. Longfellow was anxious to retire, and after approaching Lowell with the offer on January 31, he wrote in his journal that the matter was "as good as settled." It was to be a part-time appointment at a salary of twelve hundred dollars a year with duties limited to a course of lectures on literature for only two of the three college terms and no actual teaching of languages. But it permitted him to draw a salary while spending another year abroad studying German and promised to relieve him of the unremitting financial pressure from which he suffered. In the course of time, he was to discover that even part-time employment in a college demanded more hours than the contract called for, and some time before he became a full-fledged member of the faculty, he apparently found himself teaching extra classes and attending, at a presidential suggestion, the weekly faculty meetings in order to "jaw for" his "Department." But at the time he saw in the proposition nothing more than a flattering and agreeable solution to the problem of combining leisure for literature with an assurance of a livelihood, and welcomed the opportunity for a winter in Dresden without realizing how lonely he would get or how enthusiastically he would desert his studies for a long spring vacation with old friends in Italy and Sicily.

After his return, he established himself in Cambridge but not at Elmwood.

"I have been driven away," he wrote Briggs on September 18, 1856, "by reasons which perhaps you can divine—but which I do not care to trust to a letter." He found a home for his little family with Maria's sister Lois, Mrs. Estes Howe, on the "Professor's road" which is now Kirkland Street. There, Dr. Howe built him a private study with a wall full of bookshelves and an alcove bed. The domestic arrangements with the Howes continued after his marriage to Frances Dunlap in the middle of September, 1857, but he was not at ease away from Elmwood. "I have not yet got worked down here and doubt if I ever shall," he wrote Norton on the last day of December. "It is too towny. I never come away from my Elmwood visits without a pang. I have left so many roots there that I almost wonder *suckers* don't spring up from them." His younger friend evidently proposed to build the Lowells a house and allow them to occupy it for a nominal rent, but James wrote on June 13 that from something his father had recently said he hoped for the chance of living in Elmwood again, perhaps within a year. It was not until after his father's death in January, 1861, however, that he returned. "You see by my date that I am back again in the place I love best," he wrote Briggs on March 11 of that year:

> I am sitting in my old garret, at my old desk, smoking my old pipe, and loving my old friends. I begin already to feel more like my old self than I have these ten years, . . . I have been dwelling in tents for the last six years. I feel out of place and out of sorts. I believe I had grown dyspeptic, and I know I had turned blue all over, and could not get myself into right relations with men or things. I hope I shall find my old inspiration on tap here. It would not bear bottling and transportation.

The inspiration he found, however, came almost entirely from the Civil War which broke out so soon afterward with such early tragic results for the Lowell family.

The years of his exile were not unproductive. He had served as editor of the *Atlantic Monthly* from its first number of November, 1857, and before his return to Elmwood he had published more than fifty prose articles and notices and a dozen poems—old and new—in its pages. He had been a successful professor at Harvard and had been drawing a full salary from the college for a year. If he was not yet ready to publish a book of his essays, he was nevertheless a distinguished man of letters, on terms of easy friendship with Holmes, Longfellow, Emerson, and other literary celebrities of Boston and its vicinity—one who could give Harriet Beecher Stowe good advice and one who would naturally be sought out by such a young Lochinvar as William Dean Howells. He had suffered the gout and had experienced enough disillusionment to advise Howells not to "print too much" and to "read what will make you *think*, not *dream*." The new master of Elmwood was almost a great man.

But memories of his high-adventured youth continued to haunt him—even after he had become editor of the *North American Review* and should have settled down. They seem to have arisen at times when his normal buoyancy failed him, and he tried to lay the ghost of his early poetic ambitions upon more than one occasion. The essay on "The Life and Letters of James Gates Percival" in the *North American Review* for January, 1867, was probably one such effort. For the man who bore the name Lowell once tried to claim had committed the unpardonable crime of attempting to occupy the Siege Perilous under the misguided direction of his own emotions and had devoted himself too much "to telling us what poetry ought to be, as if mankind were not always more than satisfied with any one who fulfills the true office of poet, by showing them, with the least possible fuss, what it is." "Not till after he was fifty, if even then," had Percival learned the lesson that his reviewer had learned so painfully at thirty-four: "that the world never takes a man at his own valuation, and never pays money for what it does not want, or think it wants." Of course Percival was a worse sinner than his judge because his "singularly unplastic, unsympathetic, and self-involved" nature lacked the poetic faculty and the quality of imagination and his admittedly luxuriant fancy was not accompanied by any good poetic sense. Thus he was "as striking an example as could be found of the poetic temperament unballasted with those less obvious qualities which make the poetic faculty," and "his interest in poetry was always more or less scientific... forever trying experiments in matter and form." Furthermore, for a longer time than Lowell, he had been fooled by the demand for a national literature which was still alive and searching for a "brown-fisted" western poet whose Pegasus would be half-alligator. Free though he was from the taint of excessive nationalism, Lowell also had sought the poet with "toil-embrownèd" hands in his youthful "Ode"; and he could find no pity for the man who had died in the delusions that he himself had so regretfully lost.

Lowell probably had no consciousness that his assault upon Percival—even to the denunciation of his half-hearted attempt at suicide—was an attack upon the hyperbolic specter of his own youth, but the mixture of apology and bitterness with which he contemplated his early career is revealed in a little allegorical fairy tale which he wrote at about the same time. Fields had asked him early in 1865 to contribute to a new periodical, *Our Young Folks,* which his firm had started; and Lowell replied on February 2 that he had "been mulling over a fairy-story, of which something may come and something may not." That "egg," as Lowell suspected at the time, may have been "chalk"; but when Fields repeated his request nearly two years later, he immediately offered, on October 23, 1866, "a jolly little poem" entitled "Hob Gobbling's Song" which he had written for his nephews years before, and he spoke of the fairy story Fields had specifically mentioned:

I invented a kind of one at once, and yesterday and the day before continued to write it, partly to spite an infernal pain I was suffering and which got me under at last. I think I *have* told it simply enough, and was surprised to find how easy it was to write in words mostly of one syllable. I think there are some pleasant humors in it, but it may have suffered from my being in such a wretched condition while I wrote it.

"Uncle Cobus's Story" did not reach the pages of *Our Young Folks* until July of the following year, and the author had adequate time, in moments free from physical pain, to think over its substance. Yet the surviving printer's copy shows that he added a significant point to the allegory after completing it, and there can be little doubt that Lowell intended, while providing entertainment for the young folks, to ease his own mind by a public confession of failure even though the confession itself was ambiguous and was made in a form that would not be generally understood.

The story, in brief, was of the leaders of two tribes of native American fairies whose function was to attend the birth of every child and influence his disposition. If the "squaw-sachem named *Fan-ta-si-a,* or *She that bloweth bubbles*" arrived first, the children she affected became the sort who "spend most of the day in blowing bubbles, or playing on slender reed pipes, with which they make very winsome music." Such people, Lowell explained in the passage he added to the printer's copy, "are all their lives trying to string these bubbles so that they may take them to market. Of course, they always fail, but they feel so sure of great prices, if they only *could* get them thither, that they keep on trying. As for their music, nobody will pay much for that." If the "sagamore who is called *El-bo-gres,* or *He that comes out right,*" came sooner, the child was "apt to grow up into a man more willing to work, and therefore, on the whole, better fitted to live happily in this ant-hill of ours." When the hero of the story, John, was born, Fan-ta-si-a won the race to his cradle and "blew a bubble inside his head just behind the eyes"; and although El-bo-gres hurried in to rub "good-speed-wort" on his hands, he knew that it would do very little good.

> "Now this bubble that had been blown in his head did two things: it made everything he looked at seem to have a rim of rainbow round it, which, you know, it never really has; and it gave him the power of dreaming when he was wide awake, so that it was almost as good as a wishing-cap, for he could be and do and have whatever he liked, so long as the dream lasted."
>
> "Really and truly, uncle?" said Lightfoot, with plaintive doubt.
>
> "No, my dear child, not really and truly in one sense, but really and truly in another, which, so far as this world is concerned, comes to very much the same thing. But you will understand better one of these days."

So the child grew up in his rainbow world. "Perhaps Jacky might have made a pretty good poet" even though he did not have Mr. Longfellow's industry, Uncle Cobus (who had acquired the name from his nephews nearly twenty years before) observed; but, on the whole, "he could see so well what *might* be done, that he never cared much to do anything in particular; and then, if he did anything, it always had such a rainbow about it that it looked finer to him than to other people." But it made little difference until his father began to lose his money and his mother began to worry and to think sadly about her son, whose case seemed hopeless when El-bo-gres, upon consultation, reported that nothing could be done about him unless the bubbles were broken and his own magic allowed to work. When Jacky heard the news of the family's last stroke of misfortune

> it seemed to him just as if some one had hit him a smart rap on the head, and something like the very thinnest glass were broken all to pieces within it. And when he came to look at things, there was no longer any border of rainbow about them; but they all seemed very clear and sharp-edged, and had a kind of hard look at first. Likewise his palms began to prickle, as if they would fain be a-doing; for the juice of the good-speed-wort began now to work strongly on him.

He prospered of course. "But the nicest thing was, that, by degrees, whatever Mr. John looked at, (for so we must call him now,) began to get a rim to it brighter than ever."

Yet despite his little allegory, Mr. Lowell (for so, perhaps, we should call him now) was not quite willing to admit that the bubble behind his eyes was really and truly broken beyond repair. He tried again that autumn to take up "The Nooning" but wrote Fields on November 18 that he was not in the mood for it and that to supply something for the January *Atlantic* he had been obliged to "ransack" his "old notebooks" to find "In the Twilight"—

"an unfinished poem written more than twenty years ago." He was extraordinarily frank with his publisher about his efforts to string his old bubbles and take them to market. "When I am in a financial crisis, which is on an average of once in six weeks," he wrote again on March 8, 1868, "I look first to my portfolio and then to you. The verses I send you are most of them more than of age, but professors don't write poems, and I even begin to doubt if poets do always. But I suppose you will pay me for my name as you do others." And in the early autumn of the same year, when he was trying to get together the volume *Under the Willows,* he repeated a confession which had almost become habitual: "the muse will do nothing for me. I sat all last evening making pictures in the fire, but not a verse, nay, not a prose would come. I do not mean to reprint *all* I have written—but a liberal selection. Gods, how bad they seem now! But there they are and I must exploit them." The exploitation was successful, but the old notebooks could not be ransacked indefinitely, and there was not much left to exploit. To be "the good provider" that had become almost an obsession with him he had to make himself content with prose.

Lowell, as his "fairy story" shows, would have liked to believe with Coleridge that the visitations of misfortune had destroyed his "shaping spirit of Imagination." But it was not so. On the contrary, the moments of genuine imaginative excitement that occurred in his life after 1850 were almost all associated with some visitation of misfortune—the death of Maria, his failure to get back in Elmwood in 1858, the national tragedy of civil war, the death of his three nephews in the army, the assassination of Lincoln, and his failure to receive the appointment as minister to Spain at the beginning of Grant's administration. If the later poems that grew out of these events were removed from his collected works—and, with them, those that represented a reworking of his earlier inspiration—there would be little left except a collection of trivia. Misfortune affected him, but not in the way Coleridge asserted or Lowell pretended to himself.

Maria's death undoubtedly marked the end of his determination to make his life burn with a bright poetic flame, but her death was not the single cause of this observable effect. It came after a long interruption of his poetic activities and at a time when he was experiencing a serious difficulty in getting back in touch with his audience. The failure of "Our Own" was an almost paralyzing disappointment which blighted his self-confidence and placed a subtle barrier between him and his best friend. He had suffered disappointment before and with Maria's help had recovered. But this was more serious, and he was without help. The actual result of her death was a stimulation of his imagination and a disheartening of his self-esteem. What he lost in Maria was less an inspiration than an audience whose unfailing appreciation—with a few minor qualms over the grossness of his dialect writings—kept his courage up and his head high. Without her, Lowell was less certain of his poetic calling and more willing than before to write *invita Minerva* instead of venturing the precious time necessary to invite the Muse.

For the passage of time had placed the leisure for poetic dreams and reveries at a greater premium that it had been in Lowell's youth, and circumstances, normal and extraordinary, had increased the demands made upon his hours. The condition of his father and sister had put heavier responsibilities upon him after his return to Elmwood from his first trip abroad, and after Maria's death he devoted more time and thought to Mabel than would have been necessary had her mother been alive. Furthermore, he had to be more conscientious about making a living. He could no longer go into debt and be rescued by Dr. Lowell. Even while living without a family servant at the Howes, he found that out of an income of fifteen hundred dollars he was spending eleven hundred for the board and lodging of himself and family, and the annual salary of Miss Dunlap left him with a small margin for personal expenses. He had to keep his pen busy with something less speculative than poetry. A literary dinner at the Revere or Parker House might cost seven dollars or more if the diner included, as Lowell did, wines instead of bonbons among his extras; and Lowell was soon to find that he could get rid of more unbudgeted dollars during the course of twelve months than it had cost him to live during the year he spent in Boston at the beginning of his career. He found time for a weekly evening at whist with John Holmes and other friends, and he confessed to "dining out furiously" during the year preceding his second marriage; and his editorial and productive labors during the early years of the *Atlantic Monthly* and the Saturday Club show that his middle age was accompanied by no decrease in energy. But sitting around with a poet's figurative pipe at his lips, waiting for the "Mighty Mother" of song to blow through it, was neither precisely work nor exactly play; and the various pressures, financial and social, exerted upon Lowell may have made it easier for him to accuse the Muse of desertion than his family and friends of alienating her affections.

In any case, as interruptions succeeded each other—the Institute lectures and the wearisome Midwestern tour which followed, the second trip abroad and the difficulties of mastering German, and the wearing responsibilities of his professorial and editorial chairs—his devotion to poetry lost some of its fervor and it became easy for him to follow the line of least resistance into prose. The definitions and relationships he had worked out for the first of his lectures served him so well that he sometimes used them to "pump"—as Emerson suspected—his poetical inspiration, as he did in *The Cathedral.* When he wrote of "Nature" as being "but our own conceit of what we see" and "Our own reaction upon what we feel" which was so pervasive that "when our Fancy seeks analogies" they arouse only a "feigned surprise," he was playing a poetic variation on his rather fanciful definition of the Imagination as that "mysterious Nature" which lay back of the "scenery" with which the Fancy dealt. When he wrote further:

> I thank benignant Nature most for this,—
> A force of sympathy, or call it lack
> Of character firm-planted, loosing me
> From the pent chamber of habitual self
> To dwell enlarged in alien modes of thought,
> Haply distasteful, wholesomer for that,
> And through imagination to possess,
> As they were mine, the lives of other men;

he was claiming for himself the quality of "dramatic Imagination" or the power of unrestricted sympathetic identification of himself with others which he found in Shakespeare and considered "the highest form of poetic Imagination." A claim that could find so little support in his actual writings, of course, was not a modest one. Nor was there modesty in his professed "lack Of character firm-planted," for in his discussion of the "dramatic Imagination" in his lecture, he had identified it with an absence of "what we call *character.*" "The more poet, the less character," he added; "I cannot find that Shakespeare had any at all." But *The Cathedral* was Lowell's substitute for the castle in Spain, which, as he wrote at the time, he would have to build in his mind since he had lost the chance to occupy one in the body. It is not surprising that such a self-conscious "Child of an age that lectures, not creates," should have included in his lecturing some hint that his apparent faults were really virtues. He was, after all, closer to Shakespeare than was Henry S. Sanford who was nominated or Daniel E. Sickles who actually went to Spain in his stead.

But Lowell was an adaptable person who was gradually adjusting himself to his age. The old problem of his awkwardly divided personality was being resolved by a grinding away of the rough edges of his conflicting ambitions. He had even filled an unconscious gap in his wide reading by developing—as a somewhat incidental by-product of the critical theories expressed in his first Institute lecture—a theory of personality which enabled him to experience his varying moods with relaxed good humor:

> I think that every man is conscious at times that it is only his borders, his seaboard, that is civilized and subdued. Behind that narrow strip stretches the untamed domain, shaggy, unexplored, of the natural instincts. Is not this so? Then we may narrow our definition yet further, and say, that Fancy and Wit appeal to the artificial man; Imagination and Humor to the natural man. Thus each of us in his dual capacity can at once like Chaucer and Pope, Butler and Jean Paul, and bury the hatchet of one war of tastes.

In his personal world of Will and Idea, the unsubdued and unexplored Will—as was proper in a man who had been born a Lowell and forced to learn the lesson of Sir James Mackintosh in his youth—was good in its essence and in the direction toward which it compelled one's ideas. There was nothing pessimistic in his philosophy. If the untamed Will broke its bounds, if the censor relaxed its control, the result was admirable. But civilization was admirable, too; and it was inevitable that a Lowell should be ill at ease when out of touch with the seaboard. He dwelt more and more in the civilized world of Fancy and Wit, and civilization honored him for it and he learned to accept its appreciation as his due. Honorary degrees from Oxford and Cambridge marked his third trip abroad in the 1870's; and if the Latin presentation of his distinctions at Cambridge gave him a slightly "posthumous feeling," he was aware that he was a live force in contemporary politics at home. It was only proper that he should be a delegate to the national convention of his party and a presidential elector in 1876. He was offered the Russian ministry by Grant and seems to have received an intimation from the President that the State Department would be offered him "in case of a third term"; but he belonged, by principles and by interest, to the reforming element in the Republican Party, and his most effective political verse appeared in the pages of the *Nation* in support of Hayes, who sent him to Spain and afterwards to the Court of St. James's where he remained until the Democratic administration took office in 1885. He was a popular minister, except among the Irish and among those who failed to understand the obstacles that his wife's ill-health and his limited income placed in the way of elaborate entertaining; and he gracefully accepted the economic and social distinctions which had prejudiced his view of "Merry England" in his youth. He became at home in Great Britain and looked with favor upon the possibility of becoming Rector of St. Andrews University in Scotland but was forced to withdraw his name from consideration because of an opposition based upon doubts concerning the elegibility of a foreigner for the post. An anticipation of similar objections appears to have prevented him from exhibiting any interest in the professorship of Poetry at Oxford. After his wife's death, near the close of his diplomatic mission, he was ready to come back to America and eventually to settle again in Elmwood where, after other visits abroad, he died on August 12, 1891.

III

WHEN LOWELL had ascended the platform for his Institute lectures of 1855, he had been halfway through his allotted span of years but only one-third through the literary career upon which he had embarked as a junior at Harvard. The last half of his life was a success. He became a distinguished professor, a successful editor, a satisfactory diplomat, and a writer whose criticisms of literature and of life were sometimes influential, often memorable, and generally acclaimed. But the early part of his career was richer in the human element of literature, and his early writings, with all their faults, are interesting and valuable because of the insight they provide to the life of a human being and to the times in which he lived. When his history is balanced in the scales he himself designed for "St. Michael the Weigher," all the

> dreaming, doing, saying,
> All the failure and the pain,

of his youth seem more important than all his later "splendor and renoun."

The reason for this, perhaps, is not difficult to find. Lowell never achieved the quality of excellence which makes some literature so great that it possesses a life of its own, independent of time and place. He was intimately a part of nineteenth-century America, and his importance is determined by that intimacy rather than by the inherent quality of his writings. Like all earnest poets, concerned as they are with the expression of ideas primarily for the expression's sake, he was a sensitive instrument for recording the assumptions, impulses, and beliefs that directed the course of the civilization to which he belonged. Through his social background, he was in contact with the wide variety of his century's culture: it was natural for him to have a feeling for the past and a desire for progress, to know the best of the world's literature and the habits of a robin, to be equally at home in an art gallery and in a hayfield. He had forced upon him the uncertain philosophy which characterized his time: the confidence in impulses, however defined, and the uneasy compulsion to be up and doing. And in his early responses to his reading, he revealed the capricious temperament which prevented him from finding unity in the variety of his culture and from overcoming the faults of his philosophy: the tendency to lose himself in other people, the lack of "character" which he came to consider the mark of a poet.

Variable by temper and unstable in his intellectual backgrounds, Lowell faced the major disparities of his world like a weathercock, turning from one to another as the strength of each in turn pressed against his personal fortunes. Few poets have better exemplified the high-mindedness of the nineteenth century. All that poetry meant to Wordsworth, to Goethe, or to Carlyle he tried to make his own, naïvely confusing intention with accomplishment and piling ideal upon ideal in his effort to synthesize the old notion of the poet's contemplative life with the new fashion of activity. At intervals between his theorizing, he also attempted to make literature a profession to be followed through the doors opened to him by the new popular magazines which tried to make ladies pay the way for poets, and, although he would never have admitted the charge, much of the form and some of the substance of his verse were cut to the professional doors through which he hoped to pass. Lowell the ideal poet and Lowell the magazinist were both affected by the nineteenth-century desire to do good: he regularly pointed the direction from which the spirit of reform was blowing, and he was willing to sacrifice his high and his professional ambitions, and even, at times, his sincerity, to the major reform movement of his time and country. But in all his youthful works he was fighting wholeheartedly for a poet's place in a difficult world, straining at the restrictions of his environment and at the bonds of his own limitations, until he achieved for himself a place in American literature which somehow prevents his most hostile modern critics from speaking as disparagingly of his work as he himself often did when he looked back upon it.

The spontaneous wholeheartedness with which he followed his multiple interests through almost two decades of struggle is the characteristic which makes him most interesting to the historian. For he illustrates, better than any other American writer of his time, that curious capacity for self-deceit which has become the distinguishing mark of most of his countrymen and which, in fact, has often led to charges of hypocrisy and double-dealing against the people of all English-speaking countries. It is the trait of a people who make a distinction between practical and moral intelligence, who judge ability by accomplishments and honesty by intention, and who are often too confused in their righteousness to let their native shrewdness affect their doings outside the affairs of the market place. Although such a trait could have flourished only in civilizations which were so successful materially that they could afford mistakes in other relations, it does not represent a materialistic or cynical hypocrisy. On the contrary, as Lowell's writings suggest, it reflects an underlying philosophical belief in the superiority of sentiment to intelligence as a guide to moral action—a belief which has as its inevitable corollary the notion that a good man should be expected to be either stupid or irresponsible. In an age which seriously needs to examine its heritage of tacit beliefs, an author who so candidly, in the old phrase, holds a mirror up to nature—especially current human nature—should not go unvalued.

The secret of Lowell's later success was that of most professional writers who accepted the wisdom of the market place instead of pursuing something less tangible. He found his niche in the world, accepted his limitations, and wrote safely within them, yielding to his cultural environment rather than striving against it. As a poet, he applied his craftsmanship to writing up to the occasion which called forth his verses, instead of trying to compete with the best that had been thought and said in the world before him. Like the Hosea of his second series of *Biglow Papers,* he kept his judgment less "full-cocked" than it had been in his youth and became more willing to avoid the "expense" of emotion and energy by allowing events to make up his mind for him. As a critic, he settled upon a system of values and relationships that seemed sound because it had largely grown out of his earliest intellectual experiences, and he applied it with copiousness and sensitivity and usually with good humor. As a man, he settled even more solidly into the pattern of values that had been established by his early background—into an appreciation of the importance of tradition and of good connections. The writings of the latter half of his life, like those of most others who shared his secret, are more finished and in that sense better than those of his early literary career. But they are usually expressions of animated opinions rather than of living ideas, and they reveal the loss of vitality that so often accompanies the acquisition of professional ease in composition. In them, except on rare occasions, the Victorian knight-errant had quit adventuring.

Notes

A NOTE ON SOURCES

Most of the manuscript material used in this study of Lowell is in the Houghton Library at Harvard University. The largest of the collections found there includes (1) most of the correspondence, autograph poems and drafts of essays and lectures, miscellaneous papers, commonplace books, journals, and other notebooks left by Lowell to his literary executor, Charles Eliot Norton; (2) the correspondence collected by Norton for his collection of Lowell's *Letters;* and (3) considerable additions made to the collections by the university library in the course of the last fifty years. The J. B. Lowell and Rantoul collections of family papers (recently deposited in the Houghton Library) contain additional correspondence, notebooks, and business and other miscellaneous papers which constitute approximately half of the material retained by the Lowell family after Norton made his selection of papers that were primarily of literary interest. Numerous Lowell items are also to be found in other collections of autographs and correspondence, of which the most important are the two bound volumes of *Edward Morris Davis Letters.* In addition, the Houghton Library includes a number of annotated volumes from Lowell's library, a fragmentary copy of *A Year's Life* with Lowell's notes on the dates of composition for various poems, and many clippings. Unless otherwise noted, and except for an occasional phrase, all of my quotations from correspondence, manuscript poems and essays, and notebooks are from this material; and all of my references to business or miscellaneous papers, unless otherwise noted, are to it. The other important collections of manuscripts I have used are the Fields Collection in the Henry E. Huntington Library and the remaining half of the family papers (which I used from microfilm in the possession of Dixon Wecter and which will be designated in the notes that follow as "Family Papers"). I have consulted but have not quoted the Lowell manuscripts in Craigie House.

Informative correspondence which I saw only in printed form includes that in M. A. DeW. Howe's *New Letters of James Russell Lowell* (New York and London, 1932) which was not taken from the manuscript collections mentioned above, a few letters in C. E. Norton's Elmwood Edition of the *Letters* (3 vols., Boston and New York, 1904) which have not been preserved in the collection at Harvard, the correspondence of Lowell and Carter with Poe which was printed by G. E. Woodberry in *Scribner's Magazine* for August, 1894, the letters to E. A. Duyckinck in the New York Public Library *Bulletin* for October, 1900, and those in J. T. Morse's *Life and Letters of Oliver Wendell Holmes* (2 vols., Boston and New York, 1896) and in Henry James's *William Wetmore Story and his Friends*

(2 vols., Boston, 1903). Numerous other books and articles containing Lowell letters which have been of less particular value in this study may be found listed in *A Bibliography of James Russell Lowell* compiled by George W. Cooke (Boston and New York, 1906)—a book which, despite a number of inaccuracies, has been in itself an invaluable source of information concerning the first appearances in print of Lowell's individual writings.

Additional letters that were available to me only in the form of valuable excerpts or paraphases made by others include those by Charles F. Briggs used by Horace E. Scudder in *James Russell Lowell, A Biography* (2 vols., Boston and New York, 1901), some early letters from Lowell to Nathan Hale, Jr., which were evidently in the hands of Edward Everett Hale when he wrote *James Russell Lowell and His Friends* (Boston and New York, 1899), and a number of letters and papers used in *A Bibliography of the First Editions in Book Form of the Writings of James Russell Lowell* (New York, 1914), compiled by Luther S. Livingston largely from the collection and notes of Jacob C. Chamberlain—a work which is more accurate and detailed than Cooke's although it is apparently limited to "respectable" publications in book form, since it does not include volumes that reprinted, for the first time and without authorization, early magazine verse on which the copyright had expired. There are also a few fragments of letters in the Cambridge edition of Lowell's poems, and one in the Cambridge edition of Whittier, which I did not see in the originals.

For Lowell's published poems and essays I have, with two exceptions, always used the original editions of his books or, when they appeared first elsewhere, the periodicals referred to in the text. The exceptions are those contributions to the *Pennsylvania Freeman* and the *National Anti-Slavery Standard* which were printed in *The Anti-Slavery Papers of James Russell Lowell* (2 vols., Boston and New York, 1902), and the first series of *The Biglow Papers* which I used in the first edition in book form. I used the two periodicals and also the Boston *Courier,* however, for writings by Lowell which had been listed by his bibliographers but had not been collected under the above titles; but the circumstances which forced me to make exceptions to my usual procedure were unfortunate, for it was not until the files of the three periodicals were inaccessible to me that I realized the desirability of making a more careful comparison of Biglow texts or understood that Lowell made a few contributions to the *Freeman* and the *Standard* which have not yet been identified.

In addition to *The Anti-Slavery Papers of James Russell Lowell,* ed. William B. Parker (2 vols., Boston and New York, 1902), the following collections make available to the general reader certain early writings by Lowell which were not preserved in the Riverside or Elmwood editions of his *Works: Conversations on Some of the Old Poets* (Philadelphia, 1893), a reprint of the second edition with "The Plays of Thomas Middleton" and "Song-Writing" from the *Pioneer; The Power of Sound* (New York, 1896); *Lectures on English Poets* (Cleveland, 1897), the Lowell Institute Lectures as reported in the Boston *Daily Advertiser; Early Prose Writings of James Russell Lowell* (London and New York, 1902), essays from the *Boston Miscellany* and "Song-Writing" from the *Pioneer; Four*

Poems (Hingham, Mass., 1906), "The Ballad of the Stranger," "King Retro," "The Royal Pedigree," and "A Dream I Had"; *The Round Table* (Boston, 1913), early essays from the *North American Review* and the *Massachusetts Quarterly Review; The Function of the Poet and Other Essays,* ed. Albert Mordell (Boston and New York, 1920); the *Graham's Magazine* article on Poe and numerous later reviews. Miss Thelma Smith has published a volume of *Uncollected Poems of James Russell Lowell* (Philadelphia, 1950); and of the numerous unauthorized collections of his early poems (which are still useful because they print original versions which were later rejected, abbreviated, or revised), the most inclusive that I have seen is the "Vignette Edition" of *Poems* (New York, 1894). Miscellaneous unpublished poems and extracts from journals may also be found in Norton's *Letters,* in Howe's *New Letters,* in Hale's *James Russell Lowell and His Friends,* in Scudder's biography, and in Ferris Greenslet's *James Russell Lowell His Life and Work* (Boston and New York, 1905).

CHAPTER NOTES

Chapter I. The Young Squire

General information concerning Lowell's boyhood and early environment is derived from his early correspondence, his manuscript autobiography in the 1838 *Class Book* in the Harvard Archives (printed by Ethel Golann as "A Lowell Autobiography" in the *New England Quarterly,* VII [June, 1934], 356–364), his manuscript poem "Indian Summer" in a notebook in the Houghton Library (revised and partially printed as "An Indian-Summer Reverie"), and his published essay "Cambridge Thirty Years Ago" which originally appeared as "Fireside Travels"; from Everett E. Hale's *James Russell Lowell and his Friends* and *A New England Boyhood;* and from the Cambridge Historical Society *Publications,* especially Numbers I, XXIII, and XXV, which contain T. W. Higginson's Reminiscences of young Lowell and of the convent fire, Isabella B. James's "James Russell Lowell as I knew Him," and Henry W. L. Dana's "Chronicles of the Craigie House."

Contradictory accounts of the reasons for Lowell's rustication are given in T. W. Higginson's *Old Cambridge* (New York, 1899), p. 157, and in Hale's *James Russell Lowell and his Friends,* pp. 41–42; but the first is circumstantially impossible and could only have gained currency on the basis of an assumption that the Harvard senior Class Day occurred (as it did later) during the Commencement period, and the second is contradicted by a contemporary letter in which Lowell referred to his peculiar inability to get to prayers on Mondays. Neither of these versions is supported by the College records or by the correspondence (especially that with G. B. Loring, Charles W. Scates, and Eben Wright) upon which this new account is based.

The discussion of Lowell's education is based entirely upon the following manuscript sources in the Harvard Archives: the 1838 *Class Book* autobiography; the Term Books for 1834–1838 which contain the grades of each of Lowell's recitations and exhibitions, the records of his absences from classes and prayers, and notations concerning penalties assessed against him; the Minutes of the Harvard College Faculty during Lowell's undergraduate years and a certified copy of the faculty vote concerning his rustication (which was made at the request of the Lowell family, probably after hearing the story later told by Higginson); the Minutes of the Hasty Pudding Club; and the College Catalogues for the period. Lowell's troubles with Bowen are indicated by letters from his classmates during his rustication and clarified by the Term Books.

A survey of the Harvard philosophical curriculum has been made by Edgeley W. Todd, "Philosophical Ideas in Harvard College, 1817–1837," *New England Quarterly,* XVI (March, 1943), 63–90; and Merrell R. Davis, "Emerson's 'Reason' and the Scottish Philosophers," *New England Quarterly,* XVII (June, 1944), 209–228, has discussed the relationship of the Harvard curriculum to transcendentalism. My illustration of this relationship is taken from Emerson's manuscript lecture "The Head" delivered in Boston on December 20, 1837, which is now in the Emerson Memorial Association Collection deposited in the Houghton Library. Dugald Stewart's comments upon Locke's theory of knowledge may be found in Part I, chap. i, sec. iv, of any early edition of his *Elements of the Philosophy of the Human Mind*, but his distinction between the reason and the understanding is most clearly stated in Part II, chap. i, sec. i–ii. For his discussion of various aspects of the imagination and its distinctions from the fancy, see Part I, chap. iii; chap. v, sec. i–iv; and chapter vii. For the quotations and references to Sir James Mackintosh, see *A General View of the Progress of Ethical Philosophy* (Philadelphia, 1832), pp. 9, 113, 227, and *passim*. George Peirce Clark, "Lowell's Part in the Harvard Exhibition of 1837," *American Literature,* XXII (January, 1951), 497–500, gives the account of one college event that did not come into my narrative.

Chapter II. Realms of Gold

Lowell's early correspondence is full of references to his reading, but the most illuminating single source of information concerning his literary interests is the manuscript commonplace book in the Houghton Library which contains a list of books read in 1838 and numerous extracts from his reading between 1836 and 1839 and a few later notes. A considerable number of the extracts are dated, and it is possible to date others approximately by a study of the handwriting, ink, etc., and by their position in relation to other entries of known date. A list of books drawn from the College library in 1839 (in the Harvard Archives) contains supplementary information. His contributions to *Harvardiana* in 1838 contain many allusions to books that are not mentioned in his correspondence and commonplace book, and such later essays as those on Spenser and Landor (both quoted in the text) contain reminiscences which are informative if used with care. The knowledge of literature displayed in the early essays printed in the *Boston Miscellany* and the *Pioneer* clarifies certain earlier allusions. The annotated copy of *Sartor Resartus* is in the Houghton Library.

Lowell's first love affair has been treated as something of a mystery by his most recent biographer, apparently because it was touched upon lightly by Scudder and Greenslet and because Lowell's surviving letters to the young lady are represented only by typed copies of those portions which contain original poems and critical comments. They are identifiable, however, by an allusion to the recipient as "Miss Jackson." My account of the affair is based to a certain extent upon these, but more precisely upon Lowell's correspondence at the time with G. B. Loring and W. H. Shackford, upon a letter from Robert Lowell in the "Family Papers," and upon a later but undated letter from Emelyn Eldridge to Maria White. Lowell and his friends usually took pains in their intimate confidences by mail to avoid referring to young women by name, but Lowell slipped and mentioned her to Loring as his "forlorn and desolate Hannah" in a letter of August 15, 1837, and as "Hannah Jackson" (when it was all over) in another of November 24, 1840. He mentioned his quarrel with his brother in the latter and told Loring of leaving Elmwood for a room in the village in a letter of September 18, 1839. Emelyn Eldridge's letter also speaks of "Hannah Jackson." At the request of Mrs. Frederick Winslow, Mr. Charles Jackson verified my supposition that Hannah was the daughter of Patrick Tracy Jackson and therefore the younger sister of Lowell's oldest brother's wife. The account of his interest in Maria White is based upon contemporary correspondence and upon one later letter, from Lowell to Maria's sister Lois (Mrs. Estes Howe) on November 4, 1855, in which he recalls the circumstances of his engagement. The narrative took the form in which I presented it, of course, only after I had read, against the background of this correspondence, the books that Lowell read and the poetry he wrote during his two courtships.

Chapter III. Initiation

The correspondence upon which this chapter is largely based is all in the Houghton Library with the exception of the letter from Anna Lowell which is in the "Family Papers." Incorporated in this letter is a detailed criticism of the unfinished *Class Poem* with references to numbered lines which enable the reader to identify precisely all the substantial parts added by Lowell after he went to Concord. Some of the general comments on Lowell's character contained in this letter have been quoted in Scudder's biography. Hale prints a facsimile copy of the "Supper Song" written "To the Class of '38, By their Ostracized Poet, (so called,) J.R.L." facing p. 50 in *James Russell Lowell and His Friends* and also, between pp. 52–53, a facsimile of the program for the valedictory exercise of July 17 which contains the note: "On account of the absence of the Poet the [Class] Poem will be omitted." Lowell's later comments upon Emerson's Phi Beta Kappa Address are from the essay "Thoreau" in his collected *Works*.

The manuscript poems quoted are from the Lowell-Loring correspondence with the exceptions of "The Song of the Poet" which exists in a separate manuscript and the poems sent to Hannah Jackson which are from the fragmentary typed copies of the letters to her. The quotations from Daniel, Harrington, and Puttenham are all in Joseph Haslewood's editions of *Ancient Critical Essays on English Poets and Poësy* with the exception of one incomplete quotation from

Daniel which, for the sake of clarity, follows the version in Lowell's commonplace book. Heine's *Letters Auxiliary to the History of Modern Polite Literature in Germany* was used in the Boston, 1839, edition to which Lowell referred; and the quotations from Carlyle are from the first volume of his *Miscellanies* in which the essay on Burns, in particular, differs from its original form.

Chapter IV. The Field of Endeavor

For the financial condition of the *Southern Literary Messenger* at this time see W. M. Griswold, ed., *Passages from the Correspondence and other Papers of Rufus W. Griswold* (Cambridge, Mass., 1898), pp. 35 ff. Poe's interest in phrenology has been treated by Edward B. Hungerford in "Poe and Phrenology," *American Literature,* II (November, 1930), 209–231, and Peterson's is indicated in his letters to Lowell. A good many of Lowell's contributions to the *Boston Miscellany* are identified in the annotated partial table of contents reproduced by a photograph in Edward E. Hale's *James Russell Lowell and his Friends,* and "To an Aeolian Harp" is attributed to him by Cooke although it seems to me that the attribution is circumstantially improbable. The whole question of payments to magazine contributors at this time is a difficult one, for no publisher seems to have followed a consistent policy: Epes Sargent, for example, returned a poem to Mrs. Frances Osgood on December 12, 1842, with the explanation that his magazine would have to get along for a few months with articles "gratuitously furnished" (see Griswold, *op. cit.,* p. 128); and George Graham, even while prospering, was reluctant to pay for articles for which he had not contracted (cf. his handling of Thoreau's article on Carlyle, for which Horace Greeley compelled payment, as indicated by documents printed by Griswold, pp. 207–209, 222).

The familiar story of Lowell's losses as a publisher was originally told by George E. Woodberry in "Lowell's Letters to Poe," *Scribner's Magazine,* XVI (August, 1894), 171, and additional light has been shed on the enterprise by the bills, receipts, and other papers which may be found in the Rantoul collection of family papers in the Houghton Library and which are quoted extensively by Sculley Bradley in his valuable introduction to *The Pioneer* (Scholars' Facsimiles and Reprints: New York, 1947) and in his article, "Lowell, Emerson, and the *Pioneer,*" *American Literature,* IX (November, 1947), 231–244. These papers had suggested to me a version of the story somewhat different from that told by Bradley, and after the appearance of his work I consulted the records of the superior court in Boston which contained a summary of the contract (stipulated correct by both sides) between the editors and publishers, various documents relative to the suits and countersuits, and an index of judgments rendered. This chapter, accordingly, is based upon original letters by Lowell and Poe, additional information concerning the history of Poe's contributions to the *Pioneer* found in Arthur H. Quinn's *Edgar Allan Poe* (New York, 1941), business documents in the Rantoul collection and the "Family Papers," and the official court records. I followed Bradley, although using a different method, in estimating the printing costs on the basis of material provided by William A. Charvat in "A Note on

Poe's *Tales of the Grotesque and Arabesque," Publishers' Weekly,* CL (November 23, 1946), 2957–2958. Although the identification of I. B. Wright as W. W. Story was a commonplace in the circle of Lowell's friends, and was also a matter of gossip in other literary circles (cf. H. Fuller to Mrs. Osgood from Providence on February 5, 1843, Griswold, *op. cit.,* p. 137), it was apparently not made publicly until the appearance of Henry James's *William Wetmore Story and His Friends* (2 vols., Boston, 1903), for the prose "Dream Love" was attributed to Lowell himself in an anthology, *Voices of the True-Hearted,* which was published in Philadelphia in 1846. Carter's previous experience with magazine publication apparently was with Robert H. Collyer's *The Mesmeric Magazine; or Journal of Animal Magnetism* (Boston, 1842) which ran for only a single number. A copy of *The Pioneer* bearing the Drew and Scammel imprint is in the Huntington Library.

Chapter V. First Engagements

The letter from Carter to Poe was published by Woodberry, *op. cit.,* and the revised versions of Lowell's "Ode" and "An Incident in a Railway-Car" first appeared in his 1844 *Poems.* The texts of both "A Legend of Brittany" and "Rhoecus" which are discussed here differ substantially from those preserved by Lowell in his collected poems. For the revisions, see chap. viii.

Chapter VI. The Siege Perilous

The account of Lowell's relationship with the abolitionists, as given here and in chaps. vii and viii, is based upon the correspondence in the two volumes of Edward Morris Davis letters in the Houghton Library and other relevant correspondence indicated in the text, upon the *Annual Reports* of the American Anti-Slavery Society and the Massachusetts Anti-Slavery Society, and upon such miscellaneous documents as the *Proceedings of a Convention of Delegates* (Boston, 1845) and the *Proceedings of the Anti-Slavery Meeting Held in Stacy Hall* (Boston, 1855) included in the Widener Library collection of "Pamphlets on Slavery." These materials were used in connection with the *Pennsylvania Freeman* (a complete file of which is in the Swarthmore College Library), the *National Anti-Slavery Standard,* and the Boston *Courier* to which Lowell contributed with some regularity. Garrison's *The Liberator* and the New York *Anti-Slavery Examiner* were also occasionally useful, and *William Lloyd Garrison, 1805–1879. The Story of his Life told by his Children* (4 vols., New York, 1869) proved to be a practical index to the former periodical. Samuel J. May, *Some Recollections of our Anti-Slavery Conflict* (Boston, 1869); F. Byrdsall, *The History of the Loco-Foco or Equal Rights Party* (New York, 1842); Wendell Phillips, *Speeches, Lectures, and Letters* (Boston, 1863); and Elias L. Magoon, *Republican Christianity* (Boston, 1849) were useful contemporary sources of background information. Among many secondary sources consulted, John A. Krout's *The Origins of Prohibition* (New York, 1935) was useful, Gilbert H. Barnes's *The Antislavery Impulse 1830–1844* (New York, 1933) was disappointing because of the author's apparent lack of contact with the complicated details of the anti-slavery movement, and Arthur B. Darling's *Political Changes in Massachusetts, 1824–1848* (New Haven, 1925) was invaluable for its precision and attention to details.

The story of Lowell's meeting with Poe, as it is told here, seems to be the most reasonable one which can be inferred from the letters of Lowell to Briggs and the letters from Mrs. Clemm which are preserved in the Houghton Library; and the letter from Holmes defending himself against Lowell's charges may be found in John T. Morse's *Life and Letters of Oliver Wendell Holmes* (2 vols., Boston, 1896), I, 275 ff.

Chapter VII. Knight-Errant

The circumstances surrounding the composition of *The Biglow Papers* became evident from a consideration of the simple chronological order of Lowell's compositions in the light of his comments upon them in his letters and the particular historical and political events of the time. A careful examination of the printed volume with reference to its author's correspondence was also illuminating; for the pressures under which Lowell prepared a book for publication are often reflected in bibliographical or literary peculiarities of the work, and in the first series of *Biglow Papers,* Lowell's race to keep ahead of the printers had an evident effect upon the text of the introductory parts. I have not examined a sufficiently large number of copies of the first edition with reference to the circumstantial evidence concerning its publication to be certain, but I doubt whether copies containing the "Notices of an Independent Press" and bearing the George Nichols imprint should be accepted as specimens of the "first issue." For background material used in this chapter, see notes to chap. vi.

The chronology of Lowell's work on *A Fable for Critics* can be followed, for the greater part of the poem, in his notebooks and his letters to Briggs; and a comparison of the order of passages as they were composed with the rearrangements and additions made for the published work gives a clear indication of how it grew according to moods but was put together and sometimes moderated by judicious second thoughts. Lowell usually wrote out in manuscript the names represented by blanks in the published version, and his identification of Thoreau and Ellery Channing, about which there has been some controversy, is clear. There is surprisingly little direct information in Lowell's correspondence about the composition of *The Vision of Sir Launfal,* and the account of it given here, as the text indicates, is largely inferential.

Chapter VIII. The Last Tournaments

Lowell's relationship with the *National Anti-Slavery Standard* at this time is clearly indicated when his correspondence, especially that with Sidney Howard Gay, is read in connection with the various announcements of policy, etc., found in the files of the *Standard* and in the *Annual Reports* of the American Anti-Slavery Society. The 1849 edition of his *Poems* rivals the first series of *Biglow Papers* in bibliographical interest, and my comments upon it are based upon a careful and sometimes microscopic comparison between it and the earlier texts.

Chapter IX. The Waste Land

The letters to Fields referred to in this chapter are in the Fields Collection in the Huntington Library, and the account of the Commemoration Ode to which reference is made is Hamilton V. Bail's "James Russell Lowell's Ode Recited at the Commemoration of the Living and Dead Soldiers of Harvard University, July 21, 1865," *Papers of the Bibliographical Society of America,* XXXVII (Third Quarter, 1943), 169–202. Lowell's letter to Higginson is in the Huntington Library.

Chapter X. The Flowing Waters

Although there is no perfect text for Lowell's Institute lectures, they may be reproduced with some accuracy from three sources: (1) a manuscript in the Houghton Library which evidently was his actual reading copy, but which is so marked that it is difficult to tell which parts were read and which may have been omitted; (2) the reports of the lectures printed in the Boston *Daily Advertiser,* supposedly made by Robert Carter, which were verbatim copies of selected portions of the manuscript, and almost certainly represent some of the parts actually read; and (3) the reports in the Boston *Traveller* which were evidently made from stenographic notes of the speeches, and consequently indicate interpolations and platform revisions. My quotations, however, are all from the manuscript. The critical approach which Lowell developed in these lectures usually influenced the fresh opinions expressed in his later essays, but it did not greatly affect the formal structure of works designed to be generally informative, entertaining, and space-filling as well as critical. The printer's copy of "Uncle Cobus's Story," together with the correspondence concerning it, is in the Fields Collection in the Huntington Library.

Index

INDEX